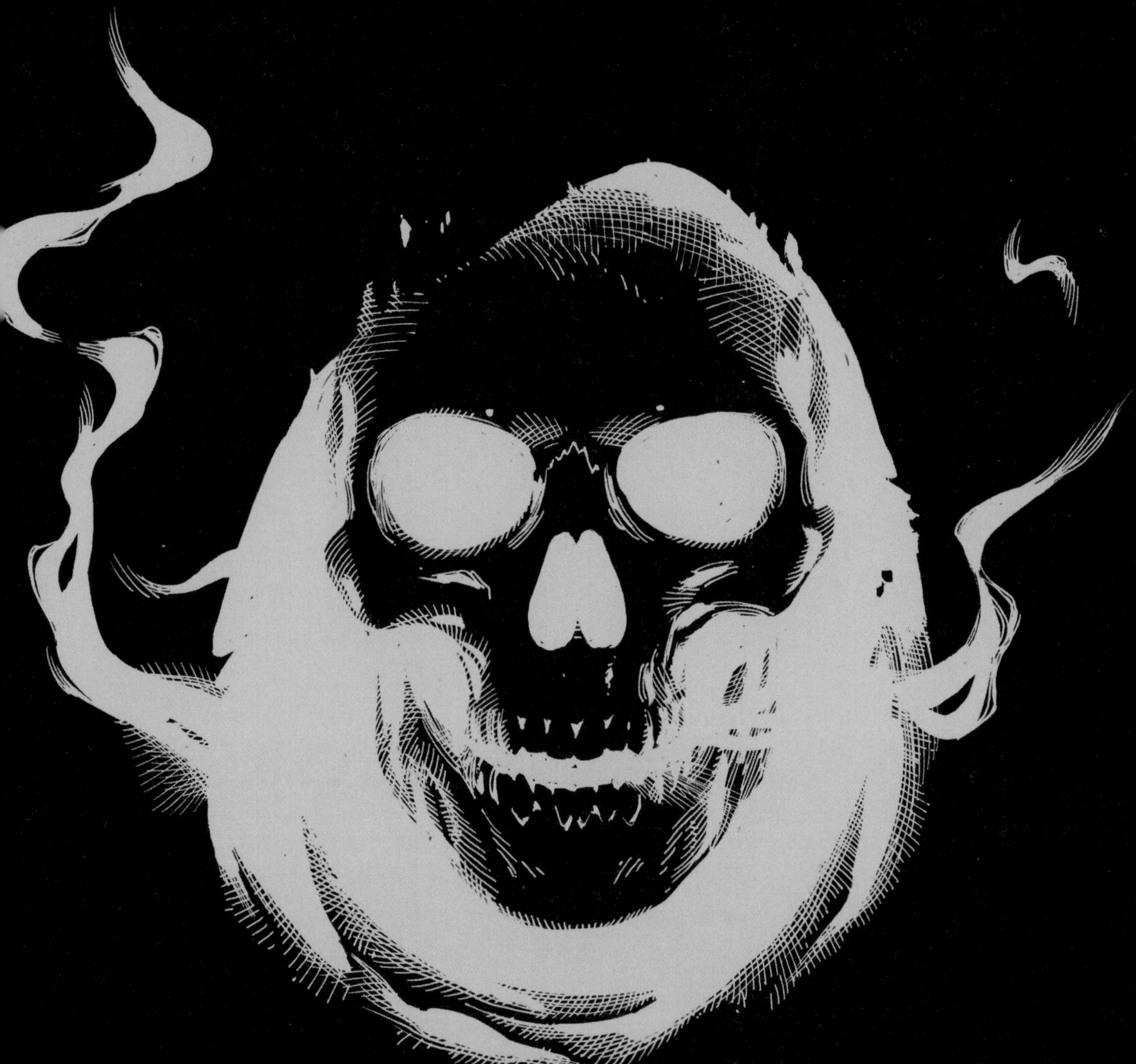

GEIGER

GEOFF JOHNS & GARY FRANK
CREATORS

BRAD ANDERSON
COLORIST

ROB LEIGH
LETTERS

BRIAN CUNNINGHAM & PAT McCALLUM
EDITORS

STEVE BLACKWELL
DESIGNER

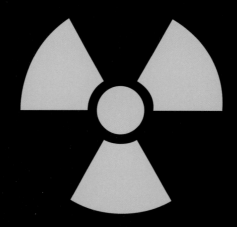

image

IMAGECOMICS, INC.

TODD McFARLANE President | **JIM VALENTINO** Vice President | **MARC SILVESTRI** Chief Executive Officer | **ERIK LARSEN** Chief Financial Officer
ROBERT KIRKMAN Chief Operating Officer | **ERIC STEPHENSON** Publisher / Chief Creative Officer | **NICOLE LAPALME** Controller | **LEANNA CAUNTER** Accounting Analyst
SUE KORPELA Accounting & HR Manager | **MARLA EIZIK** Talent Liaison | **JEFF BOISON** Director of Sales & Publishing Planning
DIRK WOOD Director of International Sales & Licensing | **ALEX COX** Director of Direct Market Sales | **CHLOE RAMOS** Book Market & Library Sales Manager
EMILIO BAUTISTA Digital Sales Coordinator | **JON SCHLAFFMAN** Specialty Sales Coordinator | **KAT SALAZAR** Director of PR & Marketing
DREW FITZGERALD Marketing Content Associate | **HEATHER DOORNINK** Production Director | **DREW GILL** Art Director | **HILARY DILORETO** Print Manager
TRICIA RAMOS Traffic Manager | **MELISSA GIFFORD** Content Manager | **ERIKA SCHNATZ** Senior Production Artist | **RYAN BREWER** Production Artist | **DEANNA PHELPS** Production Artist
IMAGECOMICS.COM

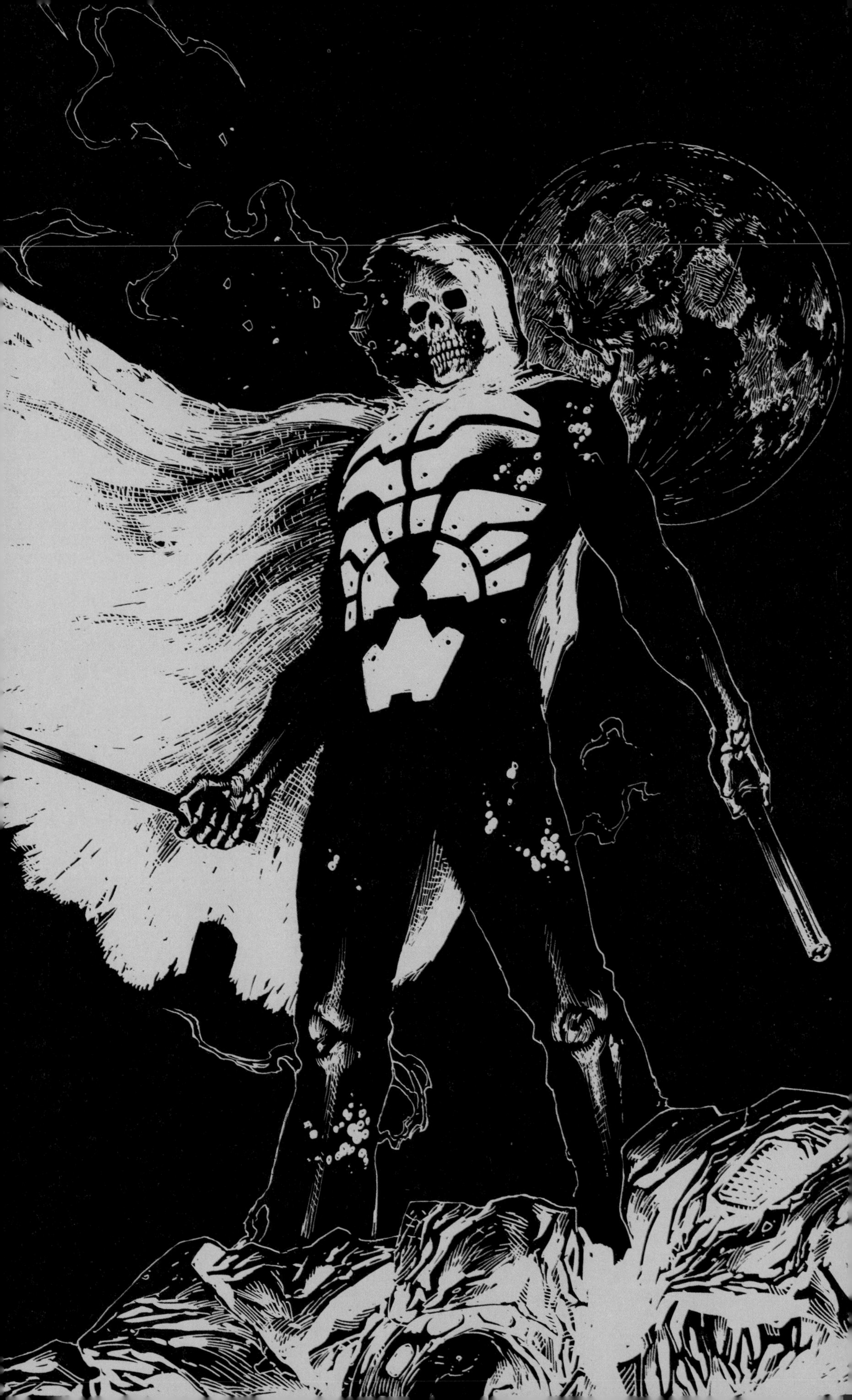

CHAPTER ONE

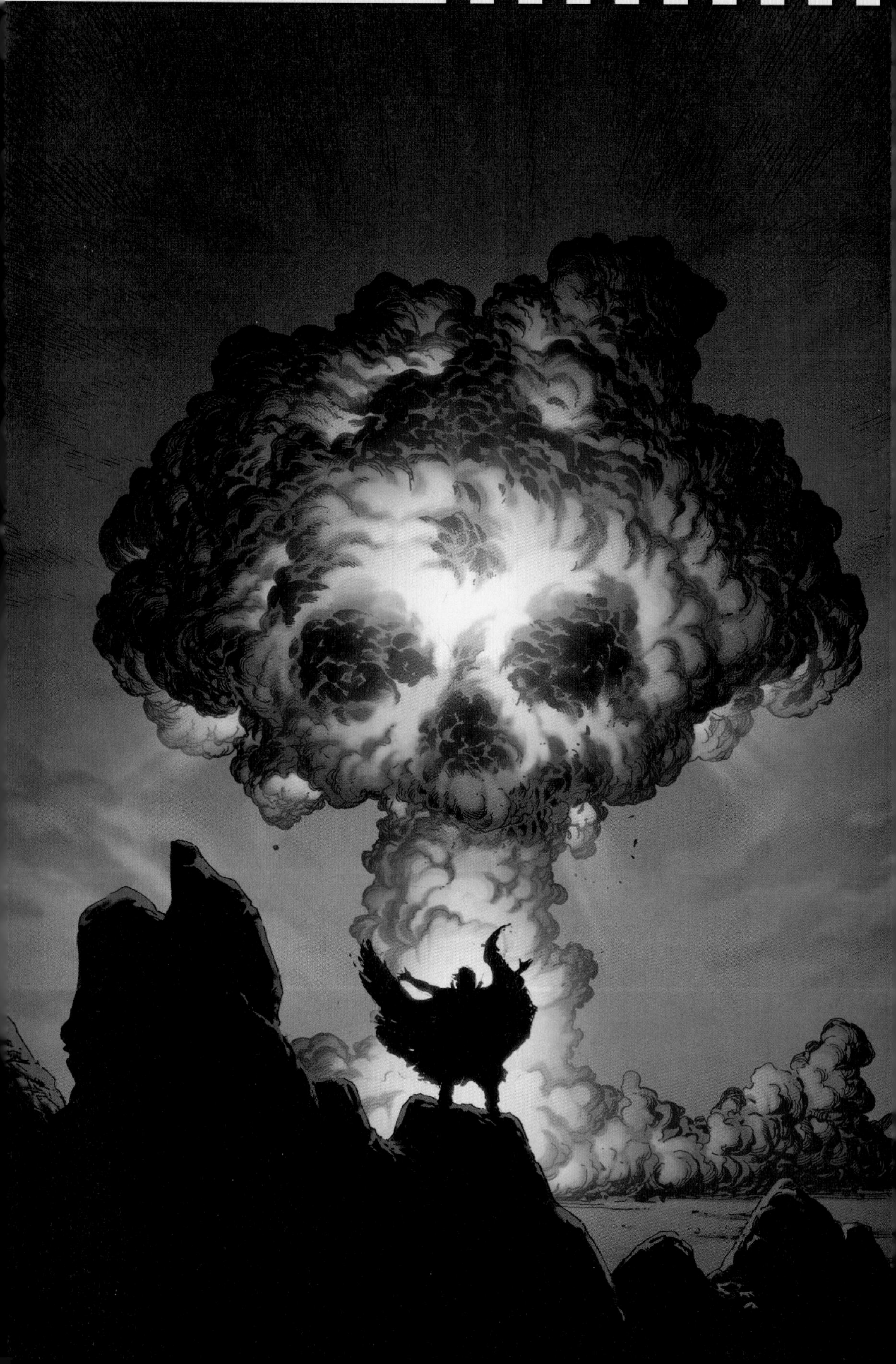

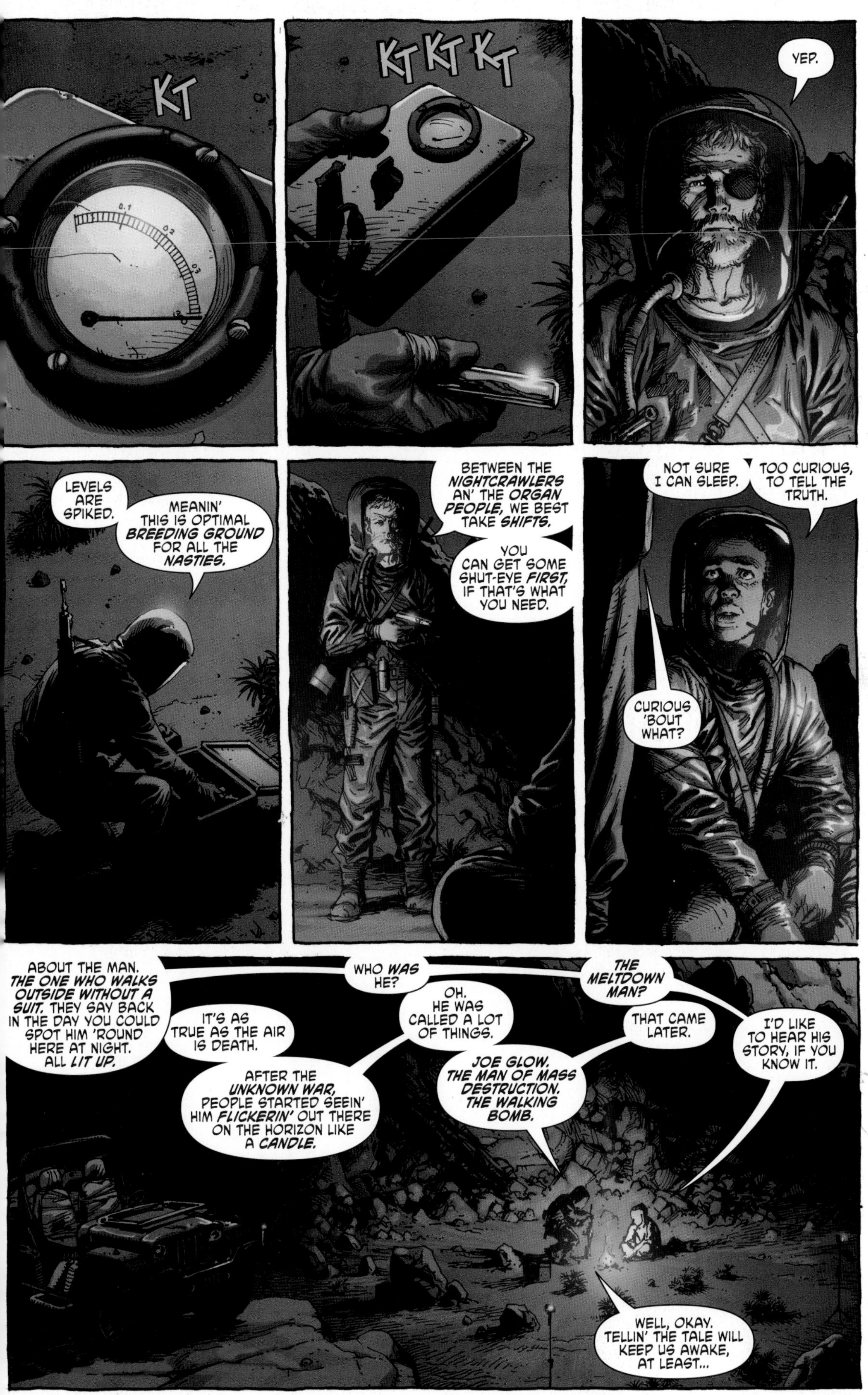
KT
KT KT KT
YEP.
LEVELS ARE SPIKED.
MEANIN' THIS IS OPTIMAL *BREEDING GROUND* FOR ALL THE *NASTIES.*
BETWEEN THE *NIGHTCRAWLERS* AN' THE *ORGAN PEOPLE,* WE BEST TAKE *SHIFTS.*
YOU CAN GET SOME SHUT-EYE *FIRST,* IF THAT'S WHAT YOU NEED.
NOT SURE I CAN SLEEP.
TOO CURIOUS, TO TELL THE TRUTH.
CURIOUS 'BOUT WHAT?
ABOUT THE MAN. *THE ONE WHO WALKS OUTSIDE WITHOUT A SUIT.* THEY SAY BACK IN THE DAY YOU COULD SPOT HIM 'ROUND HERE AT NIGHT. ALL *LIT UP.*
IT'S AS TRUE AS THE AIR IS DEATH.
WHO *WAS* HE?
THE MELTDOWN MAN?
OH. HE WAS CALLED A LOT OF THINGS.
THAT CAME LATER.
I'D LIKE TO HEAR HIS STORY, IF YOU KNOW IT.
AFTER THE *UNKNOWN WAR,* PEOPLE STARTED SEEIN' HIM *FLICKERIN'* OUT THERE ON THE HORIZON LIKE A *CANDLE.*
JOE GLOW. THE MAN OF MASS DESTRUCTION. THE WALKING BOMB.
WELL, OKAY. TELLIN' THE TALE WILL KEEP US AWAKE, AT LEAST...

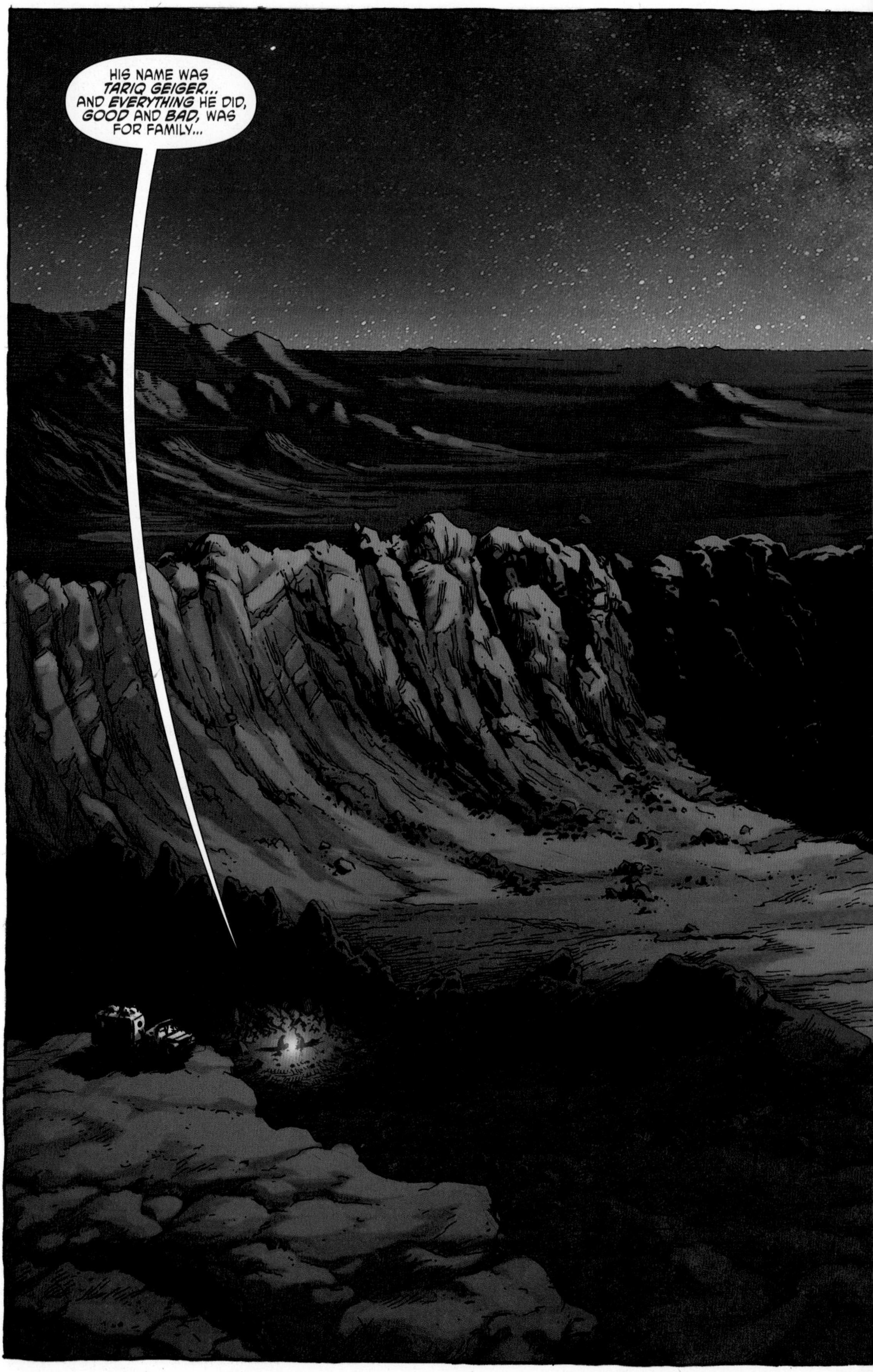
HIS NAME WAS *TARIQ GEIGER*... AND *EVERYTHING* HE DID, *GOOD* AND *BAD*, WAS FOR FAMILY...

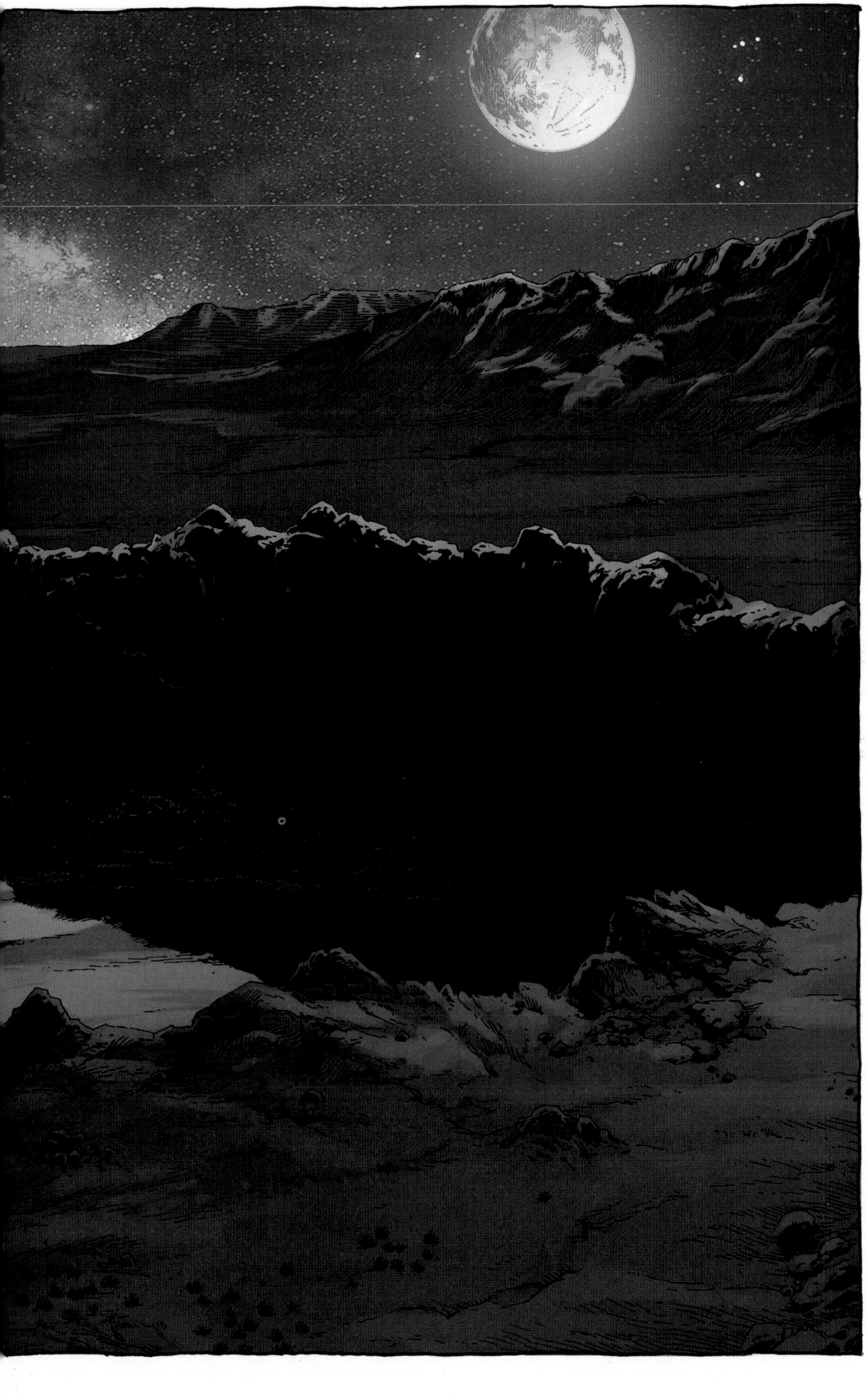

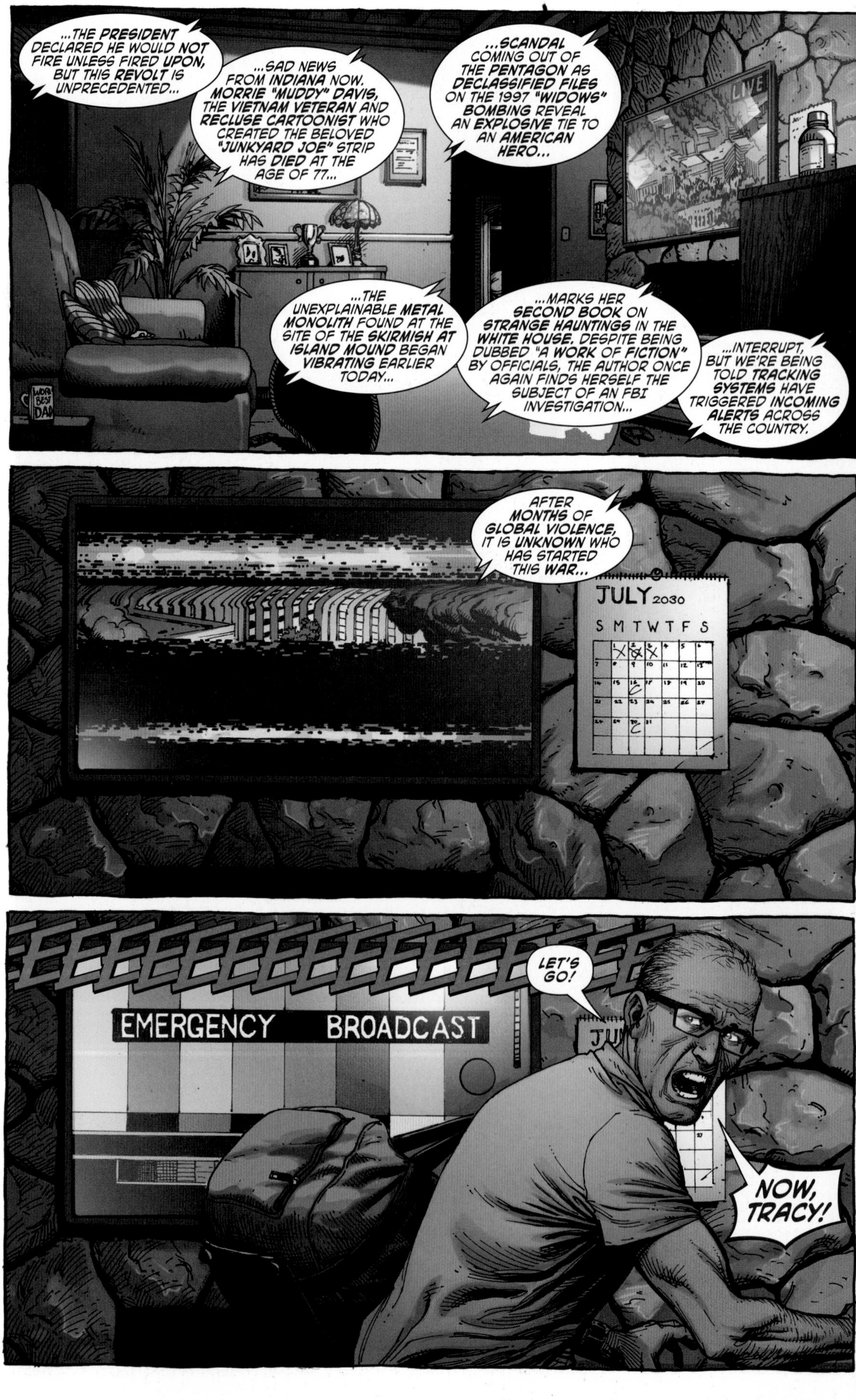
...THE PRESIDENT DECLARED HE WOULD NOT FIRE UNLESS FIRED UPON, BUT THIS REVOLT IS UNPRECEDENTED...
...SAD NEWS FROM INDIANA NOW. MORRIE "MUDDY" DAVIS, THE VIETNAM VETERAN AND RECLUSE CARTOONIST WHO CREATED THE BELOVED "JUNKYARD JOE" STRIP HAS DIED AT THE AGE OF 77...
...SCANDAL COMING OUT OF THE PENTAGON AS DECLASSIFIED FILES ON THE 1997 "WIDOWS" BOMBING REVEAL AN EXPLOSIVE TIE TO AN AMERICAN HERO...
LIVE
...THE UNEXPLAINABLE METAL MONOLITH FOUND AT THE SITE OF THE SKIRMISH AT ISLAND MOUND BEGAN VIBRATING EARLIER TODAY...
...MARKS HER SECOND BOOK ON STRANGE HAUNTINGS IN THE WHITE HOUSE. DESPITE BEING DUBBED "A WORK OF FICTION" BY OFFICIALS, THE AUTHOR ONCE AGAIN FINDS HERSELF THE SUBJECT OF AN FBI INVESTIGATION...
...INTERRUPT, BUT WE'RE BEING TOLD TRACKING SYSTEMS HAVE TRIGGERED INCOMING ALERTS ACROSS THE COUNTRY.
AFTER MONTHS OF GLOBAL VIOLENCE, IT IS UNKNOWN WHO HAS STARTED THIS WAR...
JULY 2030
S M T W T F S
EEEEEEEEEEEEEEEEEEEE
EMERGENCY BROADCAST
LET'S GO!
NOW, TRACY!

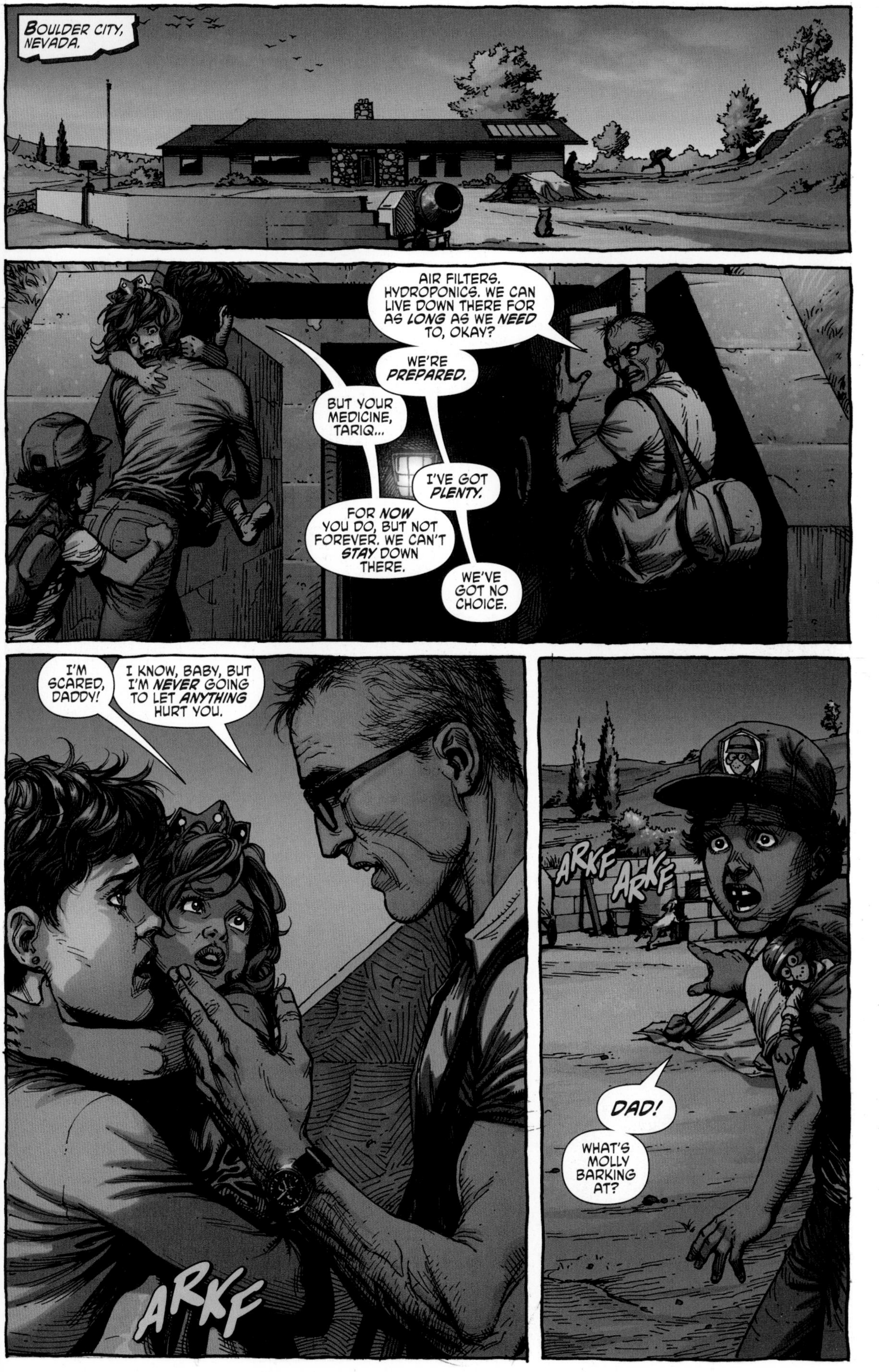
BOULDER CITY, NEVADA.
AIR FILTERS. HYDROPONICS. WE CAN LIVE DOWN THERE FOR AS LONG AS WE NEED TO, OKAY?
WE'RE PREPARED.
BUT YOUR MEDICINE, TARIQ...
I'VE GOT PLENTY.
FOR NOW YOU DO, BUT NOT FOREVER. WE CAN'T STAY DOWN THERE.
WE'VE GOT NO CHOICE.
I'M SCARED, DADDY!
I KNOW, BABY, BUT I'M NEVER GOING TO LET ANYTHING HURT YOU.
ARKF
ARKF ARKF
DAD!
WHAT'S MOLLY BARKING AT?

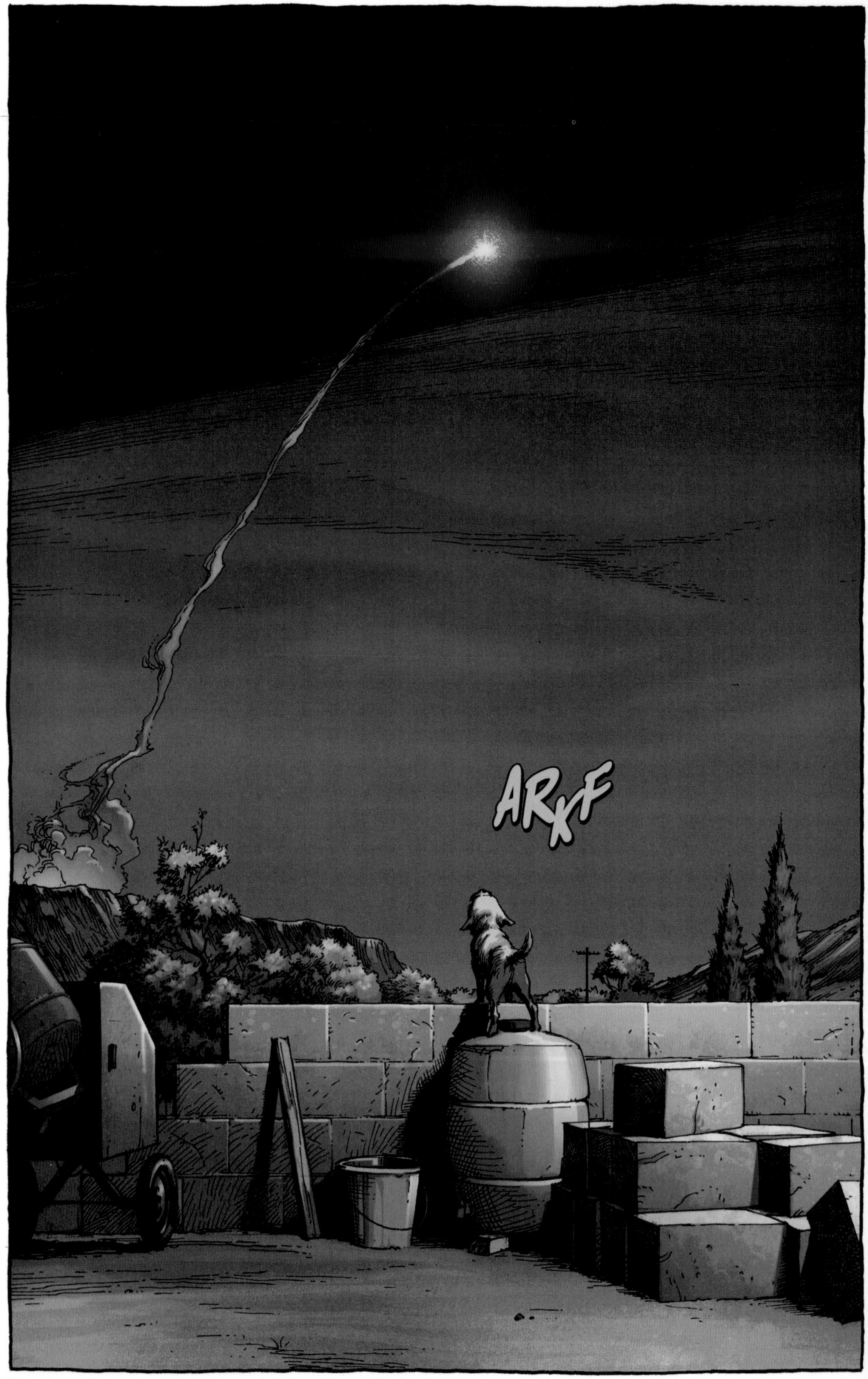
ARKF

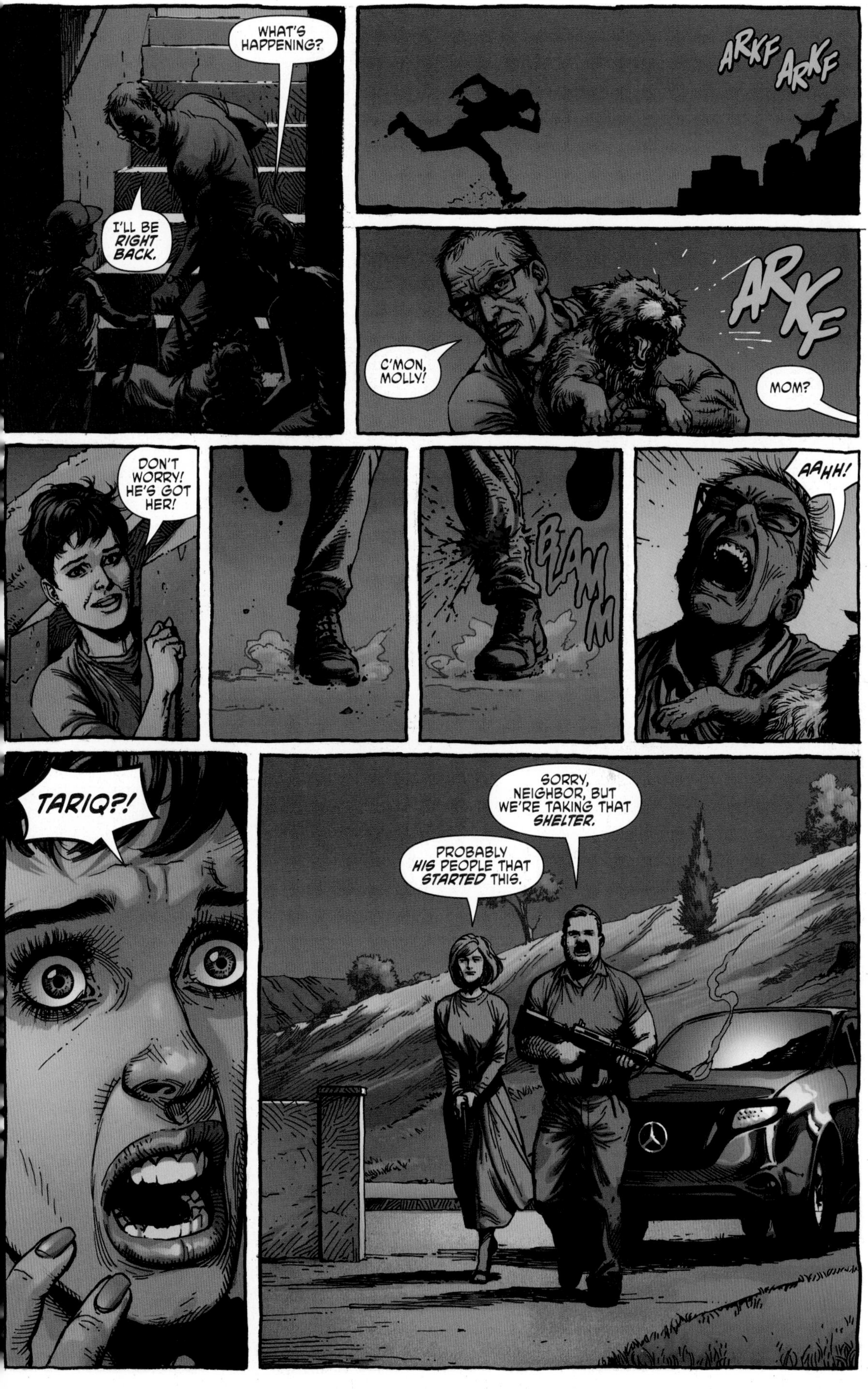
WHAT'S HAPPENING?
I'LL BE RIGHT BACK.
ARKF ARKF
ARKF
C'MON, MOLLY!
MOM?
DON'T WORRY! HE'S GOT HER!
BLAMM
AAHH!
TARIQ?!
SORRY, NEIGHBOR, BUT WE'RE TAKING THAT SHELTER.
PROBABLY HIS PEOPLE THAT STARTED THIS.

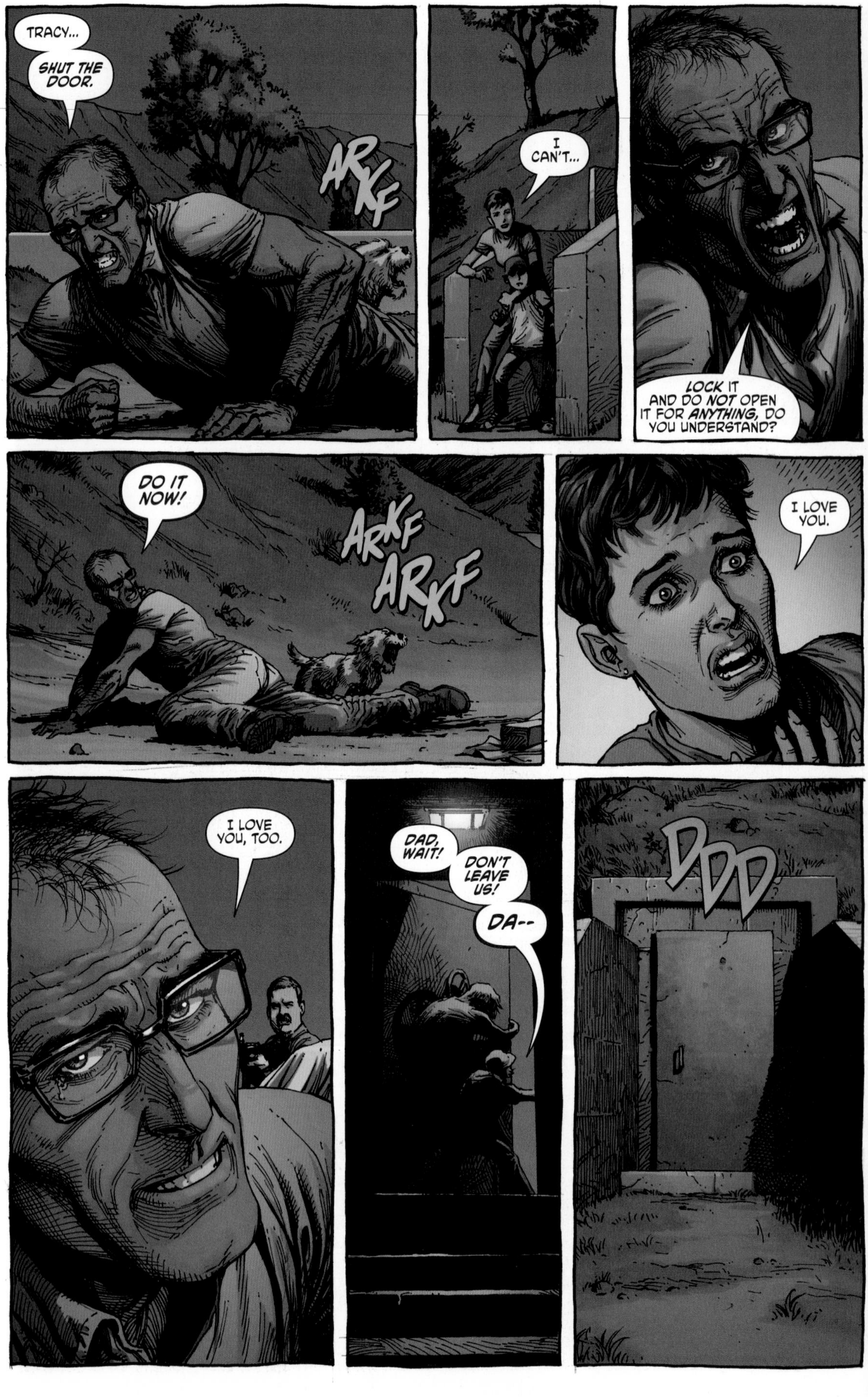
TRACY...
SHUT THE DOOR.
ARKF
I CAN'T...
LOCK IT AND DO NOT OPEN IT FOR ANYTHING, DO YOU UNDERSTAND?
DO IT NOW!
ARKF ARKF
I LOVE YOU.
I LOVE YOU, TOO.
DAD, WAIT!
DON'T LEAVE US!
DA--
DDD

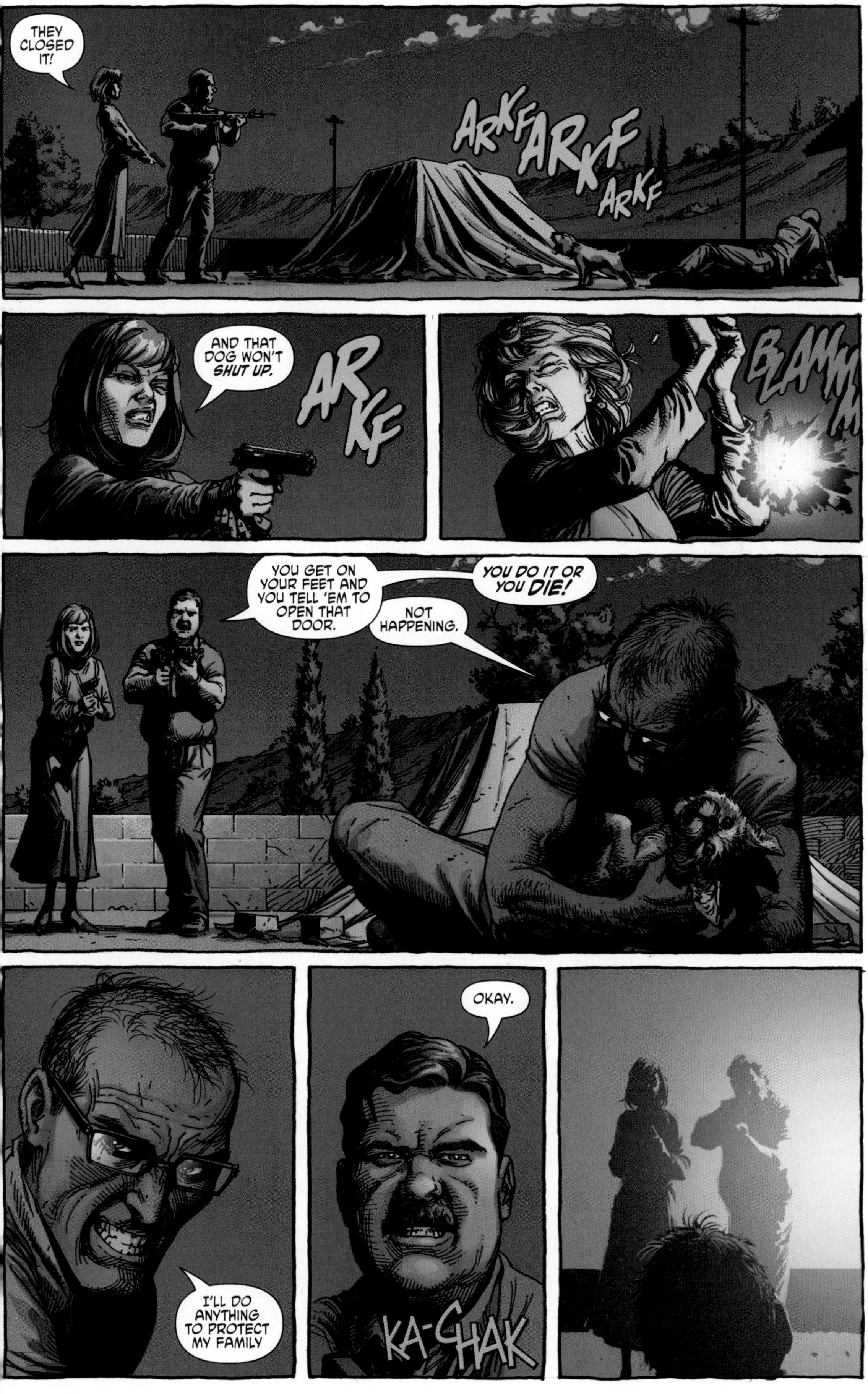

THEY CLOSED IT!
ARKF ARKF ARKF
AND THAT DOG WON'T SHUT UP.
ARKF
BLAMMM
YOU GET ON YOUR FEET AND YOU TELL 'EM TO OPEN THAT DOOR.
YOU DO IT OR YOU DIE!
NOT HAPPENING.
I'LL DO ANYTHING TO PROTECT MY FAMILY
OKAY.
KA-CHAK

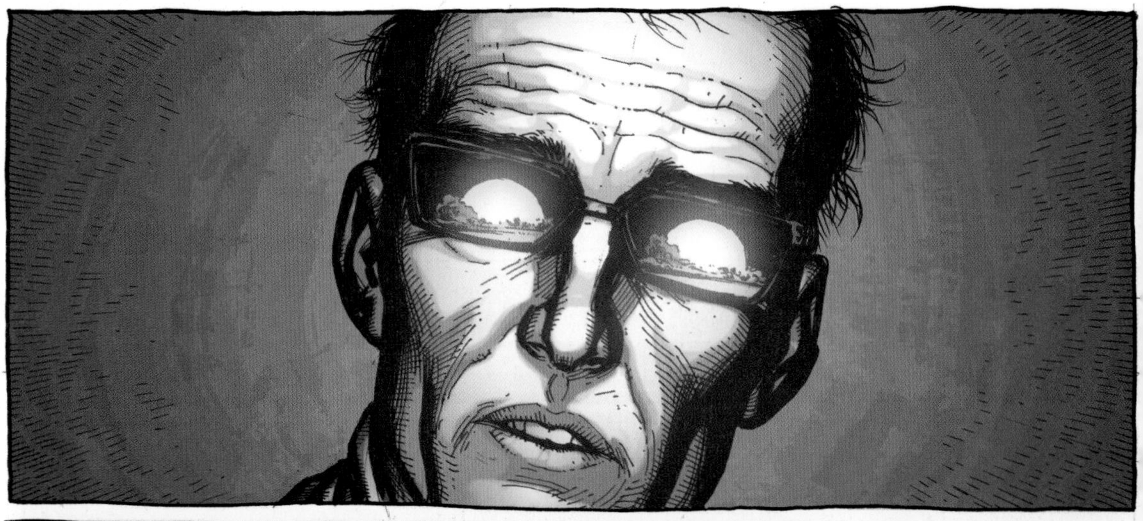

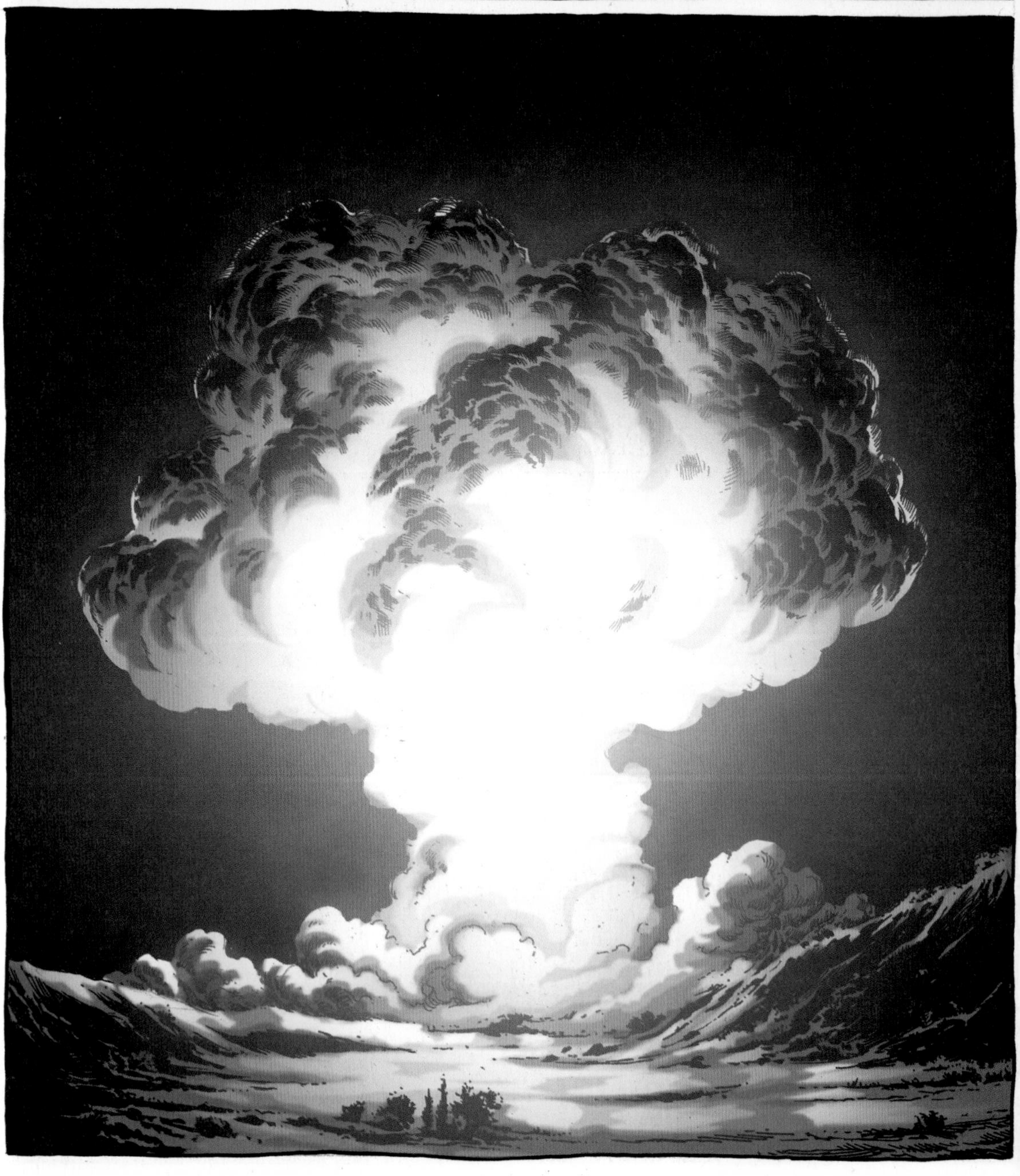

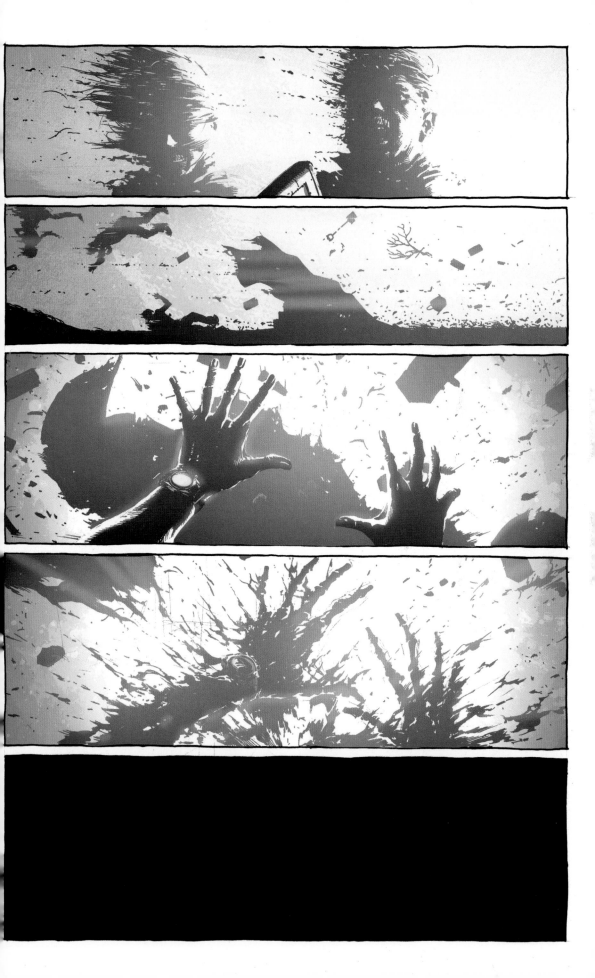

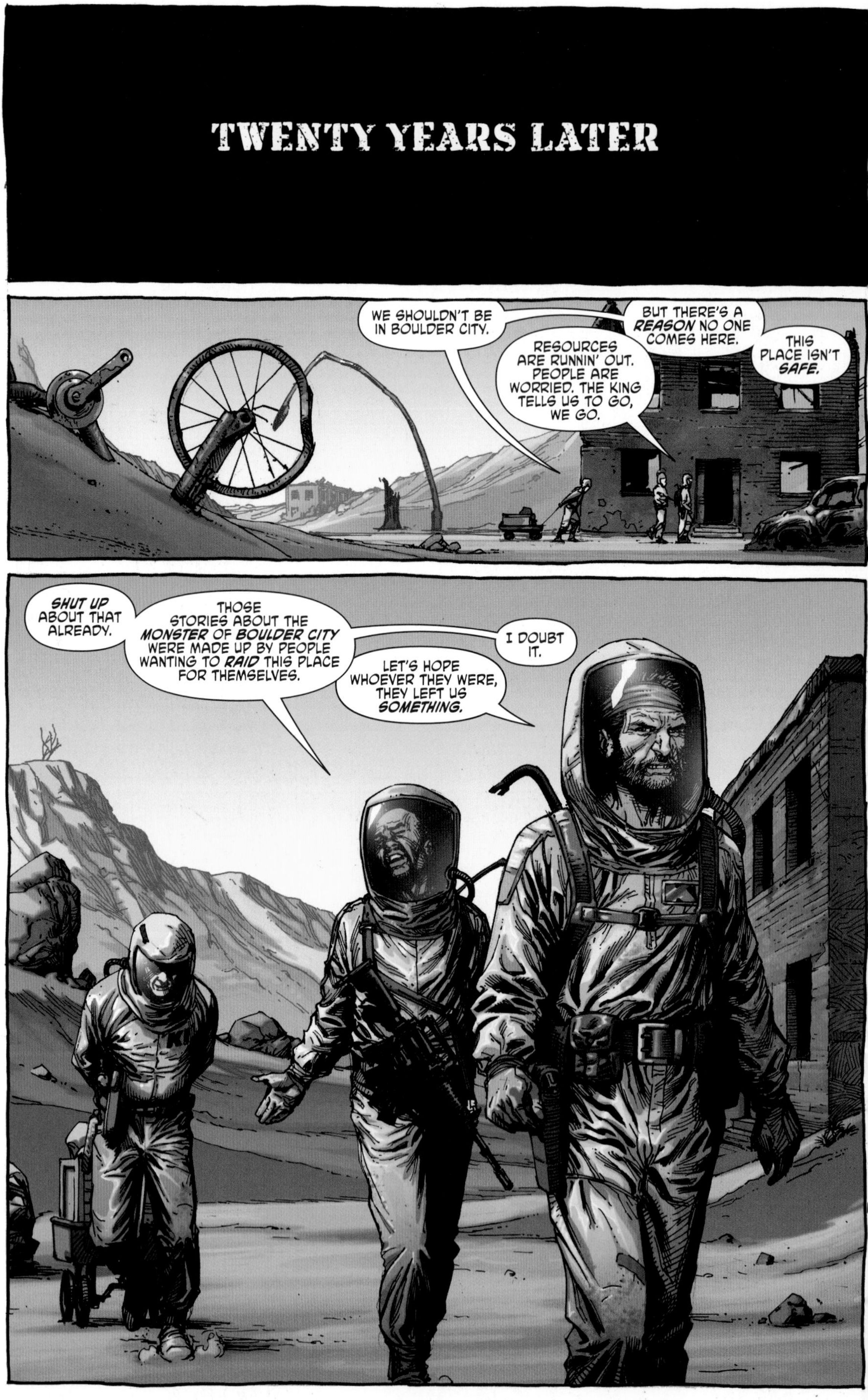
TWENTY YEARS LATER
WE SHOULDN'T BE IN BOULDER CITY.
BUT THERE'S A *REASON* NO ONE COMES HERE.
THIS PLACE ISN'T *SAFE.*
RESOURCES ARE RUNNIN' OUT. PEOPLE ARE WORRIED. THE KING TELLS US TO GO, WE GO.
SHUT UP ABOUT THAT ALREADY.
THOSE STORIES ABOUT THE *MONSTER* OF *BOULDER CITY* WERE MADE UP BY PEOPLE WANTING TO *RAID* THIS PLACE FOR THEMSELVES.
I DOUBT IT.
LET'S HOPE WHOEVER THEY WERE, THEY LEFT US *SOMETHING.*

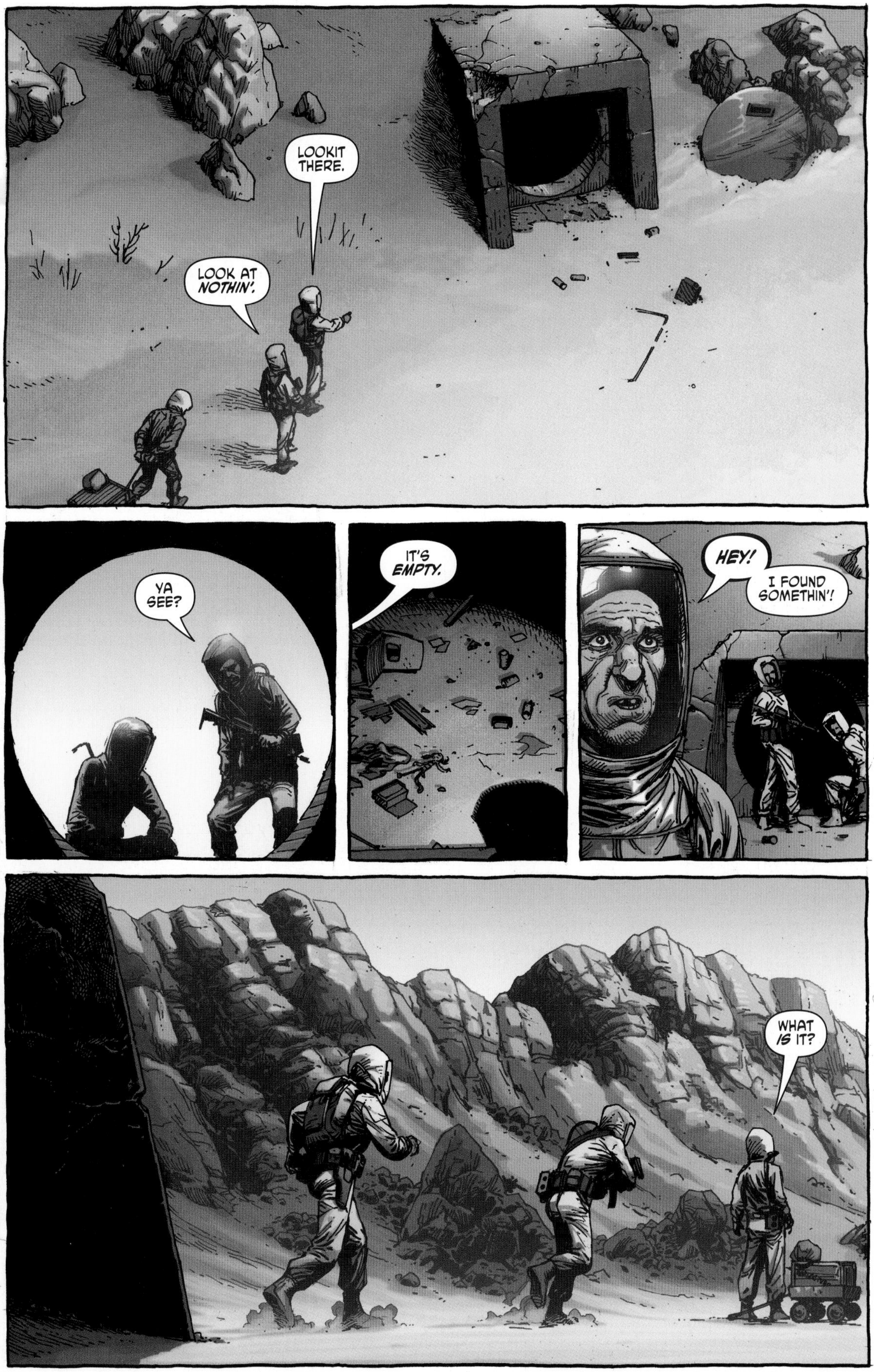
LOOKIT THERE.
LOOK AT *NOTHIN'.*
YA SEE?
IT'S *EMPTY.*
HEY!
I FOUND SOMETHIN'!
WHAT *IS* IT?

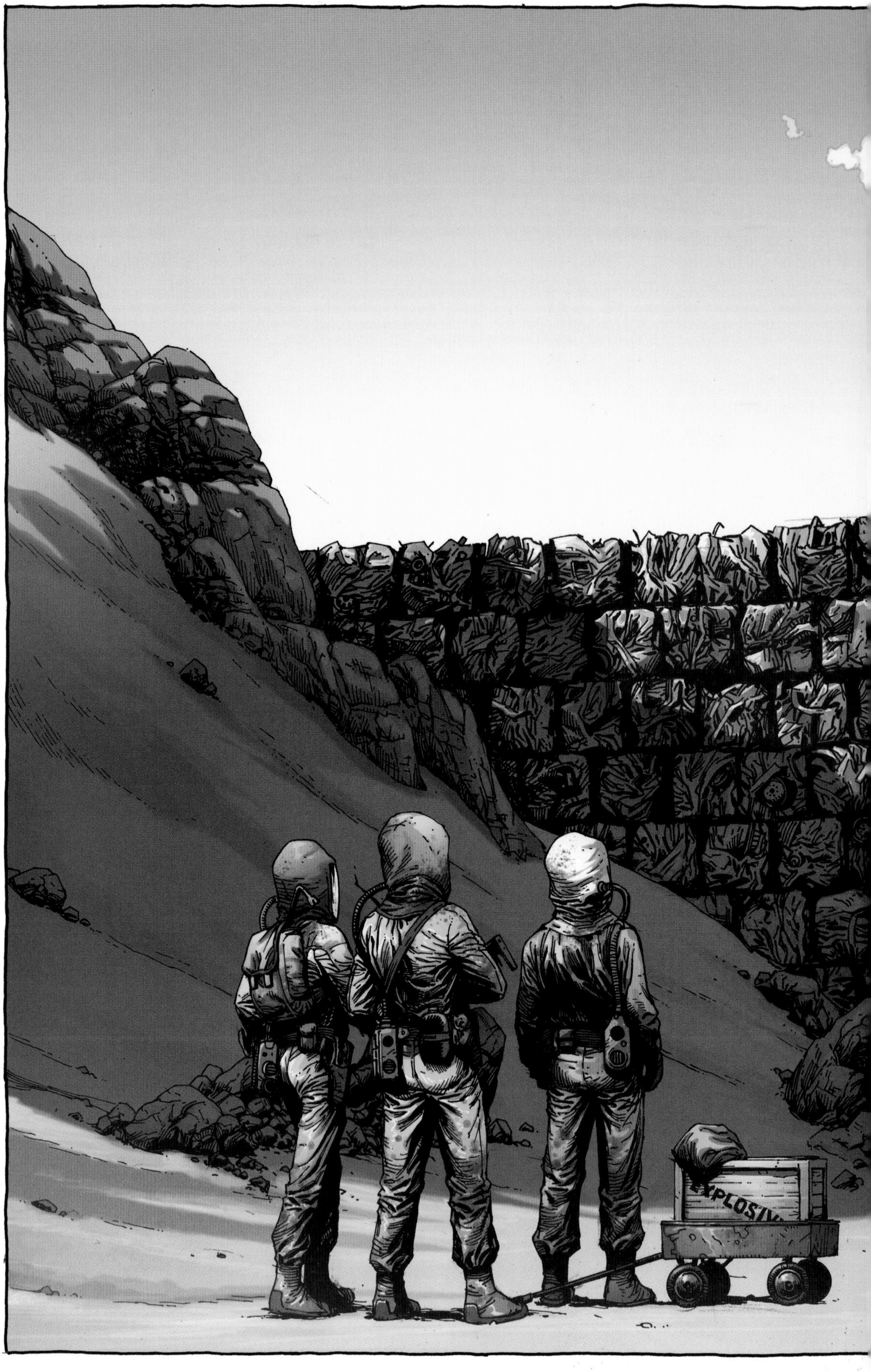

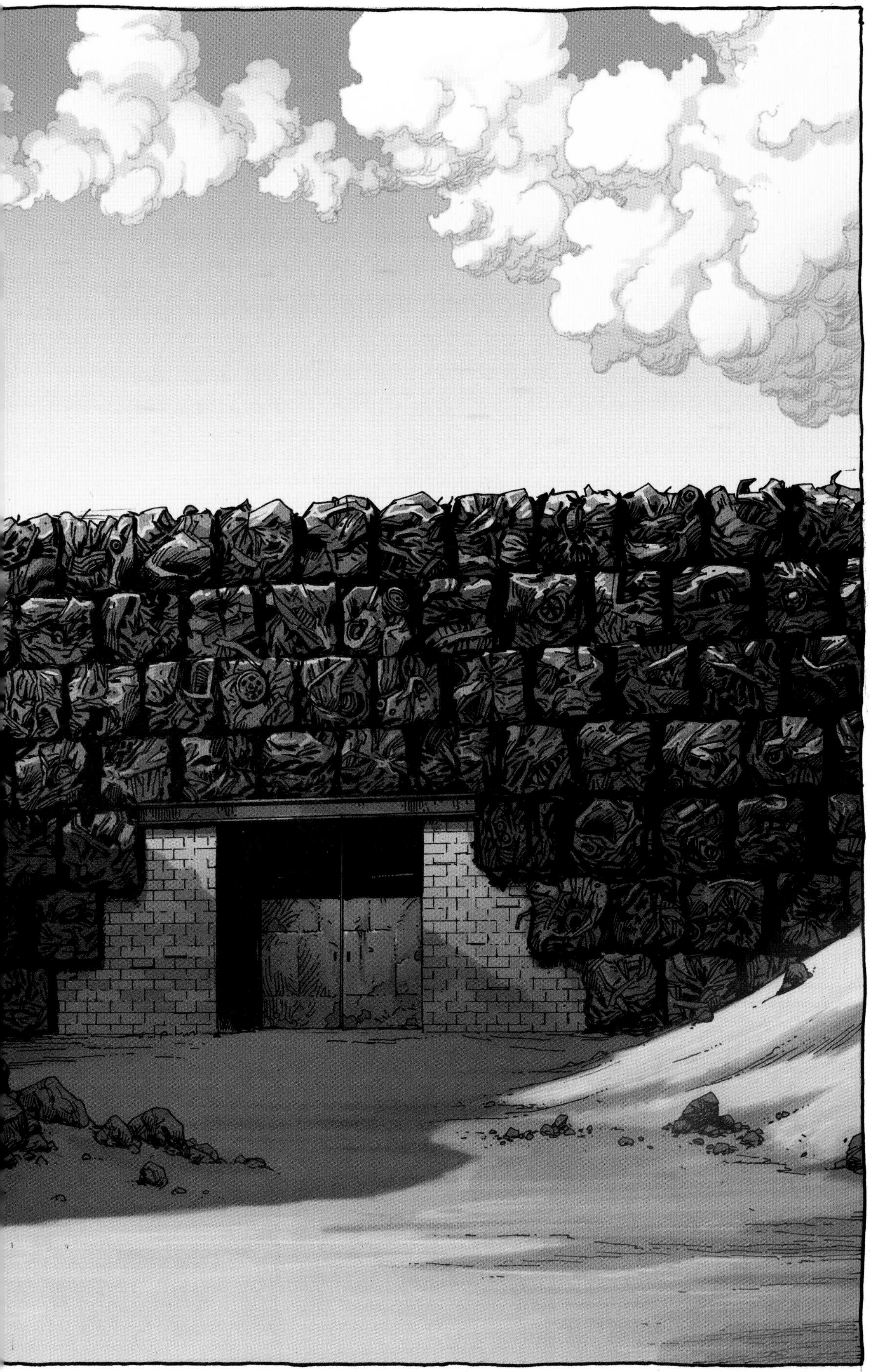

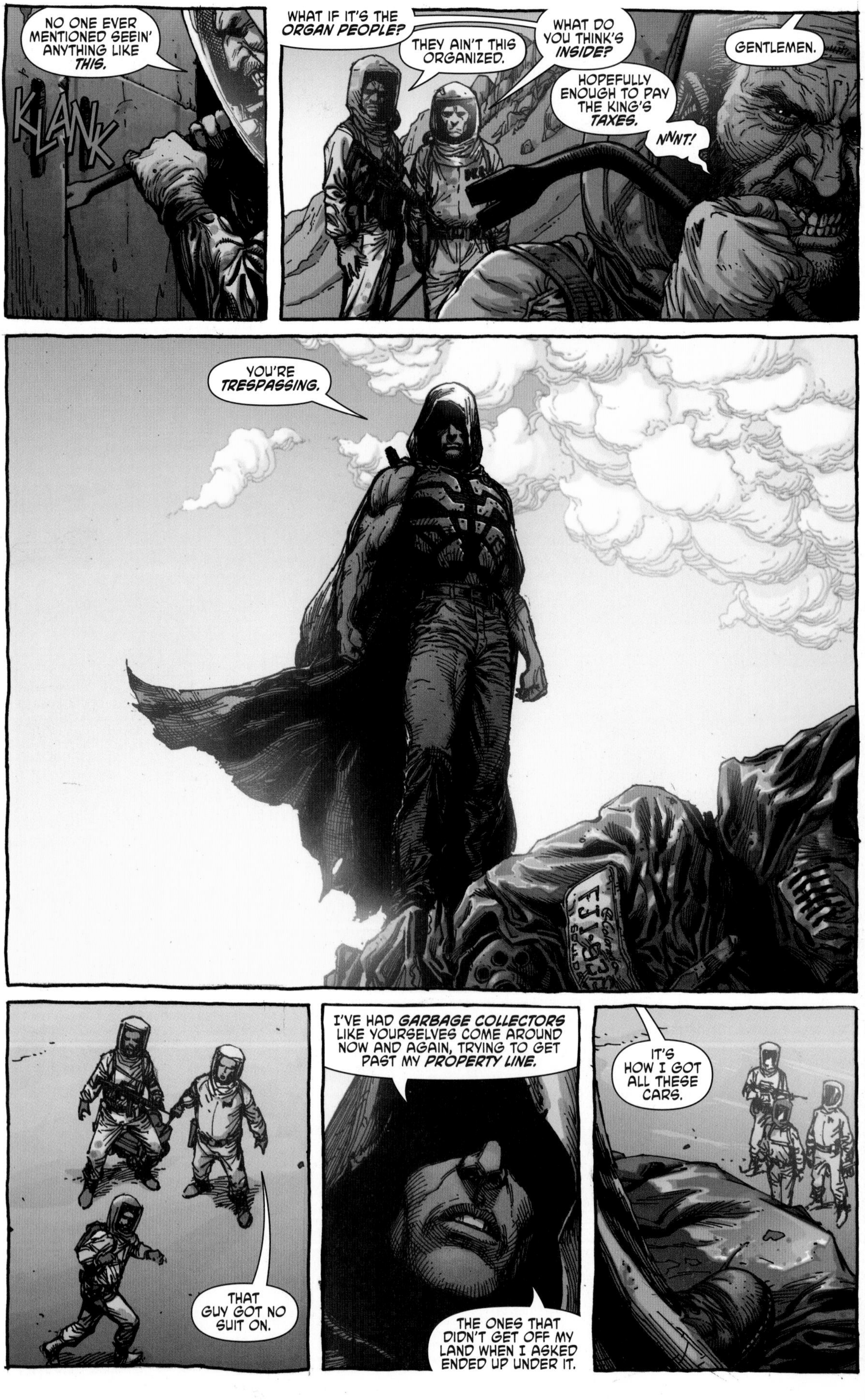
NO ONE EVER MENTIONED SEEIN' ANYTHING LIKE THIS.
KLANK
WHAT IF IT'S THE ORGAN PEOPLE?
THEY AIN'T THIS ORGANIZED.
WHAT DO YOU THINK'S INSIDE?
HOPEFULLY ENOUGH TO PAY THE KING'S TAXES.
NNNT!
GENTLEMEN.
YOU'RE TRESPASSING.
THAT GUY GOT NO SUIT ON.
I'VE HAD GARBAGE COLLECTORS LIKE YOURSELVES COME AROUND NOW AND AGAIN, TRYING TO GET PAST MY PROPERTY LINE.
THE ONES THAT DIDN'T GET OFF MY LAND WHEN I ASKED ENDED UP UNDER IT.
IT'S HOW I GOT ALL THESE CARS.

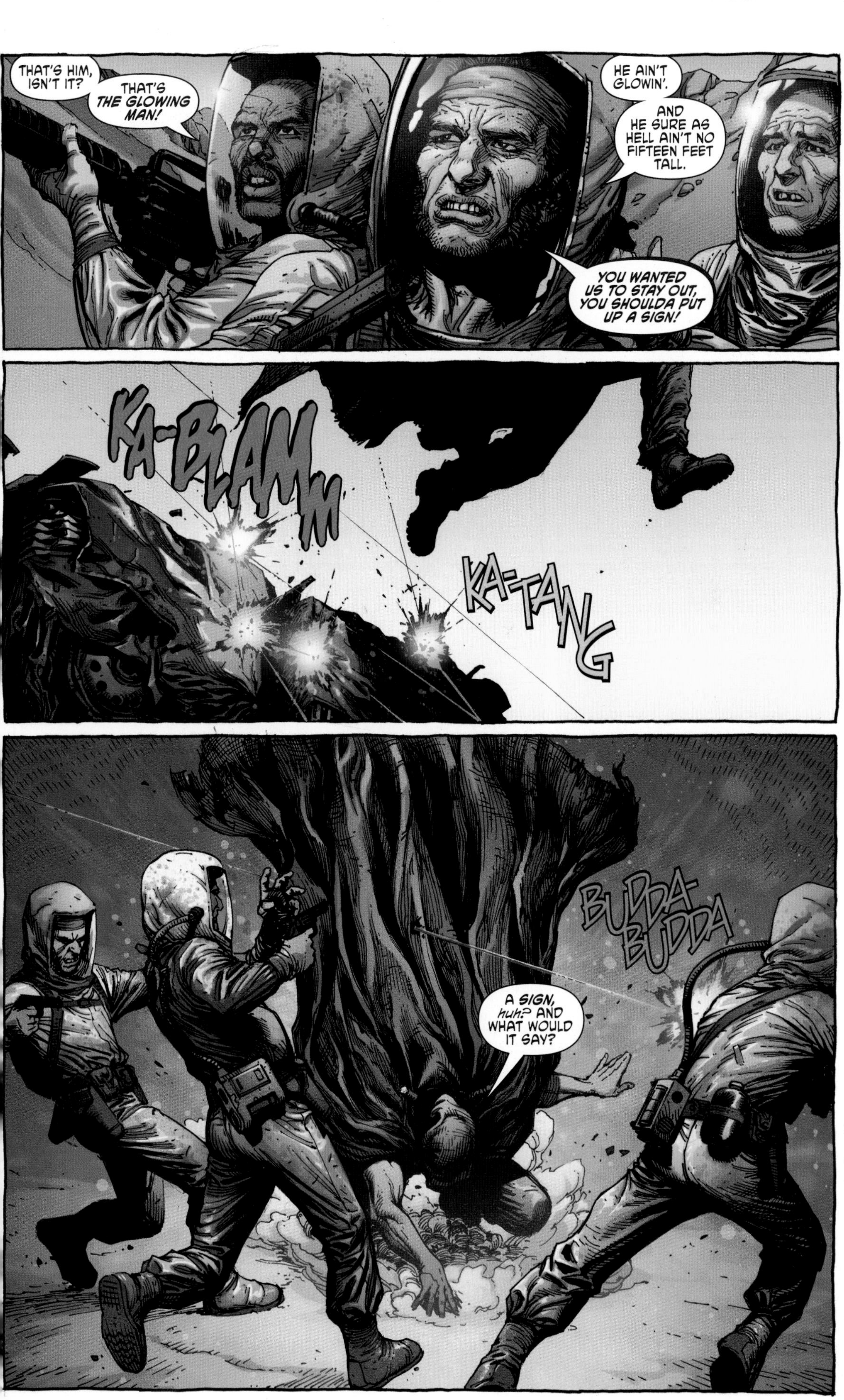
THAT'S HIM, ISN'T IT?
THAT'S *THE GLOWING MAN!*
HE AIN'T GLOWIN'.
AND HE SURE AS HELL AIN'T NO FIFTEEN FEET TALL.
YOU WANTED US TO STAY OUT, YOU SHOULDA PUT UP A SIGN!
KA-BLAMMM
KA-TANG
BUDDA-BUDDA
A *SIGN, huh?* AND WHAT WOULD IT SAY?

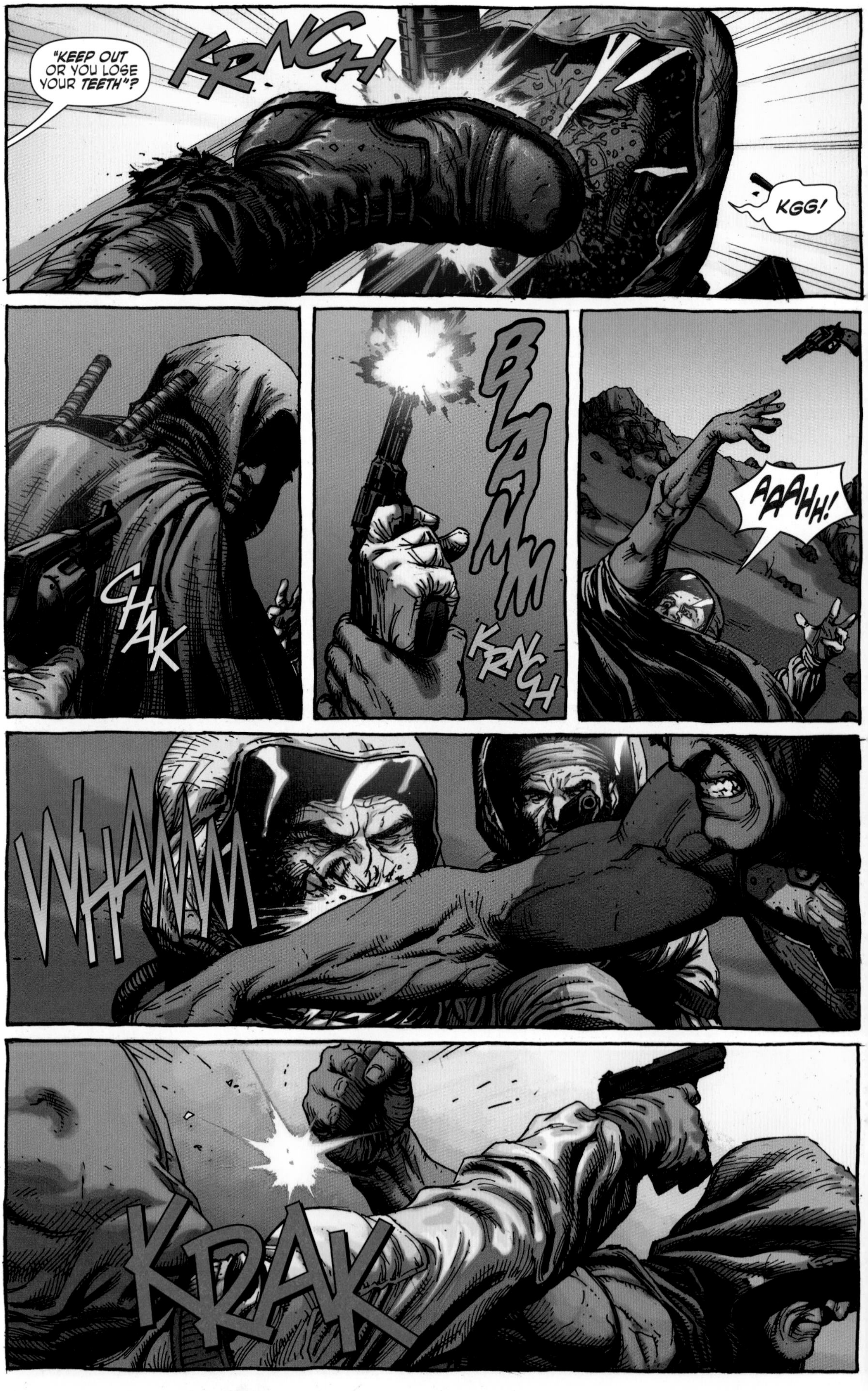
"KEEP OUT OR YOU LOSE YOUR TEETH"?
KRNCH
KGG!
CHAK
BLAMMM
KRNCH
AAAHH!
WHAMM
KRAK

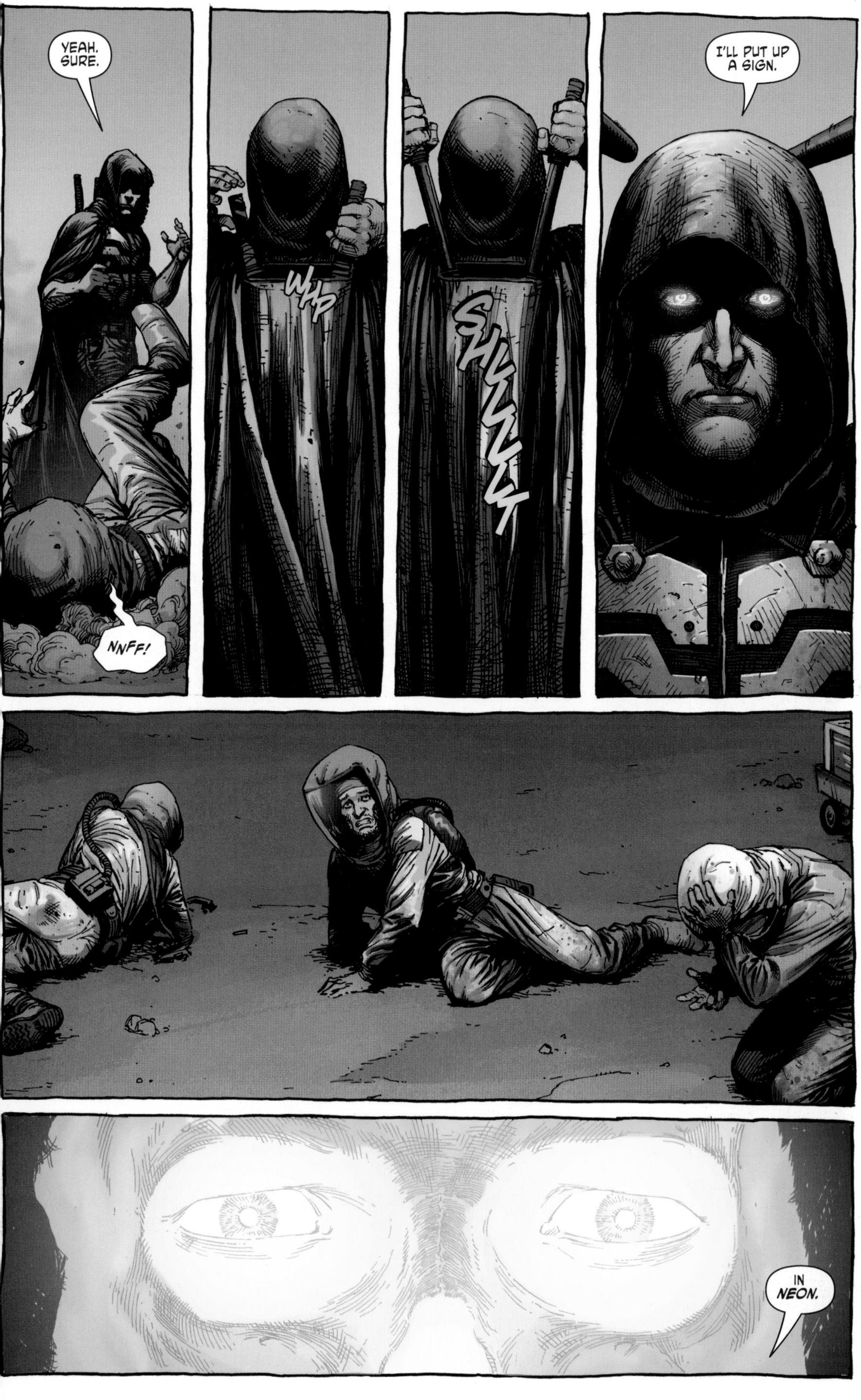
YEAH. SURE.
NNFF!
WHP
SHUKKK
I'LL PUT UP A SIGN.
IN NEON.

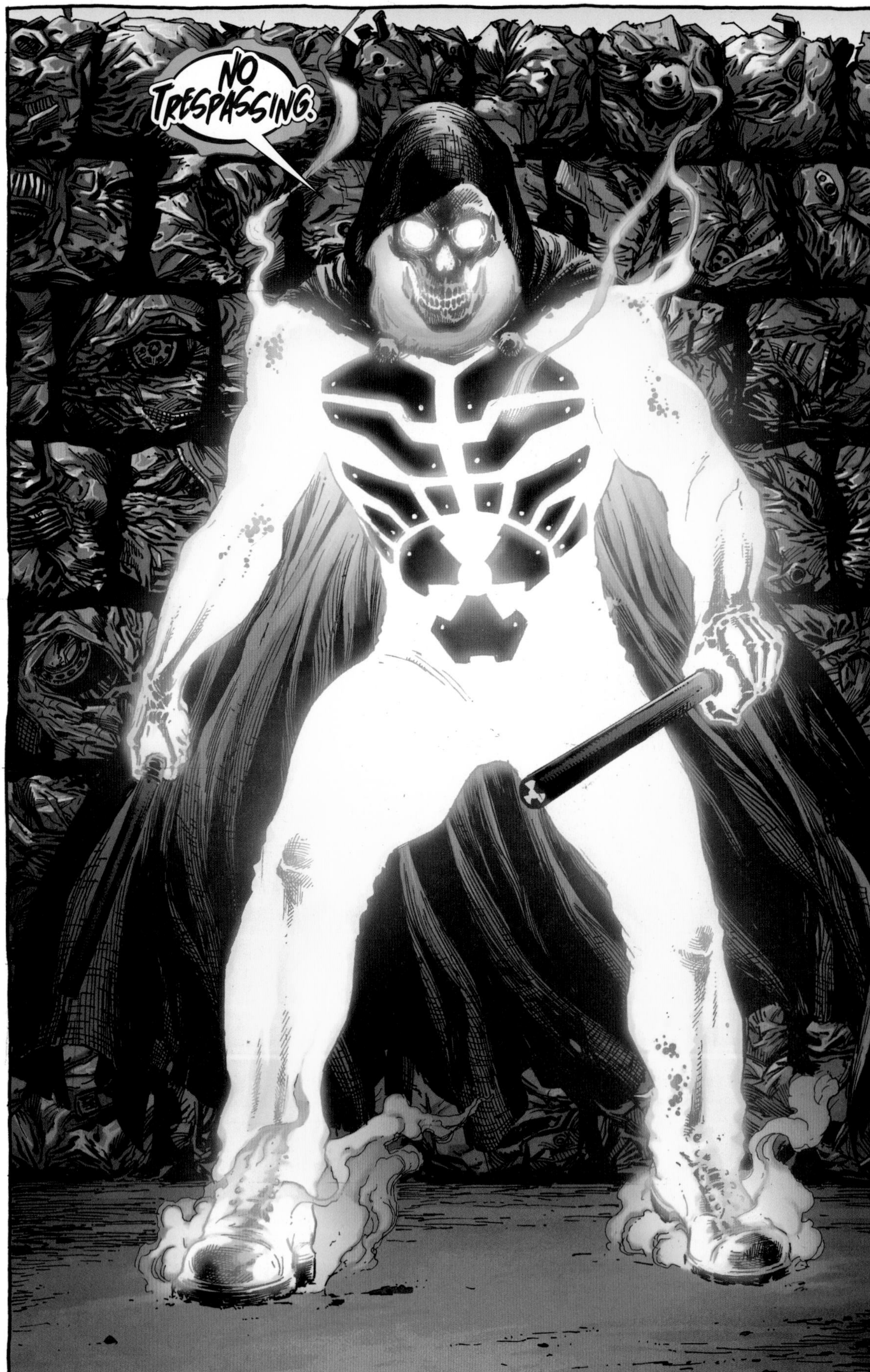
NO TRESPASSING.

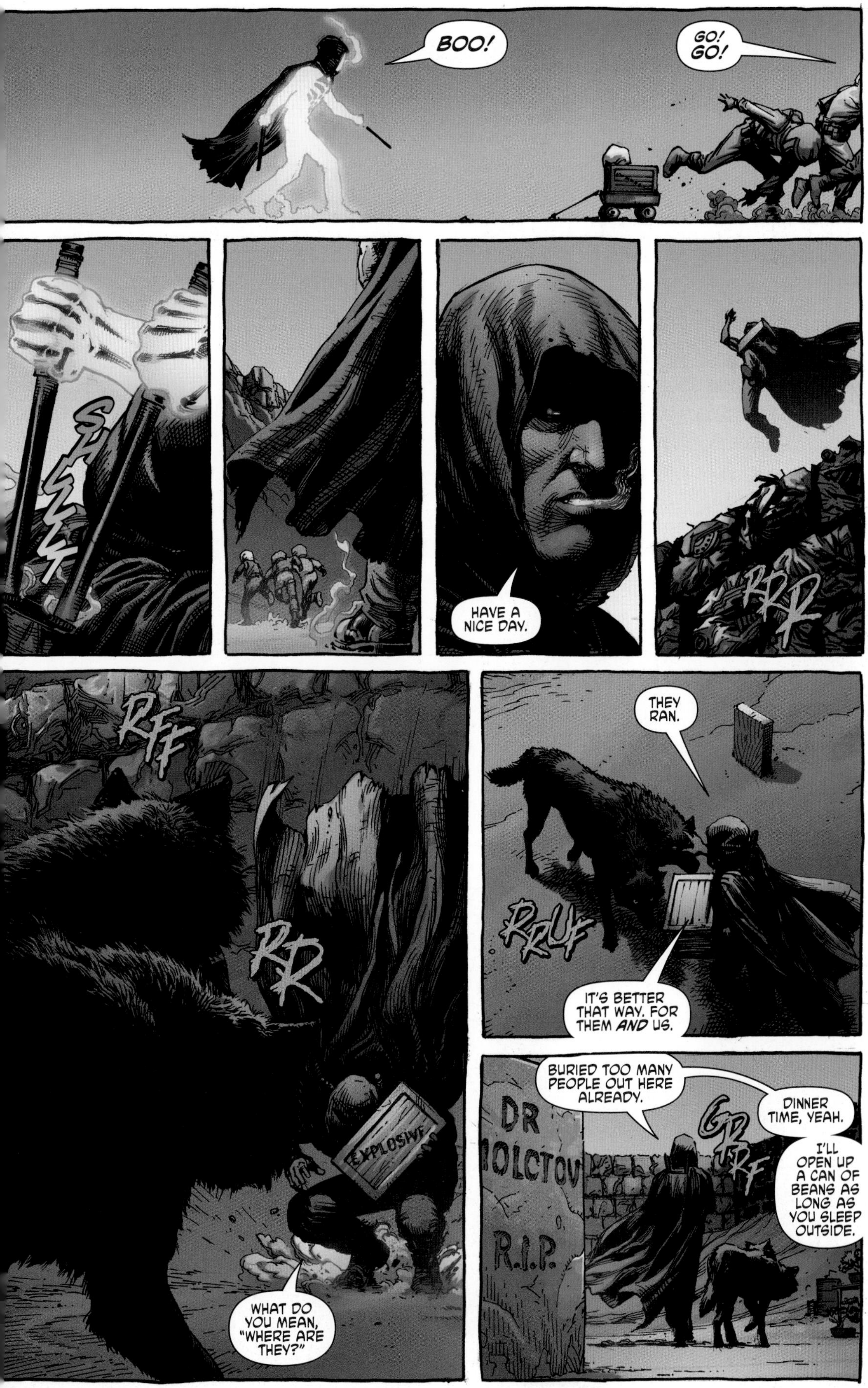
BOO!
GO! GO!
HAVE A NICE DAY.
RRR
RFF
RR
WHAT DO YOU MEAN, "WHERE ARE THEY?"
THEY RAN.
RRUF
IT'S BETTER THAT WAY. FOR THEM AND US.
BURIED TOO MANY PEOPLE OUT HERE ALREADY.
DR MOLCTOV R.I.P.
GRRF
DINNER TIME, YEAH.
I'LL OPEN UP A CAN OF BEANS AS LONG AS YOU SLEEP OUTSIDE.

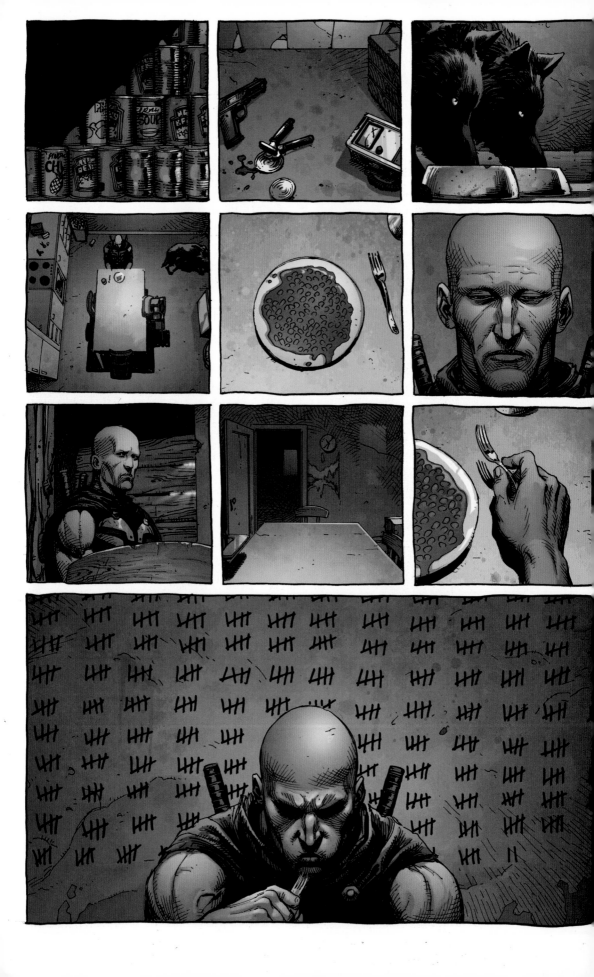

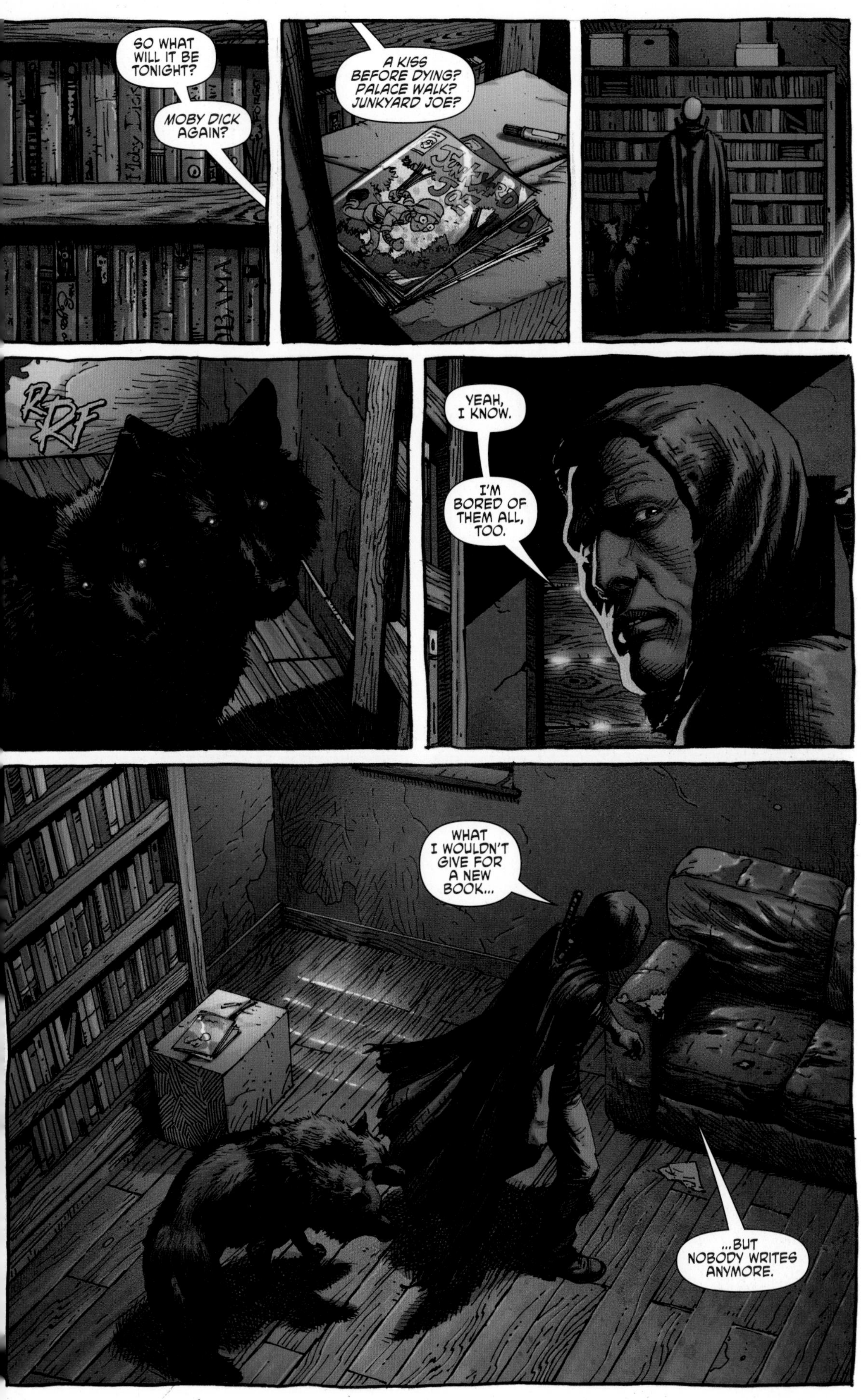
SO WHAT WILL IT BE TONIGHT?
MOBY DICK AGAIN?
A KISS BEFORE DYING? PALACE WALK? JUNKYARD JOE?
RRF
YEAH, I KNOW.
I'M BORED OF THEM ALL, TOO.
WHAT I WOULDN'T GIVE FOR A NEW BOOK...
...BUT NOBODY WRITES ANYMORE.

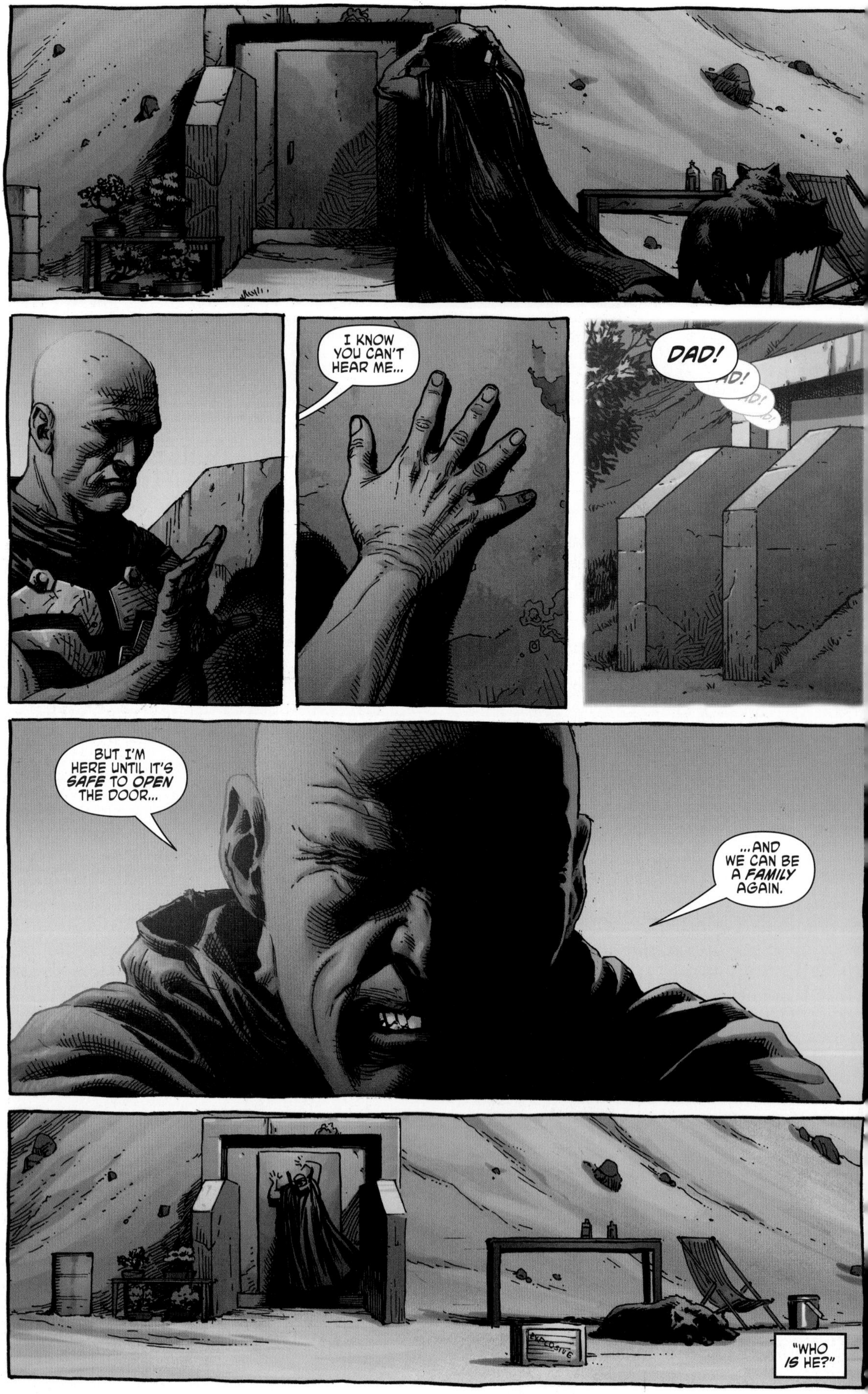
I KNOW YOU CAN'T HEAR ME...
DAD!
BUT I'M HERE UNTIL IT'S SAFE TO OPEN THE DOOR...
...AND WE CAN BE A FAMILY AGAIN.
"WHO IS HE?"

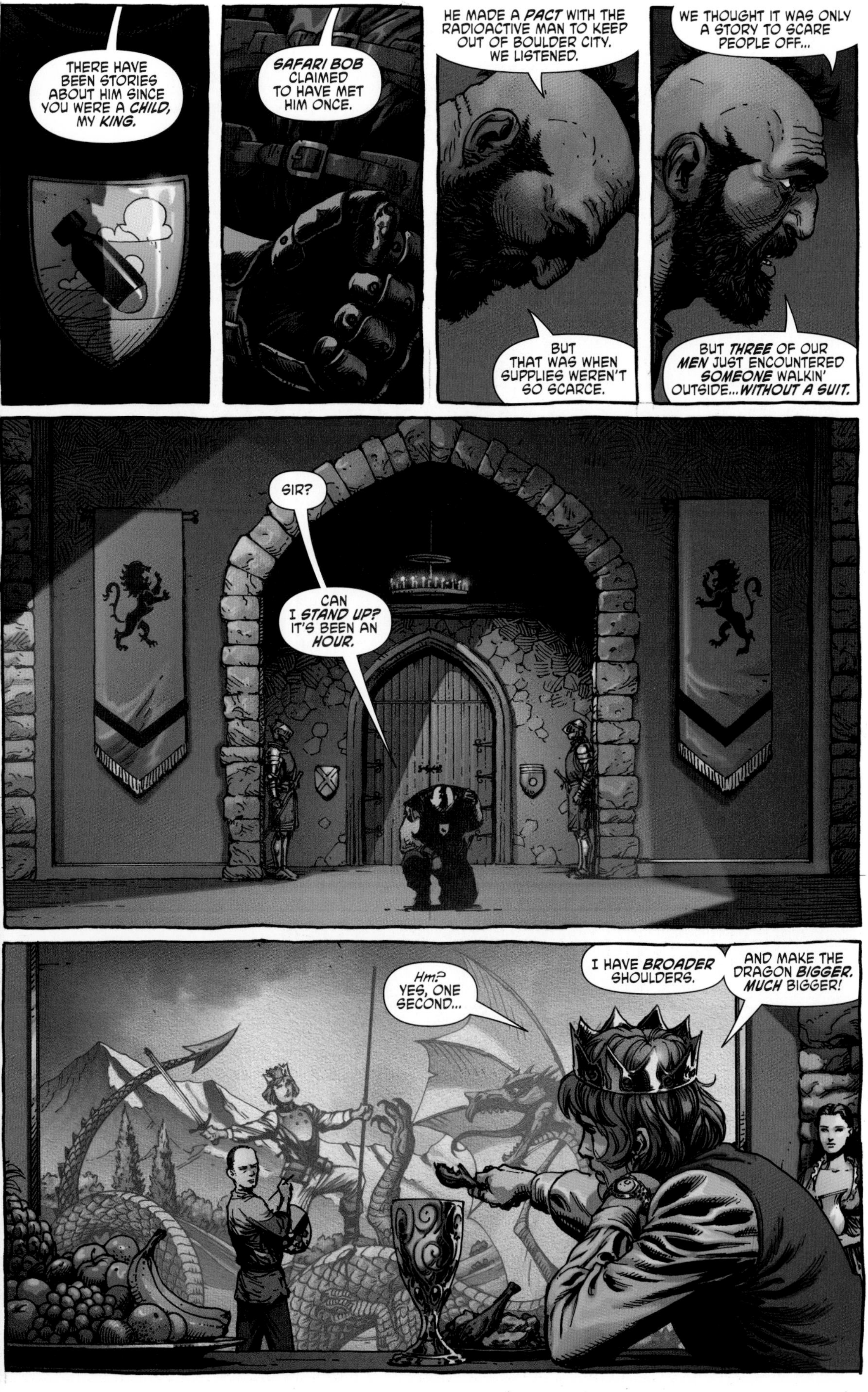
THERE HAVE BEEN STORIES ABOUT HIM SINCE YOU WERE A CHILD, MY KING.
SAFARI BOB CLAIMED TO HAVE MET HIM ONCE.
HE MADE A PACT WITH THE RADIOACTIVE MAN TO KEEP OUT OF BOULDER CITY. WE LISTENED.
BUT THAT WAS WHEN SUPPLIES WEREN'T SO SCARCE.
WE THOUGHT IT WAS ONLY A STORY TO SCARE PEOPLE OFF...
BUT THREE OF OUR MEN JUST ENCOUNTERED SOMEONE WALKIN' OUTSIDE...WITHOUT A SUIT.
SIR?
CAN I STAND UP? IT'S BEEN AN HOUR.
Hm? YES, ONE SECOND...
I HAVE BROADER SHOULDERS.
AND MAKE THE DRAGON BIGGER. MUCH BIGGER!

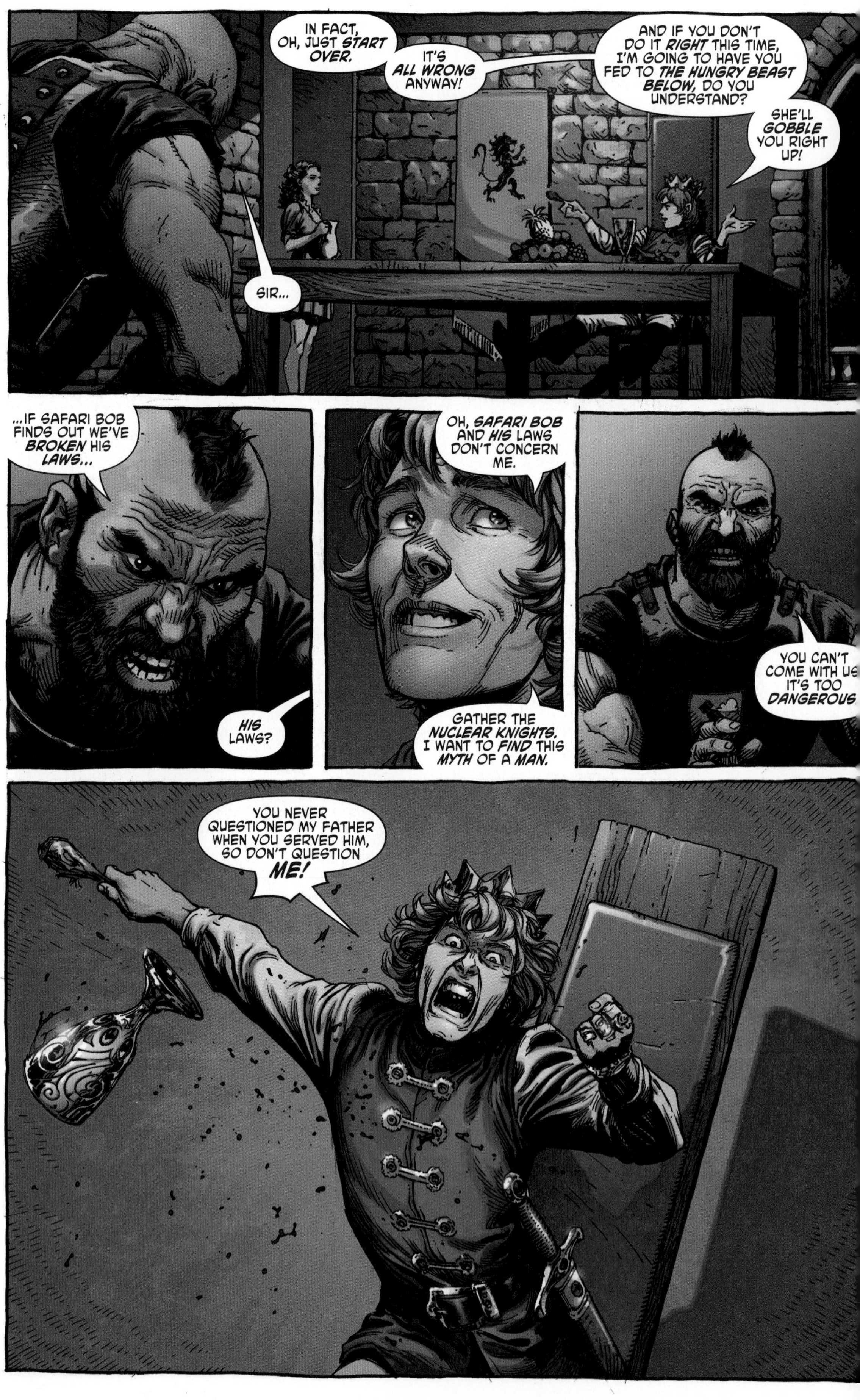
SIR...
IN FACT, OH, JUST START OVER.
IT'S ALL WRONG ANYWAY!
AND IF YOU DON'T DO IT RIGHT THIS TIME, I'M GOING TO HAVE YOU FED TO THE HUNGRY BEAST BELOW, DO YOU UNDERSTAND?
SHE'LL GOBBLE YOU RIGHT UP!
...IF SAFARI BOB FINDS OUT WE'VE BROKEN HIS LAWS...
HIS LAWS?
OH, SAFARI BOB AND HIS LAWS DON'T CONCERN ME.
GATHER THE NUCLEAR KNIGHTS. I WANT TO FIND THIS MYTH OF A MAN.
YOU CAN'T COME WITH US IT'S TOO DANGEROUS
YOU NEVER QUESTIONED MY FATHER WHEN YOU SERVED HIM, SO DON'T QUESTION ME!

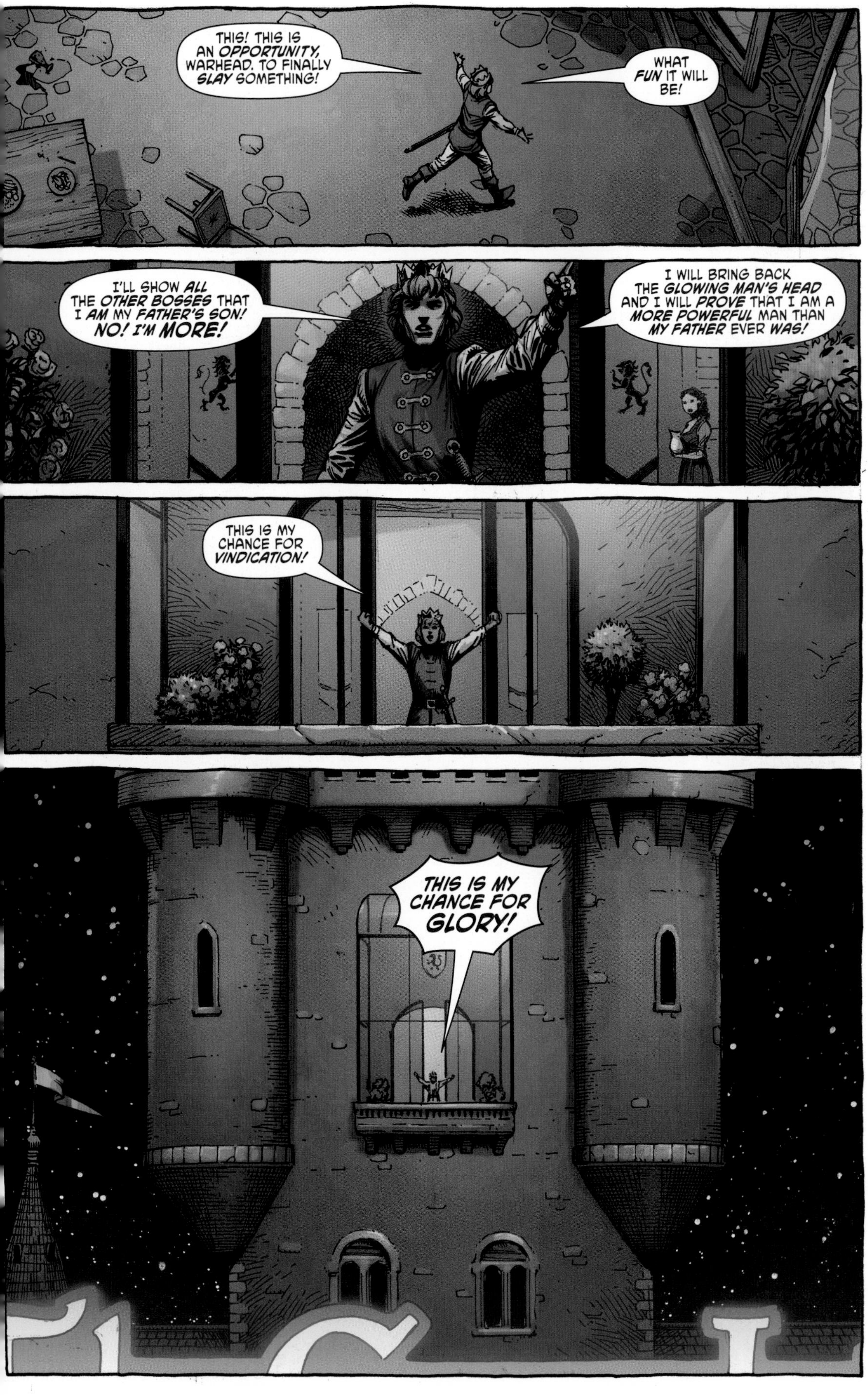
THIS! THIS IS AN OPPORTUNITY, WARHEAD, TO FINALLY SLAY SOMETHING!
WHAT FUN IT WILL BE!
I'LL SHOW ALL THE OTHER BOSSES THAT I AM MY FATHER'S SON! NO! I'M MORE!
I WILL BRING BACK THE GLOWING MAN'S HEAD AND I WILL PROVE THAT I AM A MORE POWERFUL MAN THAN MY FATHER EVER WAS!
THIS IS MY CHANCE FOR VINDICATION!
THIS IS MY CHANCE FOR GLORY!

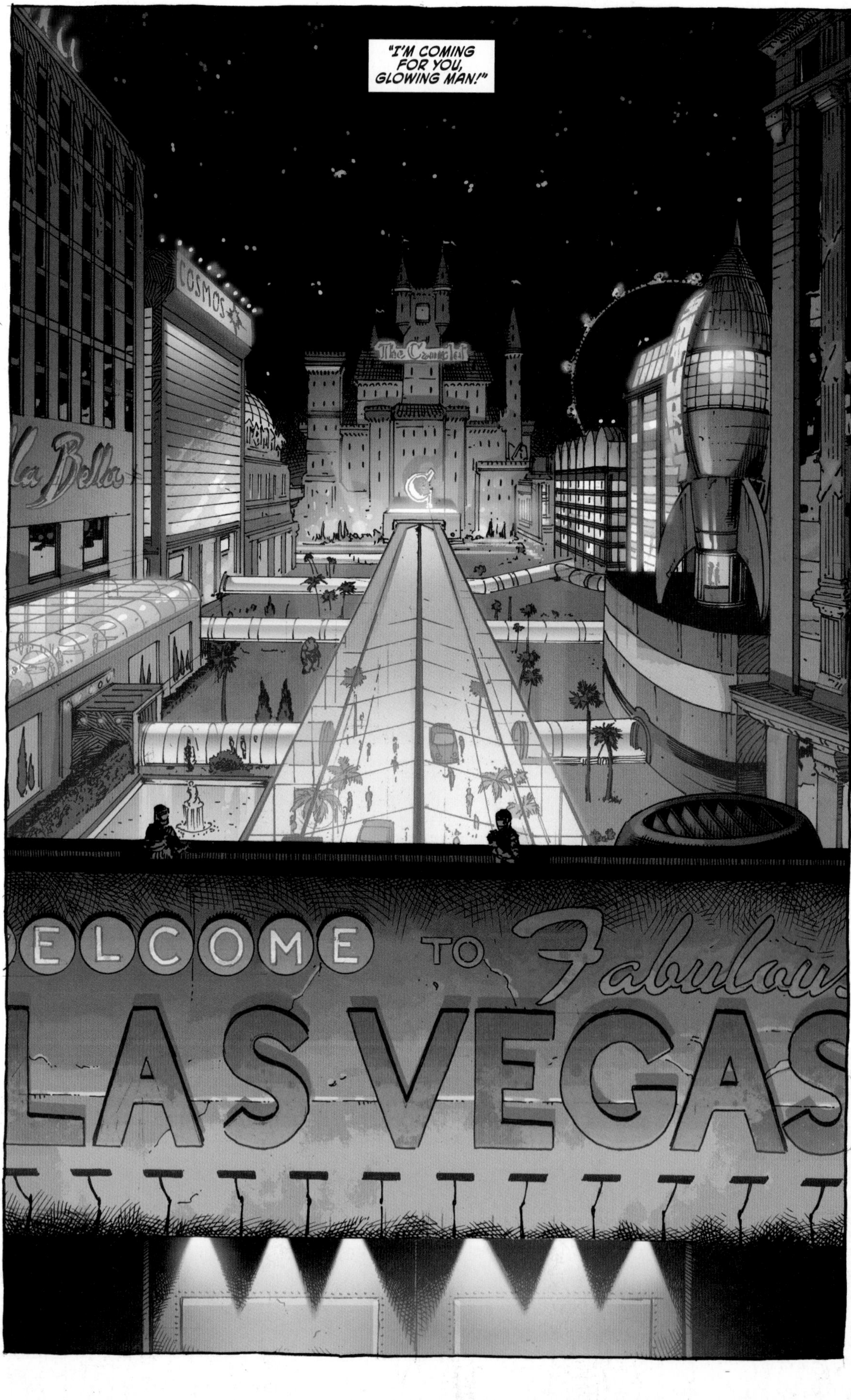
"I'M COMING FOR YOU, GLOWING MAN!"
COSMOS
la Bella
ELCOME TO
LAS VEGAS

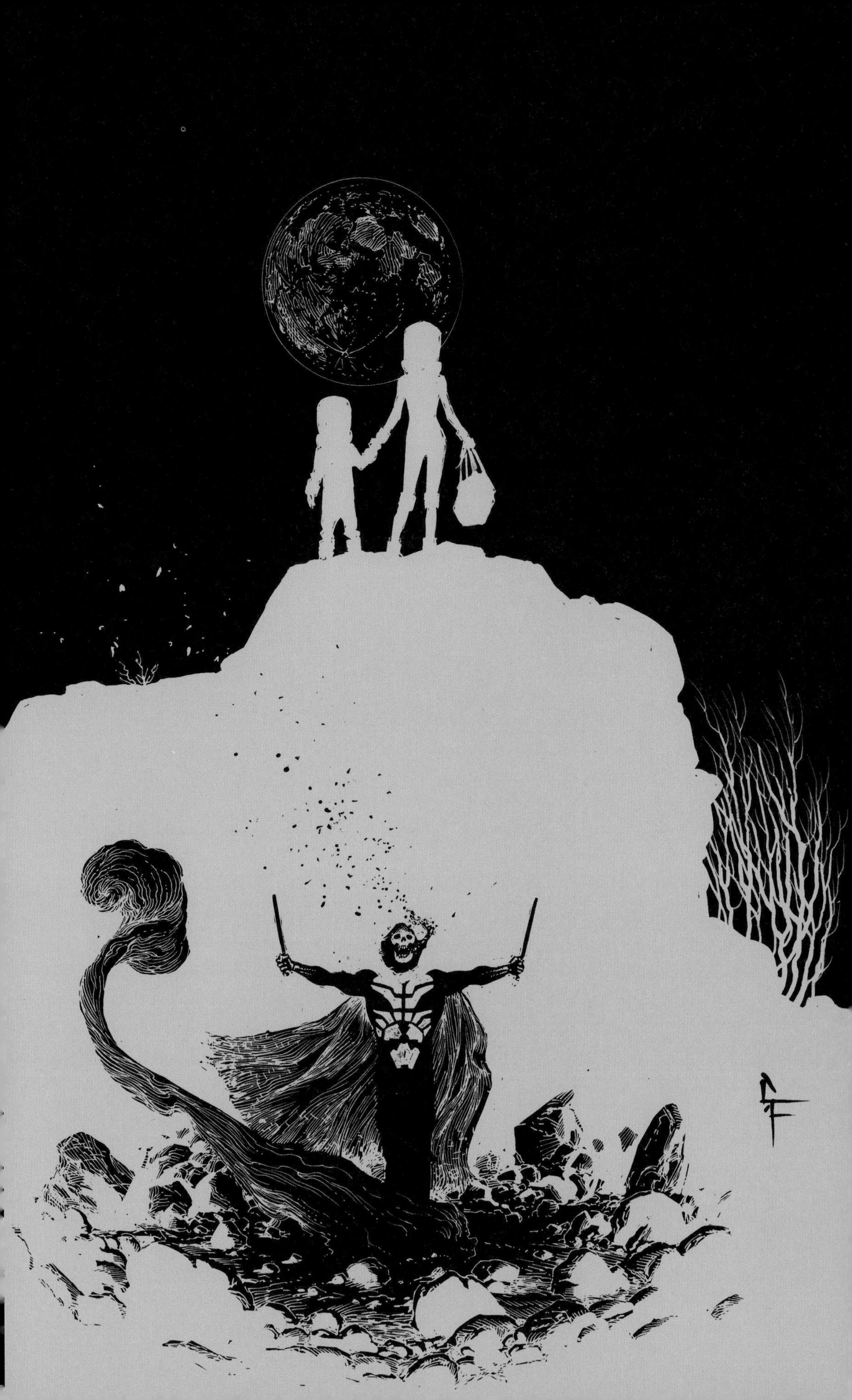

CHAPTER TWO

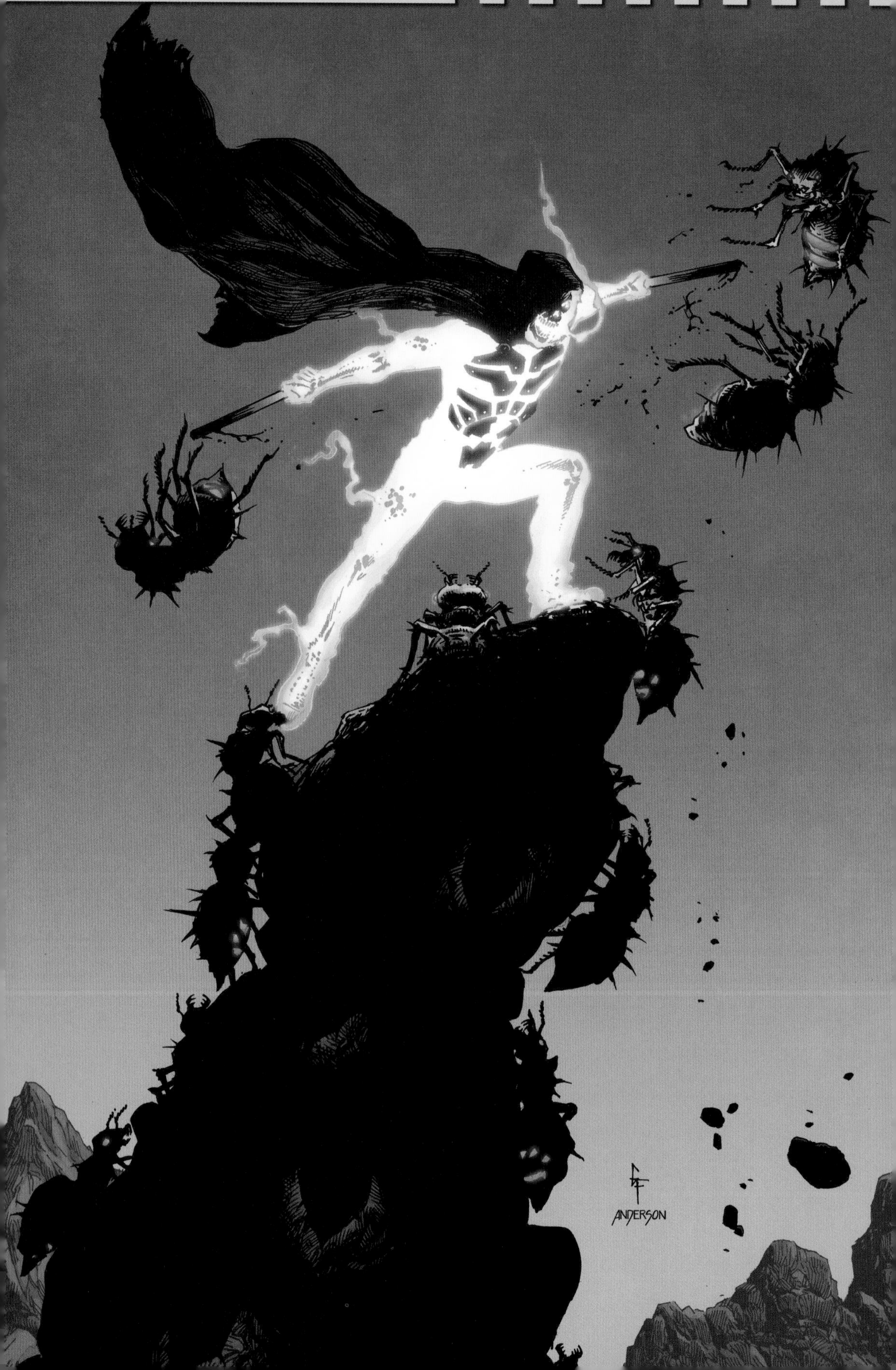

ANDERSON

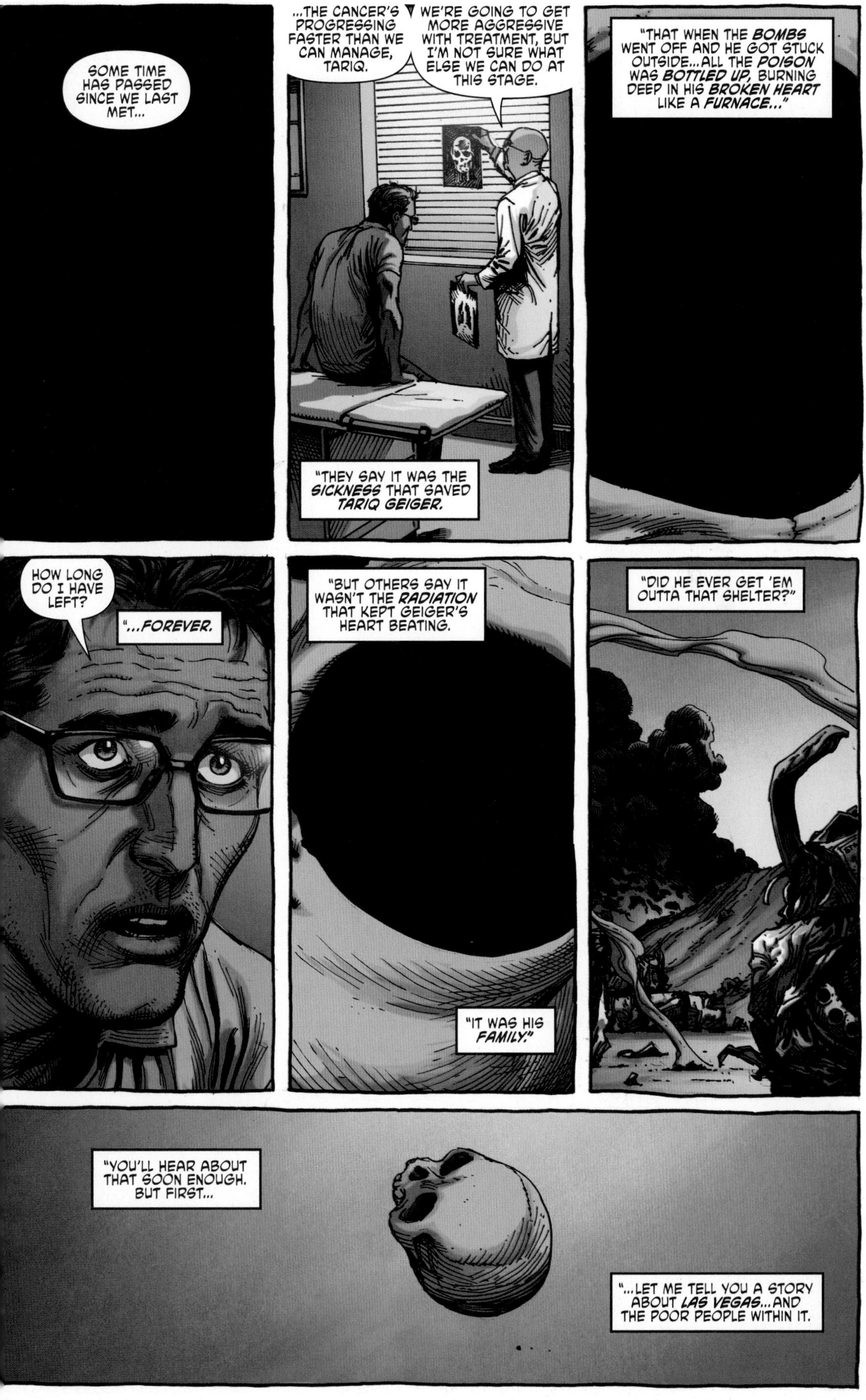
SOME TIME HAS PASSED SINCE WE LAST MET...
...THE CANCER'S PROGRESSING FASTER THAN WE CAN MANAGE, TARIQ.
WE'RE GOING TO GET MORE AGGRESSIVE WITH TREATMENT, BUT I'M NOT SURE WHAT ELSE WE CAN DO AT THIS STAGE.
"THEY SAY IT WAS THE SICKNESS THAT SAVED TARIQ GEIGER.
"THAT WHEN THE BOMBS WENT OFF AND HE GOT STUCK OUTSIDE...ALL THE POISON WAS BOTTLED UP, BURNING DEEP IN HIS BROKEN HEART LIKE A FURNACE..."
HOW LONG DO I HAVE LEFT?
"...FOREVER.
"BUT OTHERS SAY IT WASN'T THE RADIATION THAT KEPT GEIGER'S HEART BEATING.
"IT WAS HIS FAMILY."
"DID HE EVER GET 'EM OUTTA THAT SHELTER?"
"YOU'LL HEAR ABOUT THAT SOON ENOUGH. BUT FIRST...
"...LET ME TELL YOU A STORY ABOUT LAS VEGAS...AND THE POOR PEOPLE WITHIN IT.

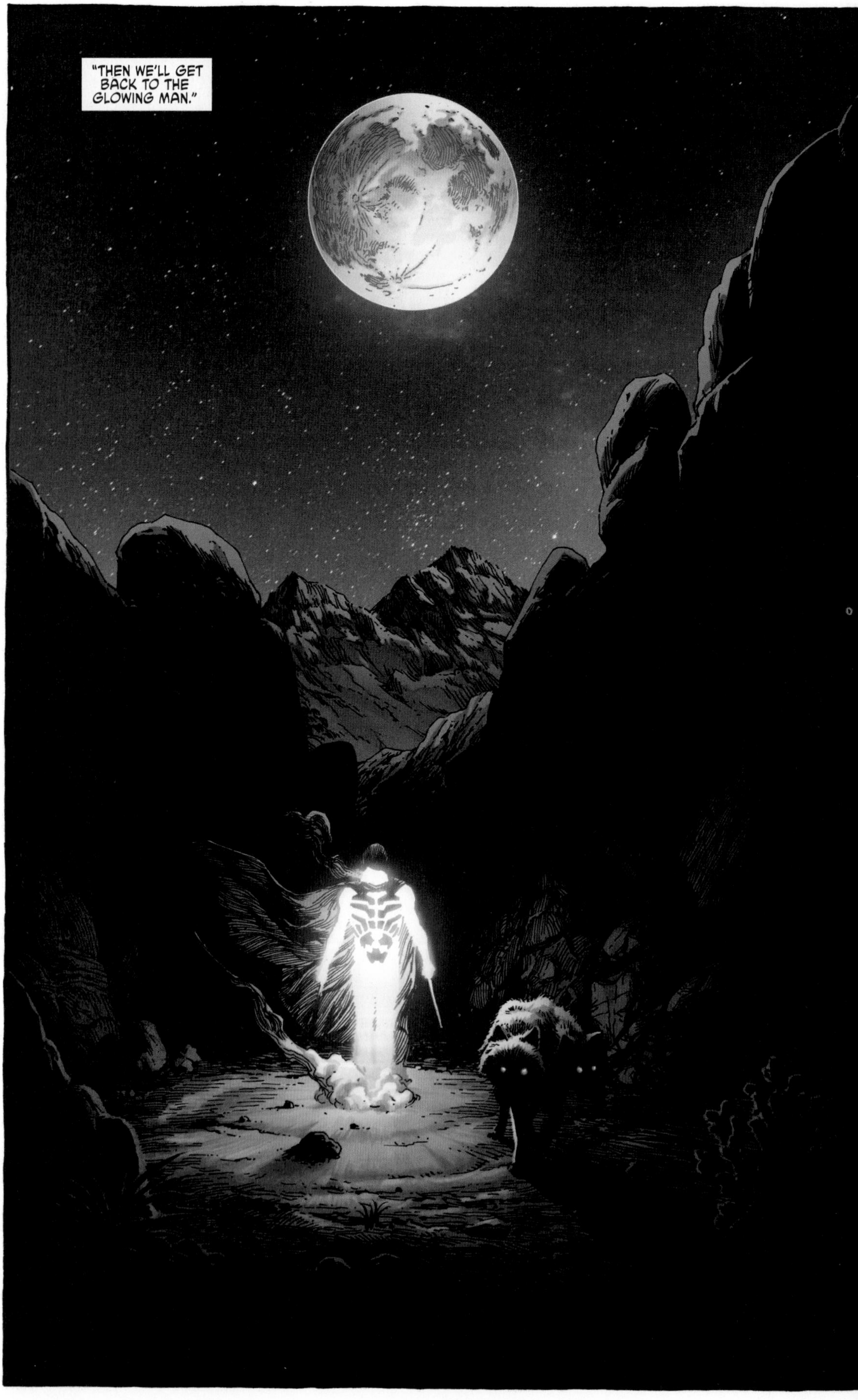
"THEN WE'LL GET BACK TO THE GLOWING MAN."

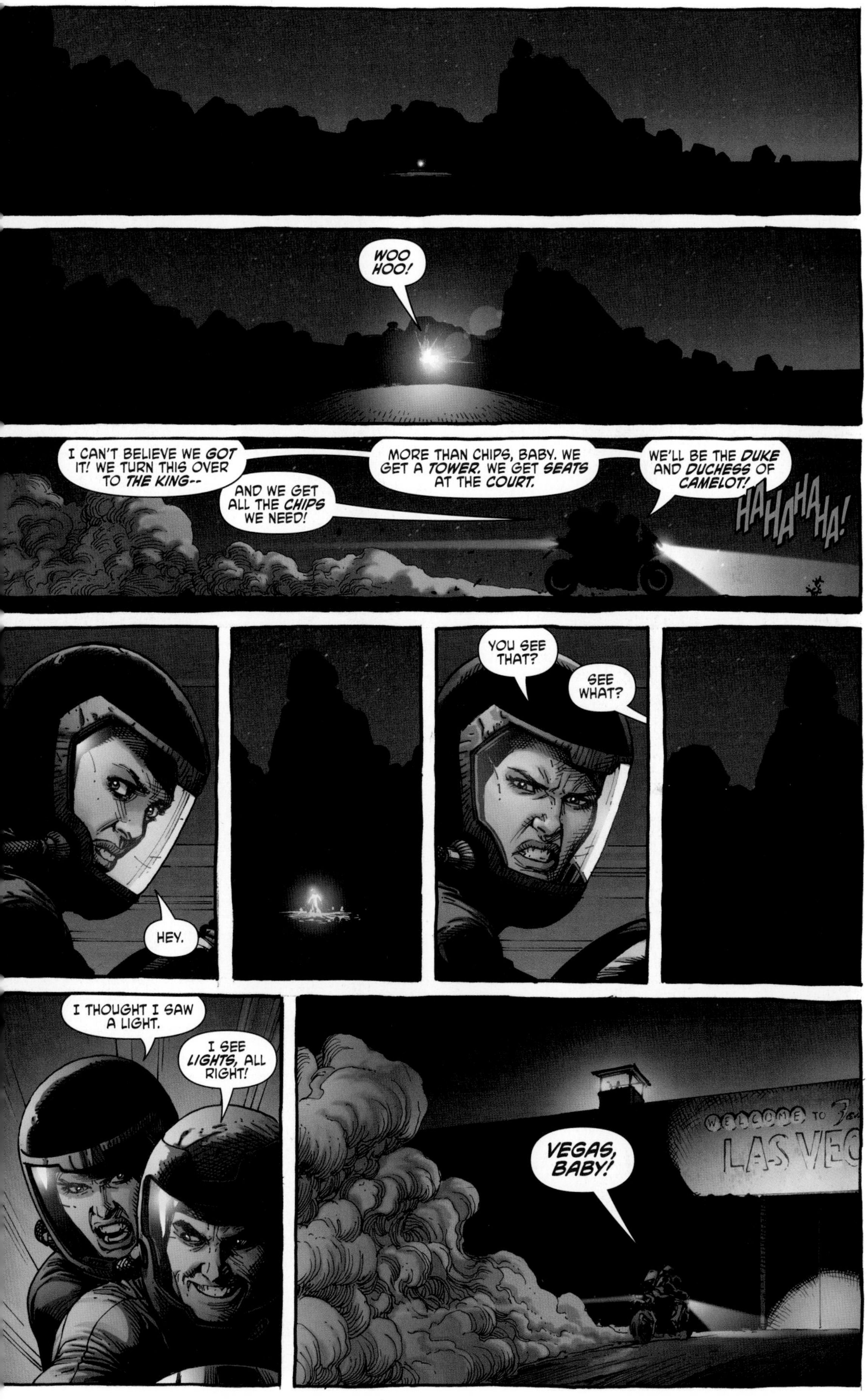
WOO HOO!
I CAN'T BELIEVE WE GOT IT! WE TURN THIS OVER TO THE KING--
AND WE GET ALL THE CHIPS WE NEED!
MORE THAN CHIPS, BABY. WE GET A TOWER. WE GET SEATS AT THE COURT.
WE'LL BE THE DUKE AND DUCHESS OF CAMELOT!
HAHAHAHA!
HEY.
YOU SEE THAT?
SEE WHAT?
I THOUGHT I SAW A LIGHT.
I SEE LIGHTS, ALL RIGHT!
VEGAS, BABY!
LAS VEG

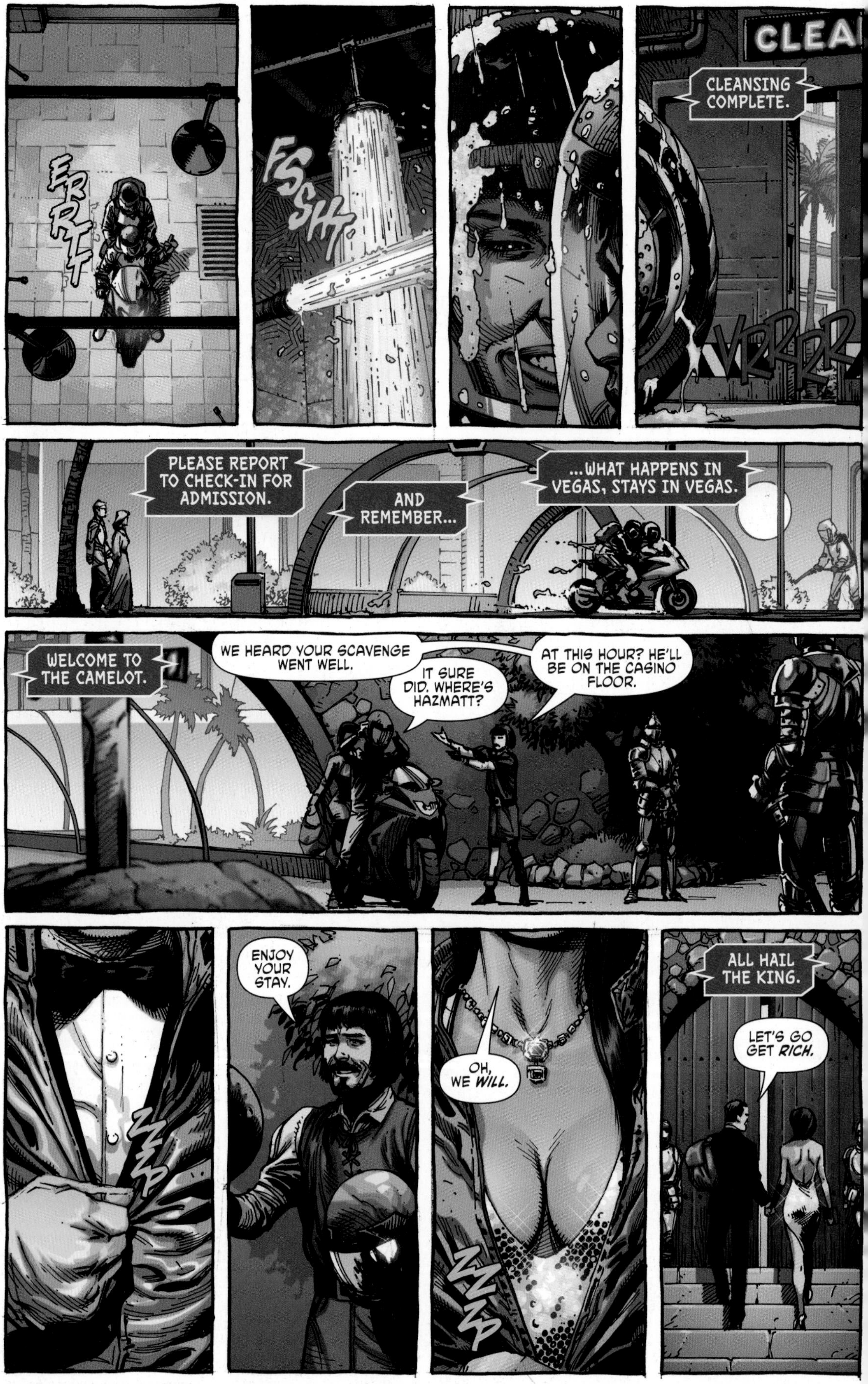
ERRIT
FSSHT
CLEA
CLEANSING COMPLETE.
VRRRR
PLEASE REPORT TO CHECK-IN FOR ADMISSION.
AND REMEMBER...
...WHAT HAPPENS IN VEGAS, STAYS IN VEGAS.
WELCOME TO THE CAMELOT.
WE HEARD YOUR SCAVENGE WENT WELL.
IT SURE DID. WHERE'S HAZMATT?
AT THIS HOUR? HE'LL BE ON THE CASINO FLOOR.
ZZZIP
ENJOY YOUR STAY.
OH, WE WILL.
ZZZIP
ALL HAIL THE KING.
LET'S GO GET RICH.

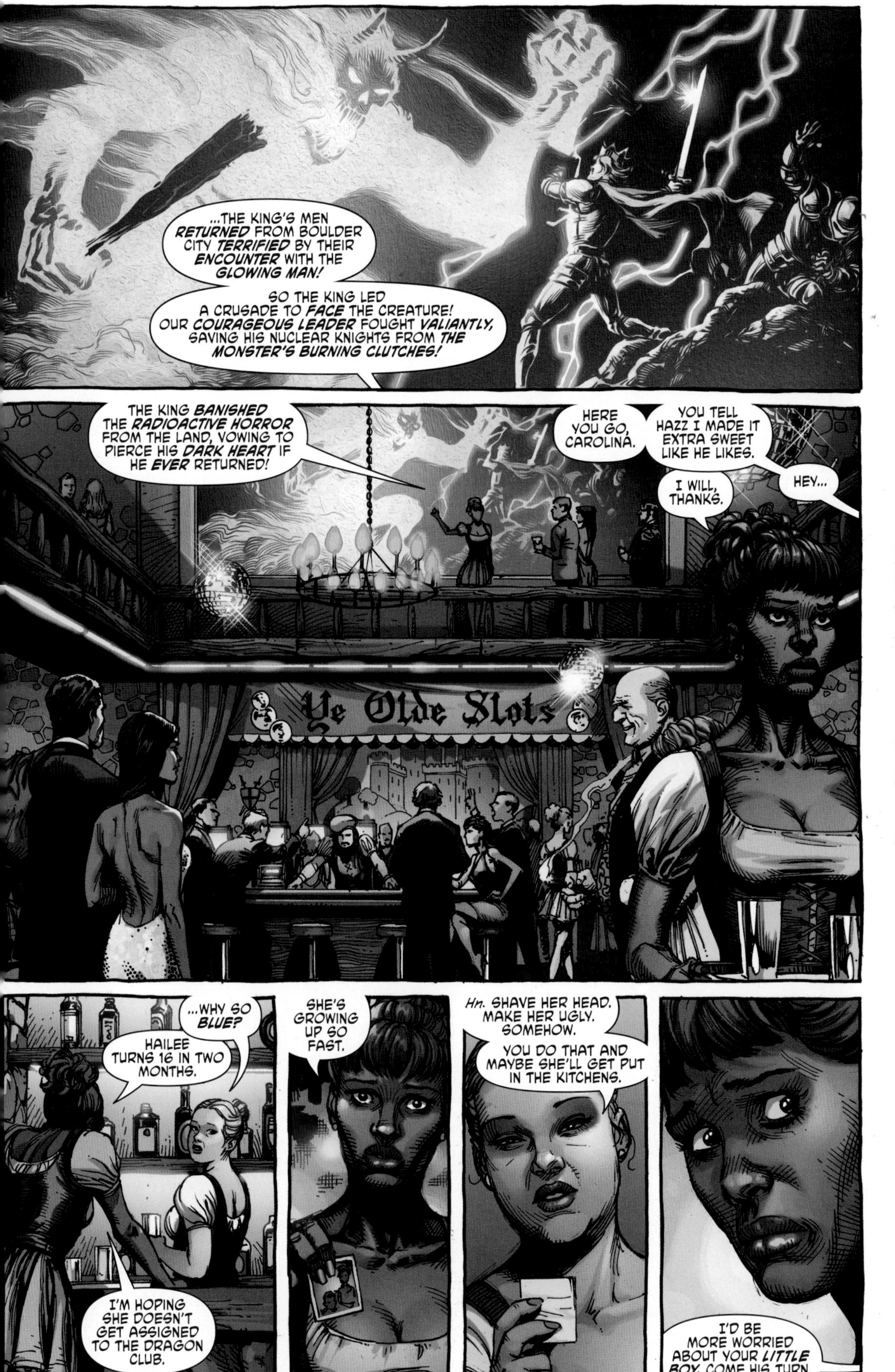
...THE KING'S MEN RETURNED FROM BOULDER CITY TERRIFIED BY THEIR ENCOUNTER WITH THE GLOWING MAN!
SO THE KING LED A CRUSADE TO FACE THE CREATURE! OUR COURAGEOUS LEADER FOUGHT VALIANTLY, SAVING HIS NUCLEAR KNIGHTS FROM THE MONSTER'S BURNING CLUTCHES!
THE KING BANISHED THE RADIOACTIVE HORROR FROM THE LAND, VOWING TO PIERCE HIS DARK HEART IF HE EVER RETURNED!
HERE YOU GO, CAROLINA.
YOU TELL HAZZ I MADE IT EXTRA SWEET LIKE HE LIKES.
I WILL, THANKS.
HEY...
Ye Olde Slots
...WHY SO BLUE?
HAILEE TURNS 16 IN TWO MONTHS.
I'M HOPING SHE DOESN'T GET ASSIGNED TO THE DRAGON CLUB.
SHE'S GROWING UP SO FAST.
Hn. SHAVE HER HEAD. MAKE HER UGLY. SOMEHOW.
YOU DO THAT AND MAYBE SHE'LL GET PUT IN THE KITCHENS.
I'D BE MORE WORRIED ABOUT YOUR LITTLE BOY, COME HIS TURN.

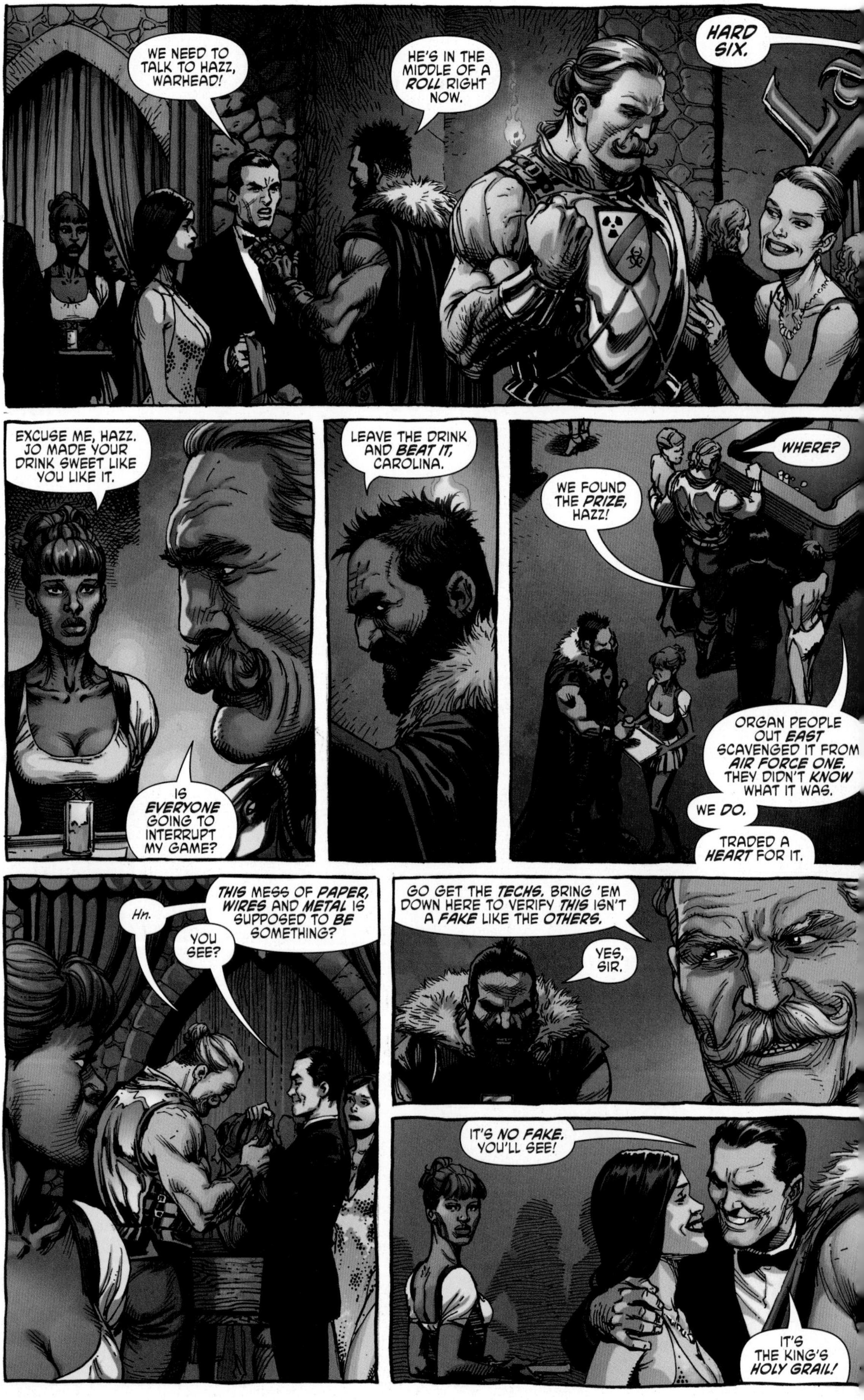
WE NEED TO TALK TO HAZZ, WARHEAD!
HE'S IN THE MIDDLE OF A ROLL RIGHT NOW.
HARD SIX.
EXCUSE ME, HAZZ. JO MADE YOUR DRINK SWEET LIKE YOU LIKE IT.
IS EVERYONE GOING TO INTERRUPT MY GAME?
LEAVE THE DRINK AND BEAT IT, CAROLINA.
WE FOUND THE PRIZE, HAZZ!
WHERE?
ORGAN PEOPLE OUT EAST SCAVENGED IT FROM AIR FORCE ONE. THEY DIDN'T KNOW WHAT IT WAS.
WE DO.
TRADED A HEART FOR IT.
Hn.
THIS MESS OF PAPER, WIRES AND METAL IS SUPPOSED TO BE SOMETHING?
YOU SEE?
GO GET THE TECHS. BRING 'EM DOWN HERE TO VERIFY THIS ISN'T A FAKE LIKE THE OTHERS.
YES, SIR.
IT'S NO FAKE. YOU'LL SEE!
IT'S THE KING'S HOLY GRAIL!

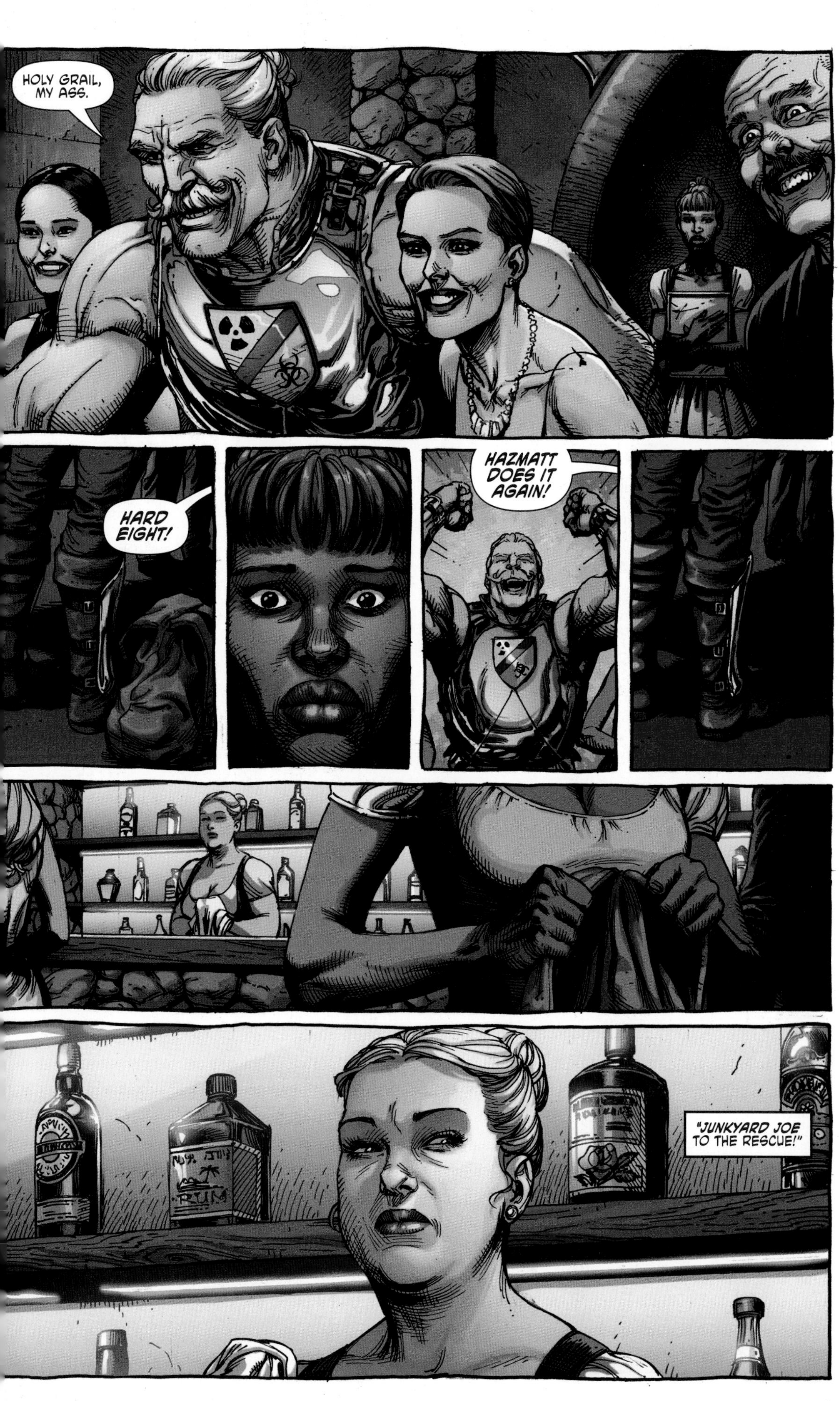
HOLY GRAIL, MY ASS.
HARD EIGHT!
HAZMATT DOES IT AGAIN!
"JUNKYARD JOE TO THE RESCUE!"
RUM

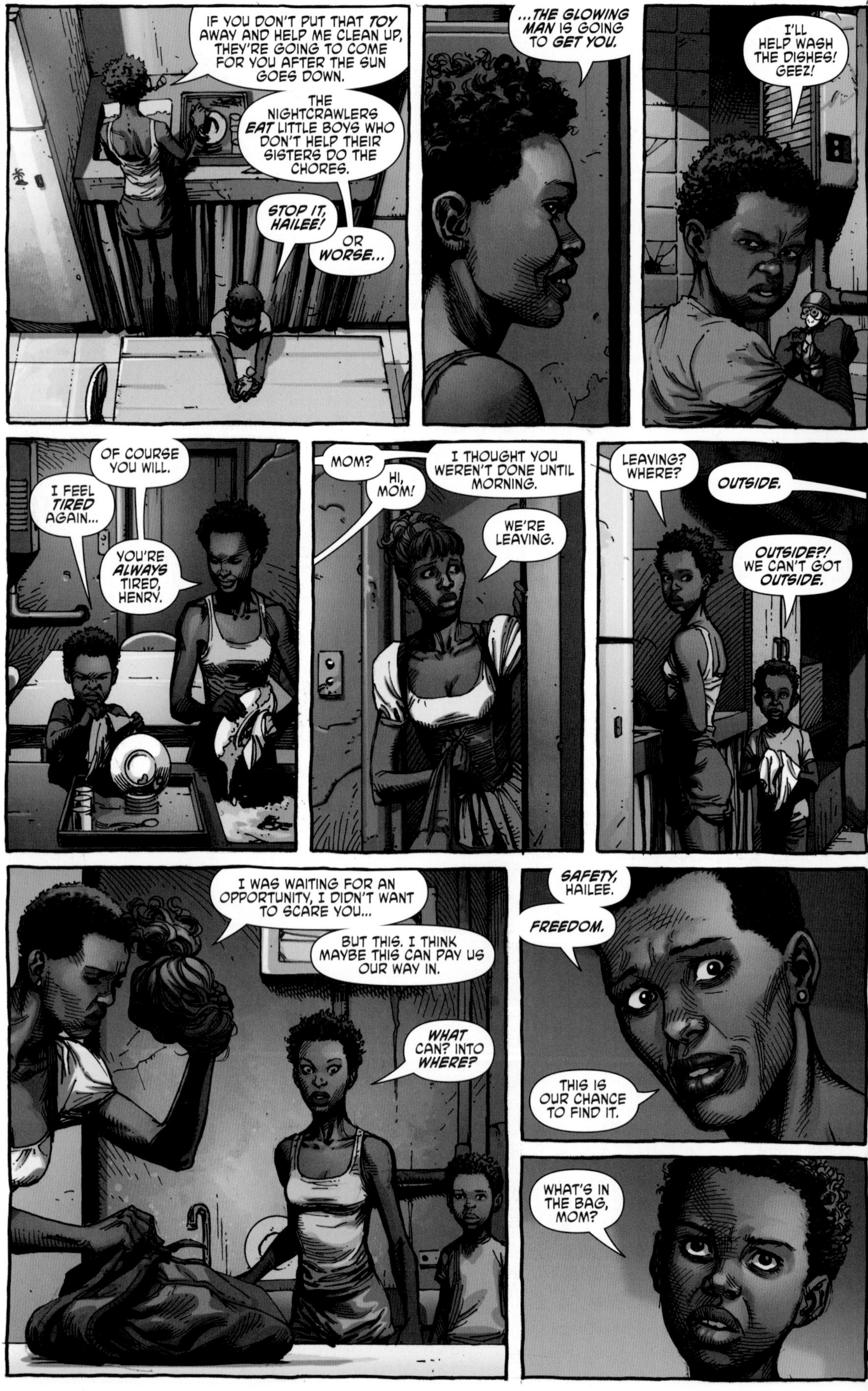
IF YOU DON'T PUT THAT TOY AWAY AND HELP ME CLEAN UP, THEY'RE GOING TO COME FOR YOU AFTER THE SUN GOES DOWN.
THE NIGHTCRAWLERS EAT LITTLE BOYS WHO DON'T HELP THEIR SISTERS DO THE CHORES.
STOP IT, HAILEE!
OR WORSE...
...THE GLOWING MAN IS GOING TO GET YOU.
I'LL HELP WASH THE DISHES! GEEZ!
I FEEL TIRED AGAIN...
OF COURSE YOU WILL.
YOU'RE ALWAYS TIRED, HENRY.
MOM?
HI, MOM!
I THOUGHT YOU WEREN'T DONE UNTIL MORNING.
WE'RE LEAVING.
LEAVING? WHERE?
OUTSIDE.
OUTSIDE?! WE CAN'T GOT OUTSIDE.
I WAS WAITING FOR AN OPPORTUNITY, I DIDN'T WANT TO SCARE YOU...
BUT THIS. I THINK MAYBE THIS CAN PAY US OUR WAY IN.
WHAT CAN? INTO WHERE?
SAFETY, HAILEE.
FREEDOM.
THIS IS OUR CHANCE TO FIND IT.
WHAT'S IN THE BAG, MOM?

IT'S A *RELIC* FROM *BEFORE* THE *UNKNOWN WAR.*

IT'S CALLED THE *NUCLEAR FOOTBALL.* THE KING'S BEEN AFTER IT FOR *YEARS.*

WHAT ARE YOU TALKING ABOUT?

LISTEN TO ME.

WE HAVE TO *GET TO NORAD.* IT'S 80 MILES SOUTH OF DENVER IN THE CHEYENNE MOUNTAINS. IT'S THE ONLY PLACE LEFT WHERE THE *AMERICAN GOVERNMENT* STILL HAS CONTROL.

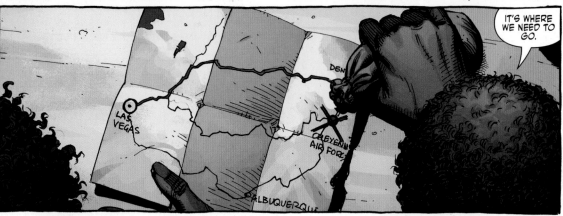

IT'S WHERE WE NEED TO GO.

BUT...?

THIS IS A *CARD* TO ACTIVATE THE *ELEVATOR.*

AND THESE *KEYS* ARE TO A *VEHICLE* IN THE GARAGE.

WE GET TO THE GARAGE, GET SUITS FROM THE CLEAN ZONE... AND WE CAN GO. WE CAN LEAVE RIGHT NOW.

WE *HAVE* TO LEAVE RIGHT NOW.

BUT I DON'T WANT TO GO OUTSIDE!

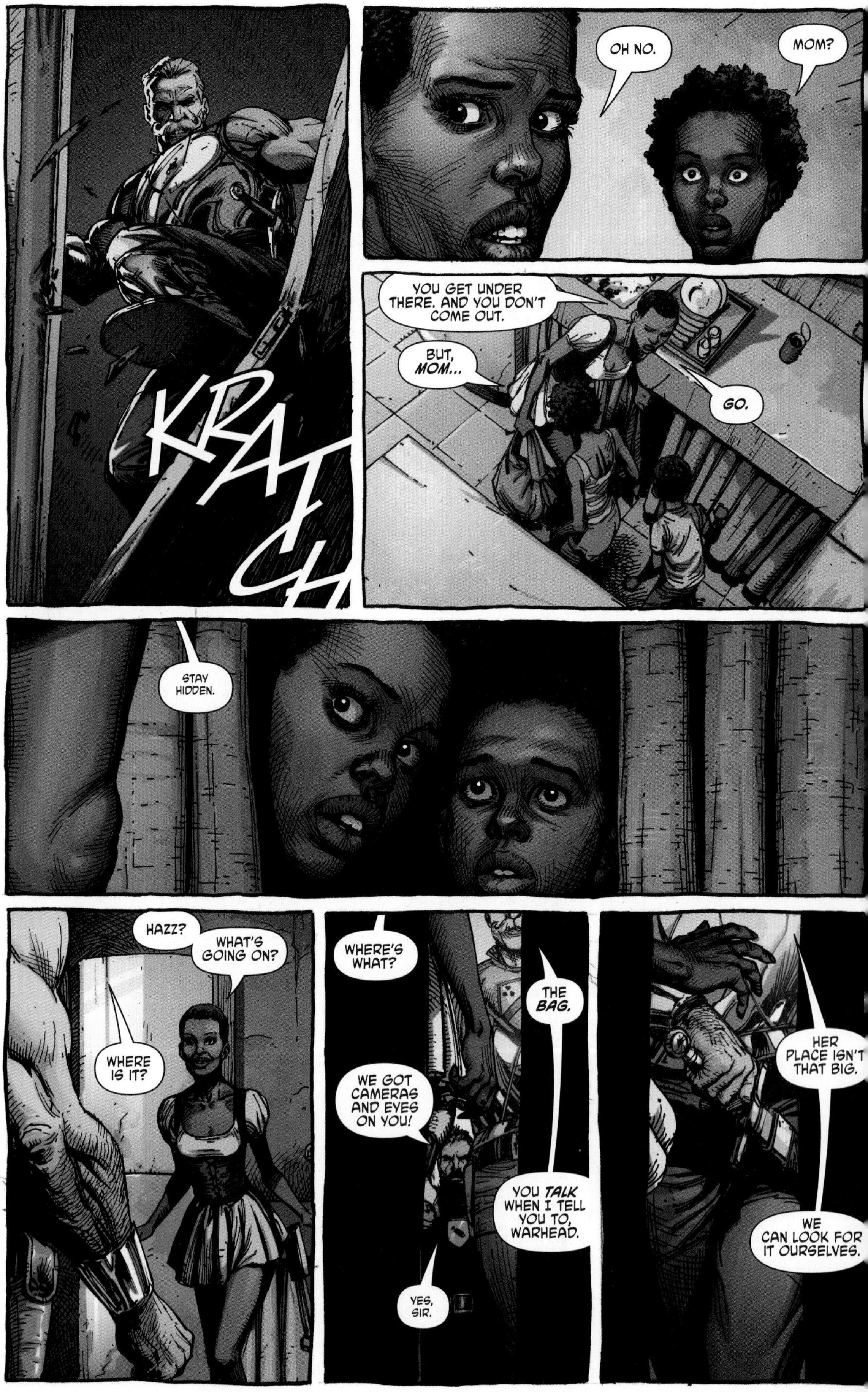
KRATCH
OH NO.
MOM?
YOU GET UNDER THERE. AND YOU DON'T COME OUT.
BUT, MOM...
GO.
STAY HIDDEN.
HAZZ?
WHAT'S GOING ON?
WHERE IS IT?
WHERE'S WHAT?
THE BAG.
WE GOT CAMERAS AND EYES ON YOU!
YOU TALK WHEN I TELL YOU TO, WARHEAD.
YES, SIR.
HER PLACE ISN'T THAT BIG.
WE CAN LOOK FOR IT OURSELVES.

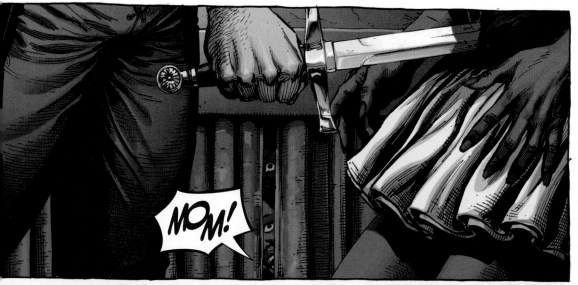

MOM!

AAAHH!

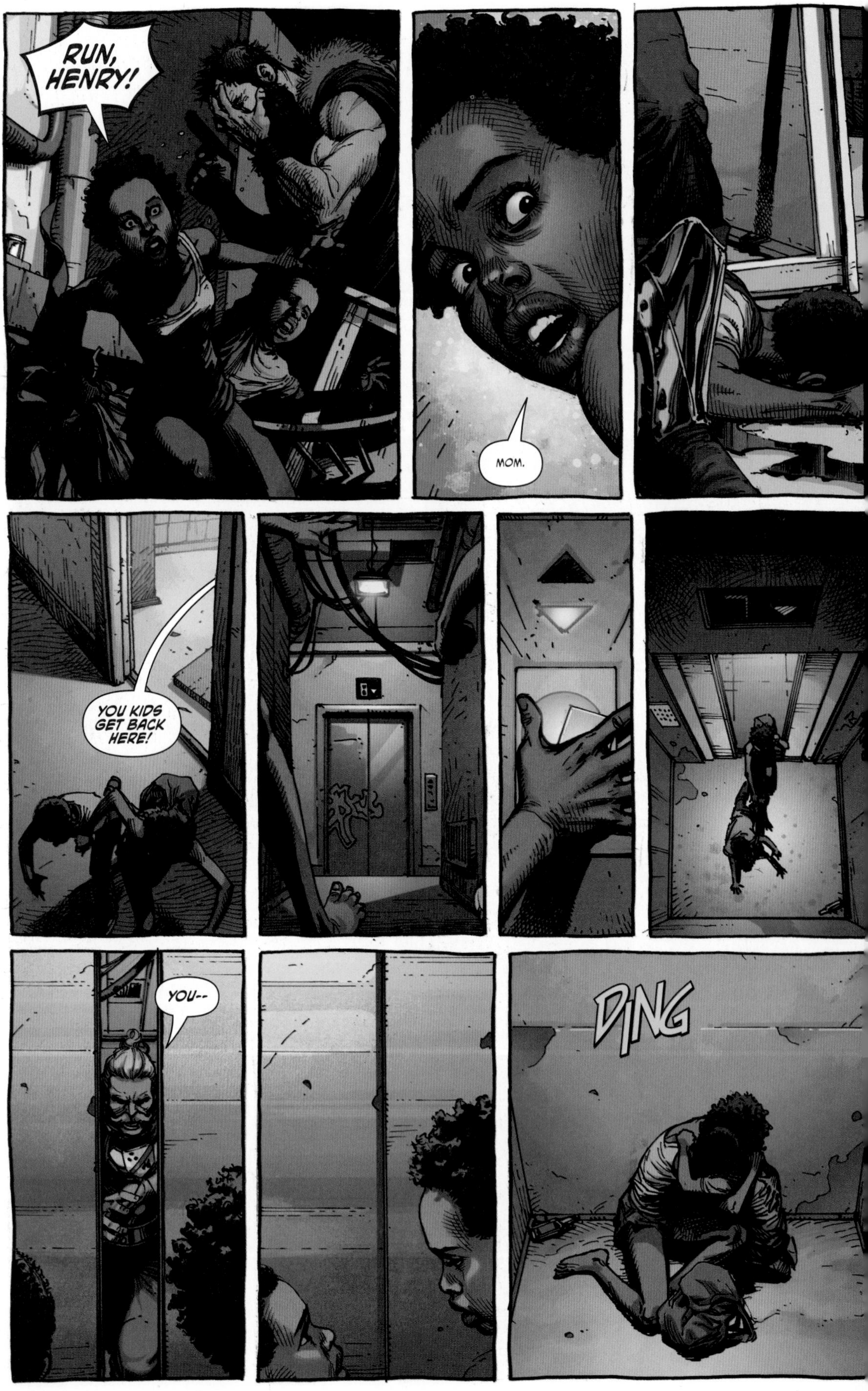
RUN, HENRY!
MOM.
YOU KIDS GET BACK HERE!
YOU--
DING

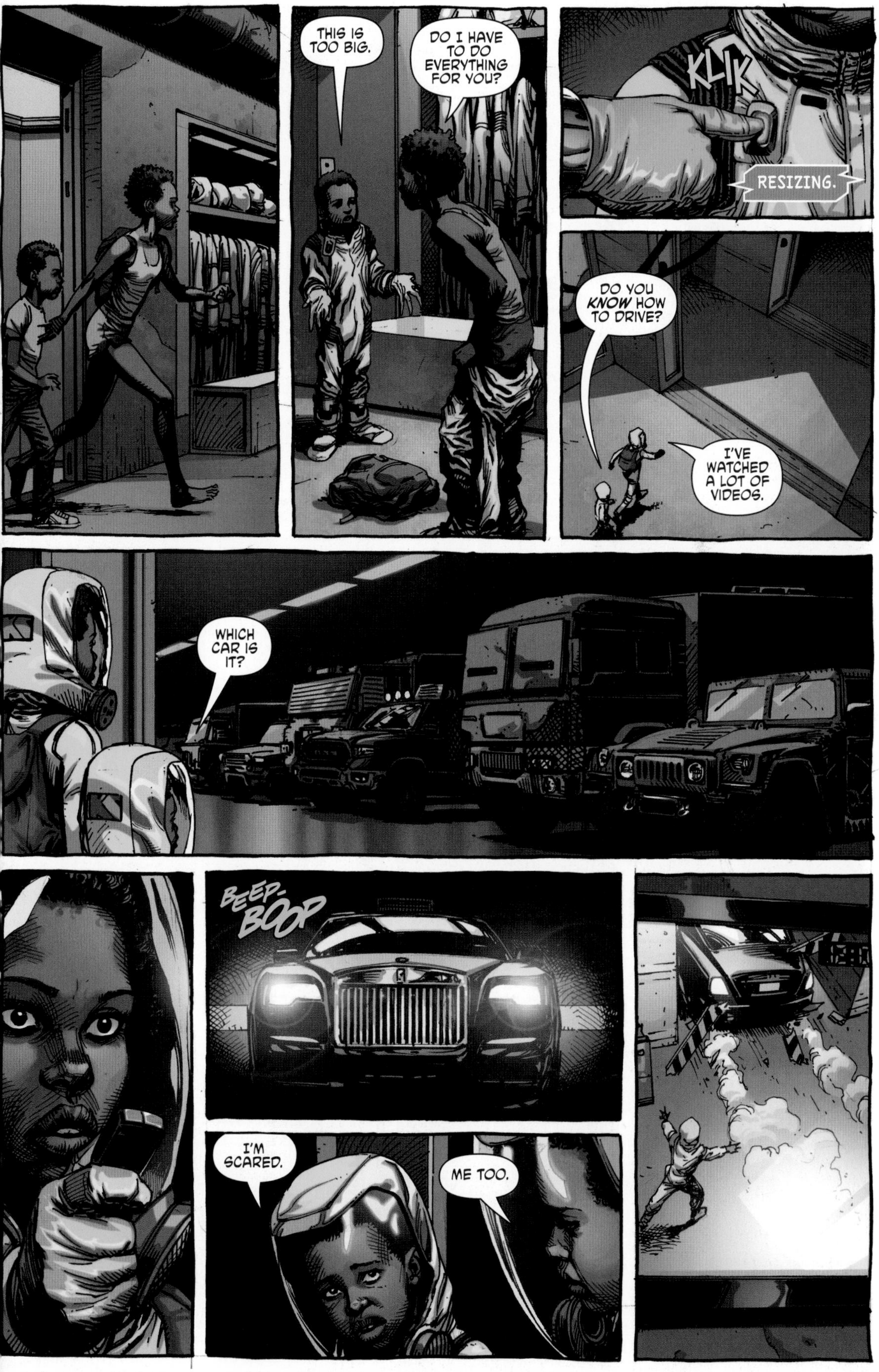
THIS IS TOO BIG.
DO I HAVE TO DO EVERYTHING FOR YOU?
KLIK
RESIZING.
DO YOU *KNOW* HOW TO DRIVE?
I'VE WATCHED A LOT OF VIDEOS.
WHICH CAR IS IT?
BEEP-BOOP
I'M SCARED.
ME TOO.

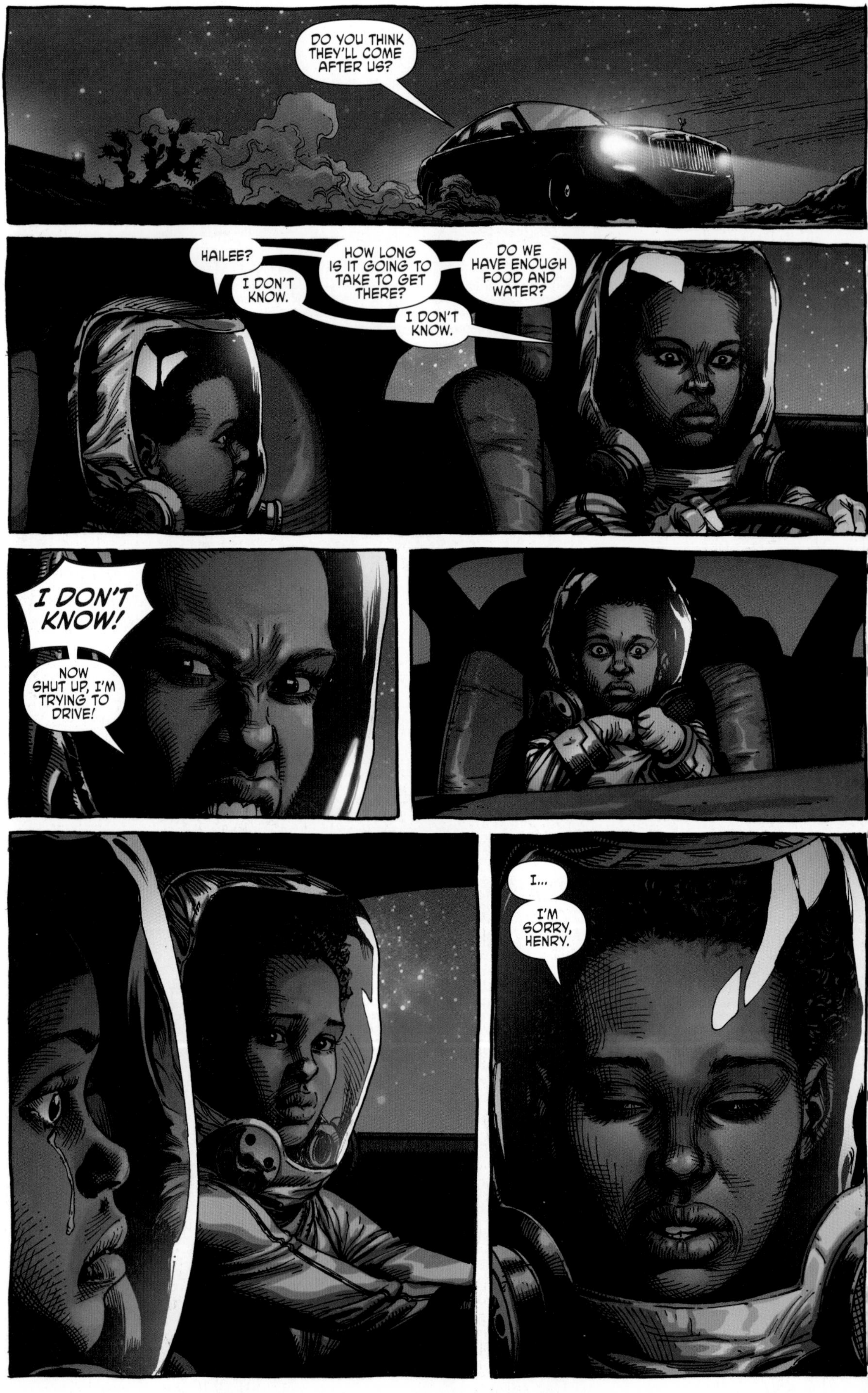
DO YOU THINK THEY'LL COME AFTER US?
HAILEE?
I DON'T KNOW.
HOW LONG IS IT GOING TO TAKE TO GET THERE?
I DON'T KNOW.
DO WE HAVE ENOUGH FOOD AND WATER?
I DON'T KNOW!
NOW SHUT UP, I'M TRYING TO DRIVE!
I...
I'M SORRY, HENRY.

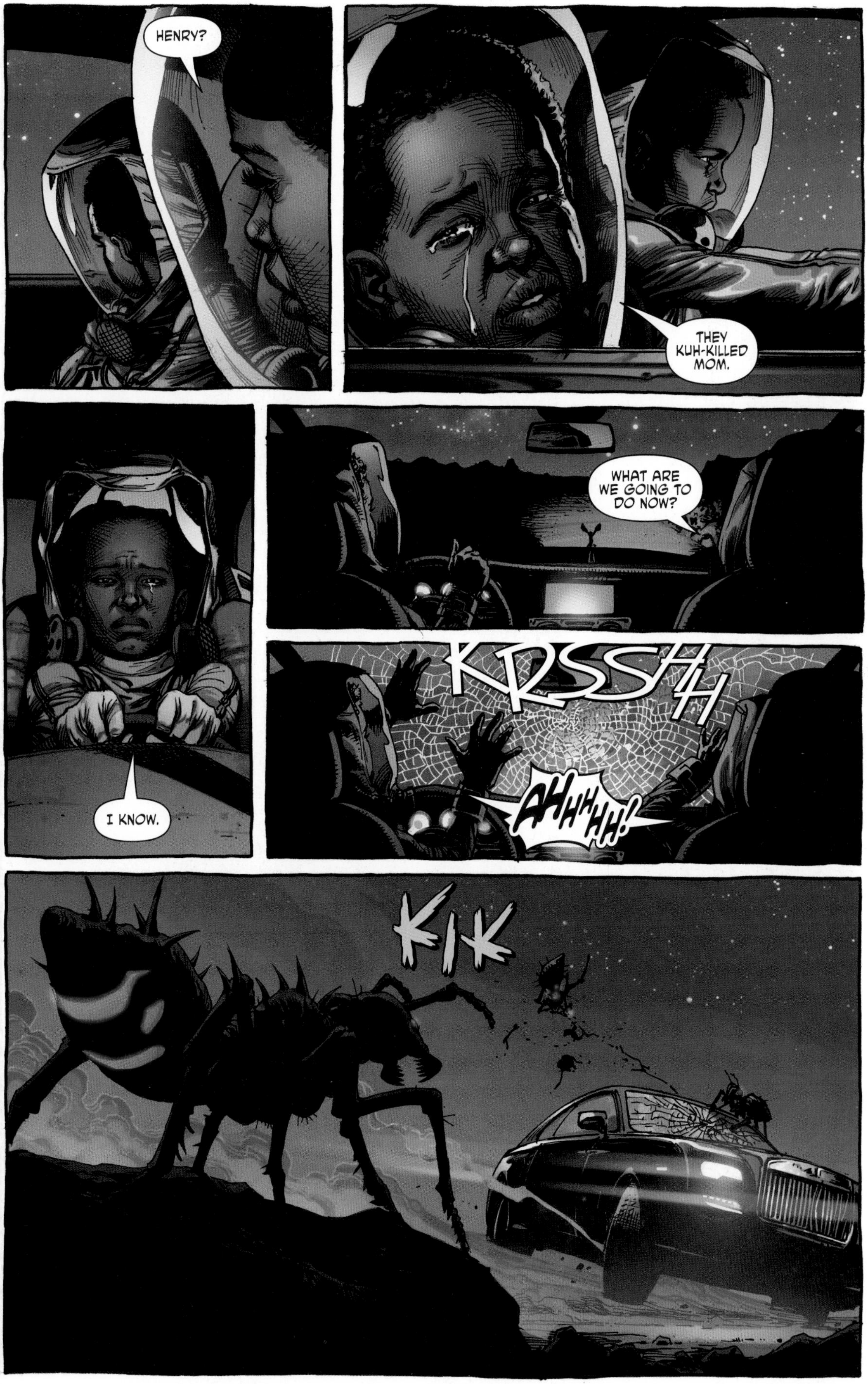
HENRY?
THEY KUH-KILLED MOM.
I KNOW.
WHAT ARE WE GOING TO DO NOW?
KRSSHH
AHHHHH!
KIK

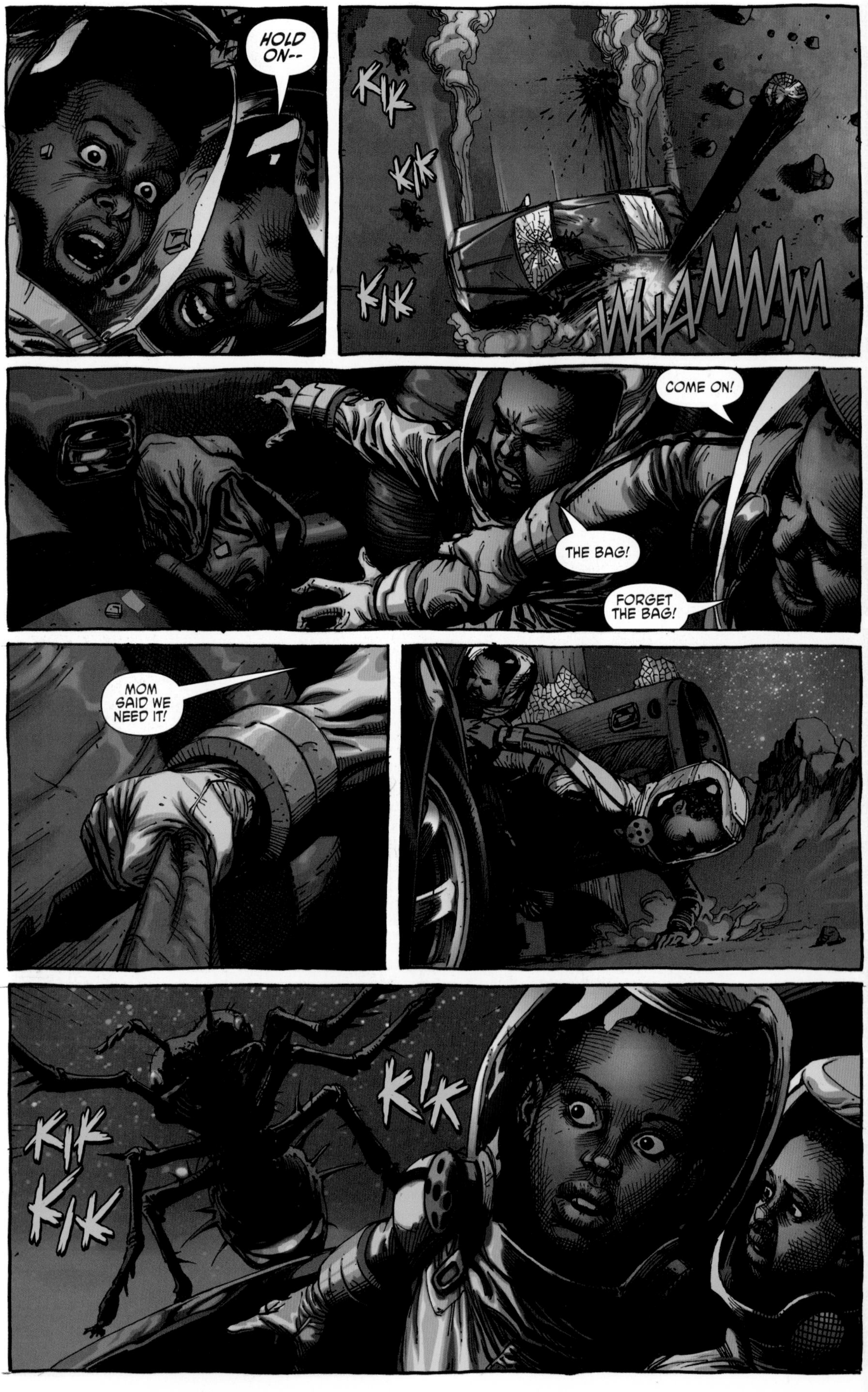
HOLD ON--
KIK
KIK
KIK
WHAMMM
COME ON!
THE BAG!
FORGET THE BAG!
MOM SAID WE NEED IT!
KIK
KIK
KIK

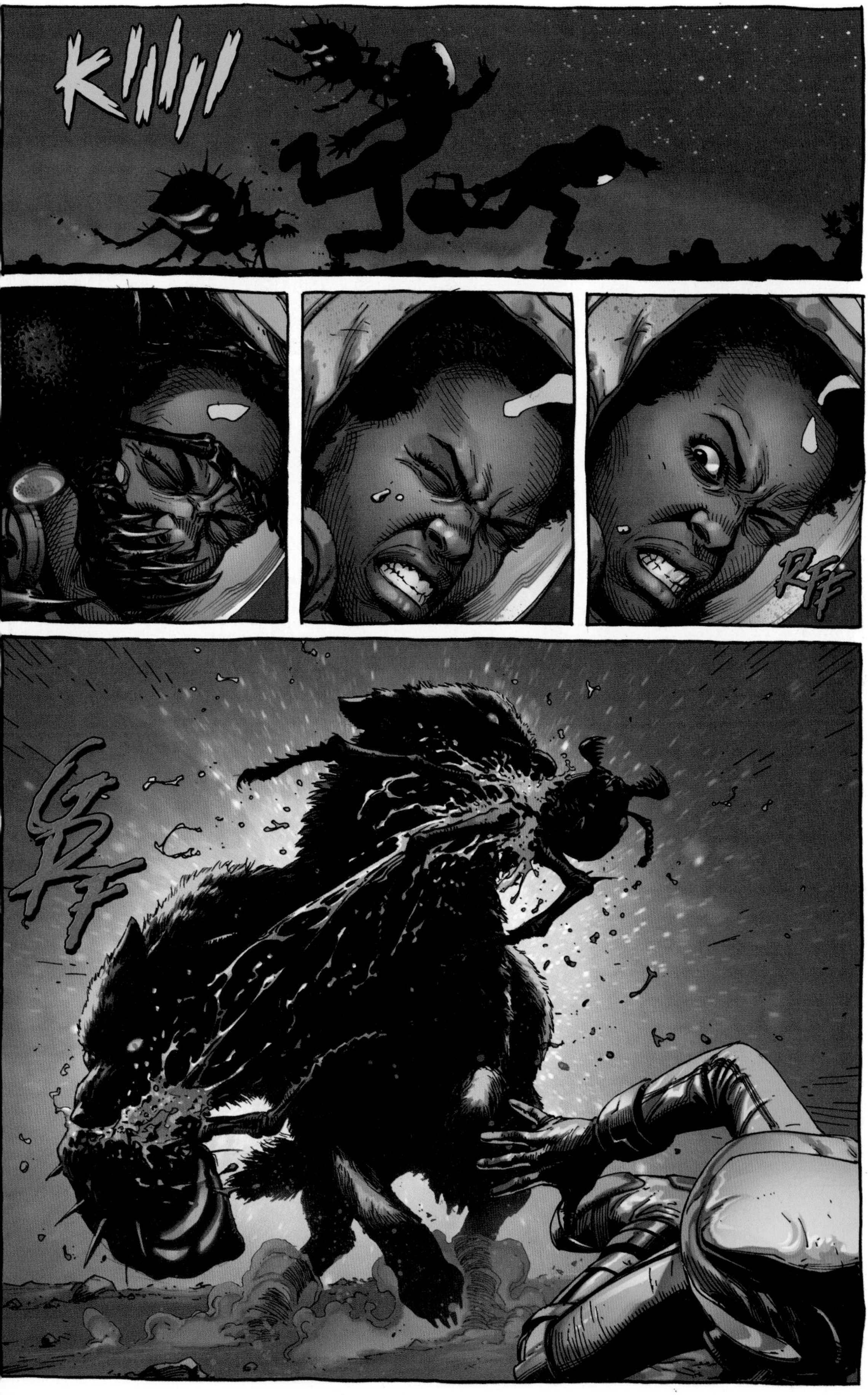
KIIIII
RFF
GRFF

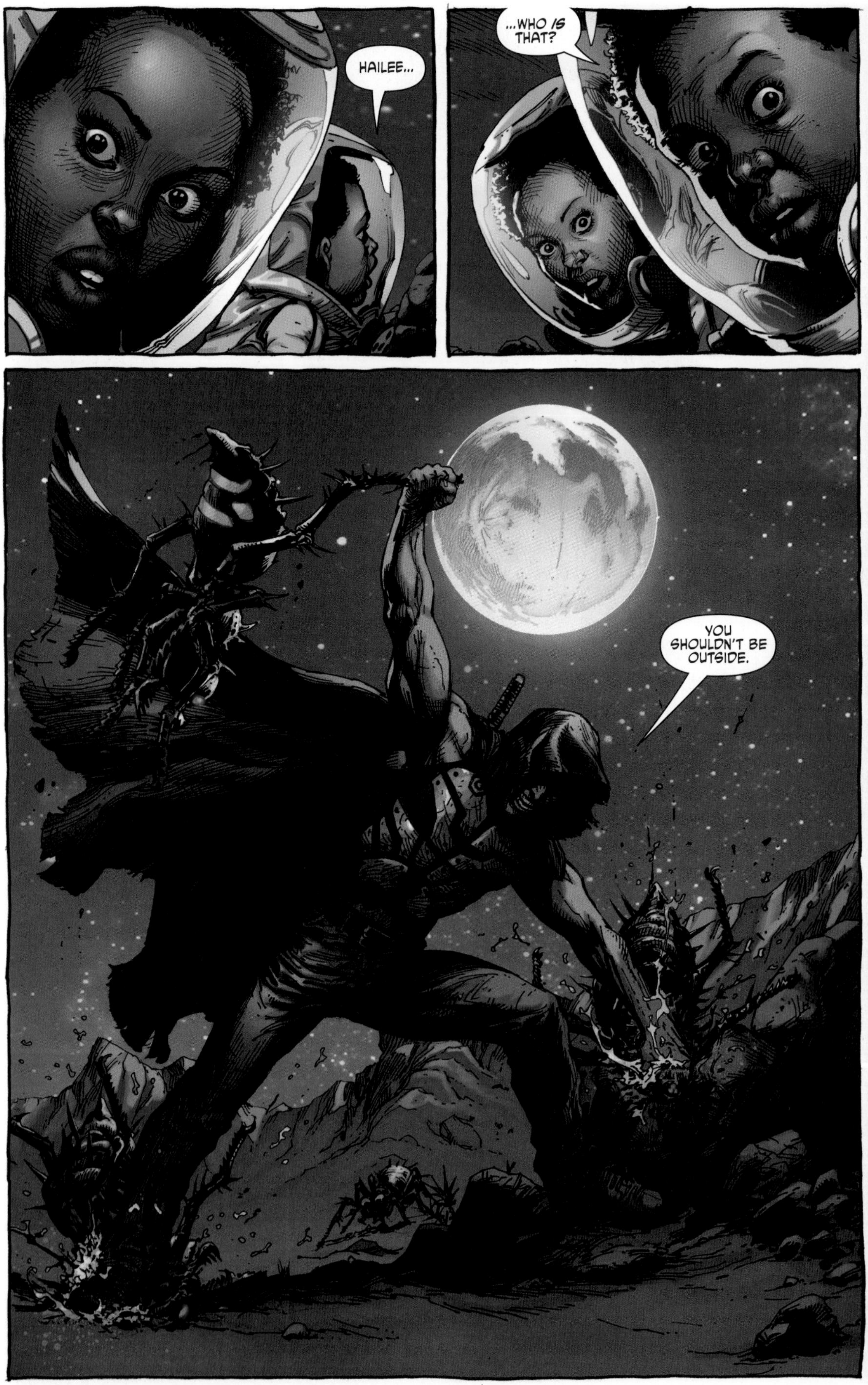
HAILEE...
...WHO IS THAT?
YOU SHOULDN'T BE OUTSIDE.

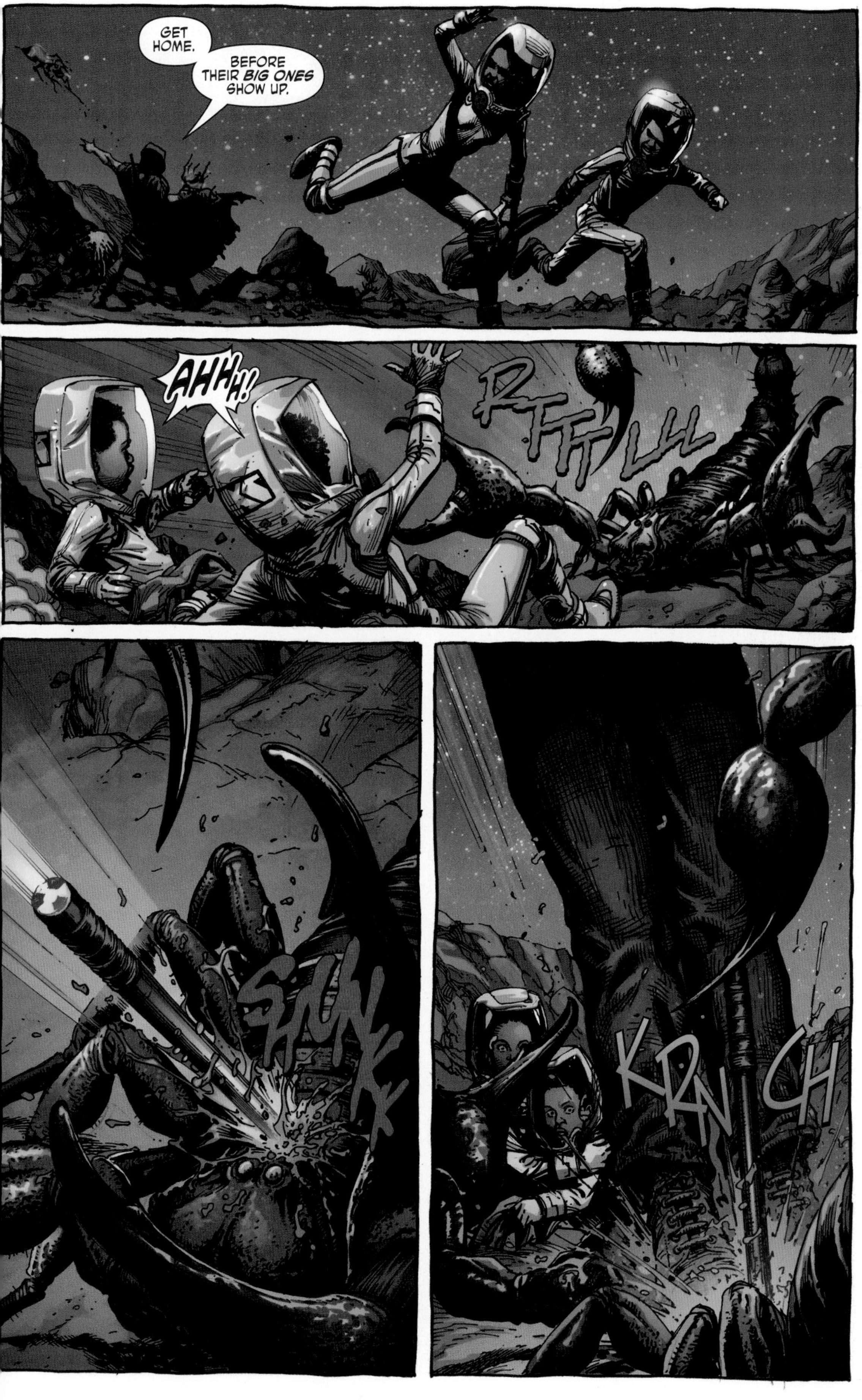
GET HOME.
BEFORE THEIR *BIG ONES* SHOW UP.
AHHH!
RTTTLLL
SHUNK
KRNCH

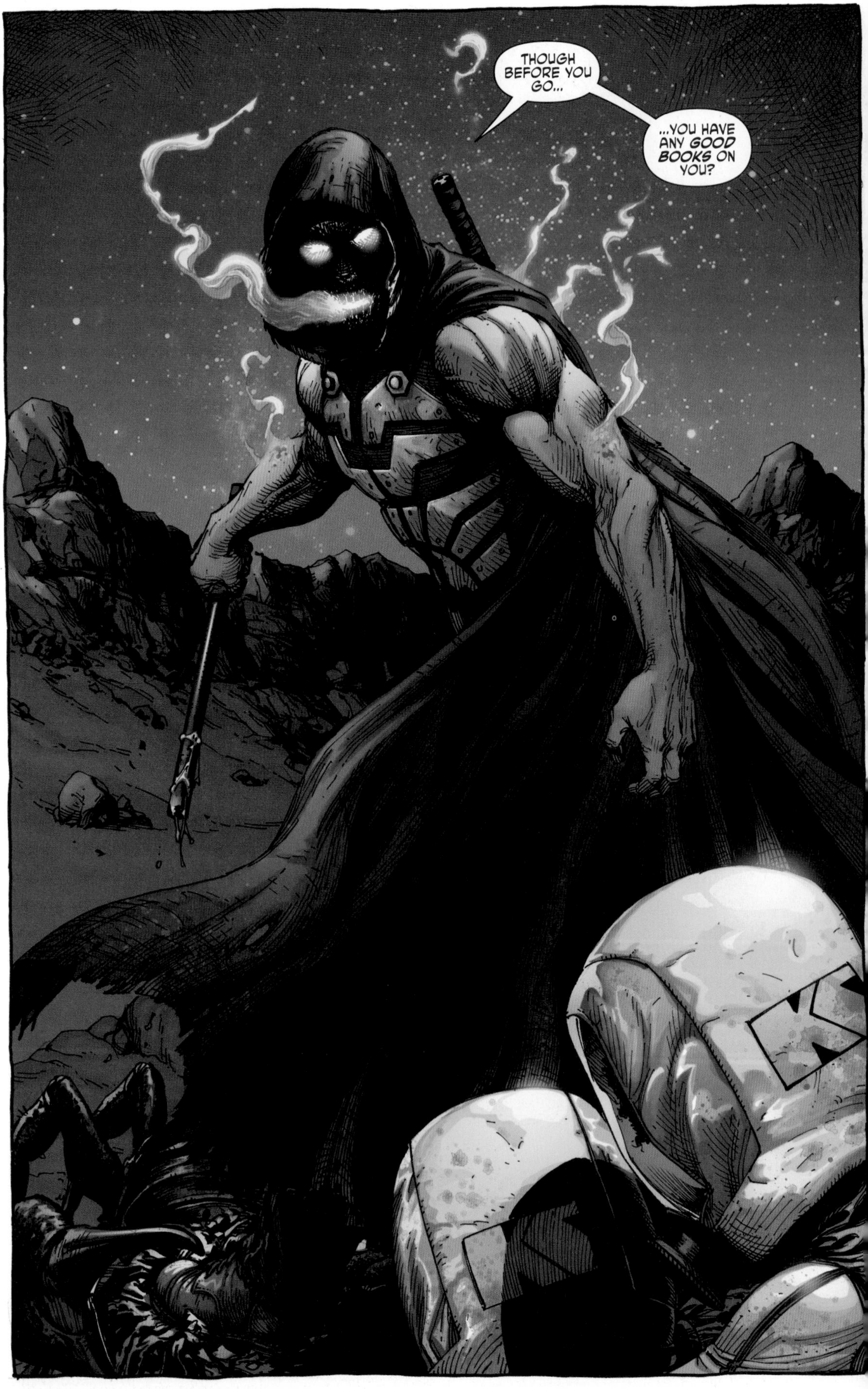
THOUGH BEFORE YOU GO...
...YOU HAVE ANY *GOOD BOOKS* ON YOU?

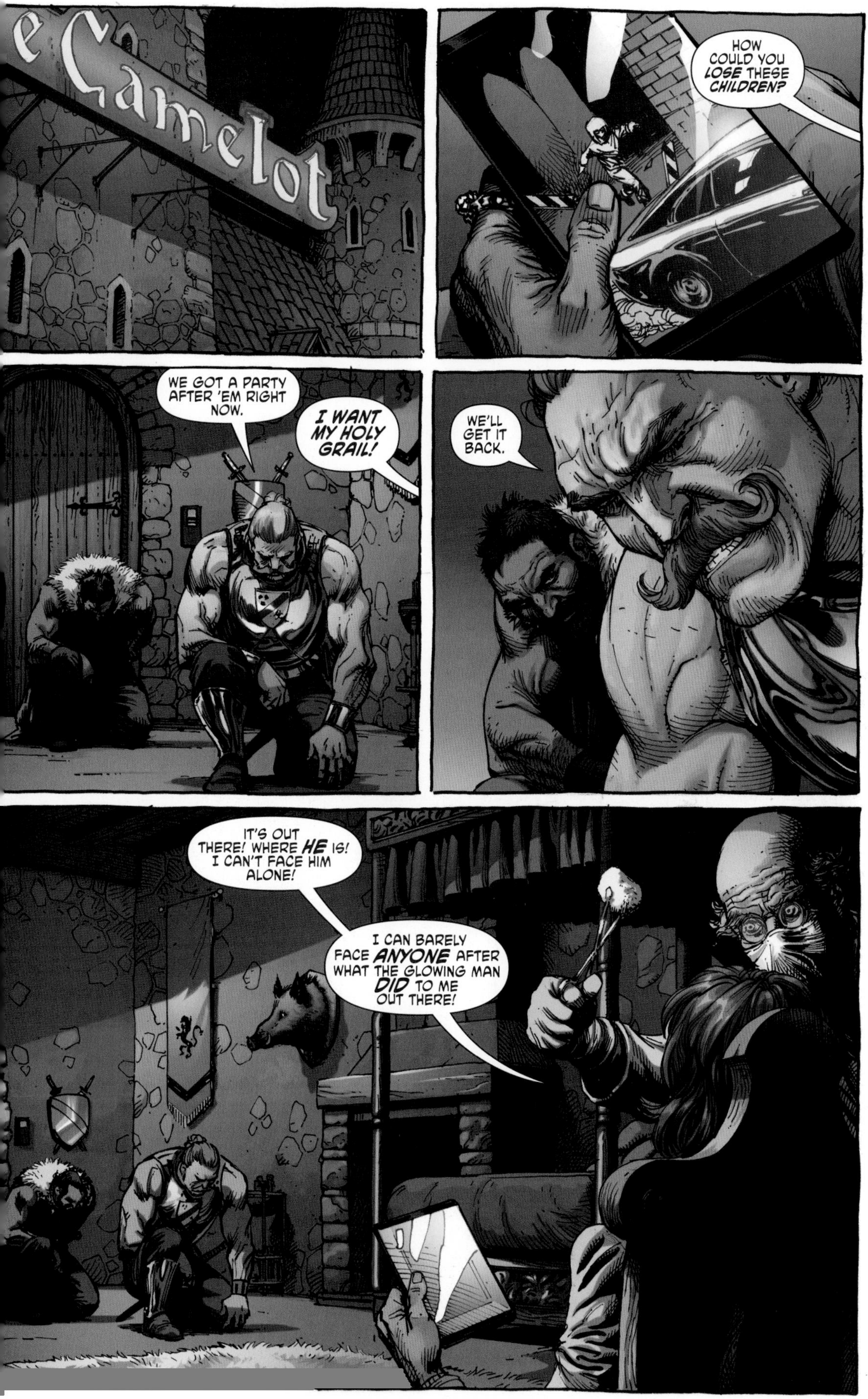
Camelot
HOW COULD YOU LOSE THESE CHILDREN?
WE GOT A PARTY AFTER 'EM RIGHT NOW.
I WANT MY HOLY GRAIL!
WE'LL GET IT BACK.
IT'S OUT THERE! WHERE HE IS! I CAN'T FACE HIM ALONE!
I CAN BARELY FACE ANYONE AFTER WHAT THE GLOWING MAN DID TO ME OUT THERE!

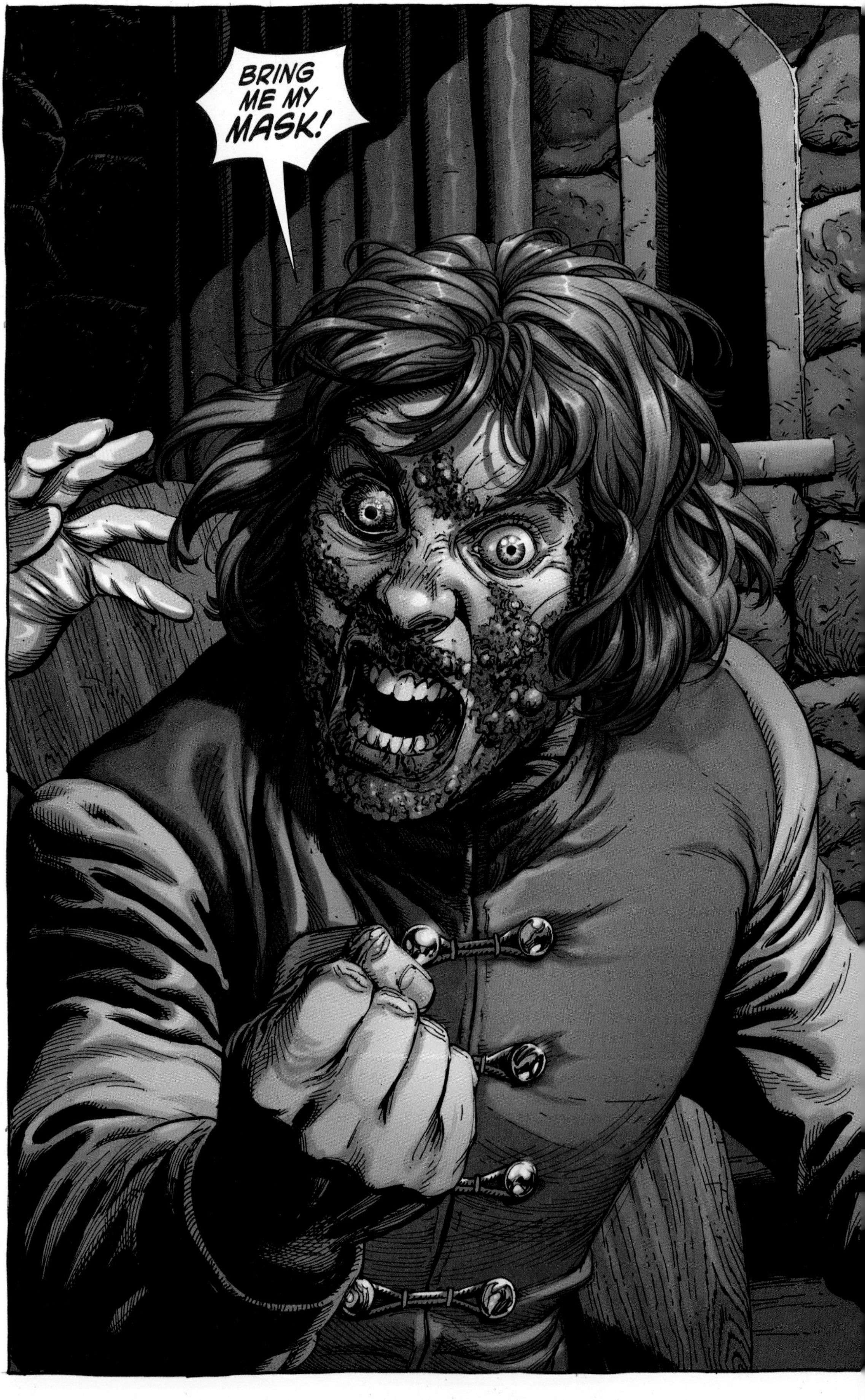
BRING ME MY MASK!

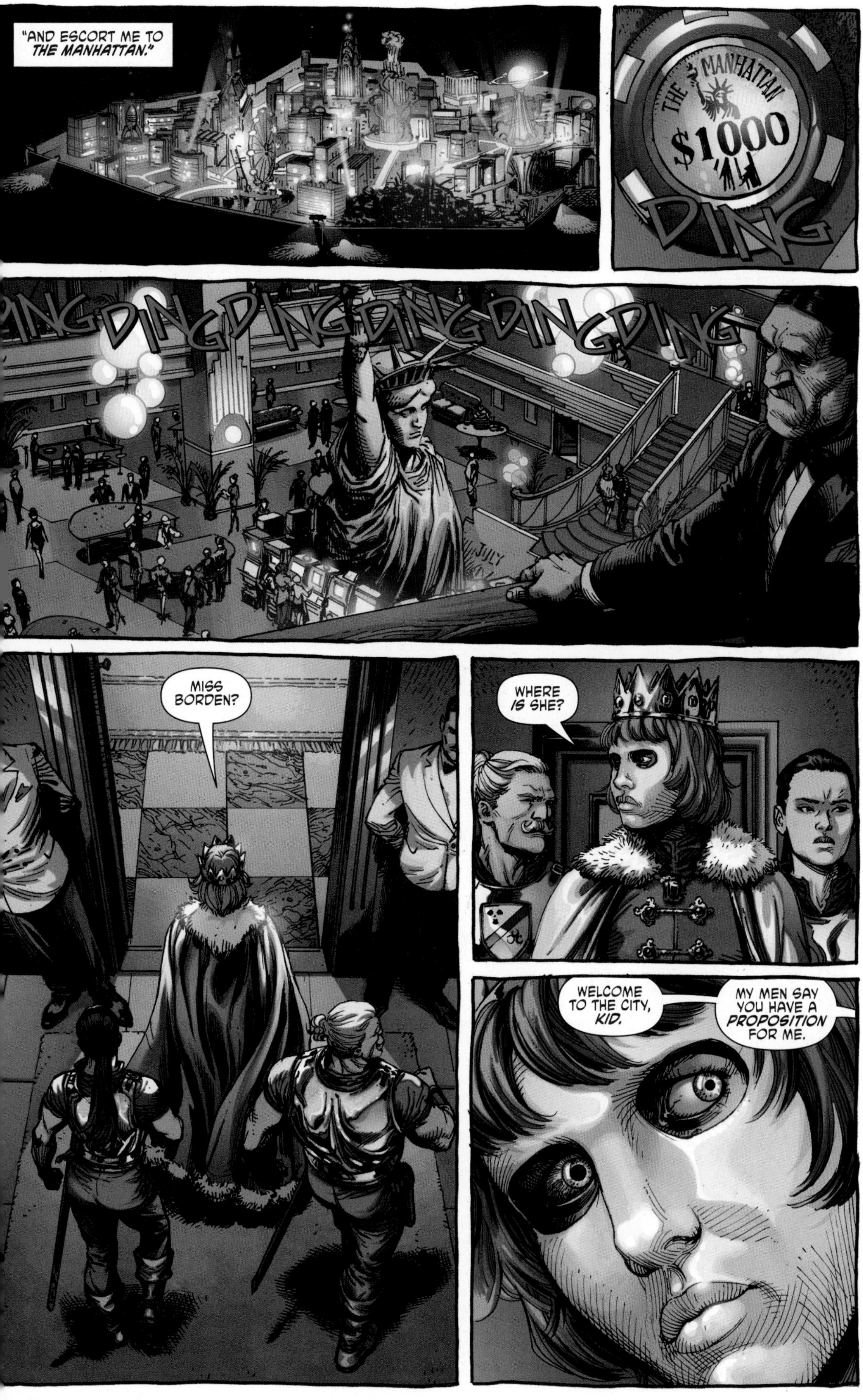
"AND ESCORT ME TO THE MANHATTAN."
THE MANHATTAN $1000
DING
DING DING DING DING DING DING
MISS BORDEN?
WHERE IS SHE?
WELCOME TO THE CITY, KID.
MY MEN SAY YOU HAVE A PROPOSITION FOR ME.

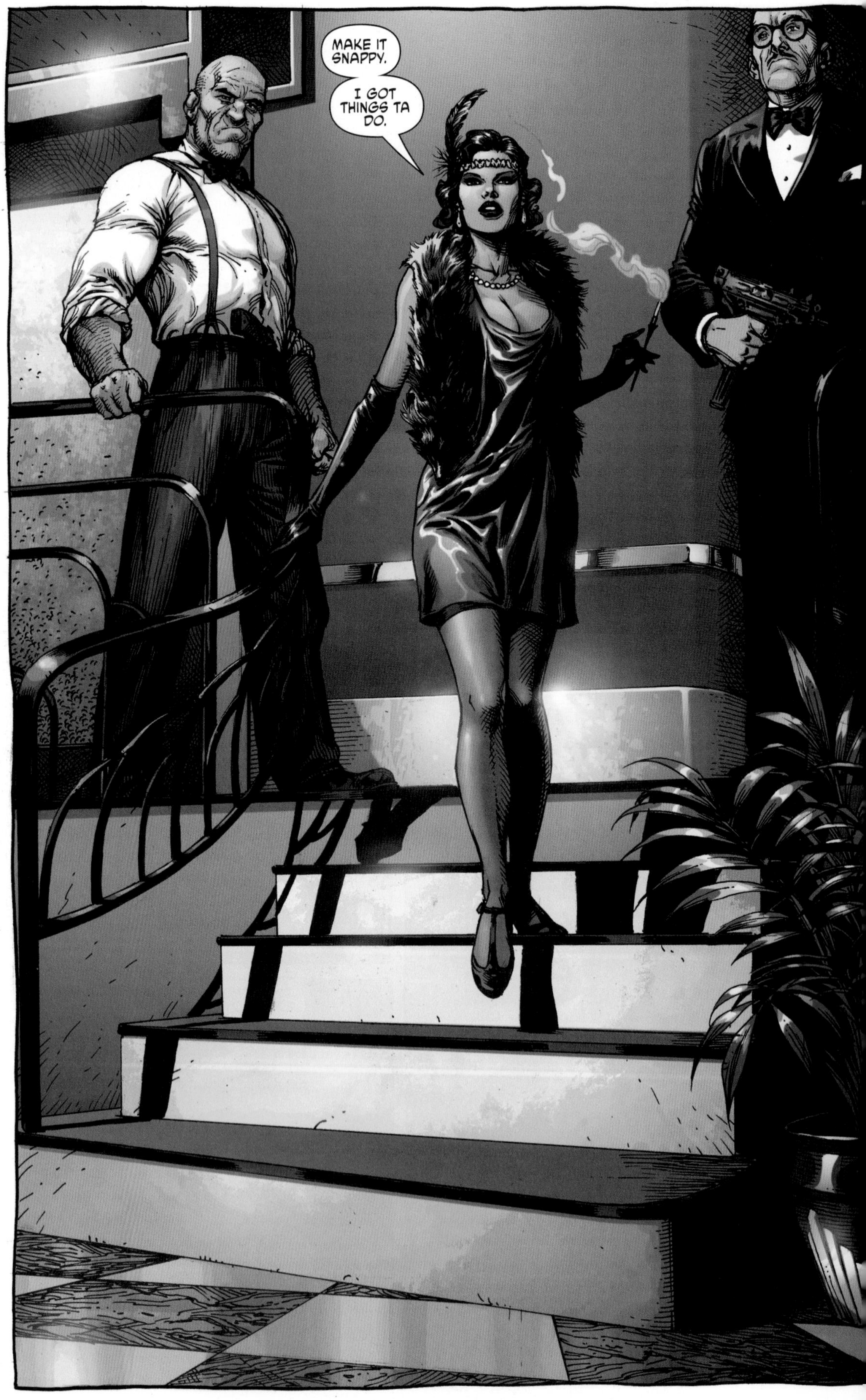
MAKE IT SNAPPY.
I GOT THINGS TA DO.

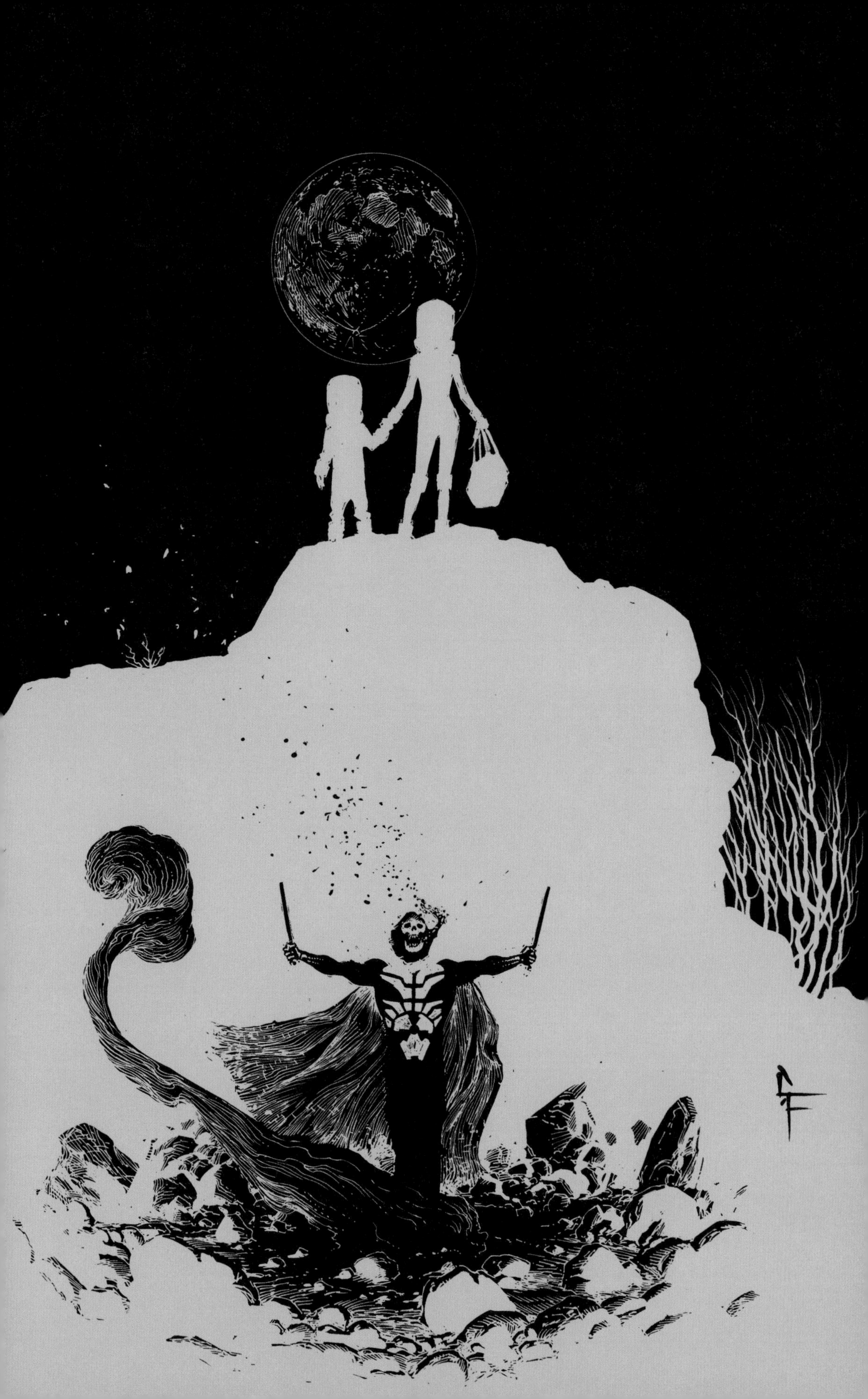

CHAPTER THREE

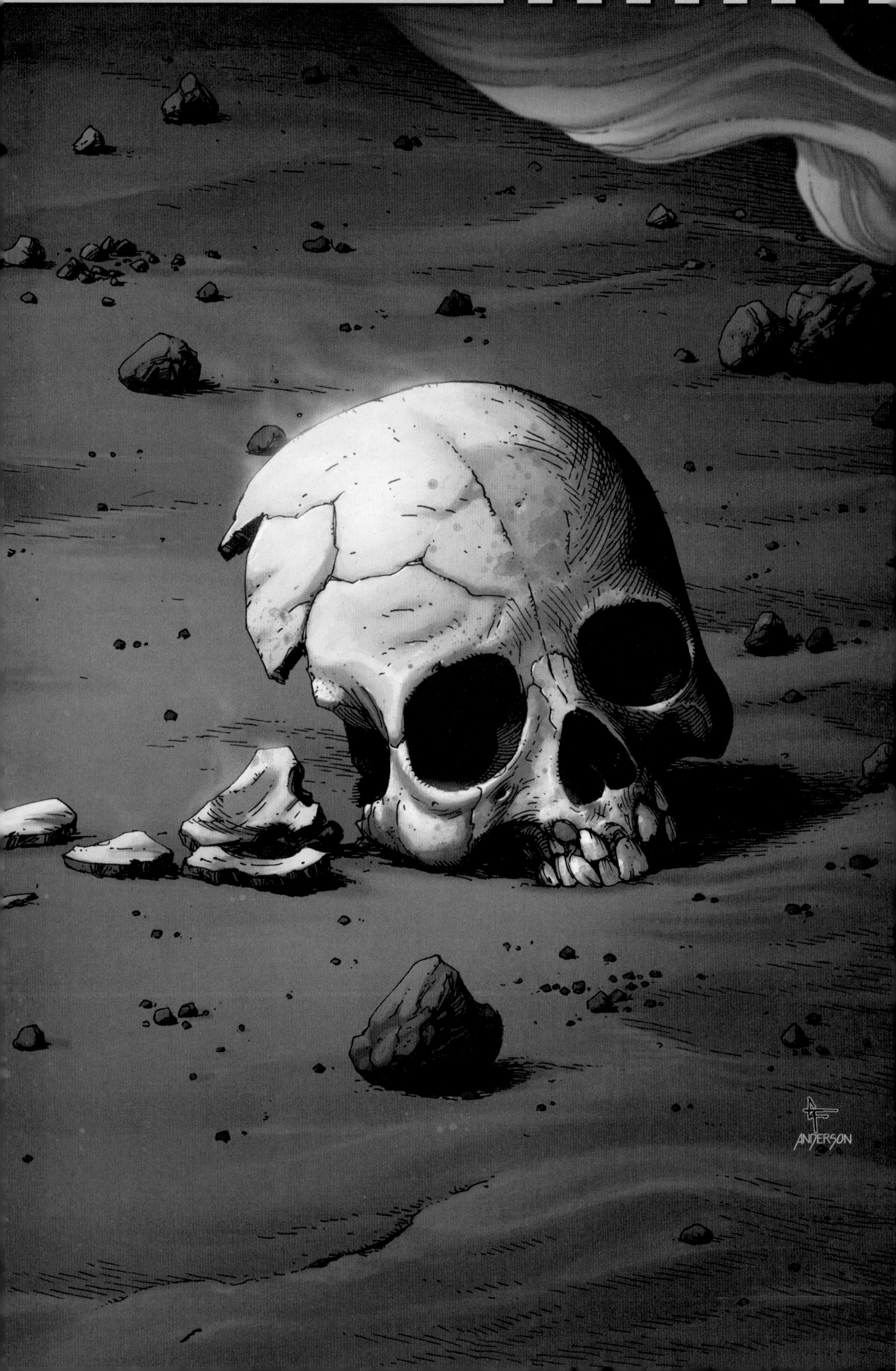
ANDERSON

"HOW DANGEROUS IS IT?"

THIS FORM OF SYSTEMIC RADIOISOTOPE THERAPY IS ADMITTEDLY EXPERIMENTAL, TRACY...

...BUT OUR SUCCESS RATE FOR REDUCING MALIGNANT TUMORS, EVEN IN THE MOST AGGRESSIVE STAGES LIKE THIS, HAS BEEN ENCOURAGING.

"THERE'S ALWAYS A RISK WITH TARGETED INTERNAL RADIATION, BUT USING IT TO ATTACK BONE METASTASIS IS NOT A NEW IDEA."

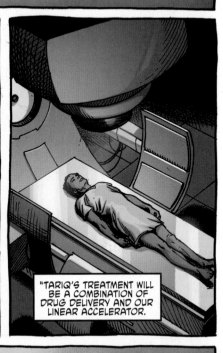

"TARIQ'S TREATMENT WILL BE A COMBINATION OF DRUG DELIVERY AND OUR LINEAR ACCELERATOR.

"OUR HOPE IS THE CANCEROUS CELLS IN YOUR HUSBAND'S BONES WILL BE AFFECTED...

"...WHILE THE HEALTHY CELLS WILL BE SPARED."

HENRY, IT'S HIM.

THE GLOWING MAN...

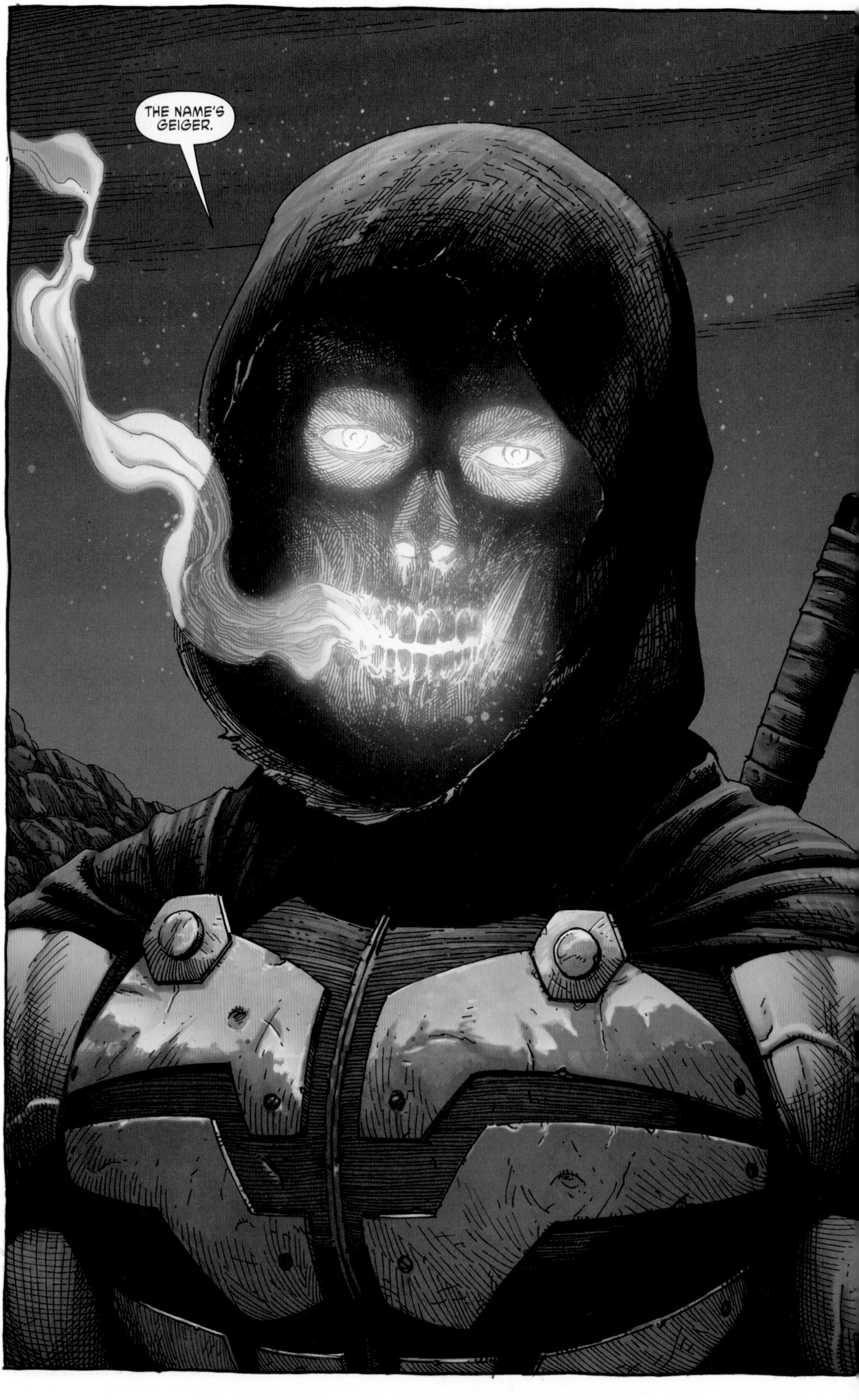
THE NAME'S GEIGER.

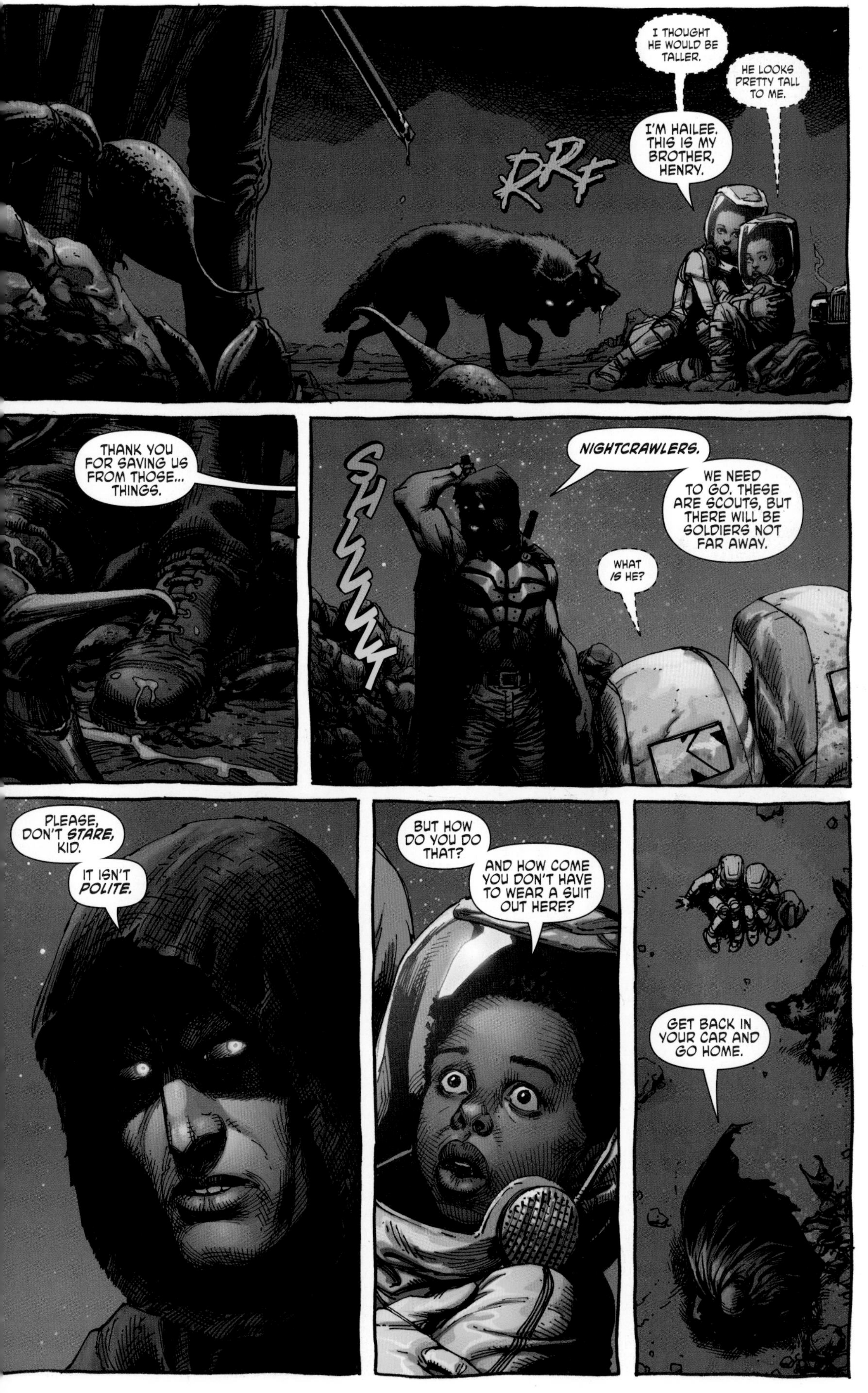

I THOUGHT HE WOULD BE TALLER.
HE LOOKS PRETTY TALL TO ME.
I'M HAILEE. THIS IS MY BROTHER, HENRY.
RRF
THANK YOU FOR SAVING US FROM THOSE... THINGS.
SHWWWK
NIGHTCRAWLERS.
WE NEED TO GO. THESE ARE SCOUTS, BUT THERE WILL BE SOLDIERS NOT FAR AWAY.
WHAT IS HE?
PLEASE, DON'T STARE, KID.
IT ISN'T POLITE.
BUT HOW DO YOU DO THAT?
AND HOW COME YOU DON'T HAVE TO WEAR A SUIT OUT HERE?
GET BACK IN YOUR CAR AND GO HOME.

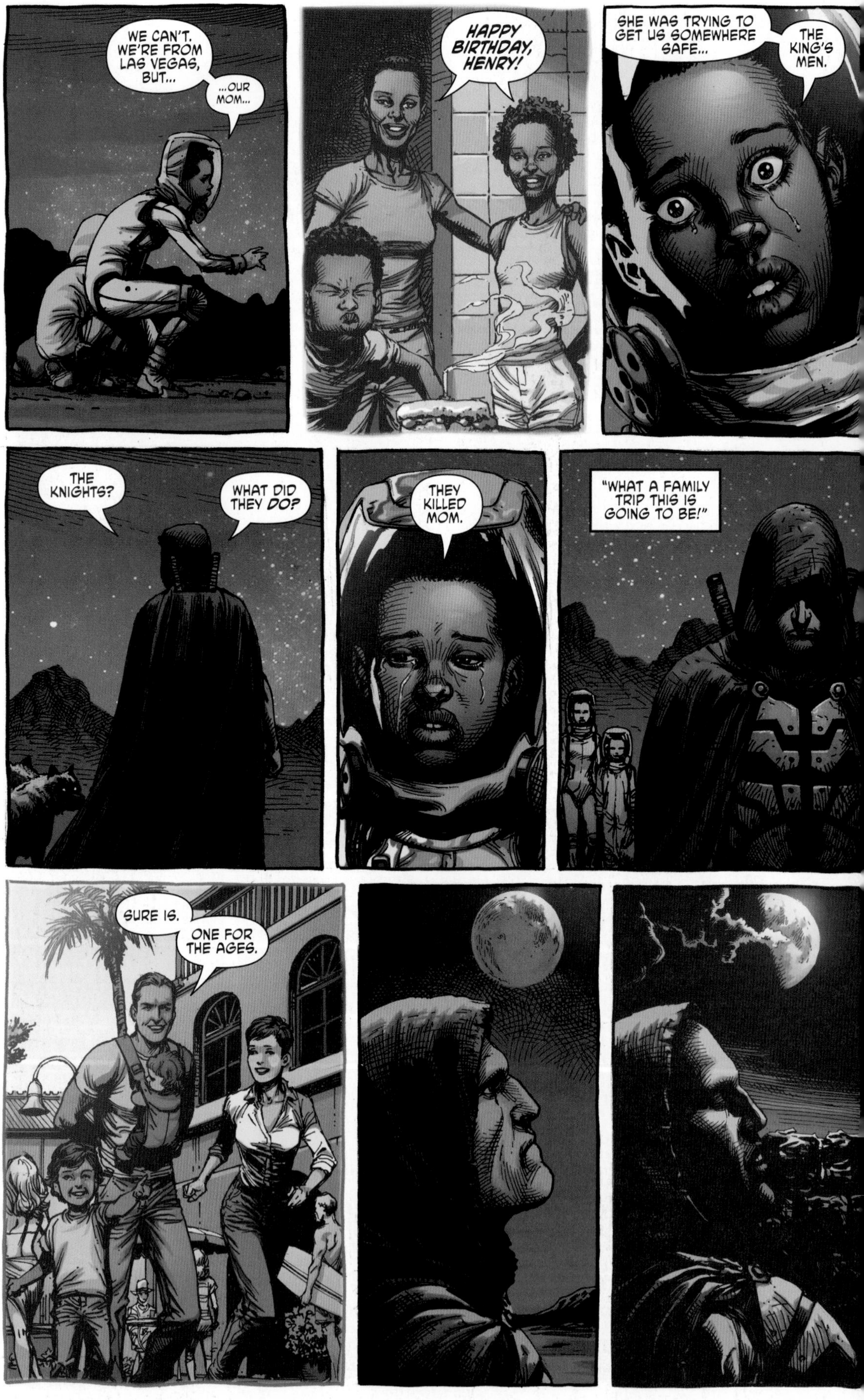

WE CAN'T. WE'RE FROM LAS VEGAS, BUT...
...OUR MOM...
HAPPY BIRTHDAY, HENRY!
SHE WAS TRYING TO GET US SOMEWHERE SAFE...
THE KING'S MEN.
THE KNIGHTS?
WHAT DID THEY DO?
THEY KILLED MOM.
"WHAT A FAMILY TRIP THIS IS GOING TO BE!"
SURE IS.
ONE FOR THE AGES.

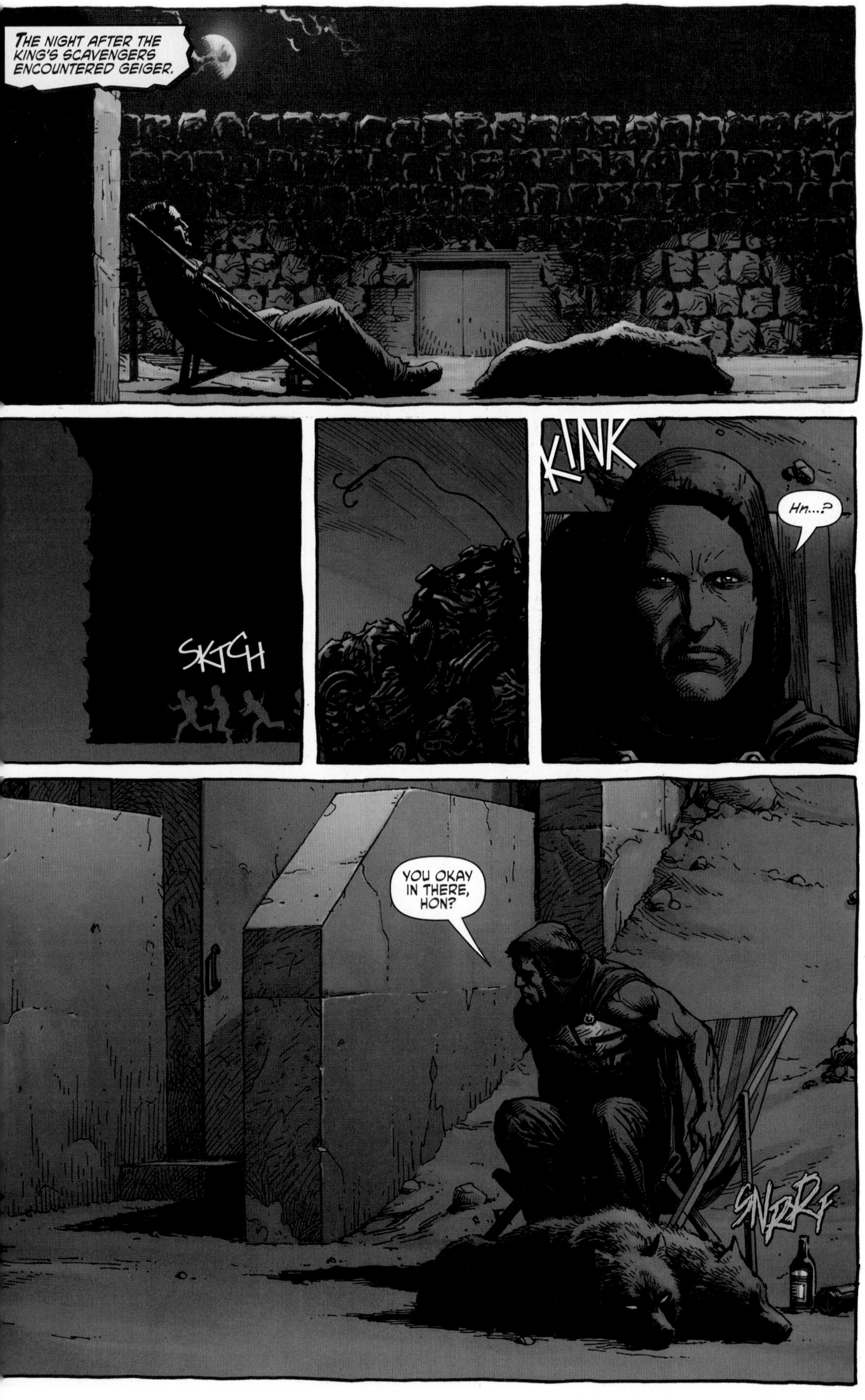
THE NIGHT AFTER THE KING'S SCAVENGERS ENCOUNTERED GEIGER.
SKTCH
KINK
Hn...?
YOU OKAY IN THERE, HON?
SNRRF

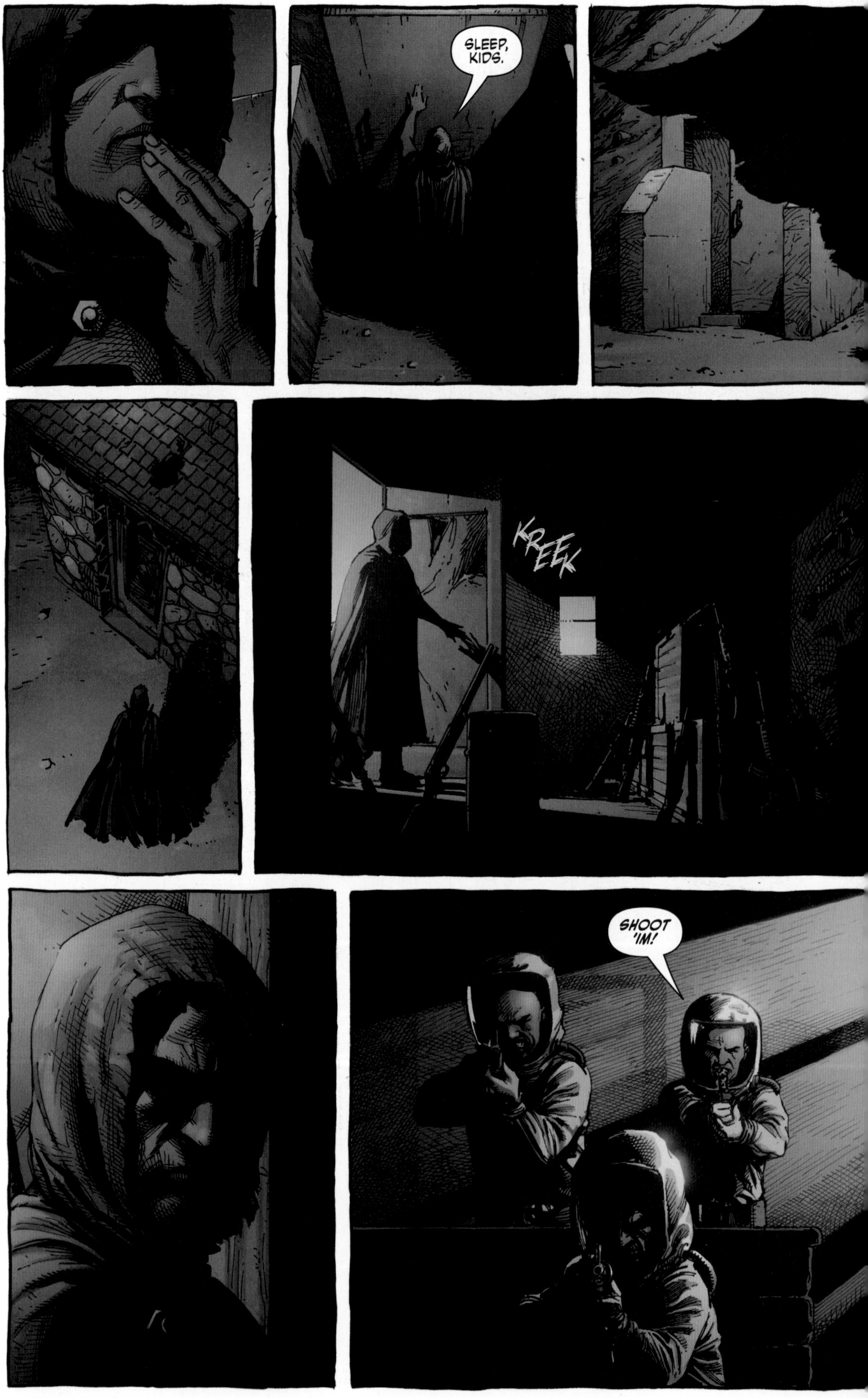
SLEEP, KIDS.
KREEK
SHOOT 'IM!

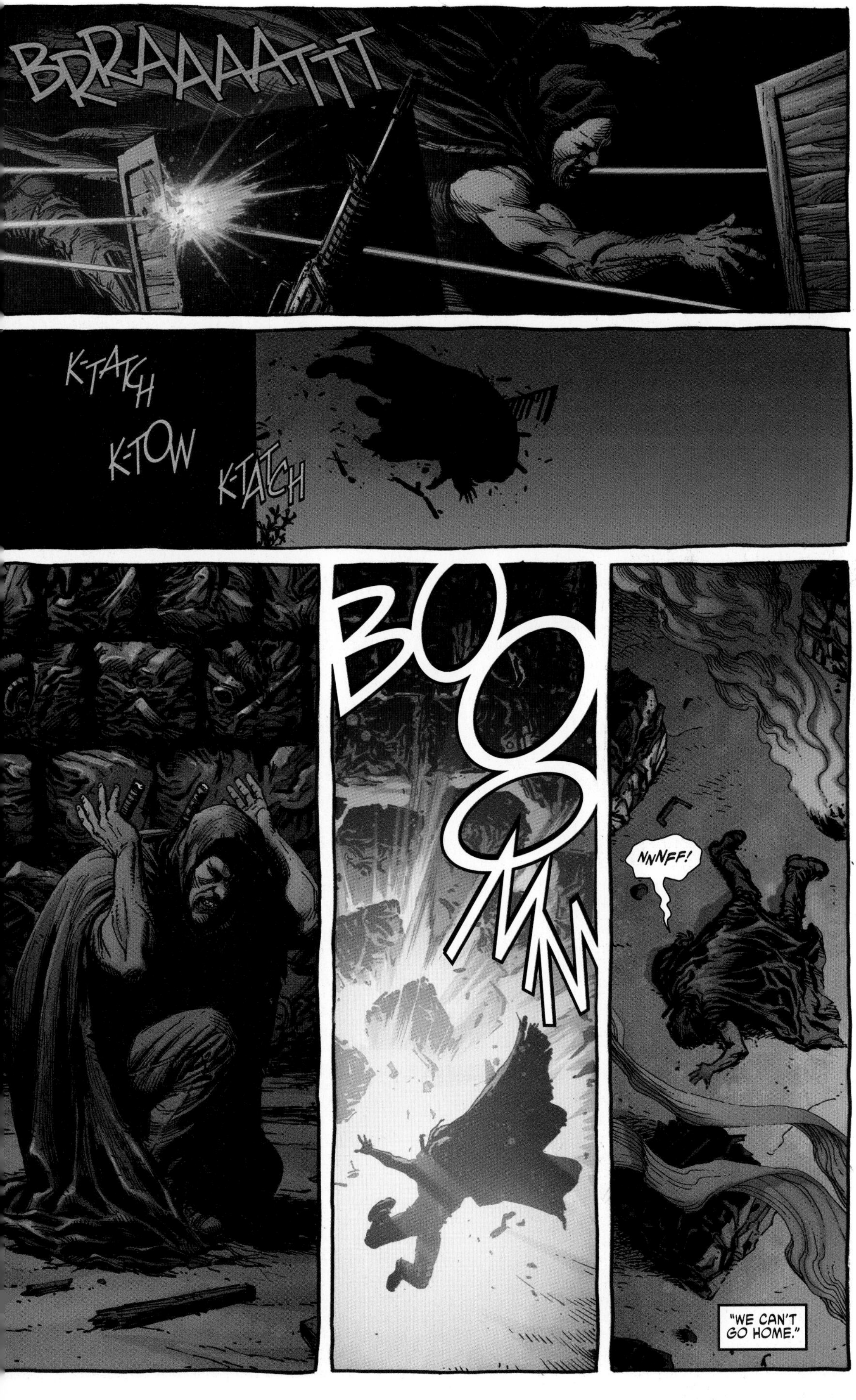
BRRAAAATTT
K-TATCH
K-TOW
K-TATCH
BOOOMM
NNNFF!
"WE CAN'T GO HOME."

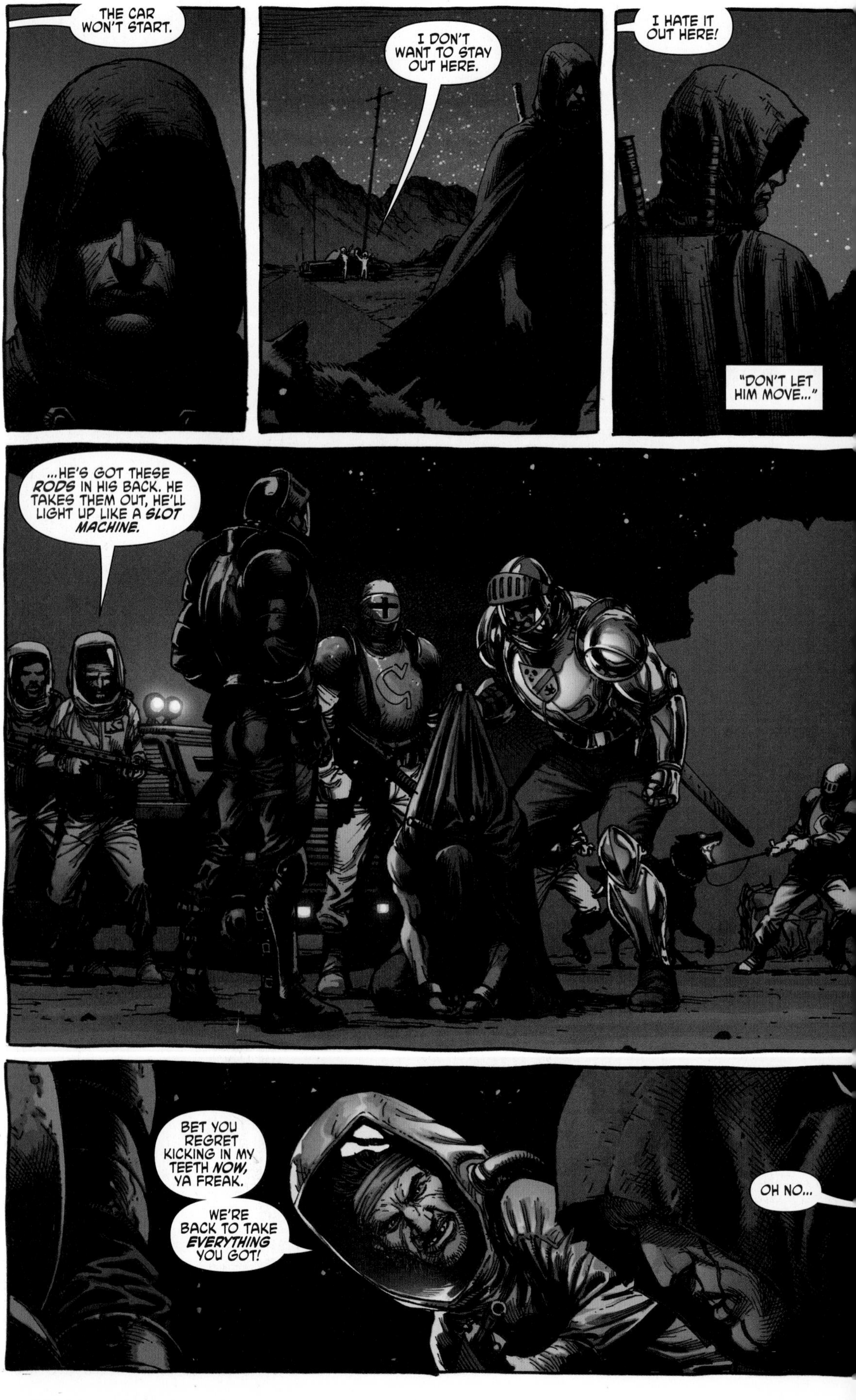
THE CAR WON'T START.
I DON'T WANT TO STAY OUT HERE.
I HATE IT OUT HERE!
"DON'T LET HIM MOVE..."
...HE'S GOT THESE *RODS* IN HIS BACK. HE TAKES THEM OUT, HE'LL LIGHT UP LIKE A *SLOT MACHINE.*
BET YOU REGRET KICKING IN MY TEETH *NOW,* YA FREAK.
WE'RE BACK TO TAKE *EVERYTHING* YOU GOT!
OH NO...

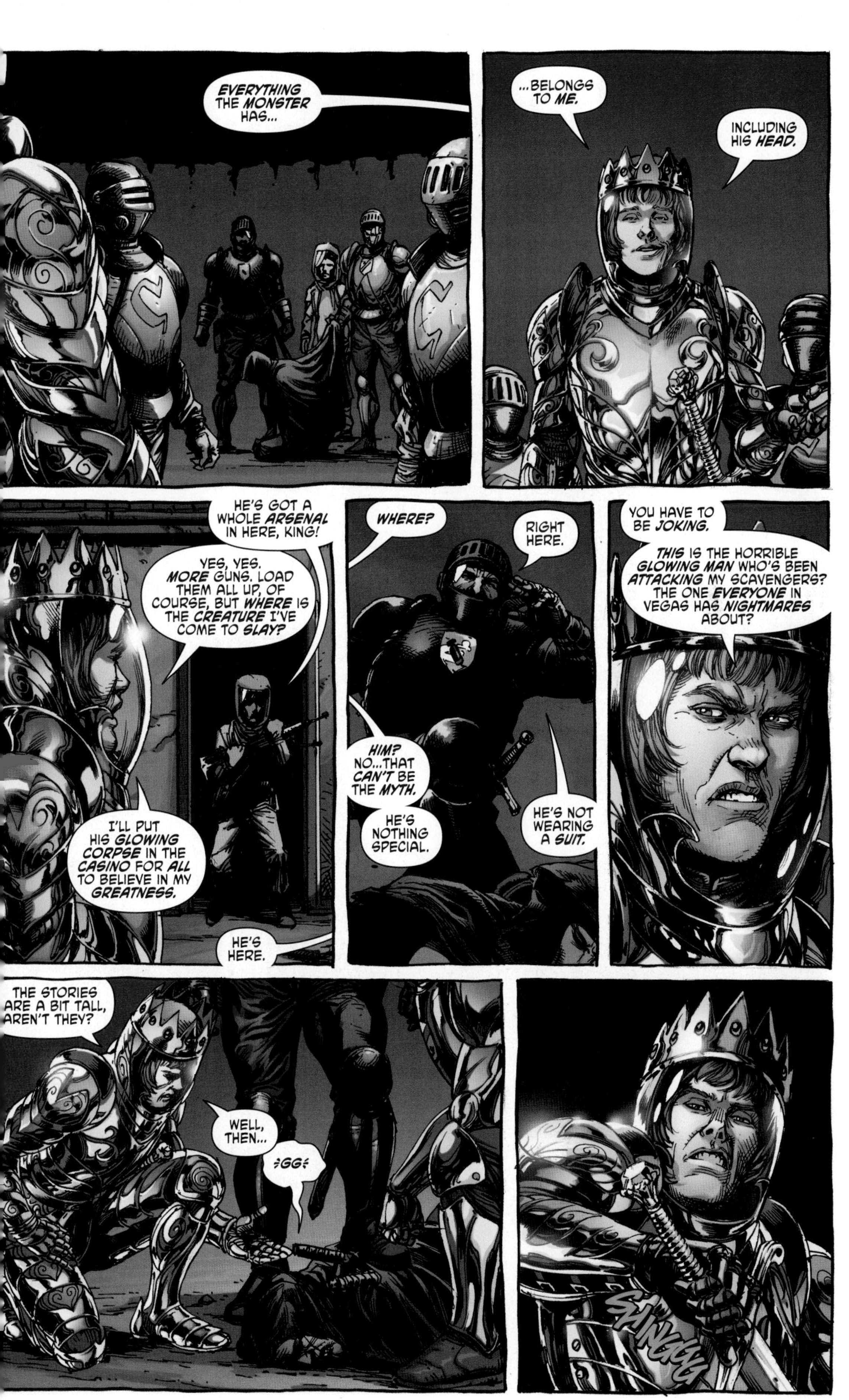
EVERYTHING THE MONSTER HAS...
...BELONGS TO ME.
INCLUDING HIS HEAD.
HE'S GOT A WHOLE ARSENAL IN HERE, KING!
YES, YES. MORE GUNS. LOAD THEM ALL UP, OF COURSE, BUT WHERE IS THE CREATURE I'VE COME TO SLAY?
I'LL PUT HIS GLOWING CORPSE IN THE CASINO FOR ALL TO BELIEVE IN MY GREATNESS.
HE'S HERE.
WHERE?
RIGHT HERE.
HIM? NO...THAT CAN'T BE THE MYTH.
HE'S NOTHING SPECIAL.
HE'S NOT WEARING A SUIT.
YOU HAVE TO BE JOKING.
THIS IS THE HORRIBLE GLOWING MAN WHO'S BEEN ATTACKING MY SCAVENGERS? THE ONE EVERYONE IN VEGAS HAS NIGHTMARES ABOUT?
THE STORIES ARE A BIT TALL, AREN'T THEY?
WELL, THEN...
GG
SWINGGGG

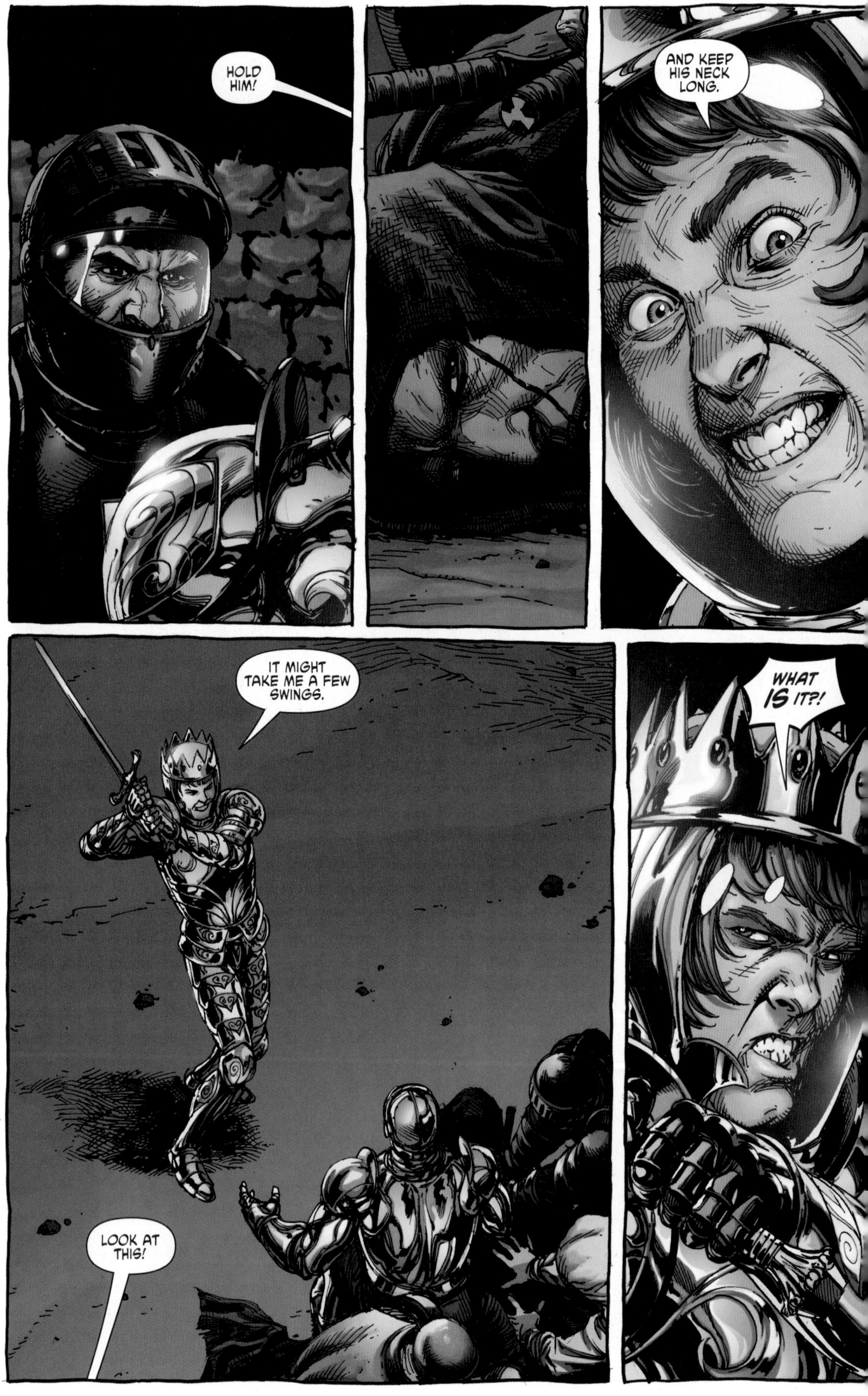
HOLD HIM!
AND KEEP HIS NECK LONG.
IT MIGHT TAKE ME A FEW SWINGS.
LOOK AT THIS!
WHAT IS IT?!

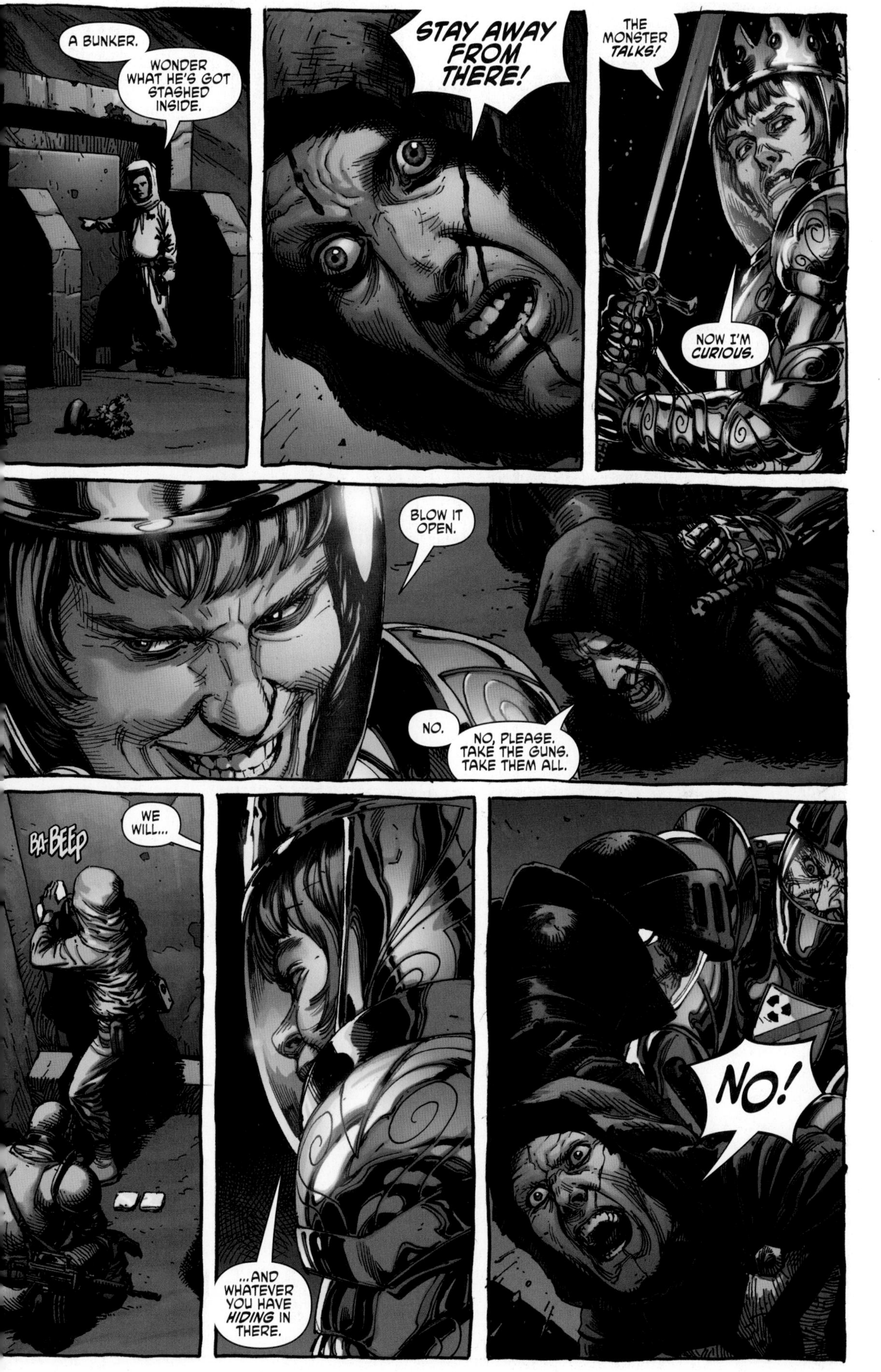
A BUNKER.
WONDER WHAT HE'S GOT STASHED INSIDE.
STAY AWAY FROM THERE!
THE MONSTER TALKS!
NOW I'M CURIOUS.
BLOW IT OPEN.
NO.
NO, PLEASE. TAKE THE GUNS. TAKE THEM ALL.
BA-BEEP
WE WILL...
...AND WHATEVER YOU HAVE HIDING IN THERE.
NO!

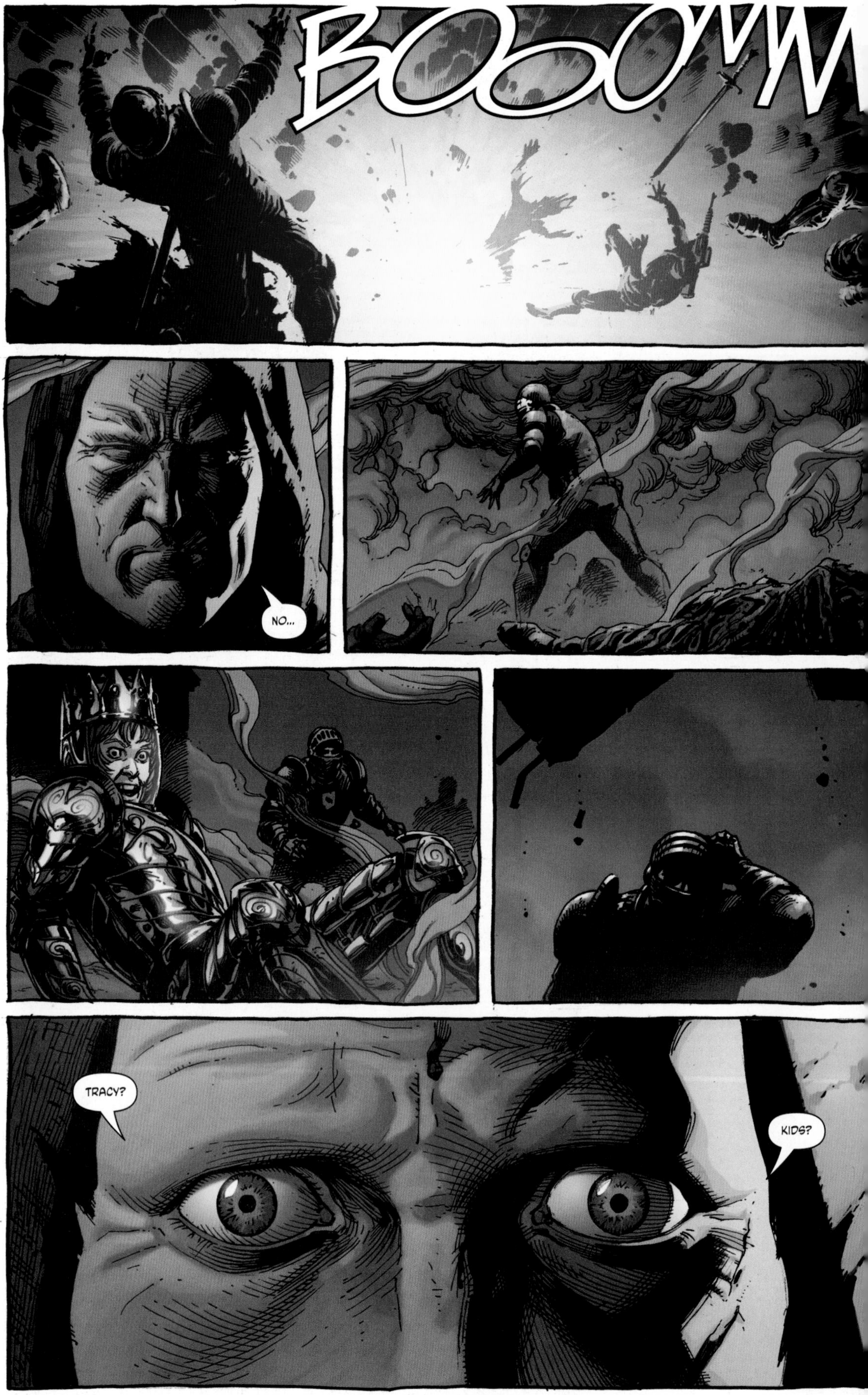
BOOOOM
NO...
TRACY?
KIDS?

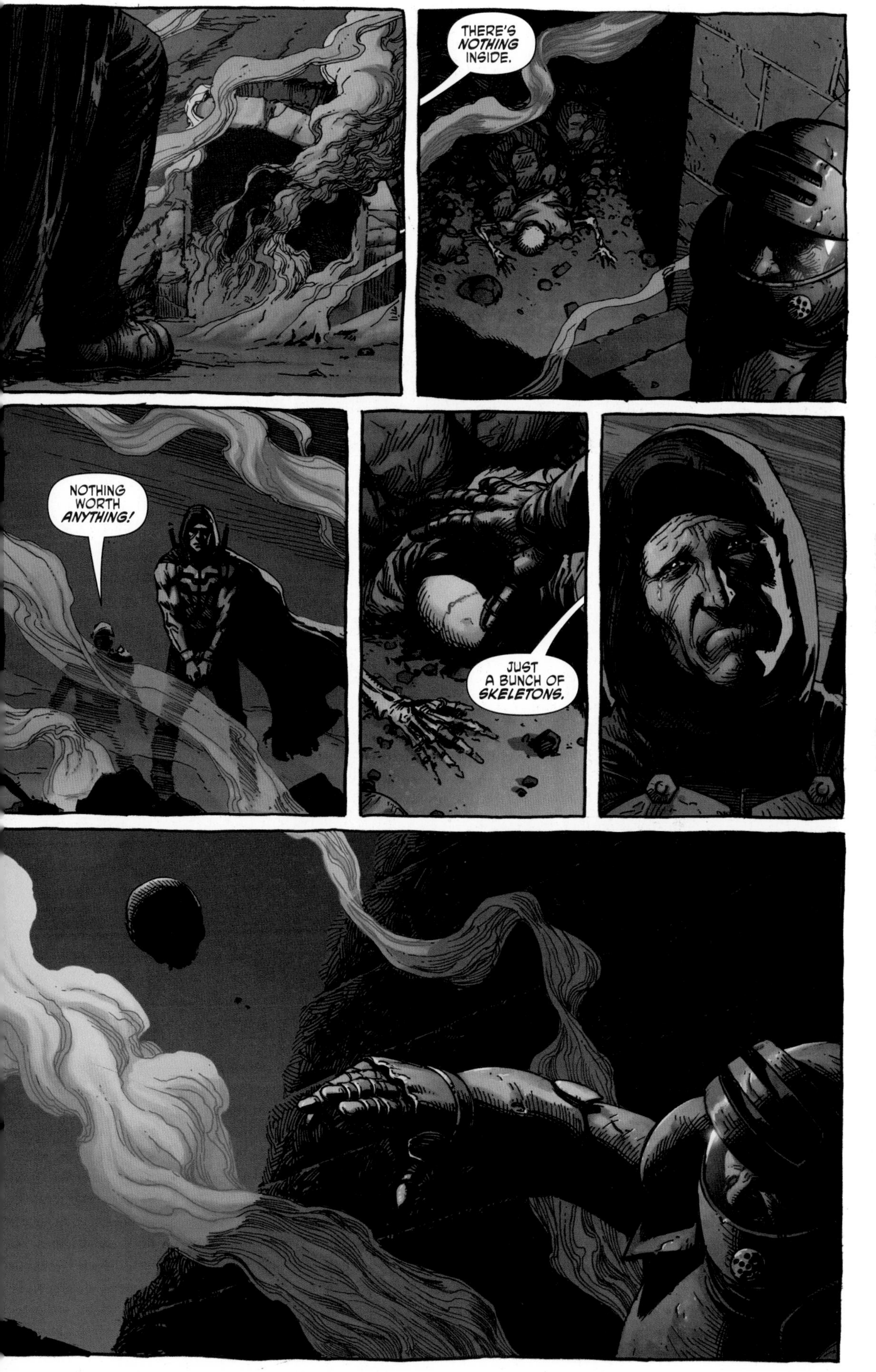
THERE'S NOTHING INSIDE.
NOTHING WORTH ANYTHING!
JUST A BUNCH OF SKELETONS.

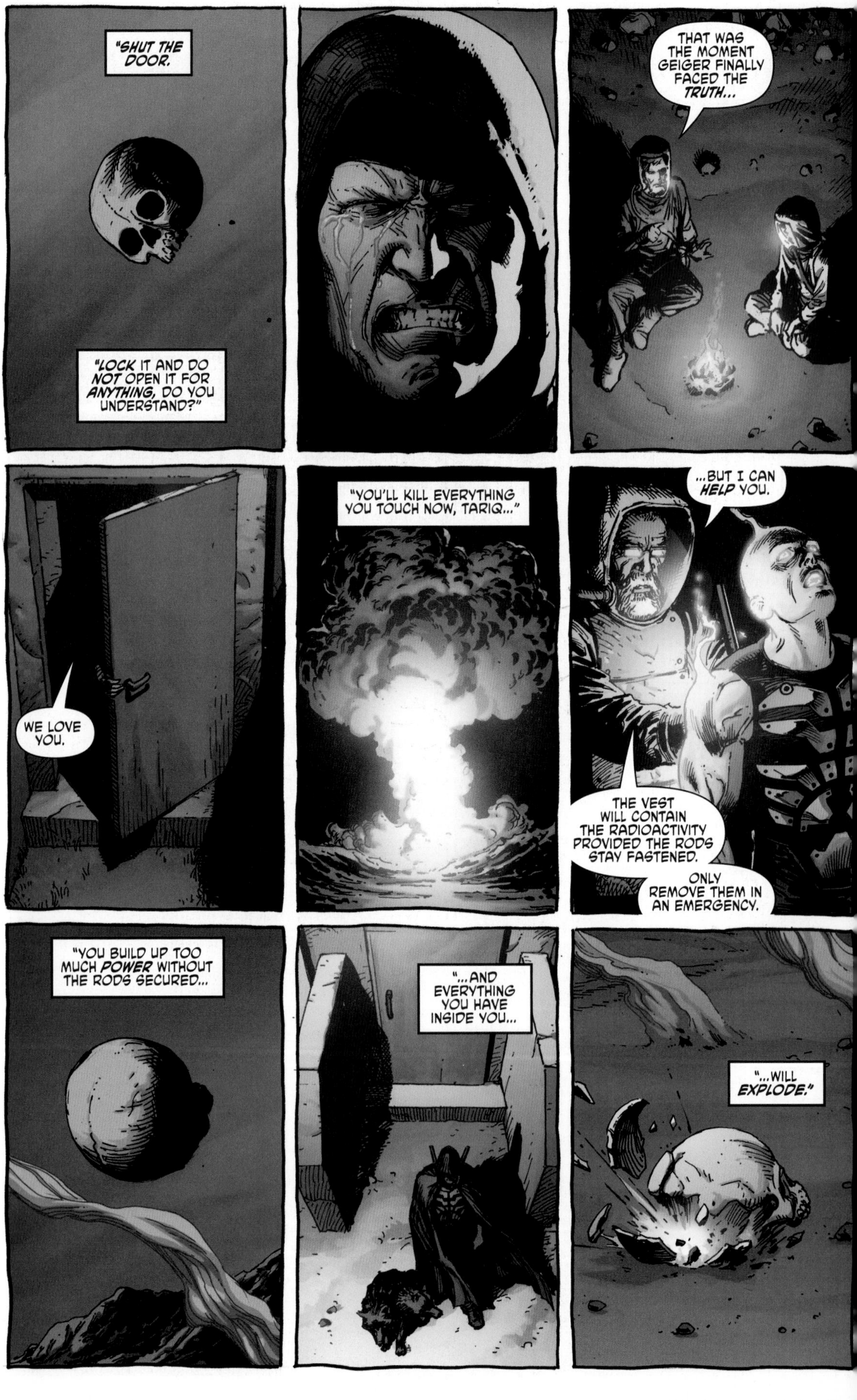
"SHUT THE DOOR.
"LOCK IT AND DO NOT OPEN IT FOR ANYTHING, DO YOU UNDERSTAND?"
THAT WAS THE MOMENT GEIGER FINALLY FACED THE TRUTH...
WE LOVE YOU.
"YOU'LL KILL EVERYTHING YOU TOUCH NOW, TARIQ..."
...BUT I CAN HELP YOU.
THE VEST WILL CONTAIN THE RADIOACTIVITY PROVIDED THE RODS STAY FASTENED.
ONLY REMOVE THEM IN AN EMERGENCY.
"YOU BUILD UP TOO MUCH POWER WITHOUT THE RODS SECURED...
"...AND EVERYTHING YOU HAVE INSIDE YOU...
"...WILL EXPLODE."

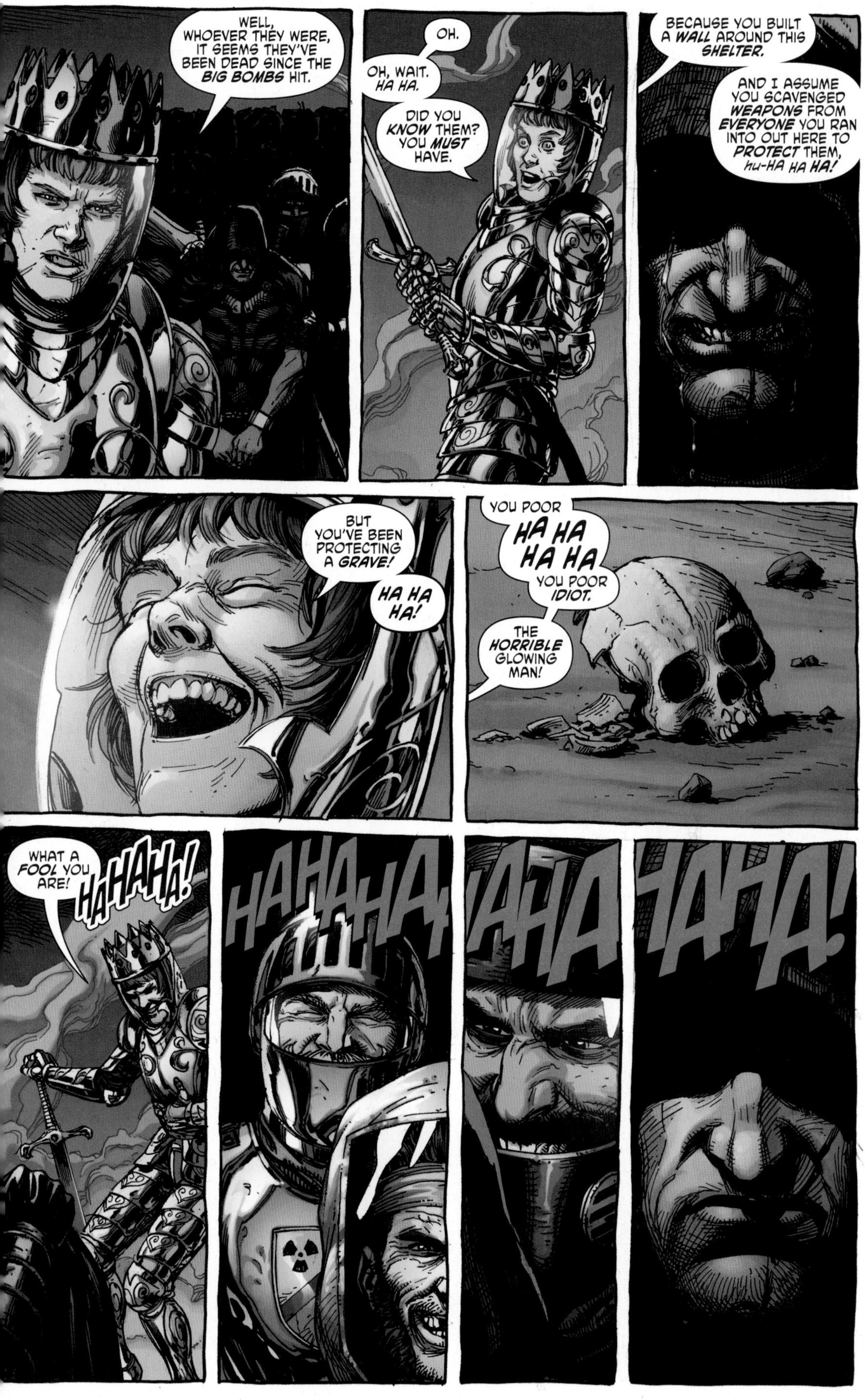
WELL, WHOEVER THEY WERE, IT SEEMS THEY'VE BEEN DEAD SINCE THE BIG BOMBS HIT.
OH.
OH, WAIT. HA HA.
DID YOU KNOW THEM? YOU MUST HAVE.
BECAUSE YOU BUILT A WALL AROUND THIS SHELTER.
AND I ASSUME YOU SCAVENGED WEAPONS FROM EVERYONE YOU RAN INTO OUT HERE TO PROTECT THEM, hu-HA HA HA!
BUT YOU'VE BEEN PROTECTING A GRAVE!
HA HA HA!
YOU POOR HA HA HA HA
YOU POOR IDIOT.
THE HORRIBLE GLOWING MAN!
WHAT A FOOL YOU ARE!
HAHAHA!
HAHAHAHAHAHAHAHA!

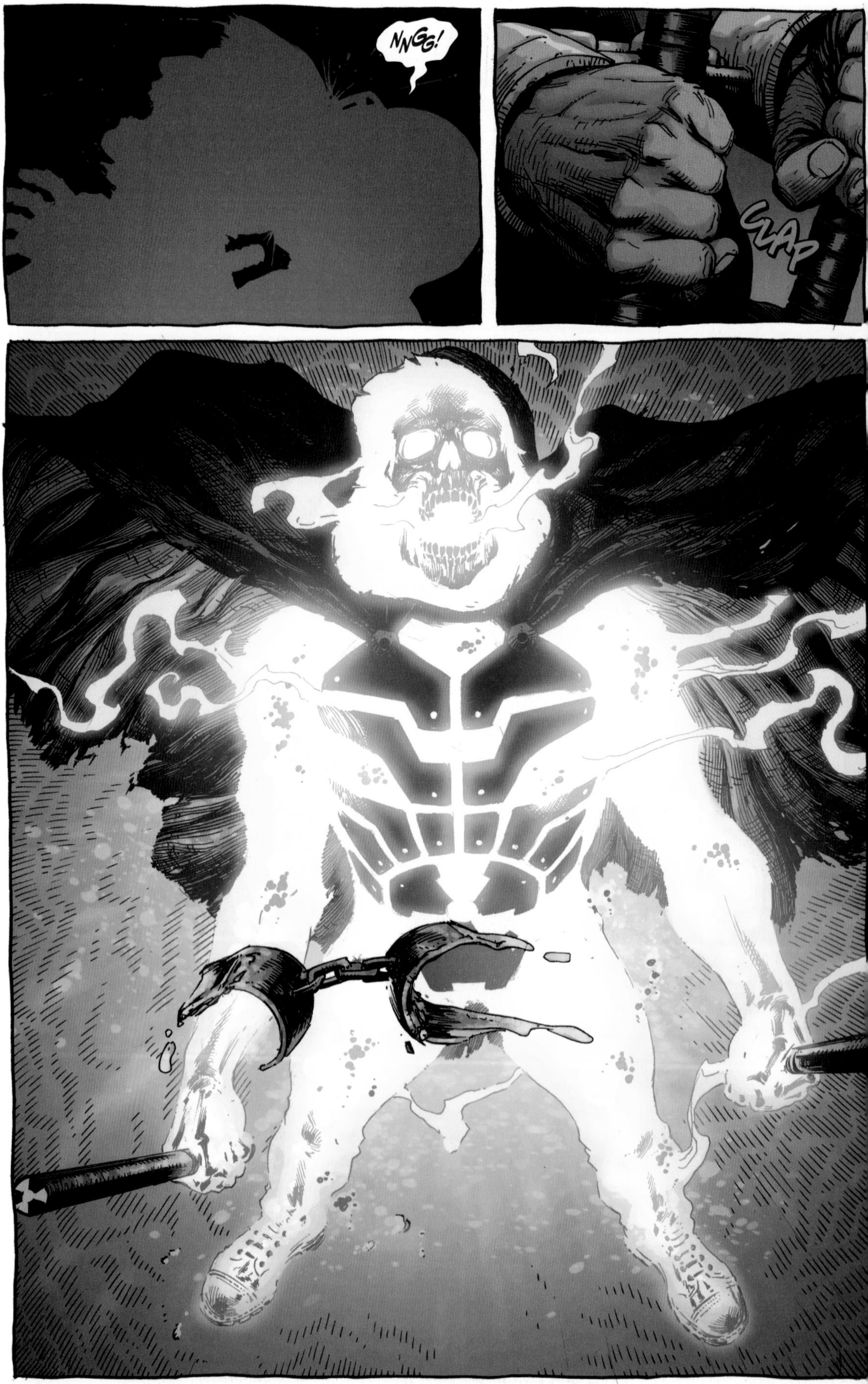
NNGG!
CLAP

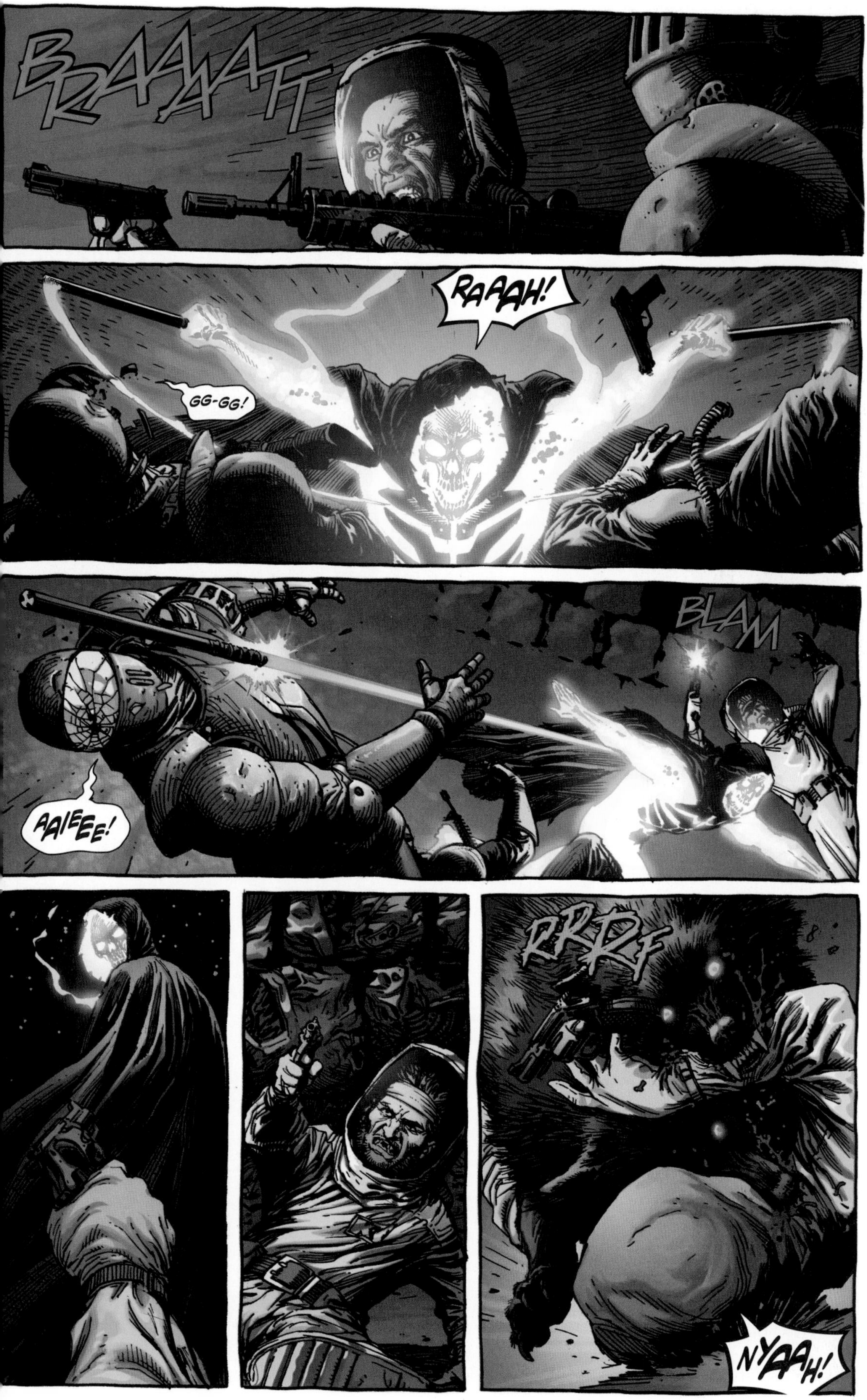
BRAAAAATT
RAAAH!
GG-GG!
BLAM
AAIEEE!
RRRF
NYAAH!

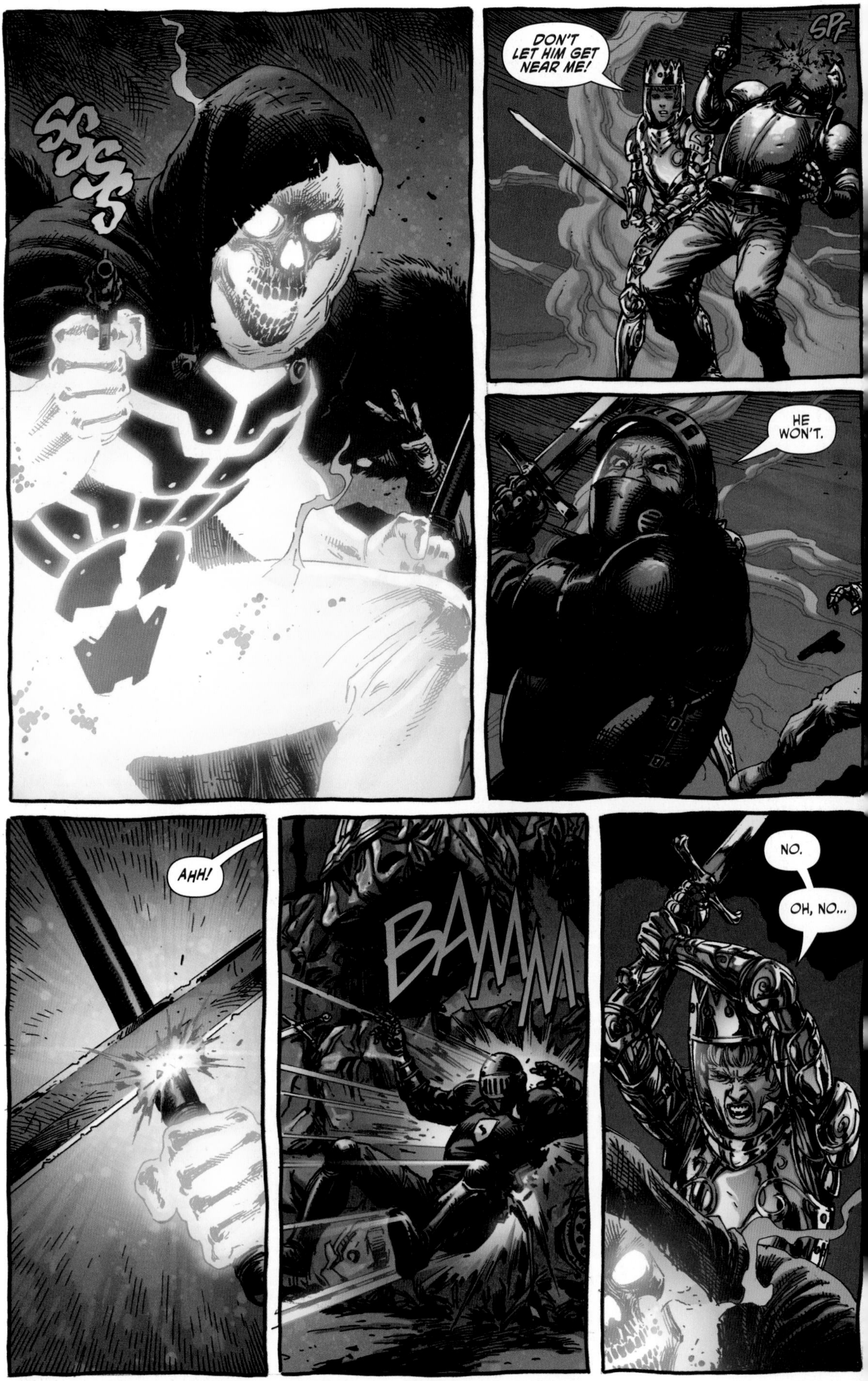
SSSSS
DON'T LET HIM GET NEAR ME!
SPF
HE WON'T.
AHH!
BAMM
NO.
OH, NO...

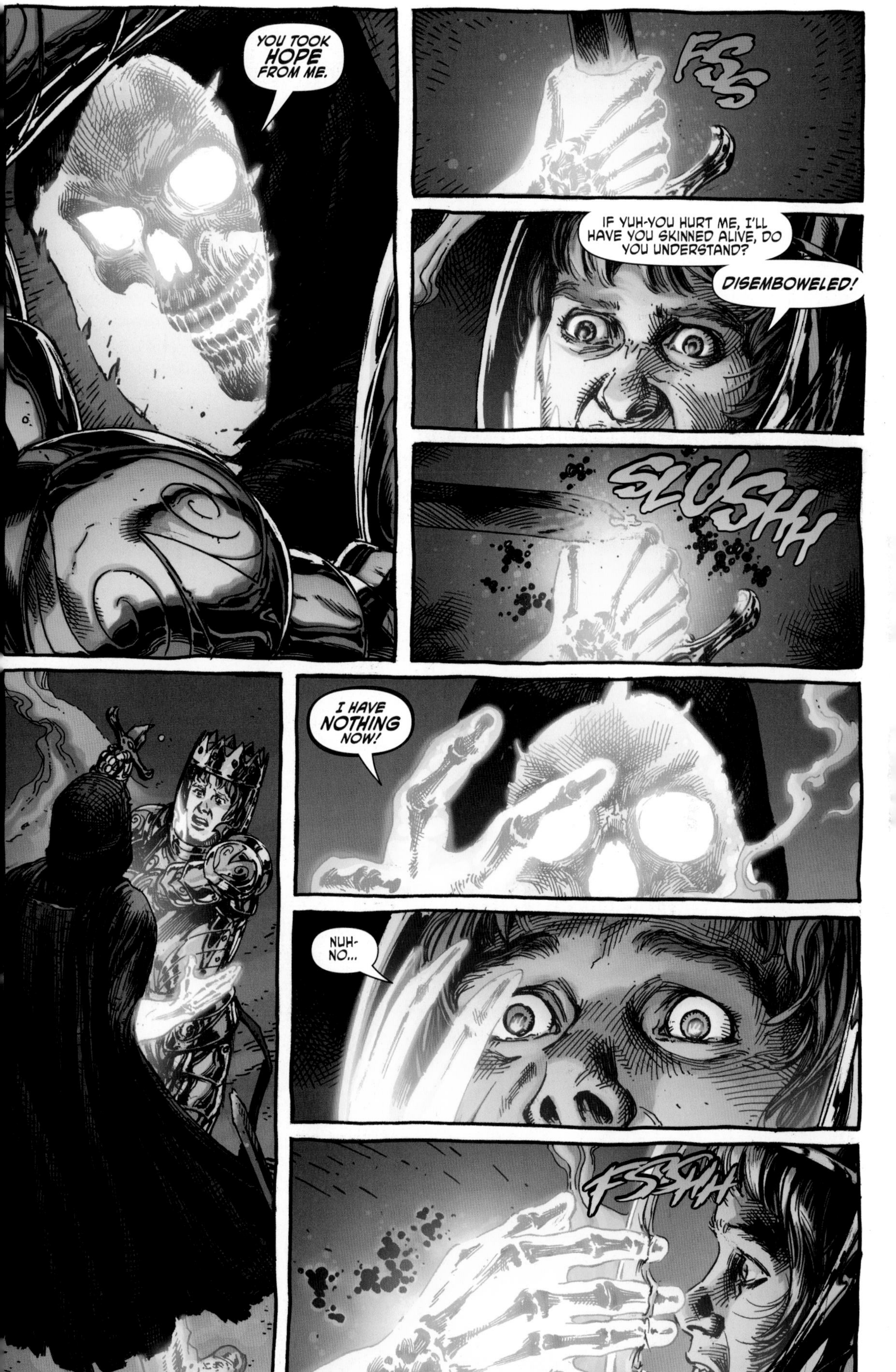
YOU TOOK HOPE FROM ME.
FSSS
IF YUH-YOU HURT ME, I'LL HAVE YOU SKINNED ALIVE, DO YOU UNDERSTAND?
DISEMBOWELED!
SLUSHH
I HAVE NOTHING NOW!
NUH-NO...
FSSHH

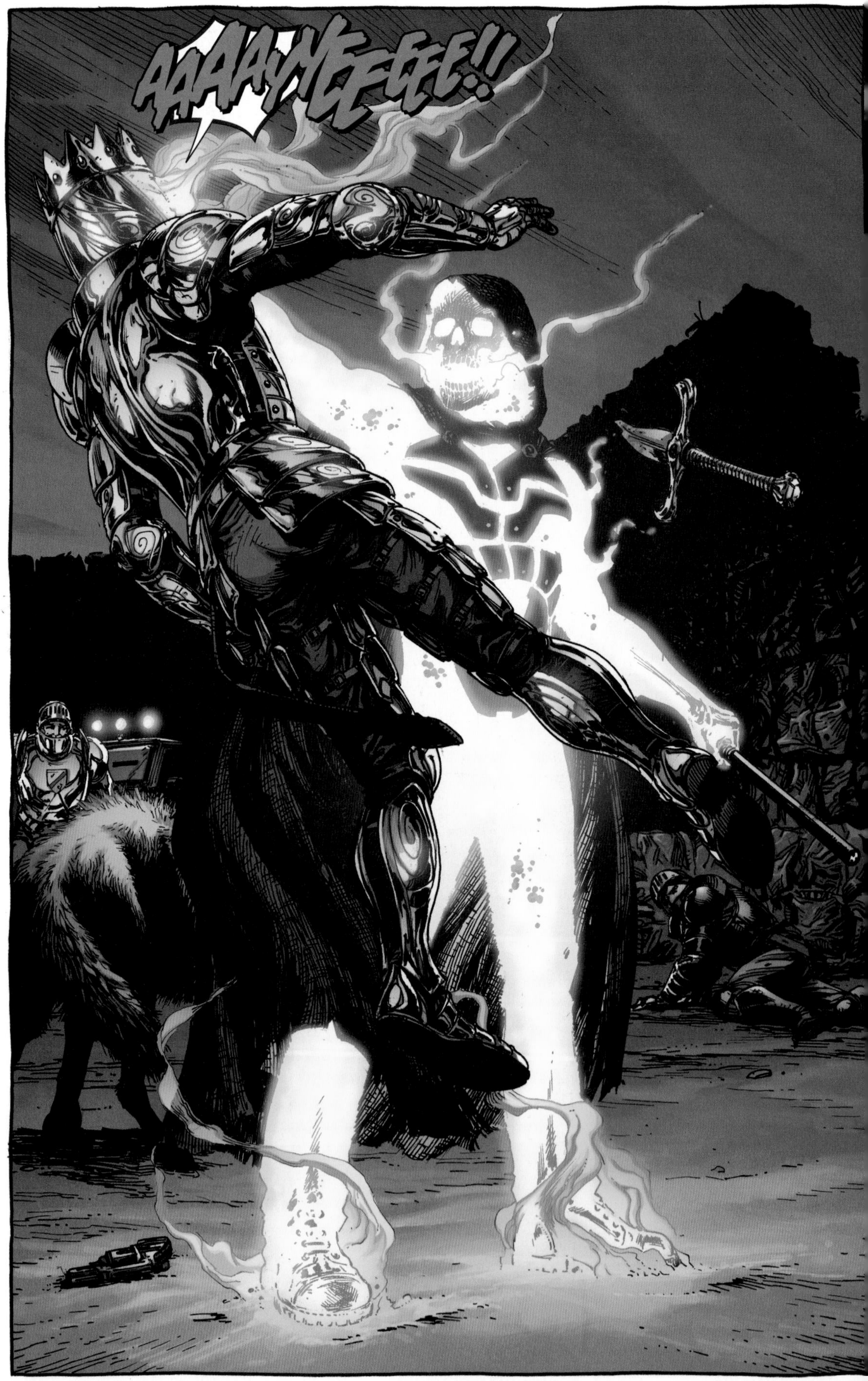
AAAAYEEEEE!!

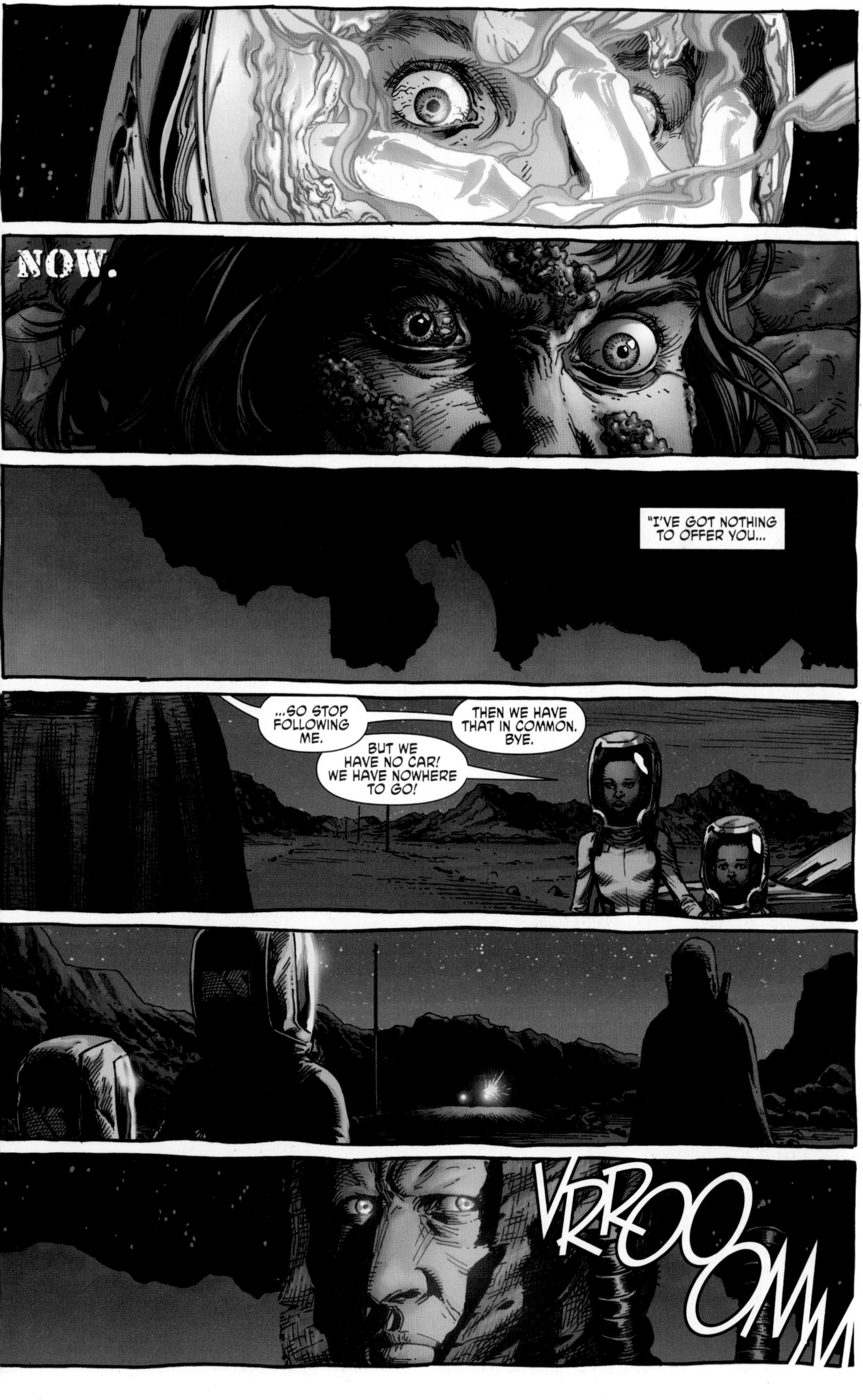
NOW.
"I'VE GOT NOTHING TO OFFER YOU...
...SO STOP FOLLOWING ME.
THEN WE HAVE THAT IN COMMON. BYE.
BUT WE HAVE NO CAR! WE HAVE NOWHERE TO GO!
VRROOOMM

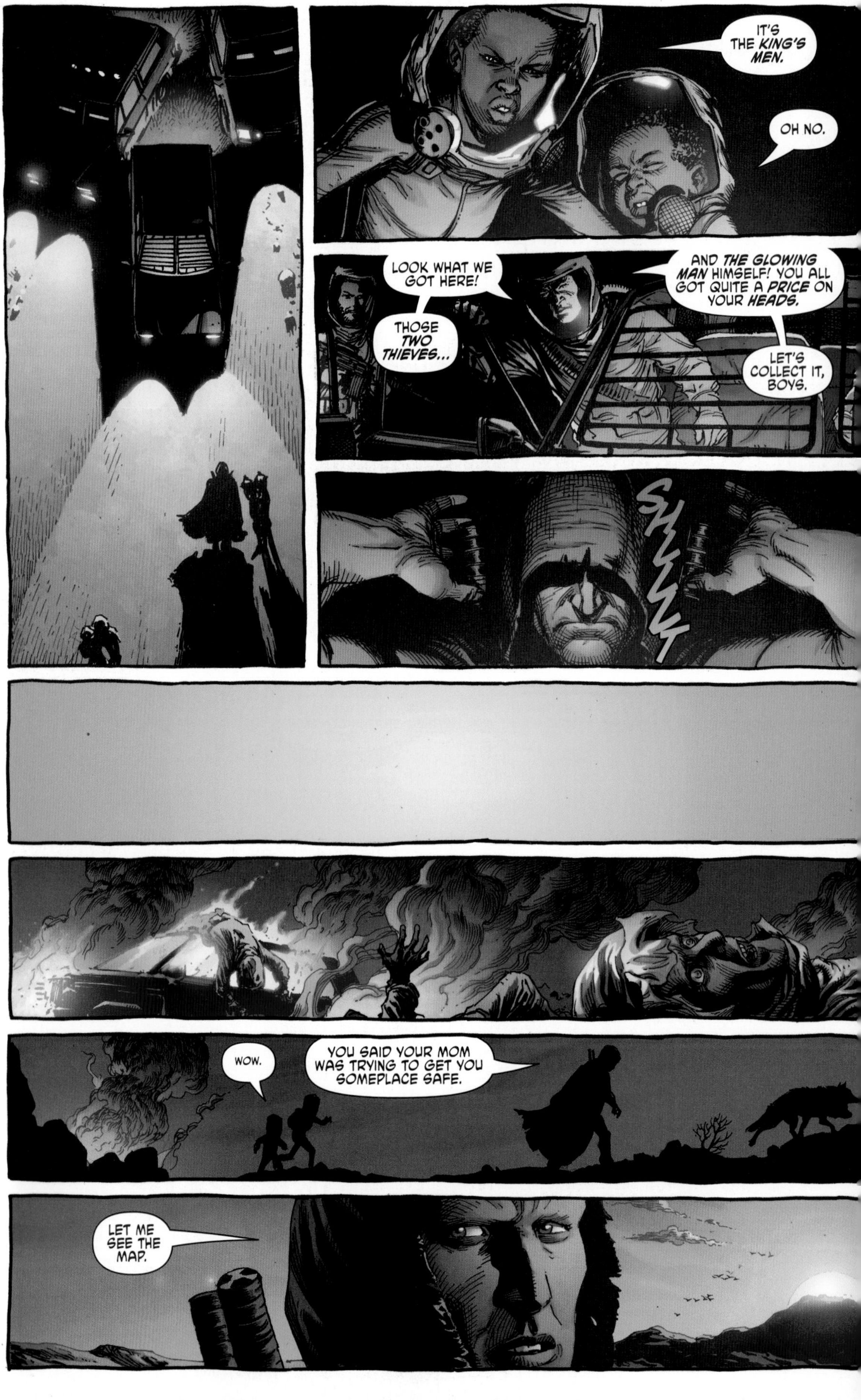
IT'S THE KING'S MEN.
OH NO.
LOOK WHAT WE GOT HERE!
THOSE TWO THIEVES...
AND THE GLOWING MAN HIMSELF! YOU ALL GOT QUITE A PRICE ON YOUR HEADS.
LET'S COLLECT IT, BOYS.
SHWWK
WOW.
YOU SAID YOUR MOM WAS TRYING TO GET YOU SOMEPLACE SAFE.
LET ME SEE THE MAP.

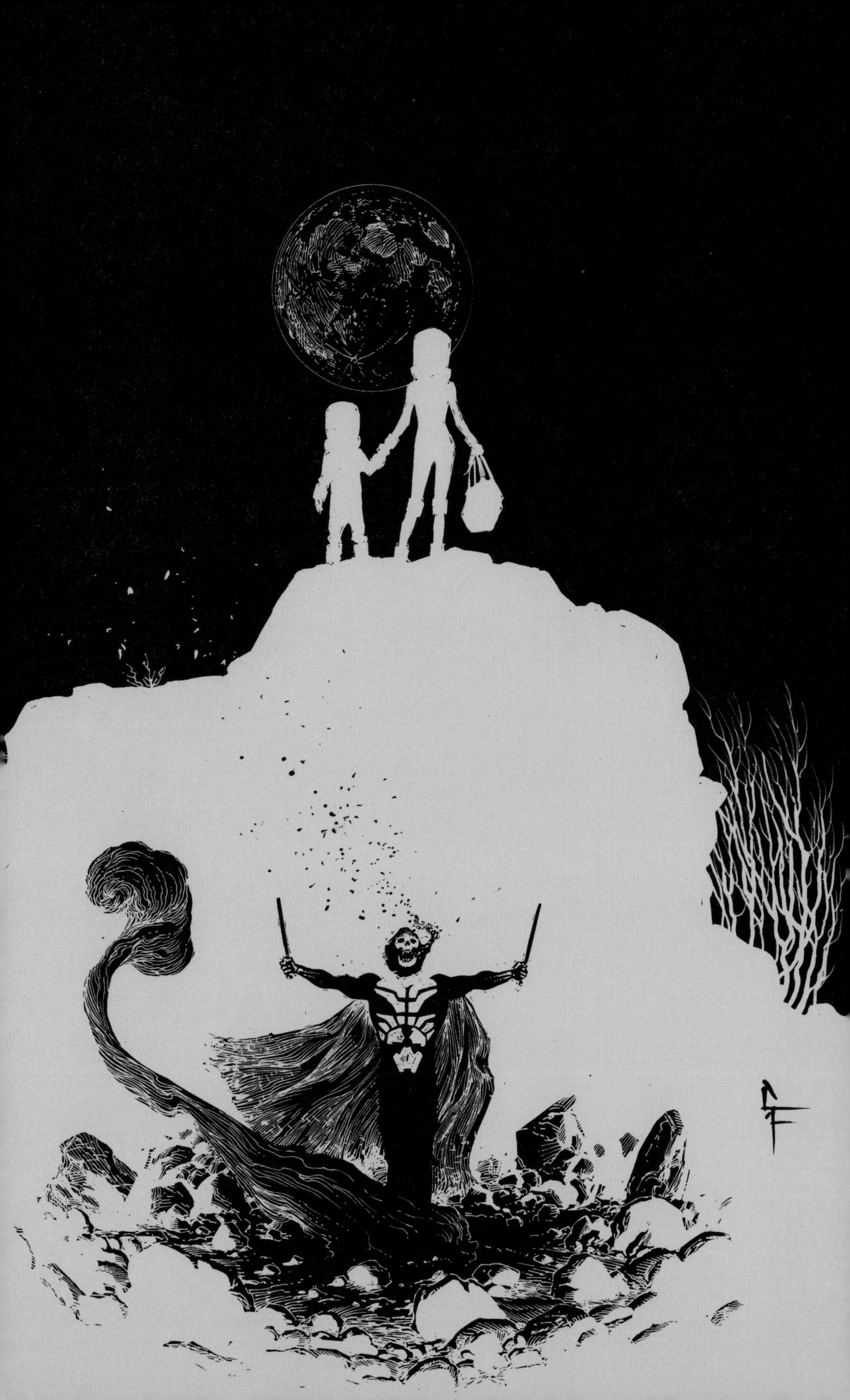

CHAPTER FOUR

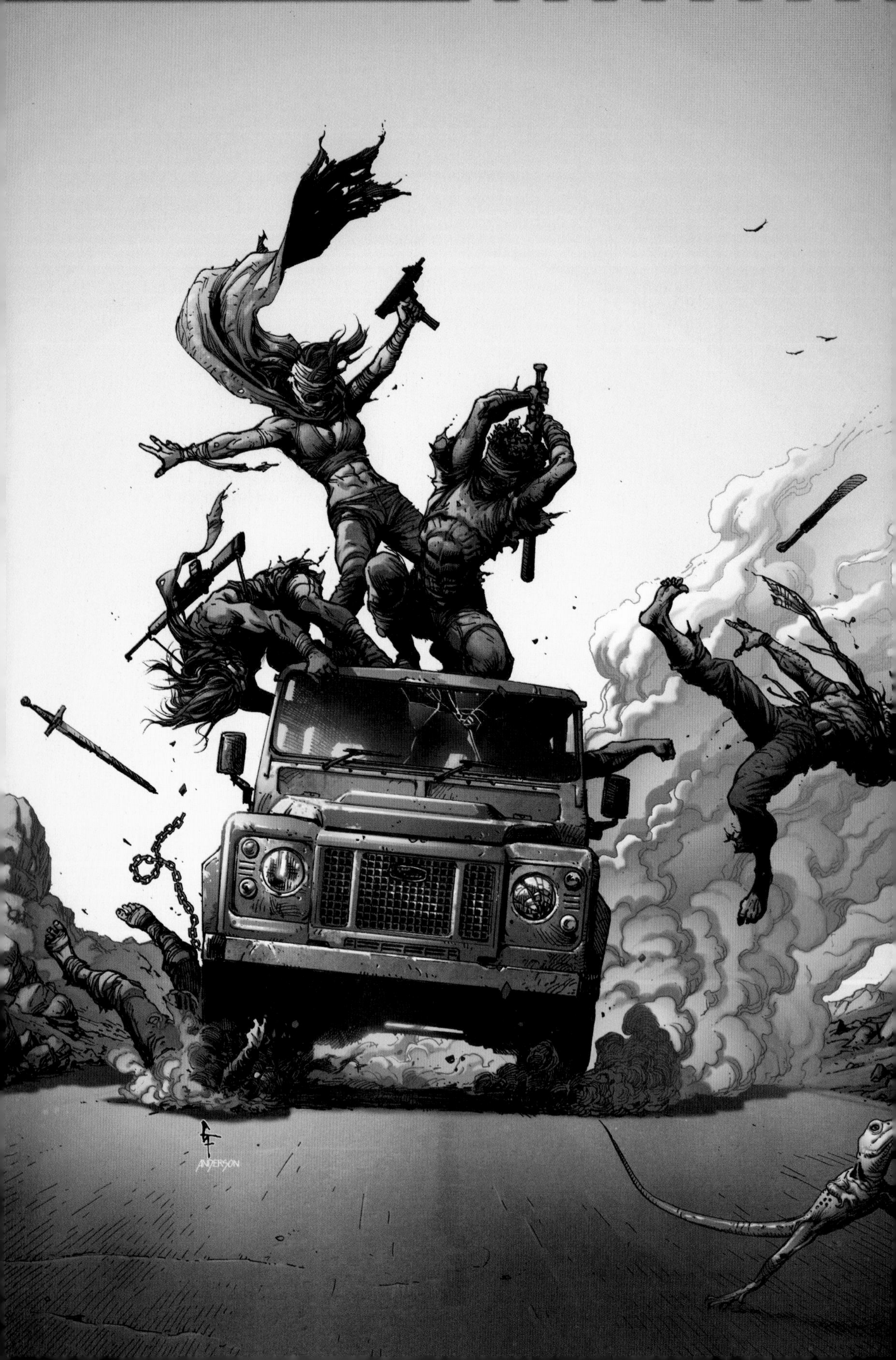
ANDERSON

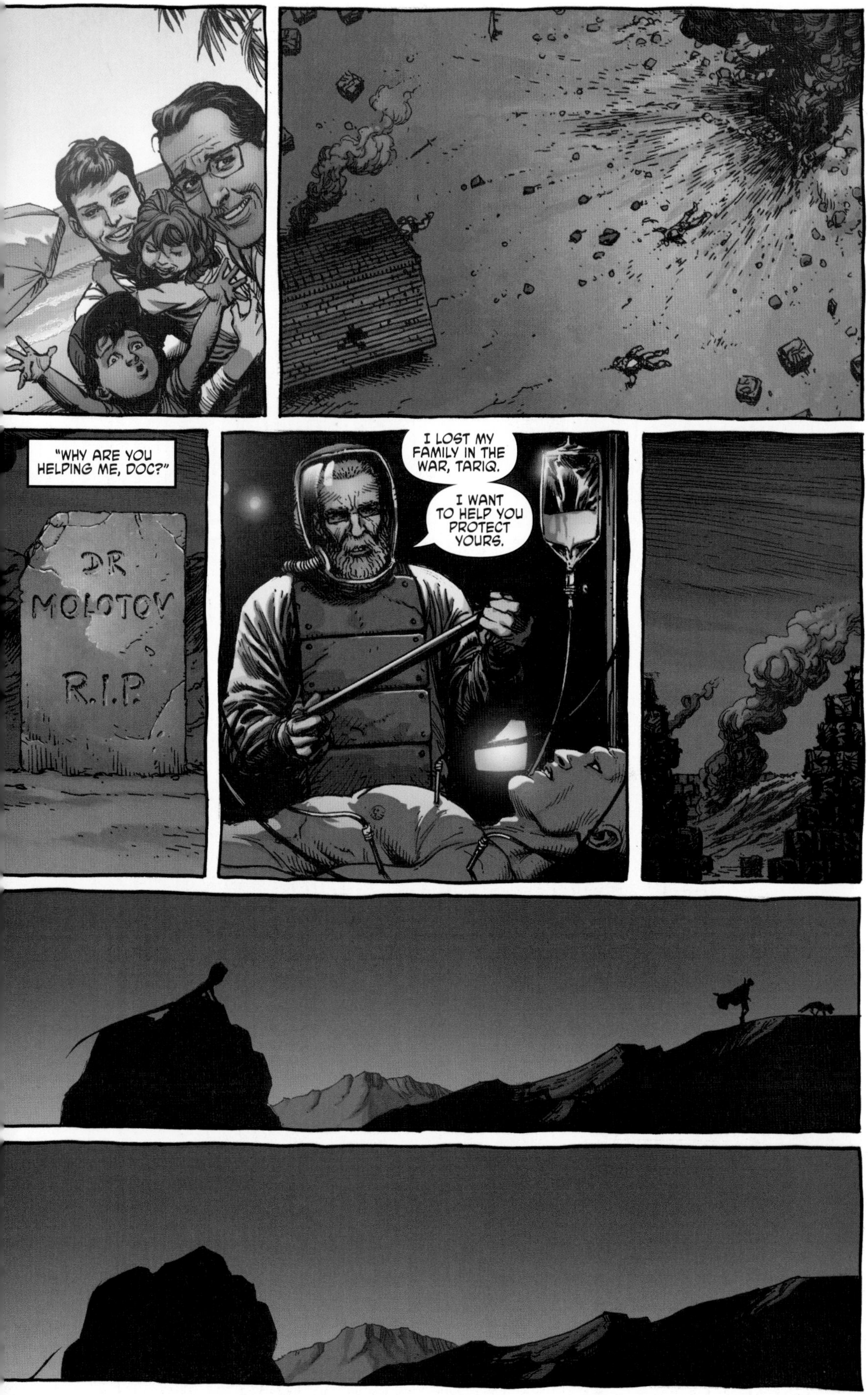
"WHY ARE YOU HELPING ME, DOC?"
DR MOLOTOV R.I.P.
I LOST MY FAMILY IN THE WAR, TARIQ.
I WANT TO HELP YOU PROTECT YOURS.

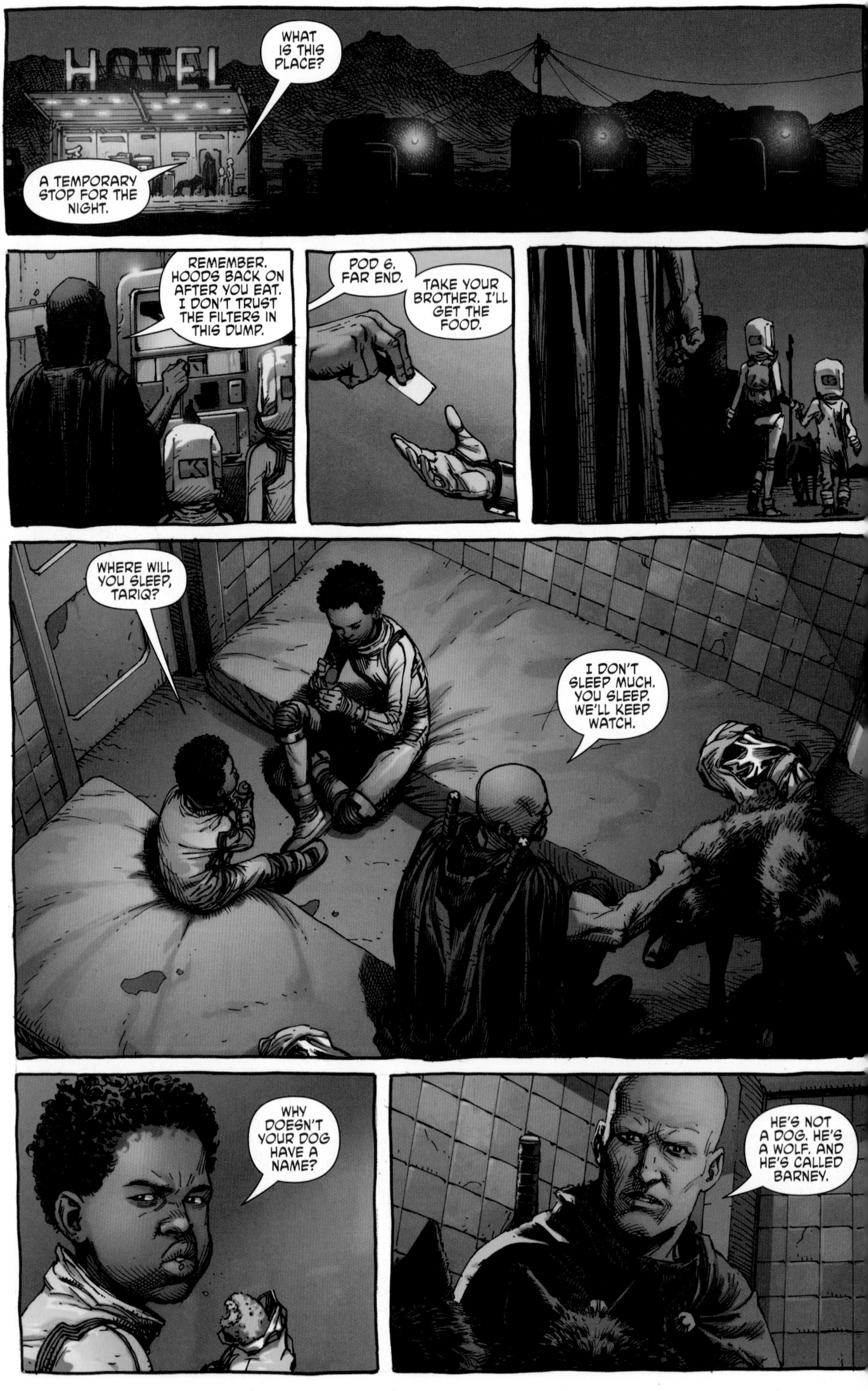

HOTEL
WHAT IS THIS PLACE?
A TEMPORARY STOP FOR THE NIGHT.
REMEMBER. HOODS BACK ON AFTER YOU EAT. I DON'T TRUST THE FILTERS IN THIS DUMP.
POD 6. FAR END.
TAKE YOUR BROTHER. I'LL GET THE FOOD.
WHERE WILL YOU SLEEP, TARIQ?
I DON'T SLEEP MUCH. YOU SLEEP. WE'LL KEEP WATCH.
WHY DOESN'T YOUR DOG HAVE A NAME?
HE'S NOT A DOG. HE'S A WOLF. AND HE'S CALLED BARNEY.

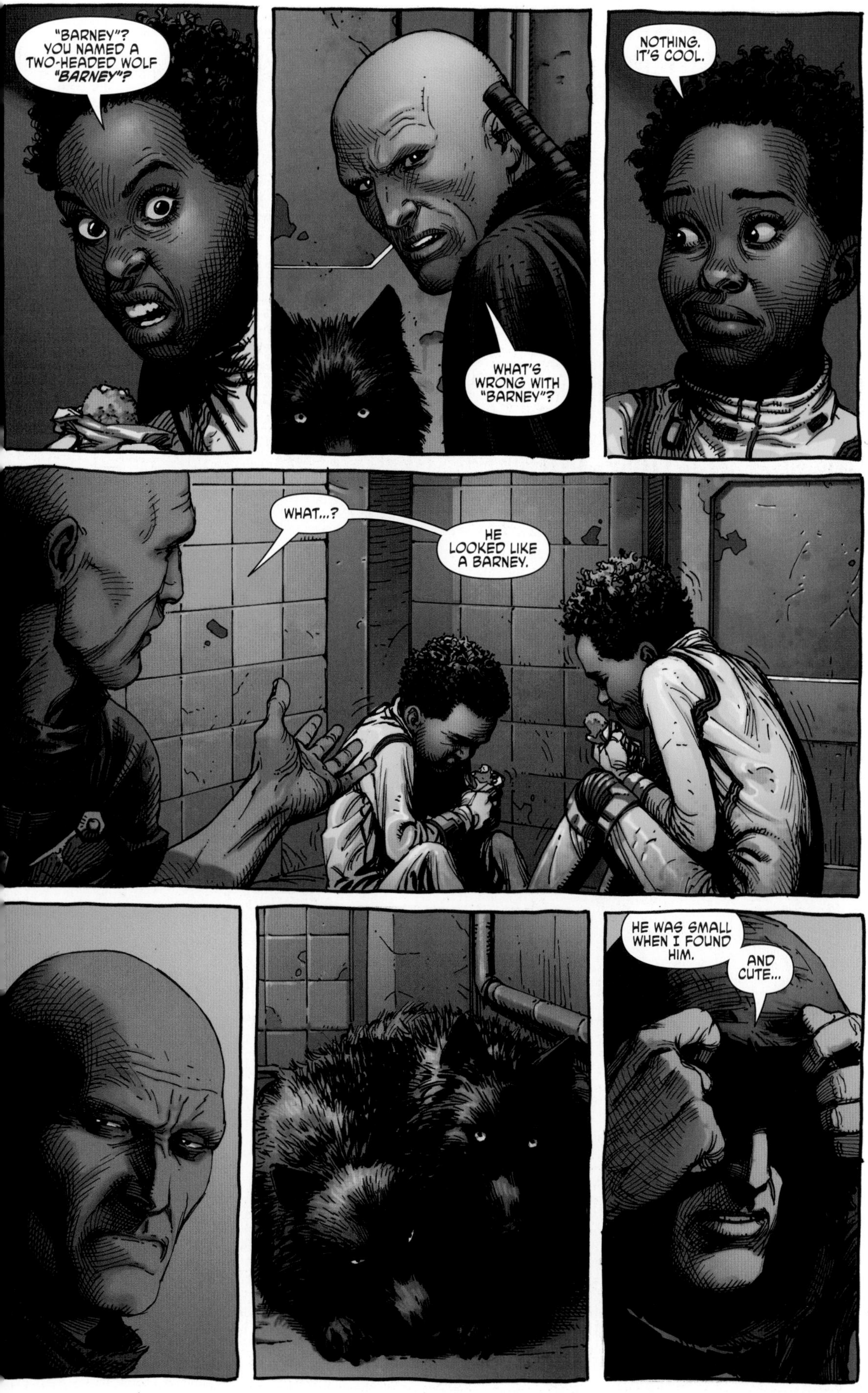
"BARNEY"? YOU NAMED A TWO-HEADED WOLF *"BARNEY"*?
WHAT'S WRONG WITH "BARNEY"?
NOTHING. IT'S COOL.
WHAT...?
HE LOOKED LIKE A BARNEY.
HE WAS SMALL WHEN I FOUND HIM.
AND CUTE...

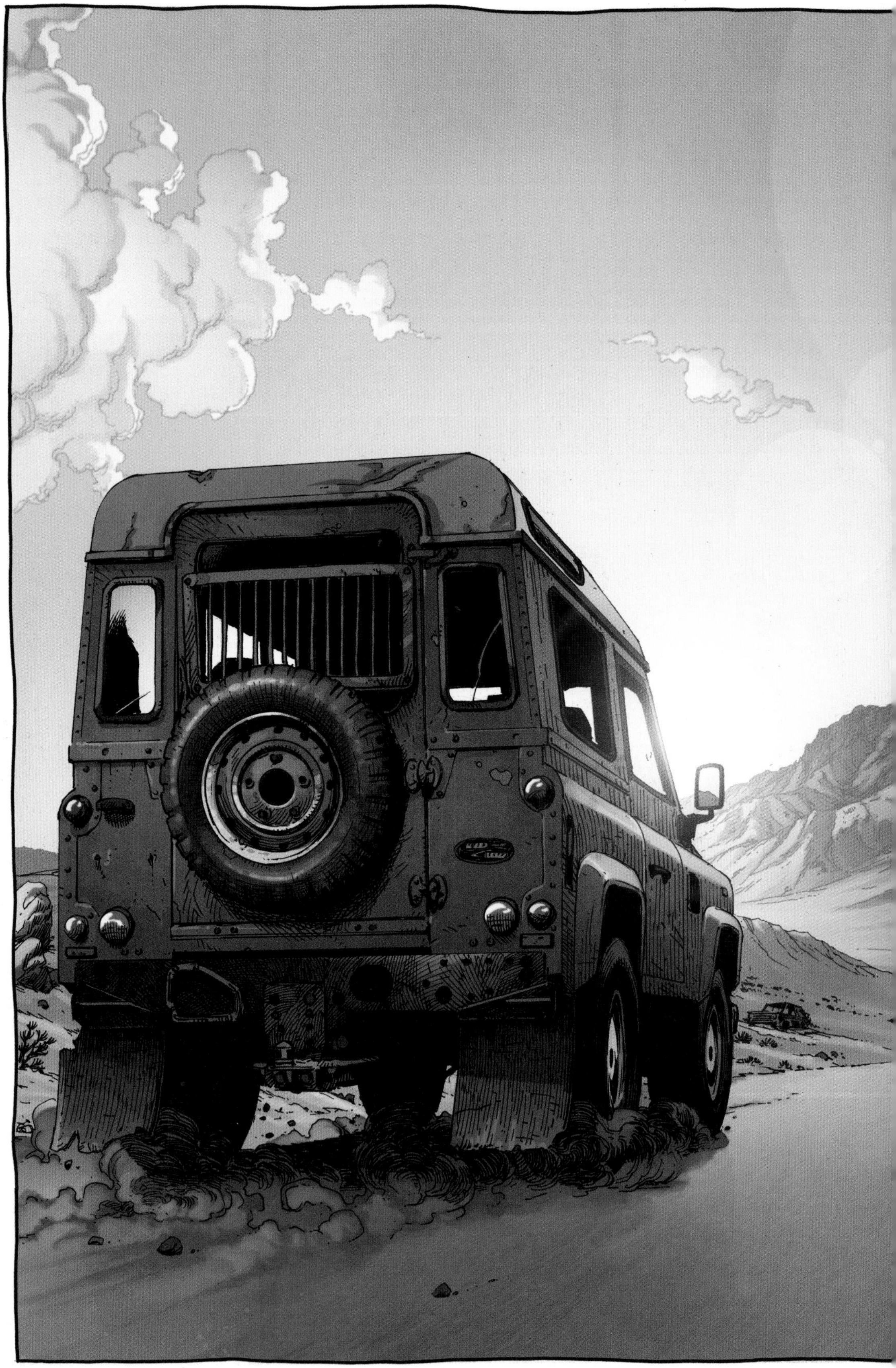

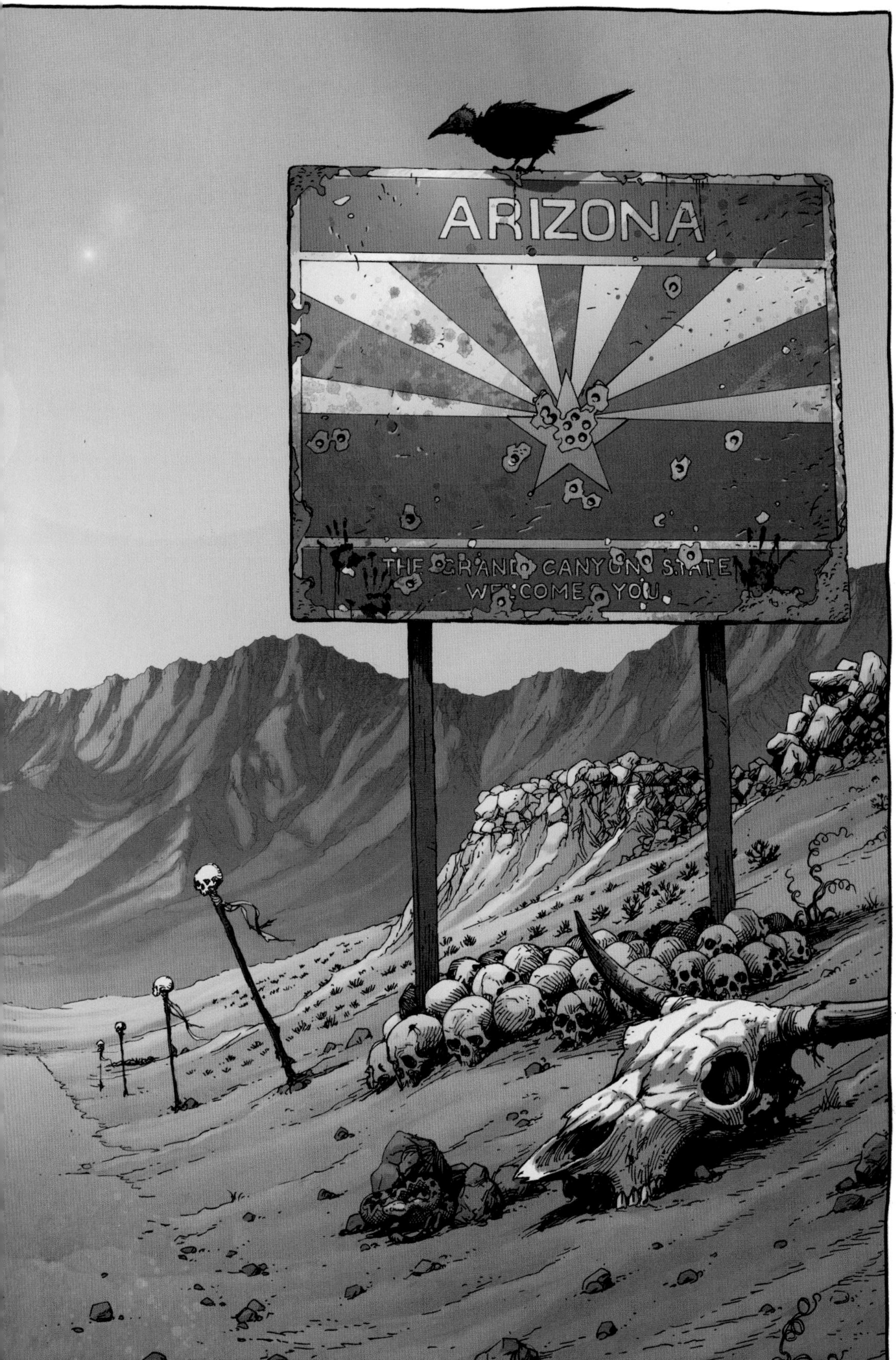

ARIZONA
THE GRAND CANYON STATE
WELCOMES YOU

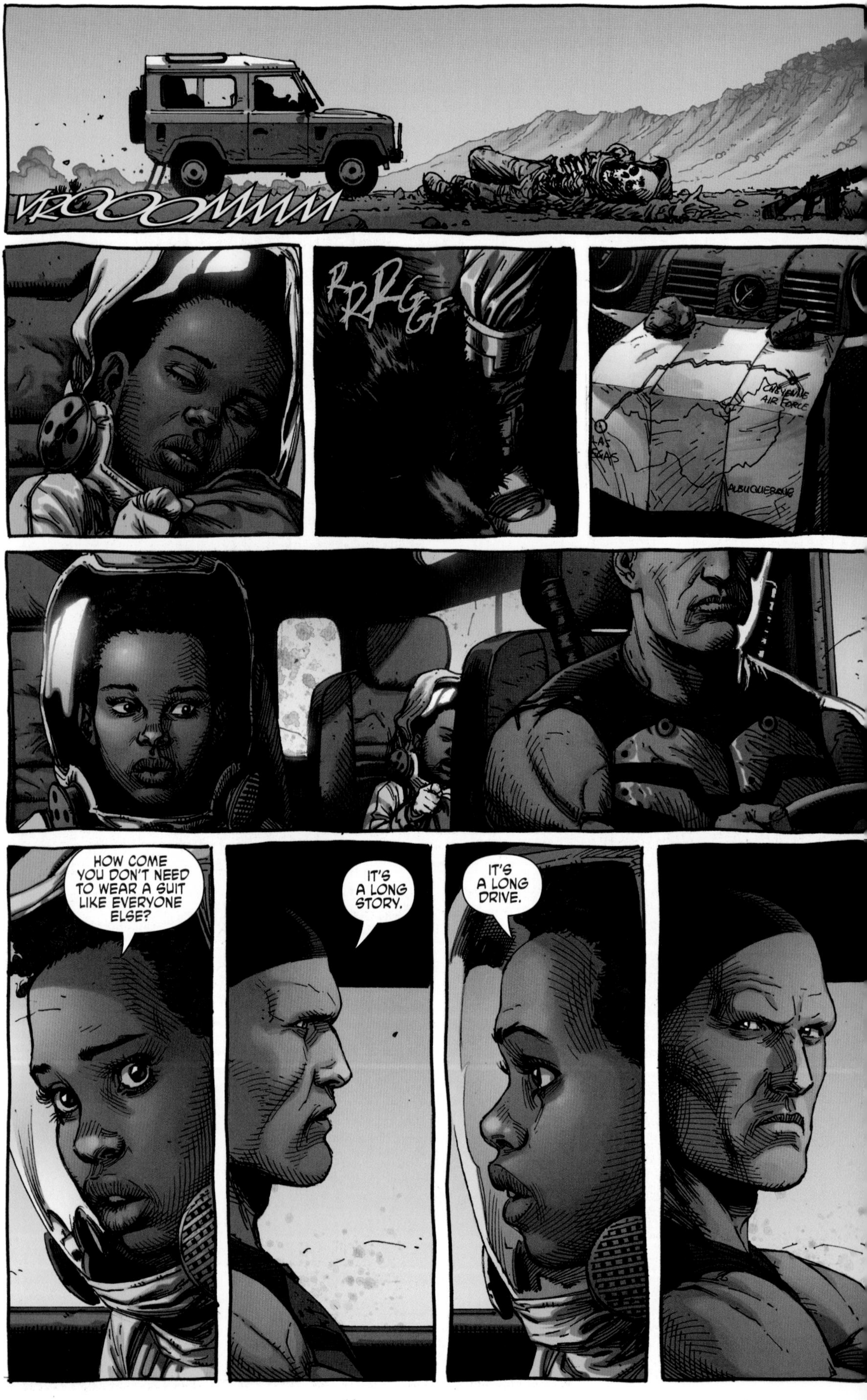
VROOOMMMM
RRRGGF
CHEYENNE AIR FORCE
LAS
EGAS
ALBUQUERQUE
HOW COME YOU DON'T NEED TO WEAR A SUIT LIKE EVERYONE ELSE?
IT'S A LONG STORY.
IT'S A LONG DRIVE.

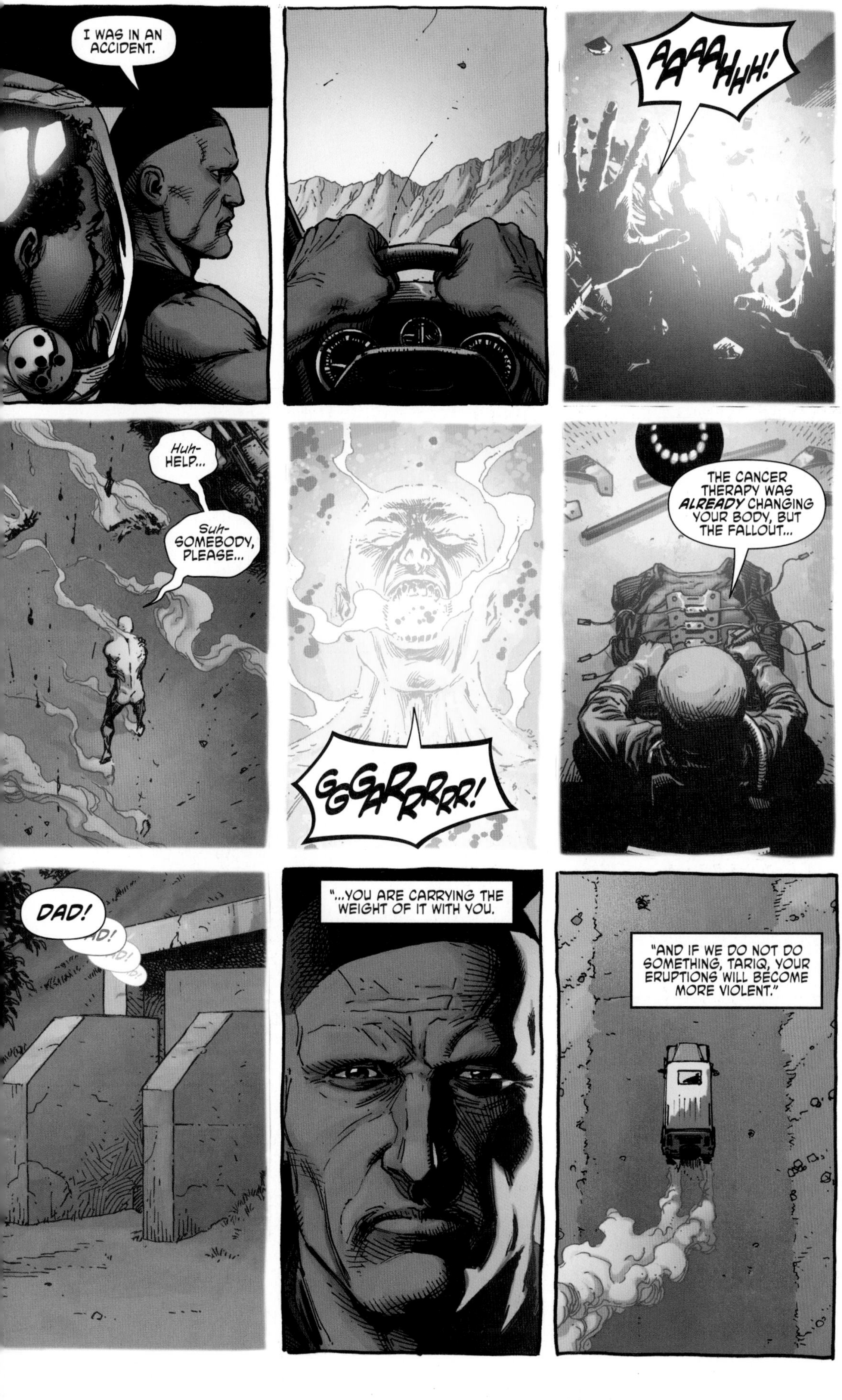
I WAS IN AN ACCIDENT.
AAAAHHH!
Huh- HELP...
Suh- SOMEBODY, PLEASE...
GGGARRRRR!
THE CANCER THERAPY WAS ALREADY CHANGING YOUR BODY, BUT THE FALLOUT...
DAD!
"...YOU ARE CARRYING THE WEIGHT OF IT WITH YOU.
"AND IF WE DO NOT DO SOMETHING, TARIQ, YOUR ERUPTIONS WILL BECOME MORE VIOLENT."

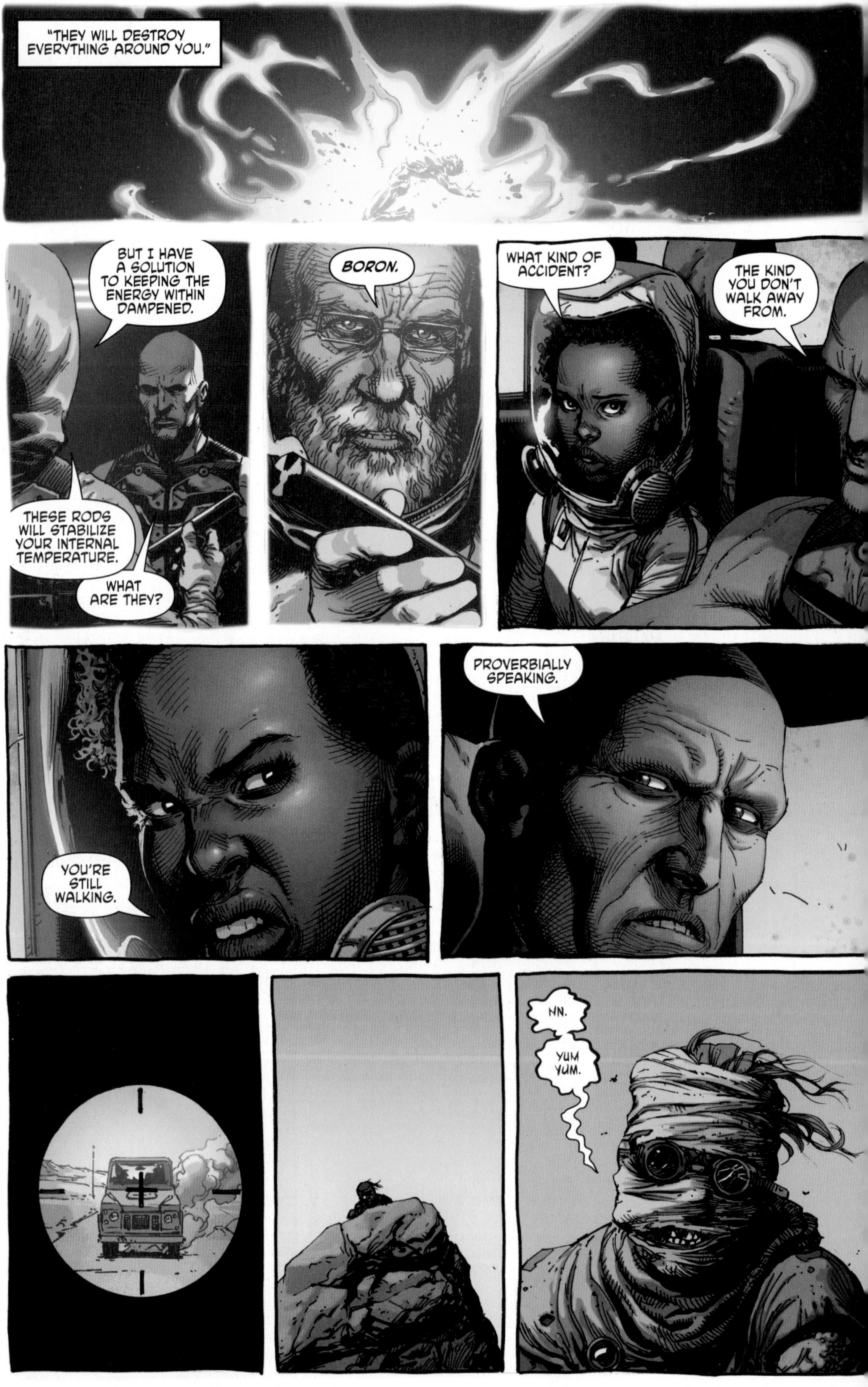
"THEY WILL DESTROY EVERYTHING AROUND YOU."
BUT I HAVE A SOLUTION TO KEEPING THE ENERGY WITHIN DAMPENED.
THESE RODS WILL STABILIZE YOUR INTERNAL TEMPERATURE.
WHAT ARE THEY?
BORON.
WHAT KIND OF ACCIDENT?
THE KIND YOU DON'T WALK AWAY FROM.
PROVERBIALLY SPEAKING.
YOU'RE STILL WALKING.
NN.
YUM YUM.

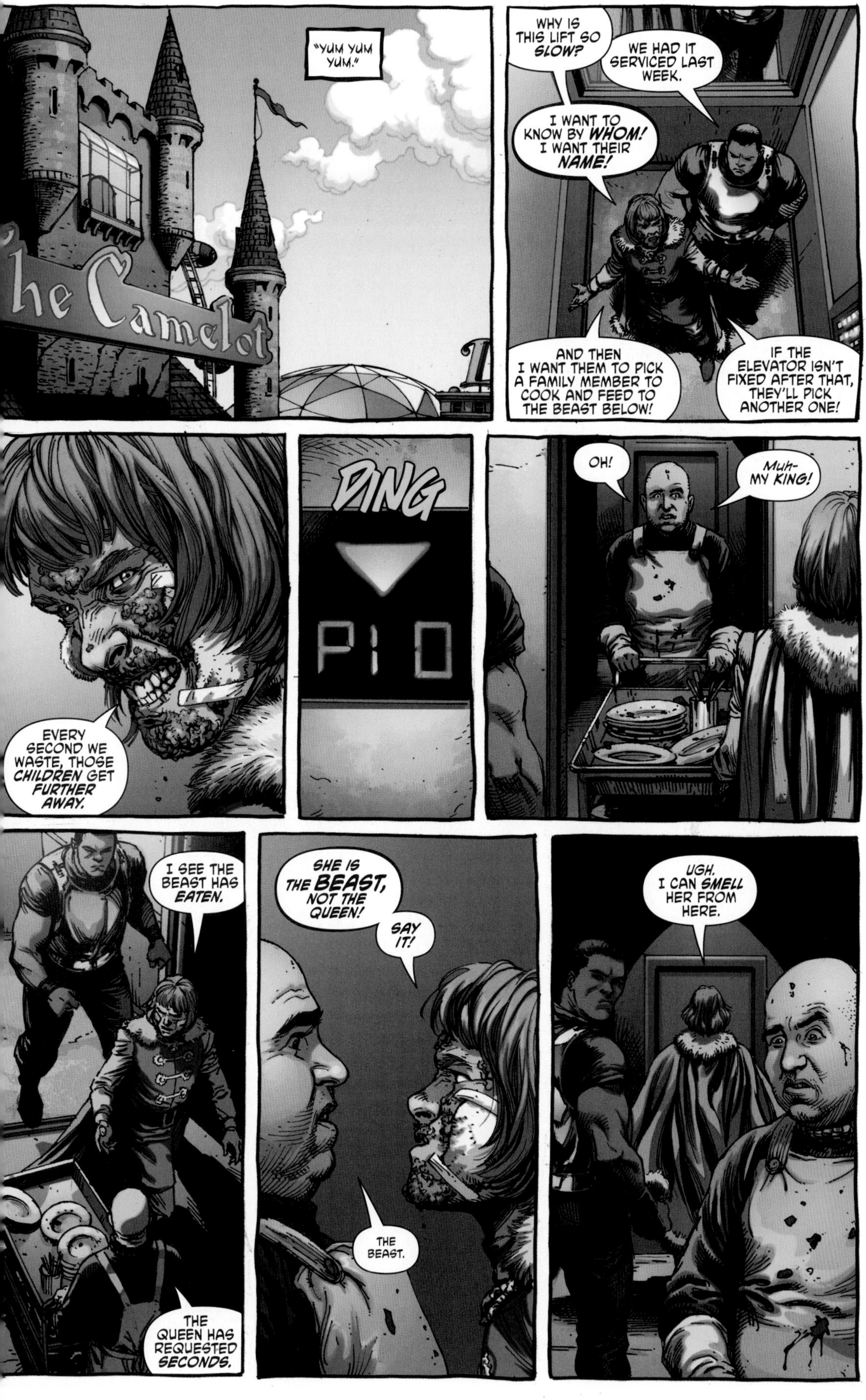

"YUM YUM YUM."
The Camelot
WHY IS THIS LIFT SO SLOW?
WE HAD IT SERVICED LAST WEEK.
I WANT TO KNOW BY WHOM! I WANT THEIR NAME!
AND THEN I WANT THEM TO PICK A FAMILY MEMBER TO COOK AND FEED TO THE BEAST BELOW!
IF THE ELEVATOR ISN'T FIXED AFTER THAT, THEY'LL PICK ANOTHER ONE!
EVERY SECOND WE WASTE, THOSE CHILDREN GET FURTHER AWAY.
DING
P10
OH!
Muh- MY KING!
I SEE THE BEAST HAS EATEN.
THE QUEEN HAS REQUESTED SECONDS.
SHE IS THE BEAST, NOT THE QUEEN!
SAY IT!
THE BEAST.
UGH. I CAN SMELL HER FROM HERE.

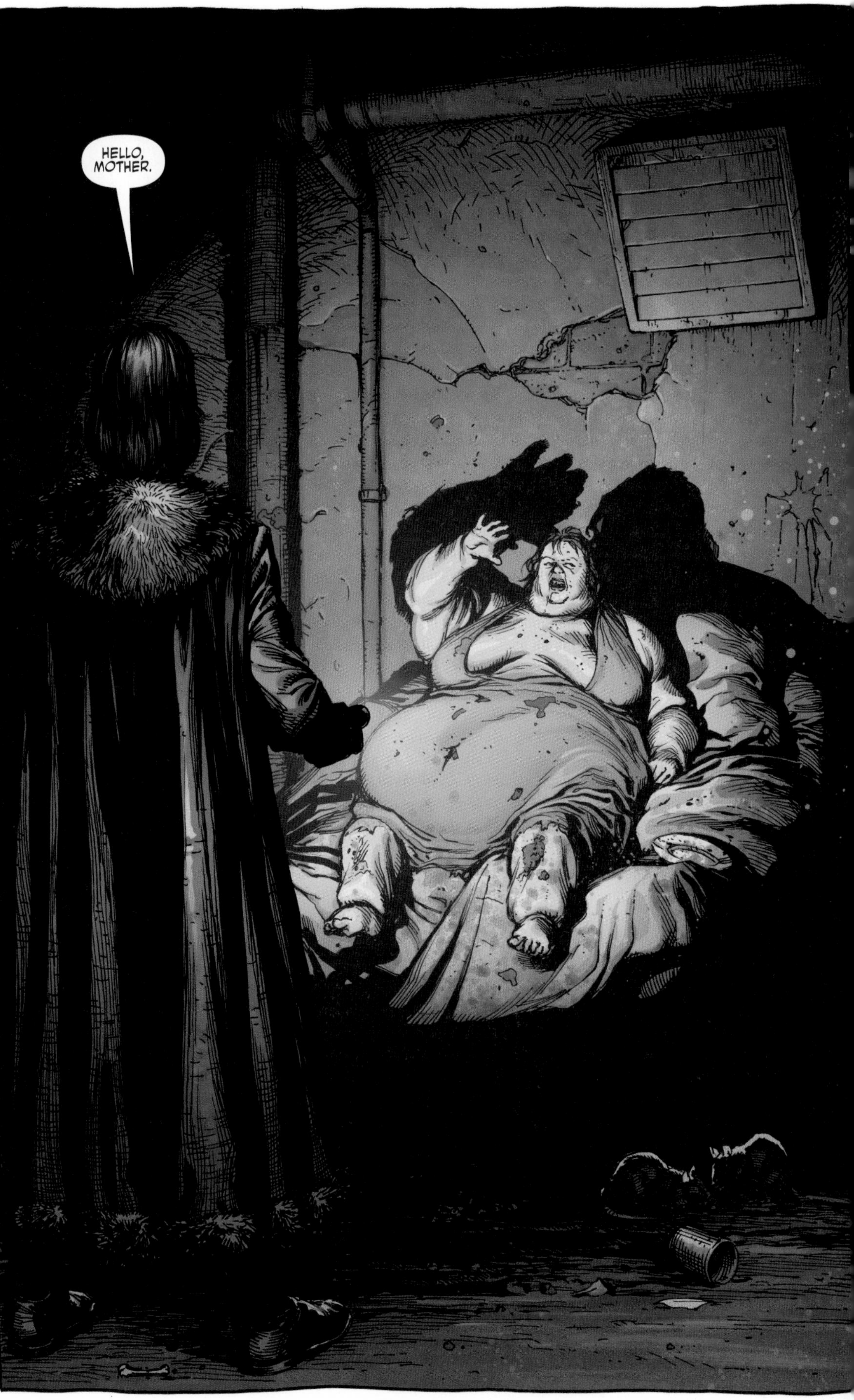
HELLO, MOTHER.

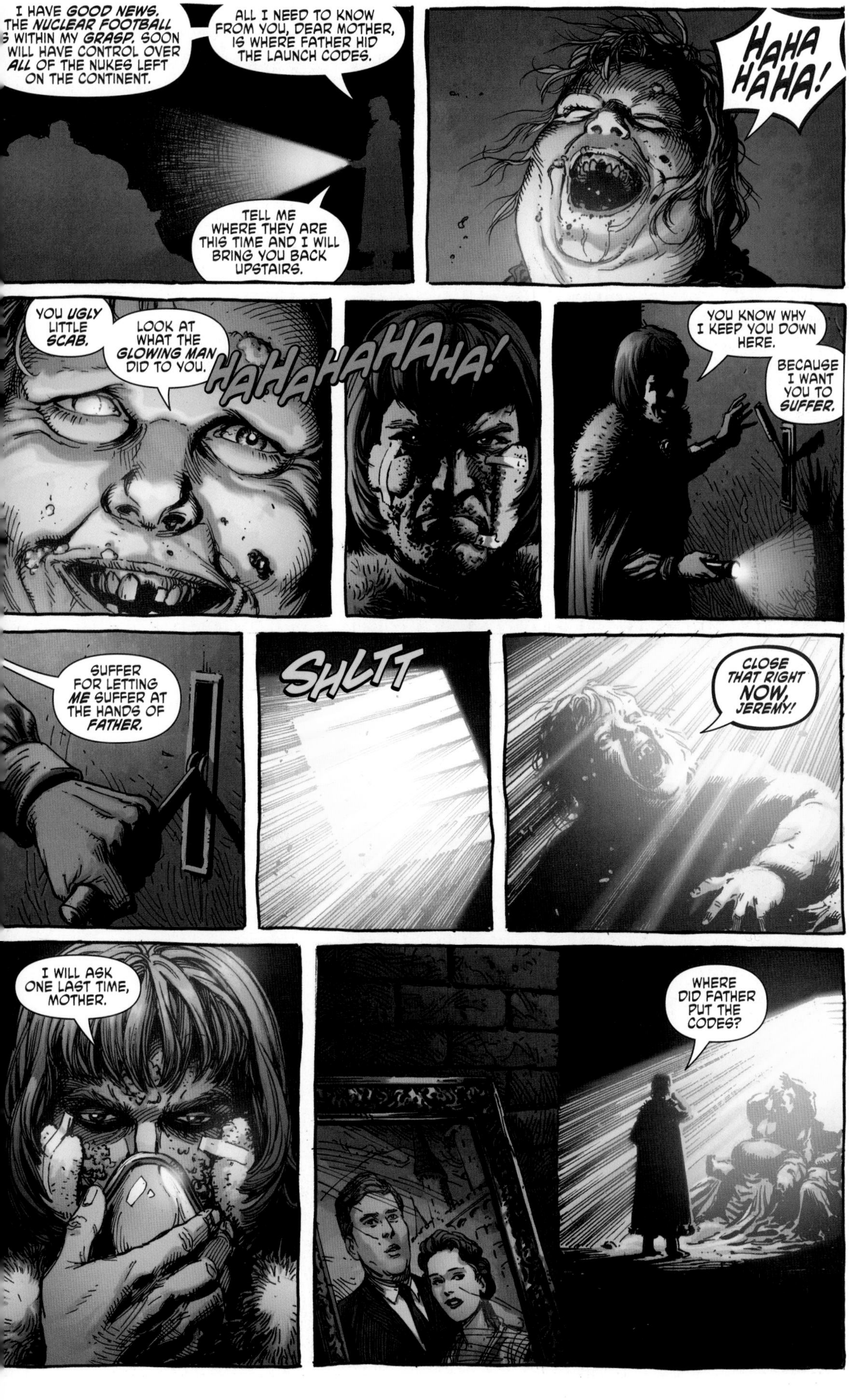

I HAVE GOOD NEWS. THE NUCLEAR FOOTBALL IS WITHIN MY GRASP. SOON I WILL HAVE CONTROL OVER ALL OF THE NUKES LEFT ON THE CONTINENT.
ALL I NEED TO KNOW FROM YOU, DEAR MOTHER, IS WHERE FATHER HID THE LAUNCH CODES.
TELL ME WHERE THEY ARE THIS TIME AND I WILL BRING YOU BACK UPSTAIRS.
HAHA HAHA!
YOU UGLY LITTLE SCAB.
LOOK AT WHAT THE GLOWING MAN DID TO YOU.
HAHAHAHAHAHAHA!
YOU KNOW WHY I KEEP YOU DOWN HERE.
BECAUSE I WANT YOU TO SUFFER.
SUFFER FOR LETTING ME SUFFER AT THE HANDS OF FATHER.
SHLTT
CLOSE THAT RIGHT NOW, JEREMY!
I WILL ASK ONE LAST TIME, MOTHER.
WHERE DID FATHER PUT THE CODES?

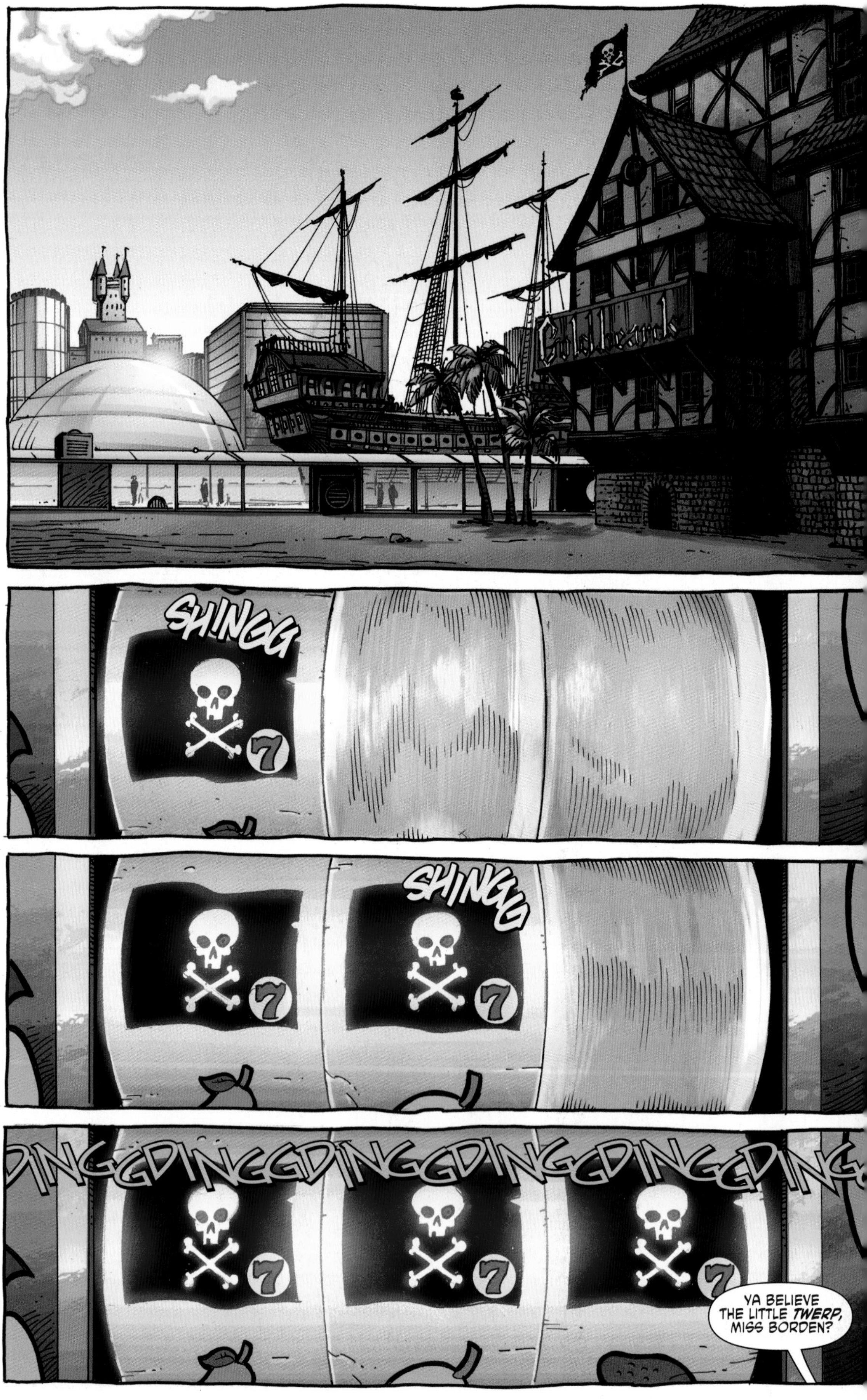
Goldbeards
SHINGG
SHINGG
DINGGDINGGDINGGDINGGDINGG
YA BELIEVE THE LITTLE *TWERP,* MISS BORDEN?

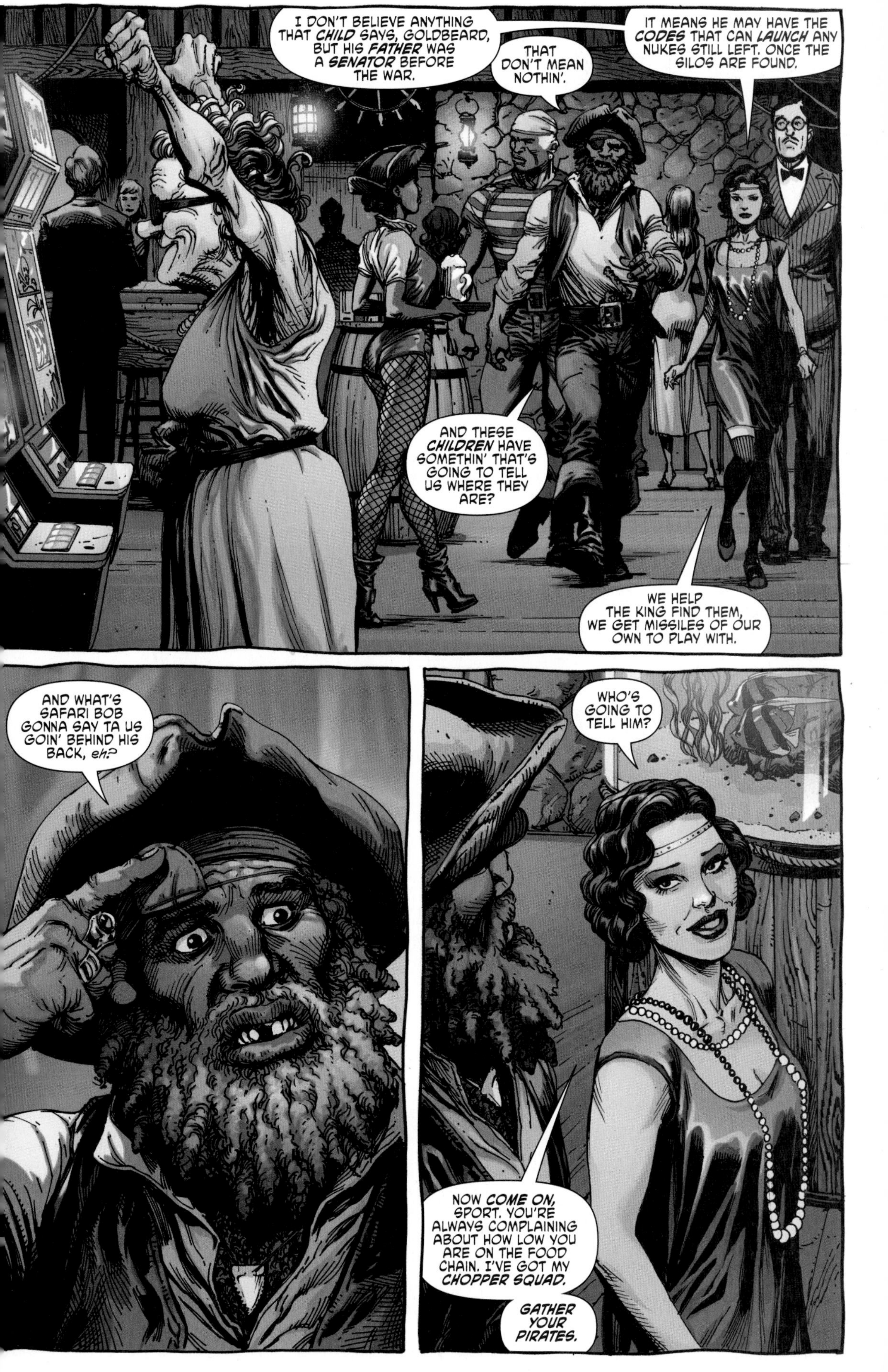
I DON'T BELIEVE ANYTHING THAT CHILD SAYS, GOLDBEARD, BUT HIS FATHER WAS A SENATOR BEFORE THE WAR.
THAT DON'T MEAN NOTHIN'.
IT MEANS HE MAY HAVE THE CODES THAT CAN LAUNCH ANY NUKES STILL LEFT. ONCE THE SILOS ARE FOUND.
AND THESE CHILDREN HAVE SOMETHIN' THAT'S GOING TO TELL US WHERE THEY ARE?
WE HELP THE KING FIND THEM, WE GET MISSILES OF OUR OWN TO PLAY WITH.
AND WHAT'S SAFARI BOB GONNA SAY TA US GOIN' BEHIND HIS BACK, eh?
WHO'S GOING TO TELL HIM?
NOW COME ON, SPORT. YOU'RE ALWAYS COMPLAINING ABOUT HOW LOW YOU ARE ON THE FOOD CHAIN. I'VE GOT MY CHOPPER SQUAD.
GATHER YOUR PIRATES.

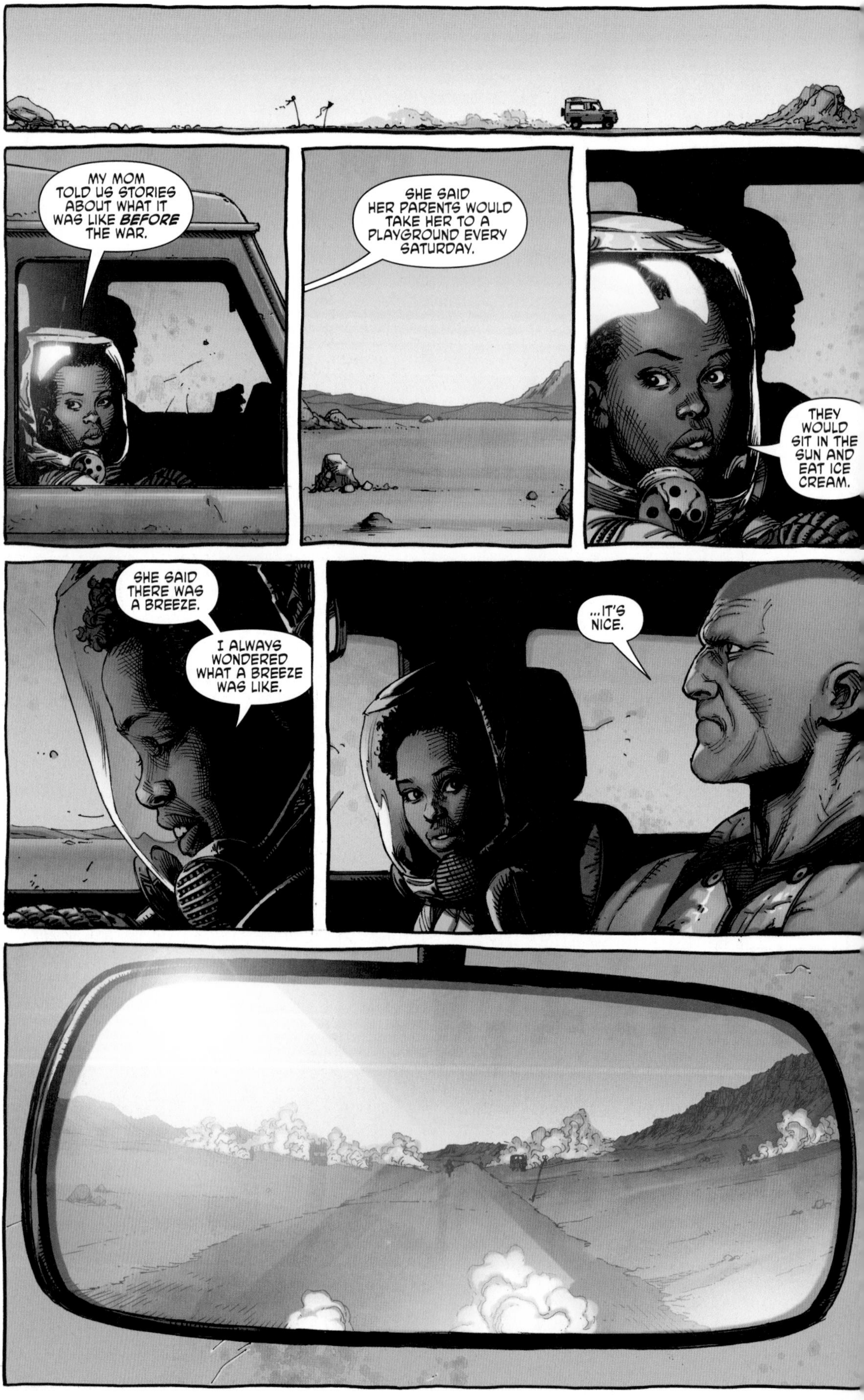
MY MOM TOLD US STORIES ABOUT WHAT IT WAS LIKE *BEFORE* THE WAR.
SHE SAID HER PARENTS WOULD TAKE HER TO A PLAYGROUND EVERY SATURDAY.
THEY WOULD SIT IN THE SUN AND EAT ICE CREAM.
SHE SAID THERE WAS A BREEZE.
I ALWAYS WONDERED WHAT A BREEZE WAS LIKE.
...IT'S NICE.

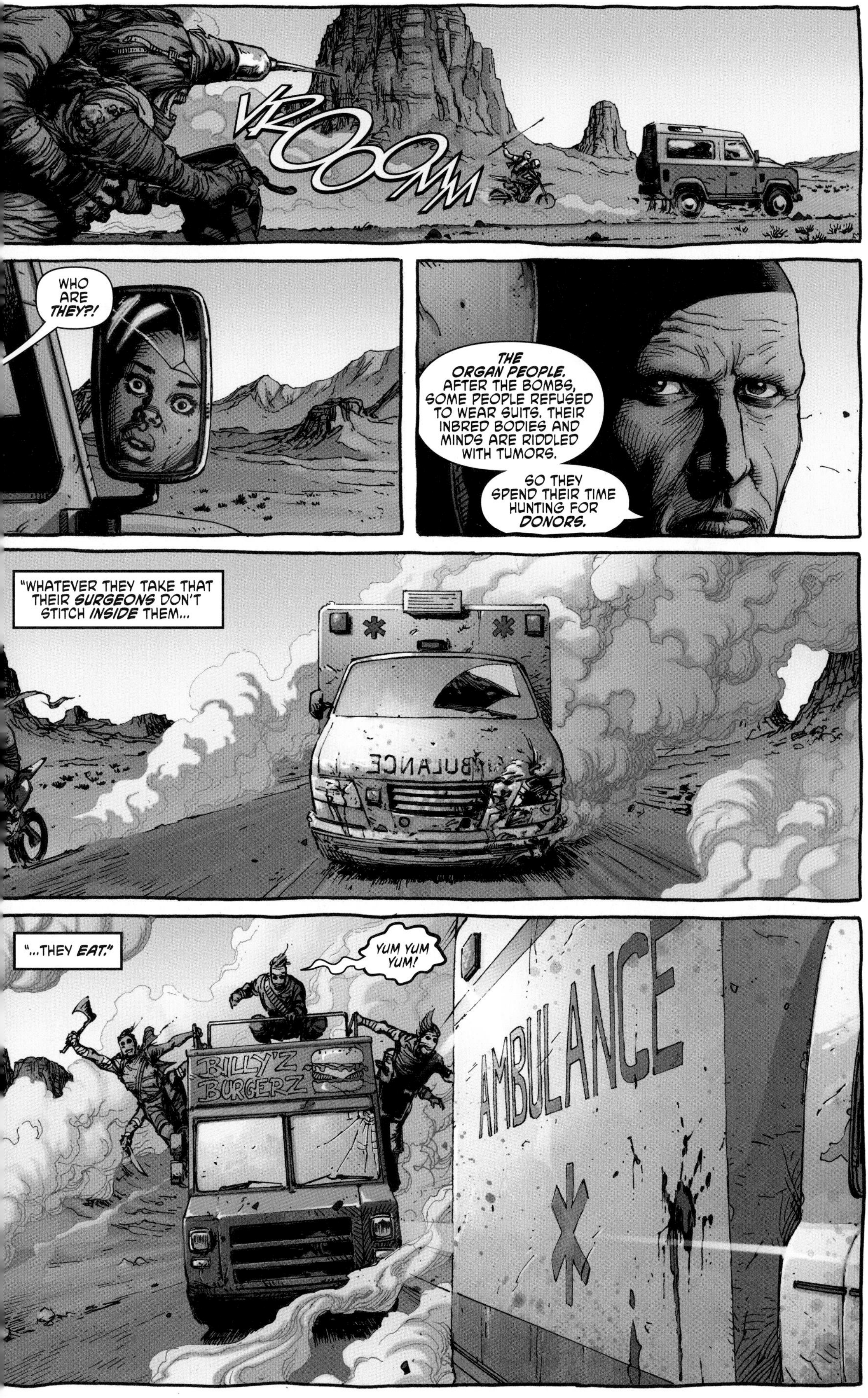

VROOOMM
WHO ARE *THEY?!*
THE ORGAN PEOPLE. AFTER THE BOMBS, SOME PEOPLE REFUSED TO WEAR SUITS. THEIR INBRED BODIES AND MINDS ARE RIDDLED WITH TUMORS.
SO THEY SPEND THEIR TIME HUNTING FOR *DONORS.*
"WHATEVER THEY TAKE THAT THEIR *SURGEONS* DON'T STITCH *INSIDE* THEM...
"...THEY *EAT.*"
YUM YUM YUM!
BILLY'Z BURGERZ
AMBULANCE

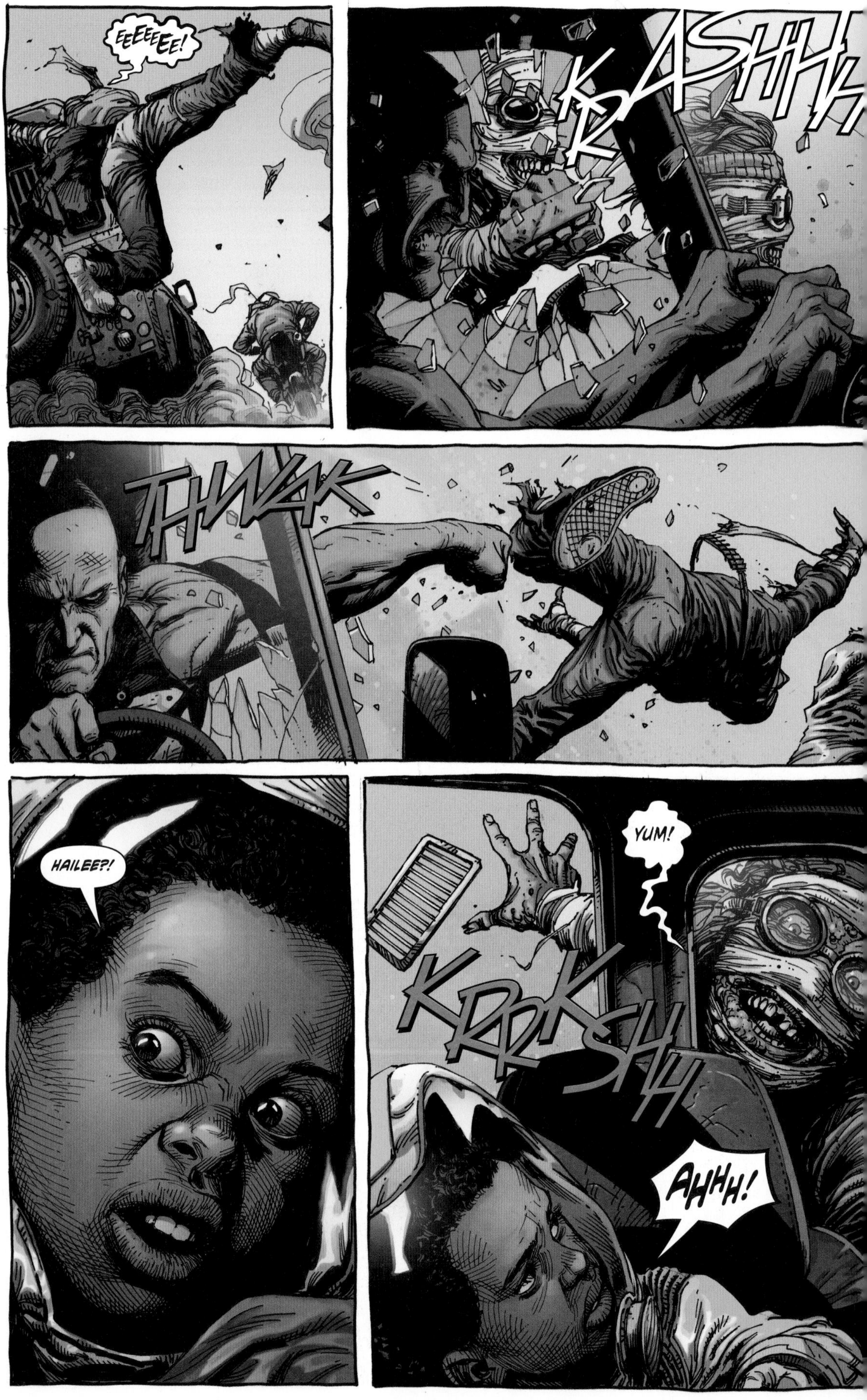
EEEEEEE!
KRASHHH
THWAK
HAILEE?!
YUM!
KRRKSHH
AHHH!

HENRY!

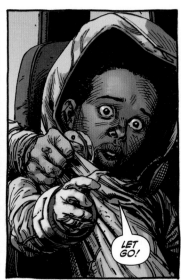

LET GO!

WEEOOWEEOOWEEOO

BAMMM

I NEED YOU TO TAKE THE WHEEL.

WHAT?

NOW, HAILEE.

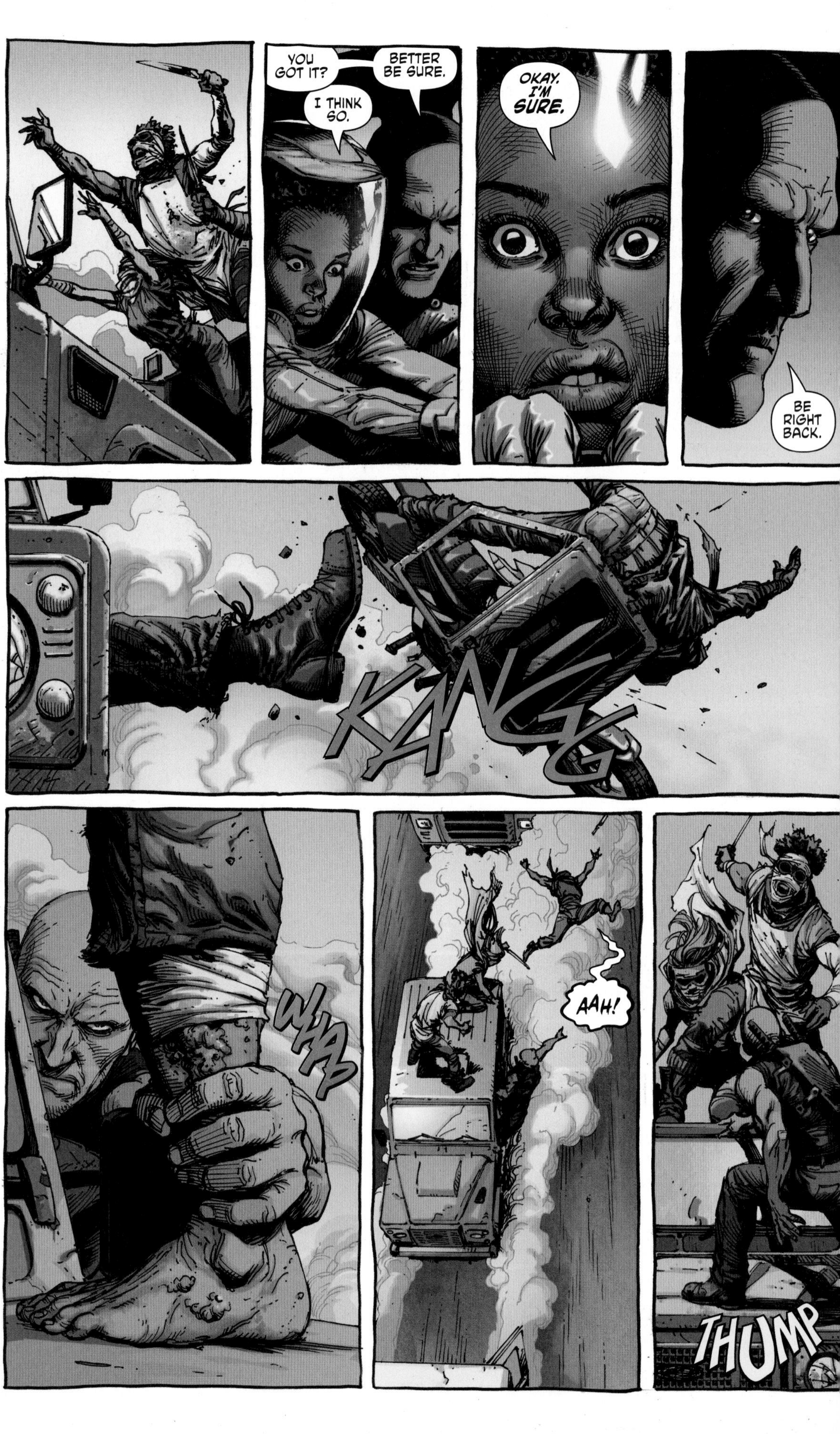
YOU GOT IT?
BETTER BE SURE.
I THINK SO.
OKAY. I'M SURE.
BE RIGHT BACK.
KANGG
WHAP
AAH!
THUMP

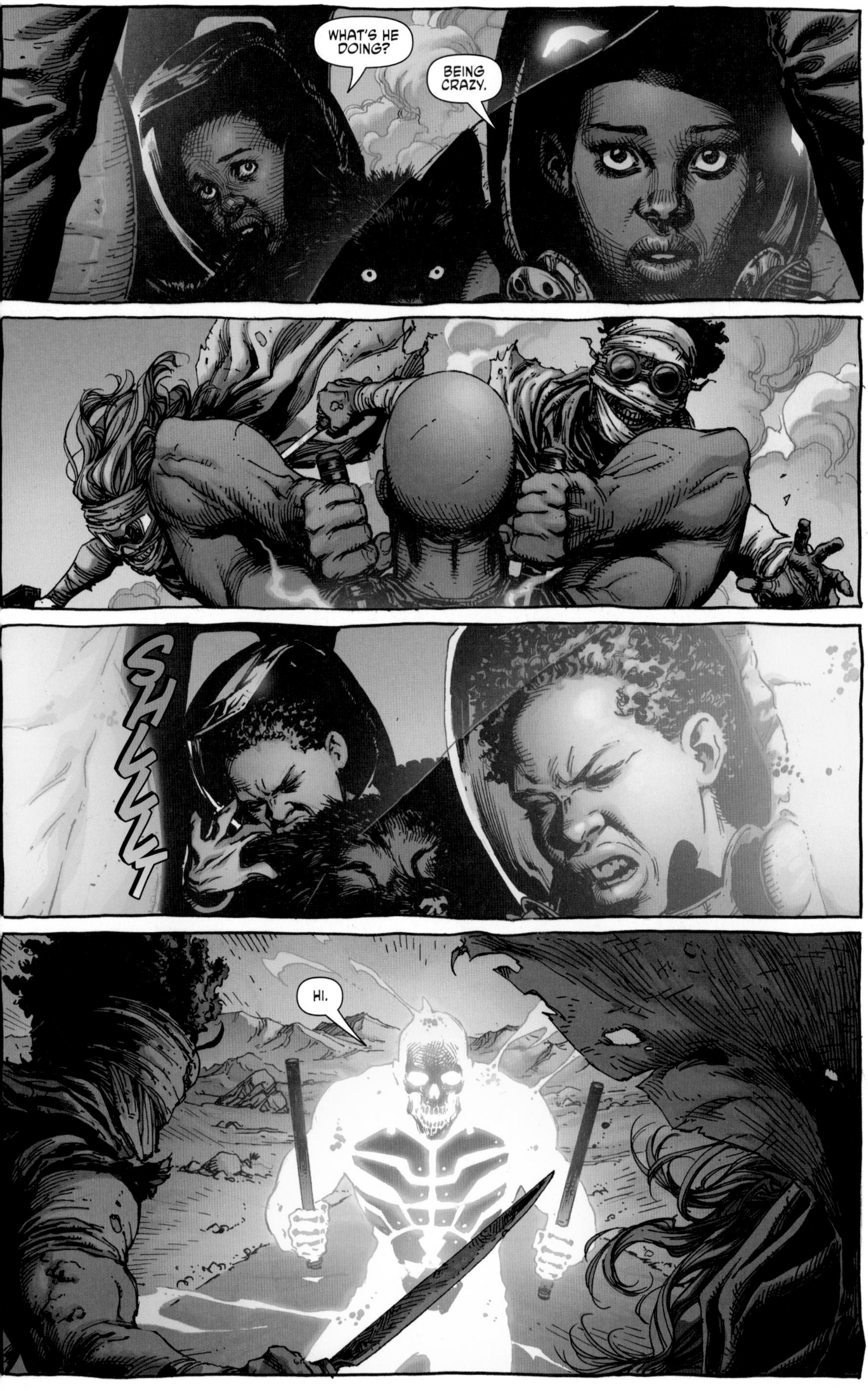
WHAT'S HE DOING?
BEING CRAZY.
SHLLLT
HI.

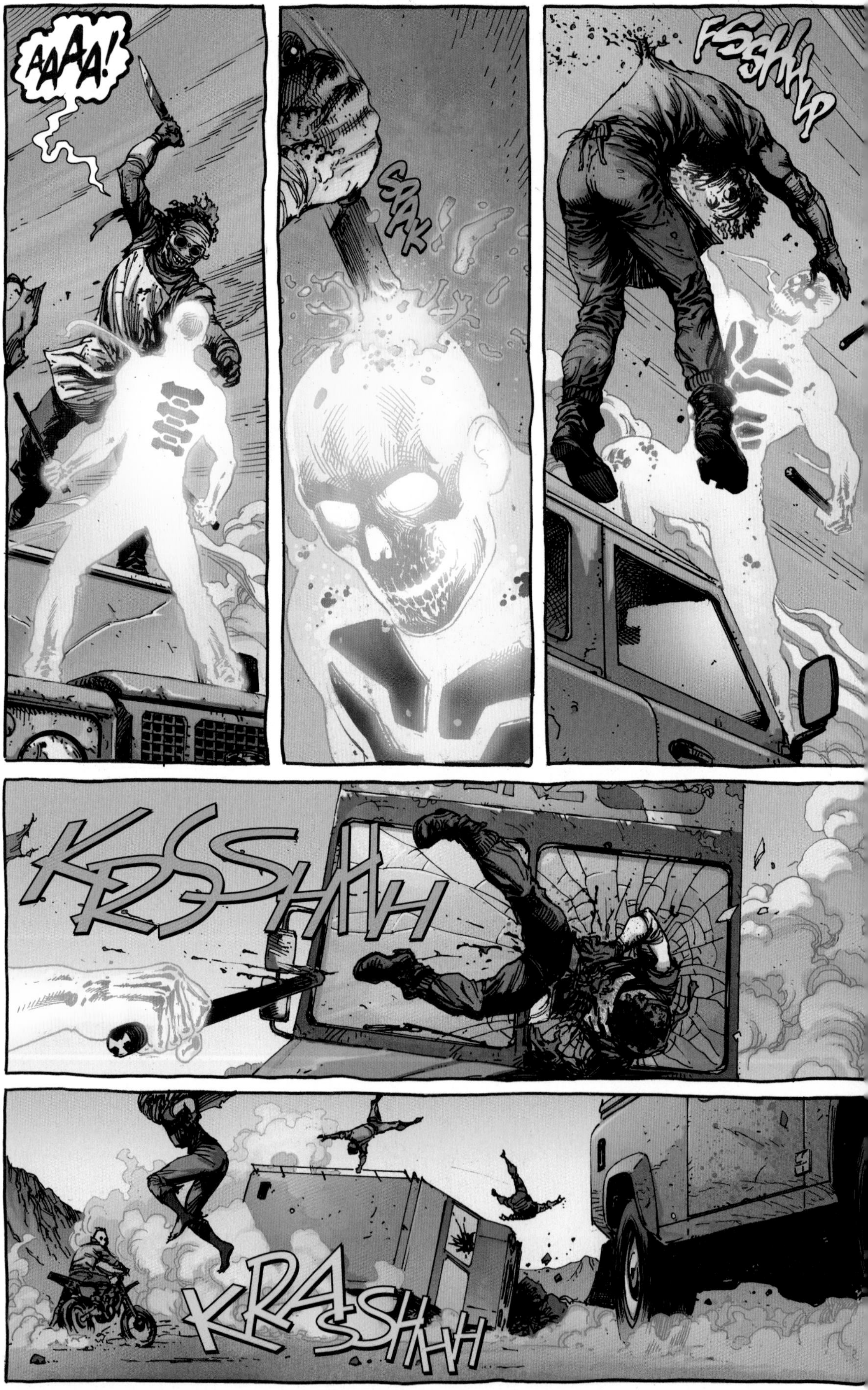

AAAAA!
SPAK!
FSSHHHP
KRSSHHHH
KRASHHHH

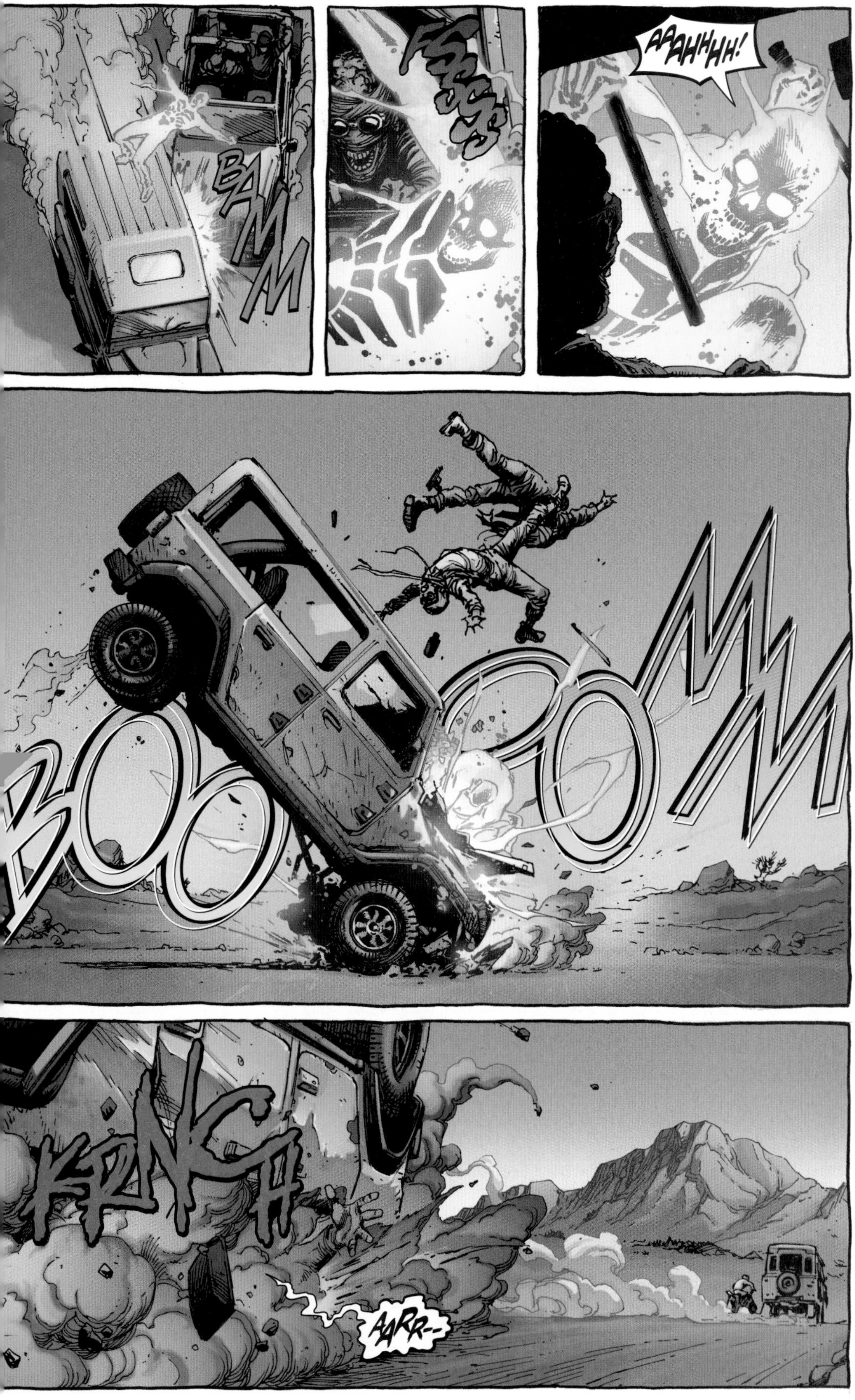

BAMM
FSSSSS
AAAHHHH!
BOOOOMM
KRNCH
AARR--

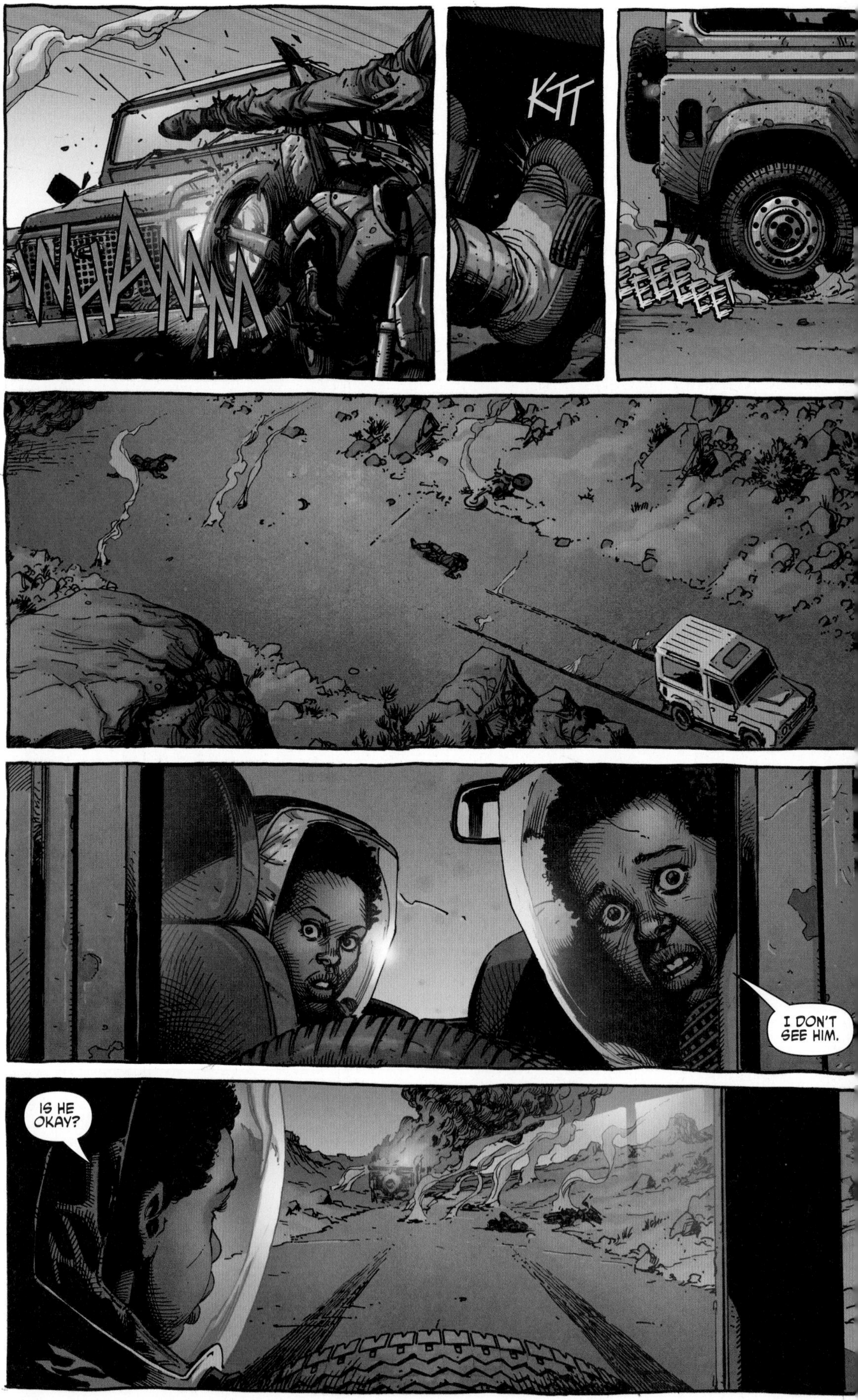
WHAMM
KTT
EEEEEEET
I DON'T SEE HIM.
IS HE OKAY?

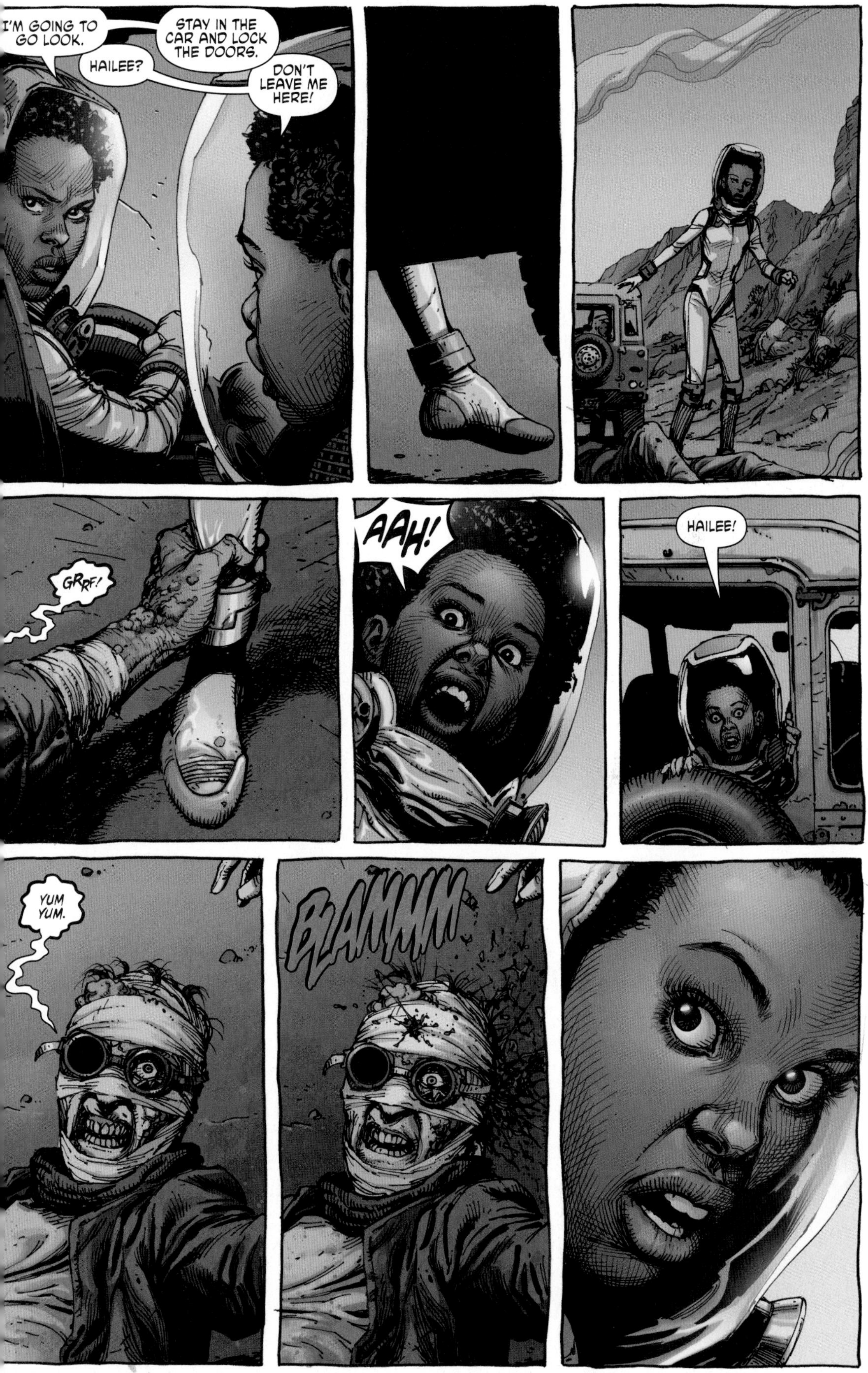
I'M GOING TO GO LOOK.
STAY IN THE CAR AND LOCK THE DOORS.
HAILEE?
DON'T LEAVE ME HERE!
GRRRF!
AAH!
HAILEE!
YUM YUM.
BLAMMM

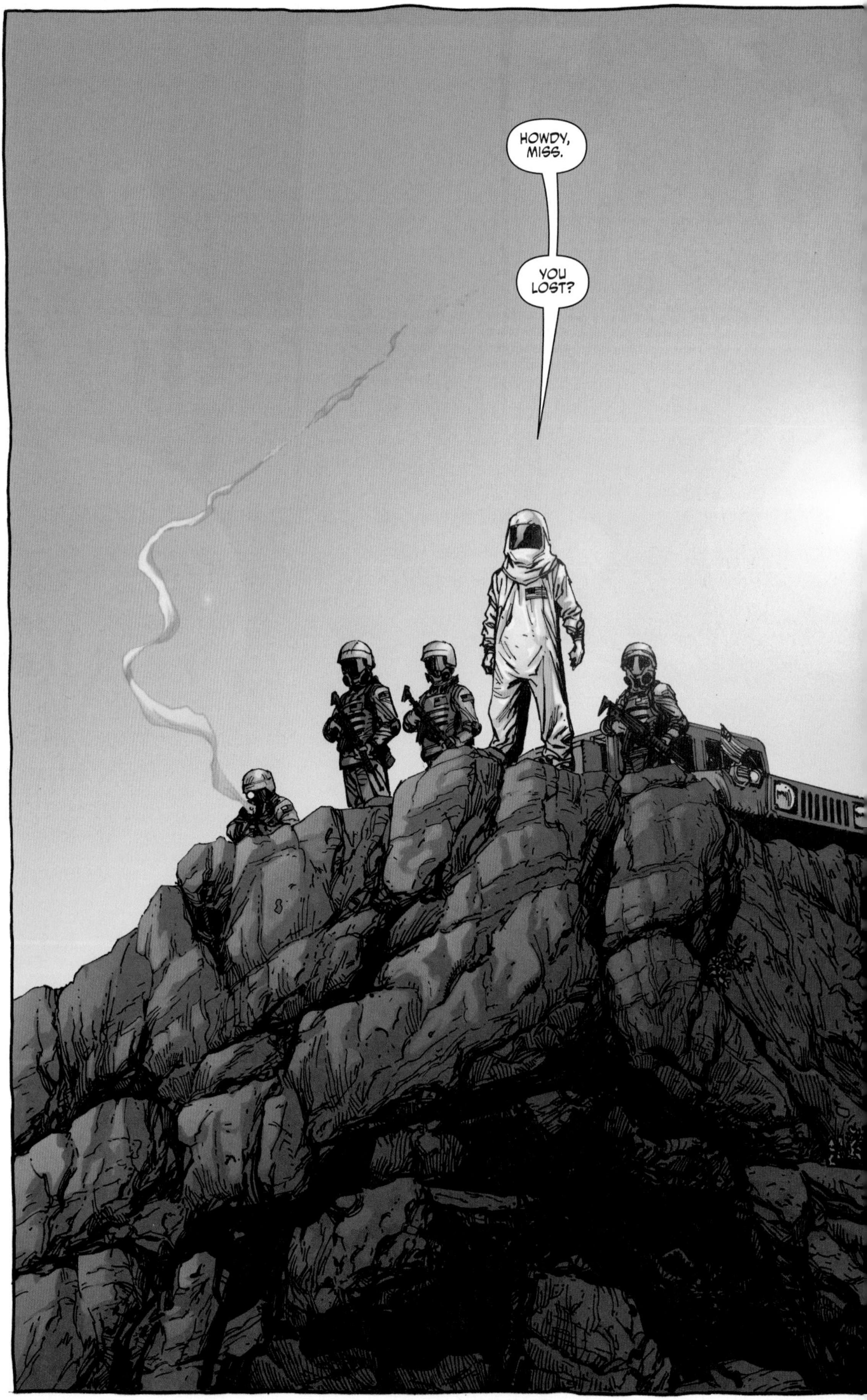
HOWDY, MISS.
YOU LOST?

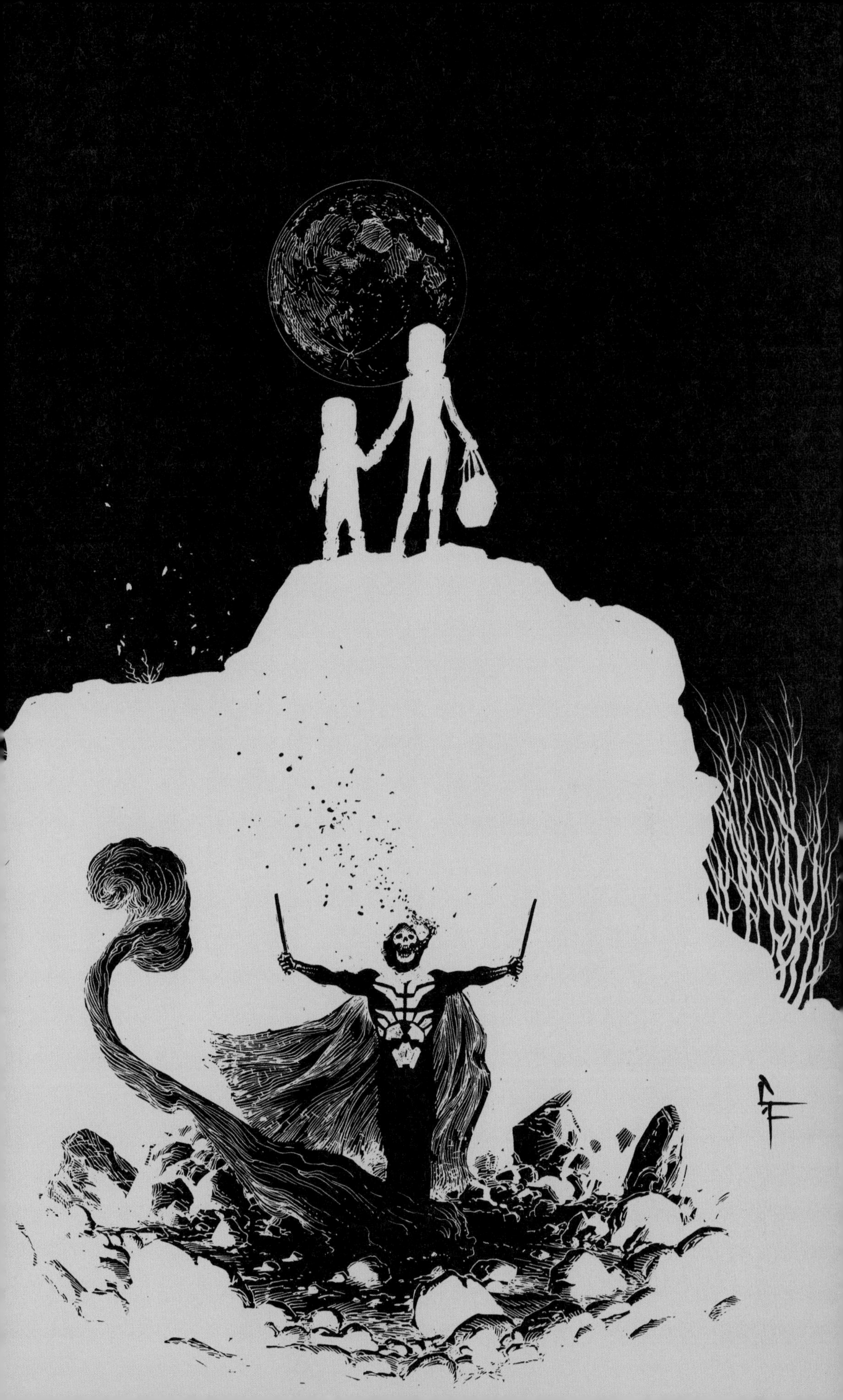

CHAPTER FIVE

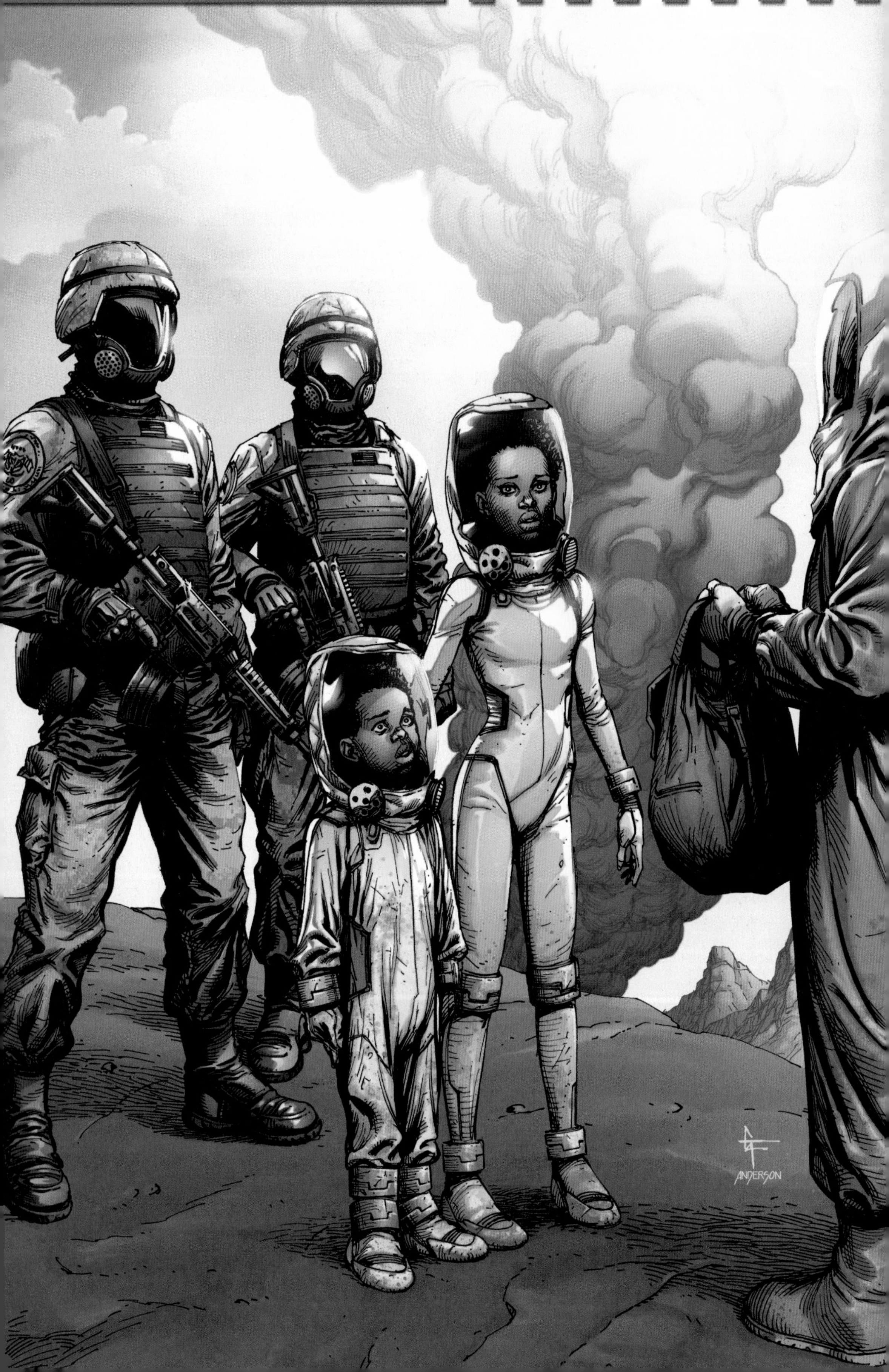
ANDERSON

GEIGER'S FAMILY WAS *LOCKED* INSIDE THE SHELTER WHILE HE WAS CAUGHT IN THE *FALLOUT.*

SOMEHOW, WHETHER IT WAS BECAUSE OF THE *EXPERIMENTAL CANCER TREATMENT* HE'D UNDERGONE OR HIS *WILL TO SURVIVE,* HE WAS TURNED INTO A *HUMAN GLOWSTICK.*

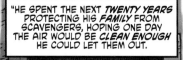

"HE SPENT THE NEXT *TWENTY YEARS* PROTECTING HIS *FAMILY* FROM SCAVENGERS, HOPING ONE DAY THE AIR WOULD BE *CLEAN ENOUGH* HE COULD LET THEM OUT.

"BUT *THE KING OF LAS VEGAS* LED HIS *NUCLEAR KNIGHTS* IN AN ATTACK.

"THE KNIGHTS BLEW OPEN THE SHELTER AND GEIGER WAS FACED WITH THE *HORRIBLE TRUTH...*

"HIS FAMILY HAD BEEN *DEAD* FOR YEARS, THE SHELTER *CAVED IN* BY THE *BOMBS* THAT STARTED THE *UNKNOWN WAR.*

"HE'D BEEN PROTECTING A *GRAVE.*

"AND IT NEARLY DROVE HIM *MAD.*

"GEIGER KILLED MOST OF THE KNIGHTS, BUT HE LEFT THE KING *ALIVE...*

"...SCARRED FOREVER, LIKE GEIGER HIMSELF.

"AFTER THAT, *THE GLOWING MAN* HEADED OUT INTO THE DESERT WITH NOWHERE TO GO."

UNTIL HE MET *TWO CHILDREN* ON THE RUN FROM THE KING, HOPING TO GET SOMEPLACE *SAFE.*

WHERE WAS THAT?

THE LAST HOLDOUT OF THE *UNITED STATES.*

IT WAS CALLED *NORAD.*

GEIGER AGREED TO TAKE THEM THERE...

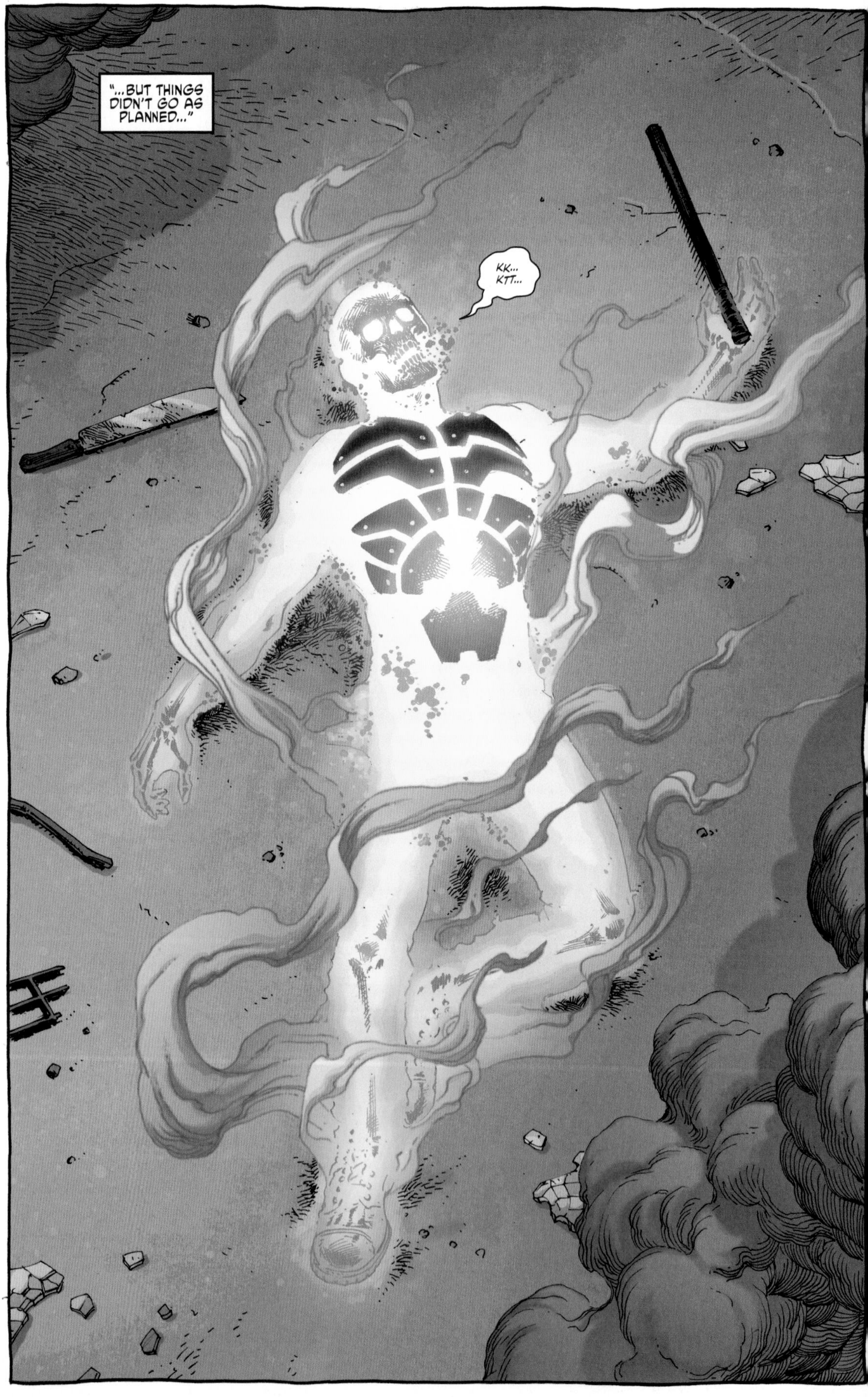
"...BUT THINGS DIDN'T GO AS PLANNED..."
KK... KTT...

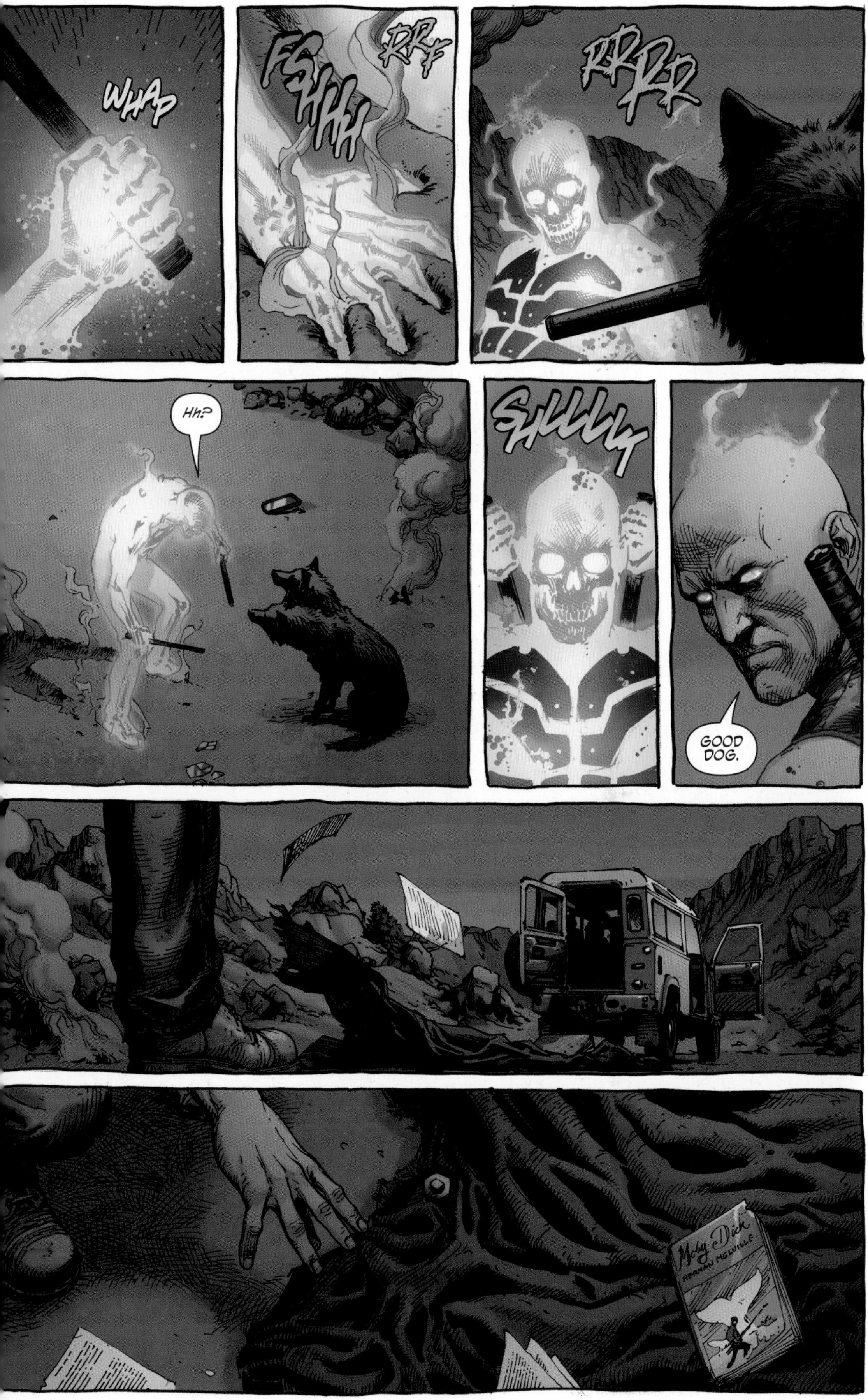
WHAP
FSHHH
RRF
RRRRR
Hh?
SHLLLL
GOOD DOG.
Moby Dick
HERMAN MELVILLE

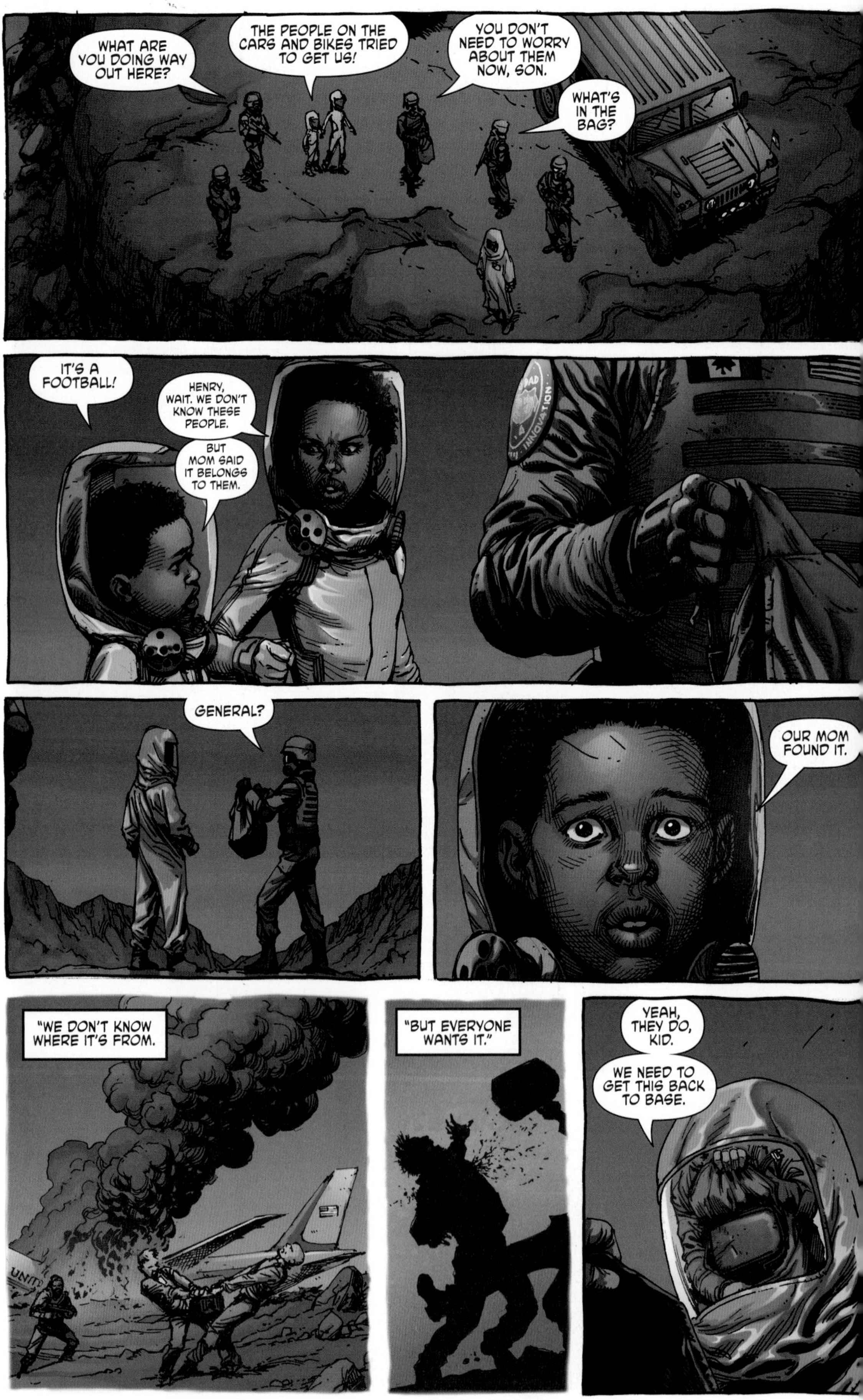
WHAT ARE YOU DOING WAY OUT HERE?
THE PEOPLE ON THE CARS AND BIKES TRIED TO GET US!
YOU DON'T NEED TO WORRY ABOUT THEM NOW, SON.
WHAT'S IN THE BAG?
IT'S A FOOTBALL!
HENRY, WAIT. WE DON'T KNOW THESE PEOPLE.
BUT MOM SAID IT BELONGS TO THEM.
INNOVATION
GENERAL?
OUR MOM FOUND IT.
"WE DON'T KNOW WHERE IT'S FROM.
"BUT EVERYONE WANTS IT."
YEAH, THEY DO, KID.
WE NEED TO GET THIS BACK TO BASE.

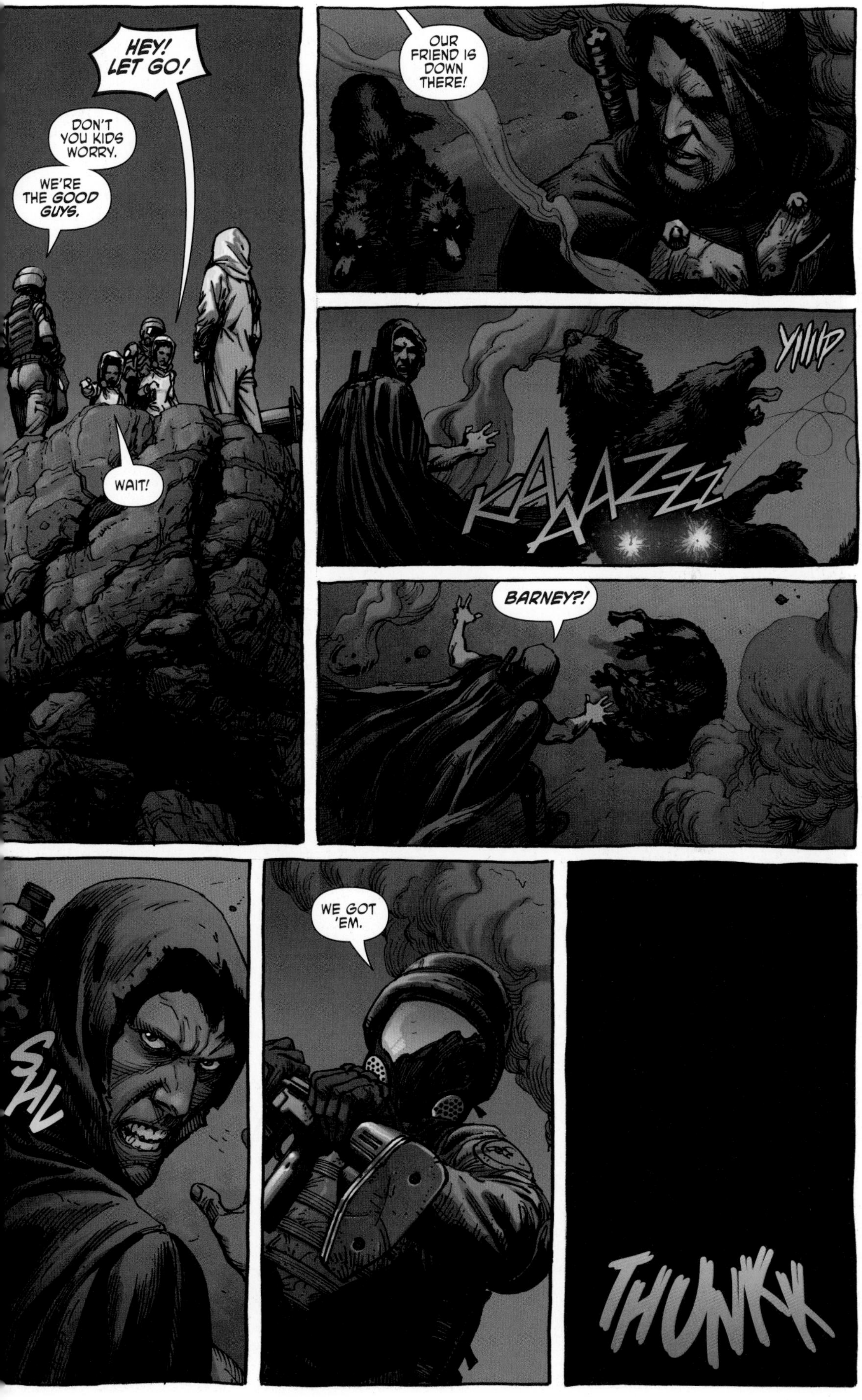
HEY! LET GO!
DON'T YOU KIDS WORRY.
WE'RE THE GOOD GUYS.
WAIT!
OUR FRIEND IS DOWN THERE!
YIIIP
KAAAZZZ
BARNEY?!
SHU
WE GOT 'EM.
THUNKK

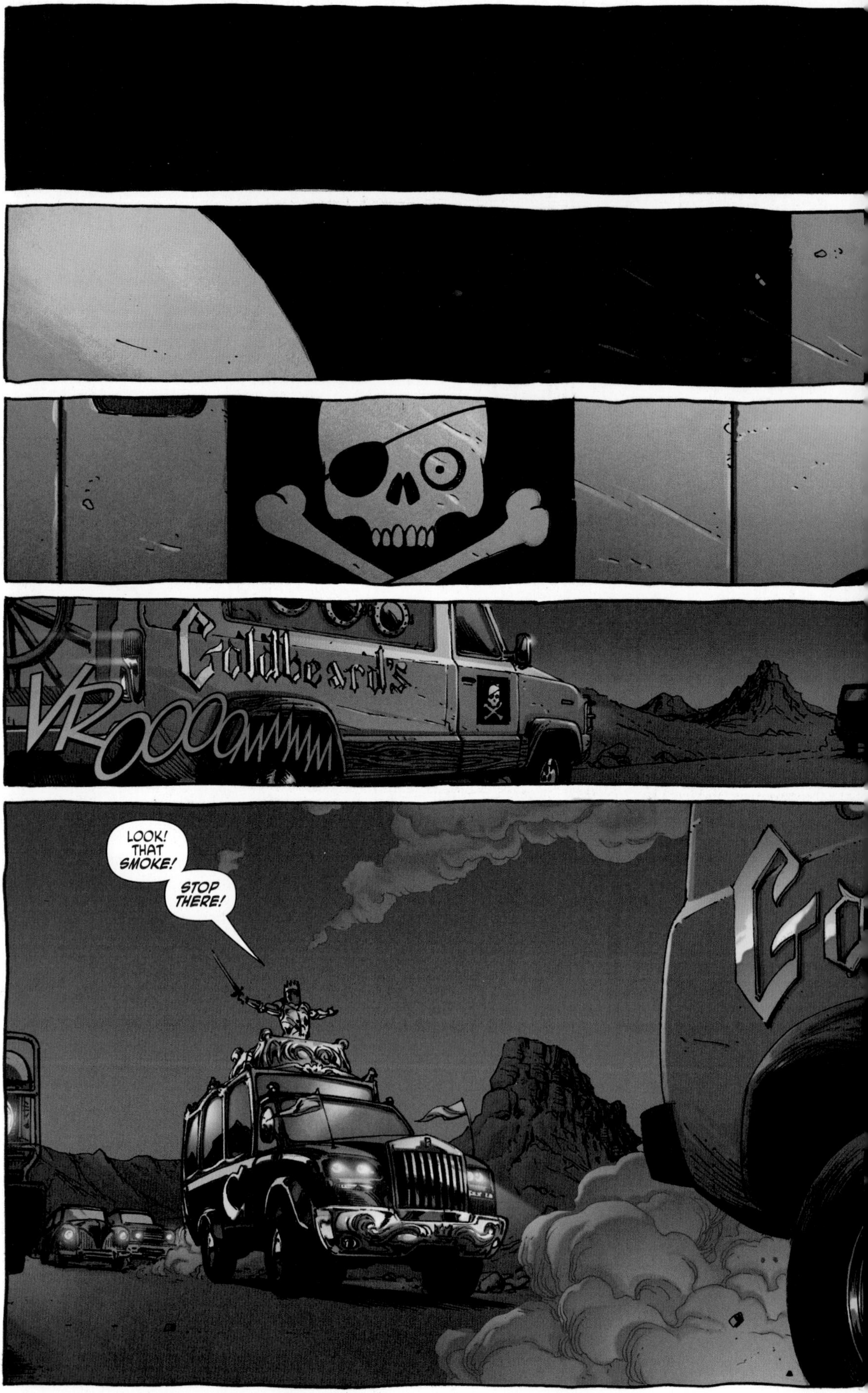
Coldbeard's
VROOOOOMMMMM
LOOK! THAT SMOKE!
STOP THERE!

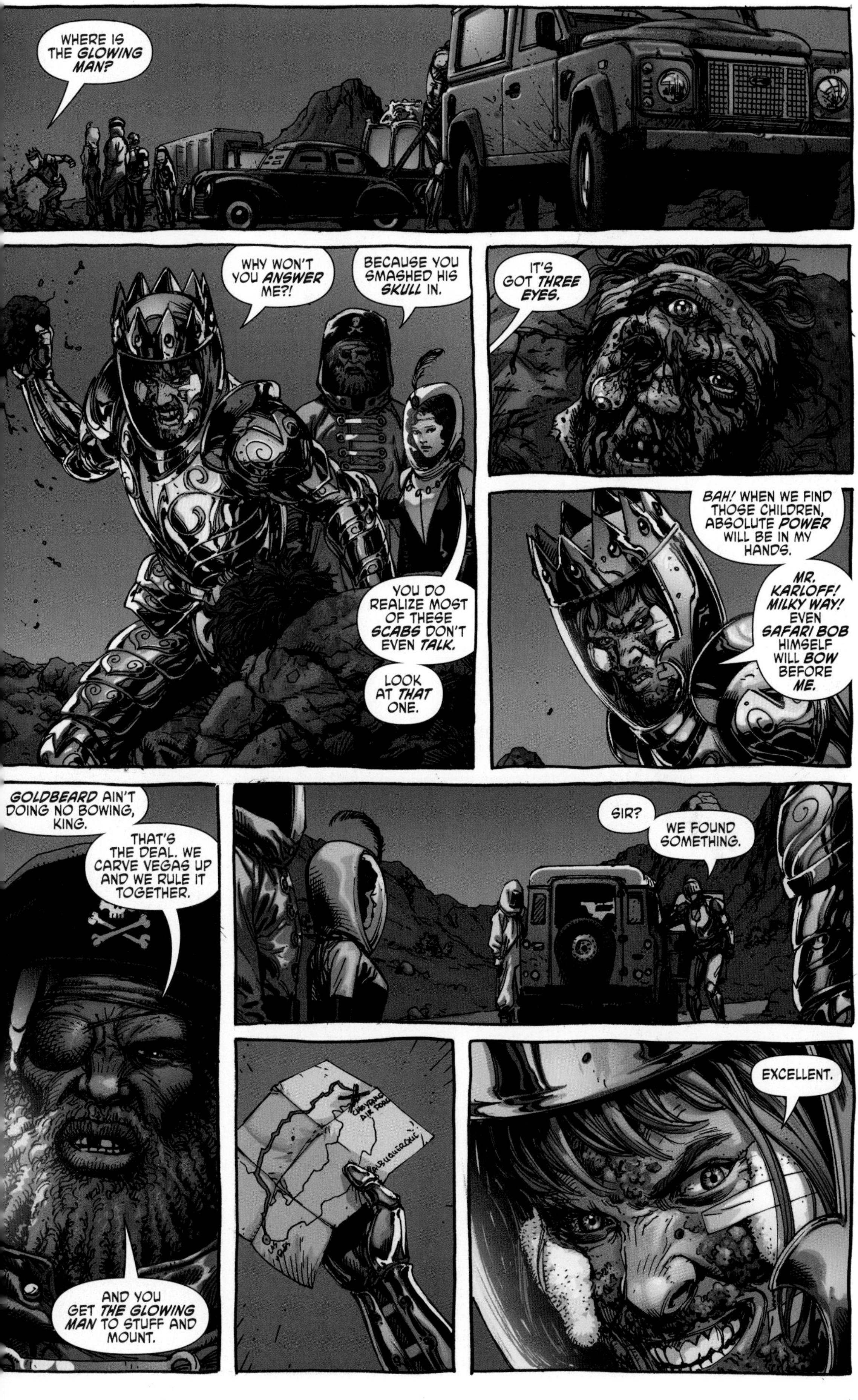
WHERE IS THE *GLOWING MAN?*
WHY WON'T YOU *ANSWER* ME?!
BECAUSE YOU SMASHED HIS *SKULL* IN.
YOU DO REALIZE MOST OF THESE *SCABS* DON'T EVEN *TALK.*
LOOK AT *THAT* ONE.
IT'S GOT *THREE EYES.*
BAH! WHEN WE FIND THOSE CHILDREN, ABSOLUTE *POWER* WILL BE IN MY HANDS.
MR. KARLOFF! MILKY WAY! EVEN *SAFARI BOB* HIMSELF WILL *BOW* BEFORE *ME.*
GOLDBEARD AIN'T DOING NO BOWING, KING.
THAT'S THE DEAL. WE CARVE VEGAS UP AND WE RULE IT TOGETHER.
AND YOU GET *THE GLOWING MAN* TO STUFF AND MOUNT.
SIR?
WE FOUND SOMETHING.
EXCELLENT.

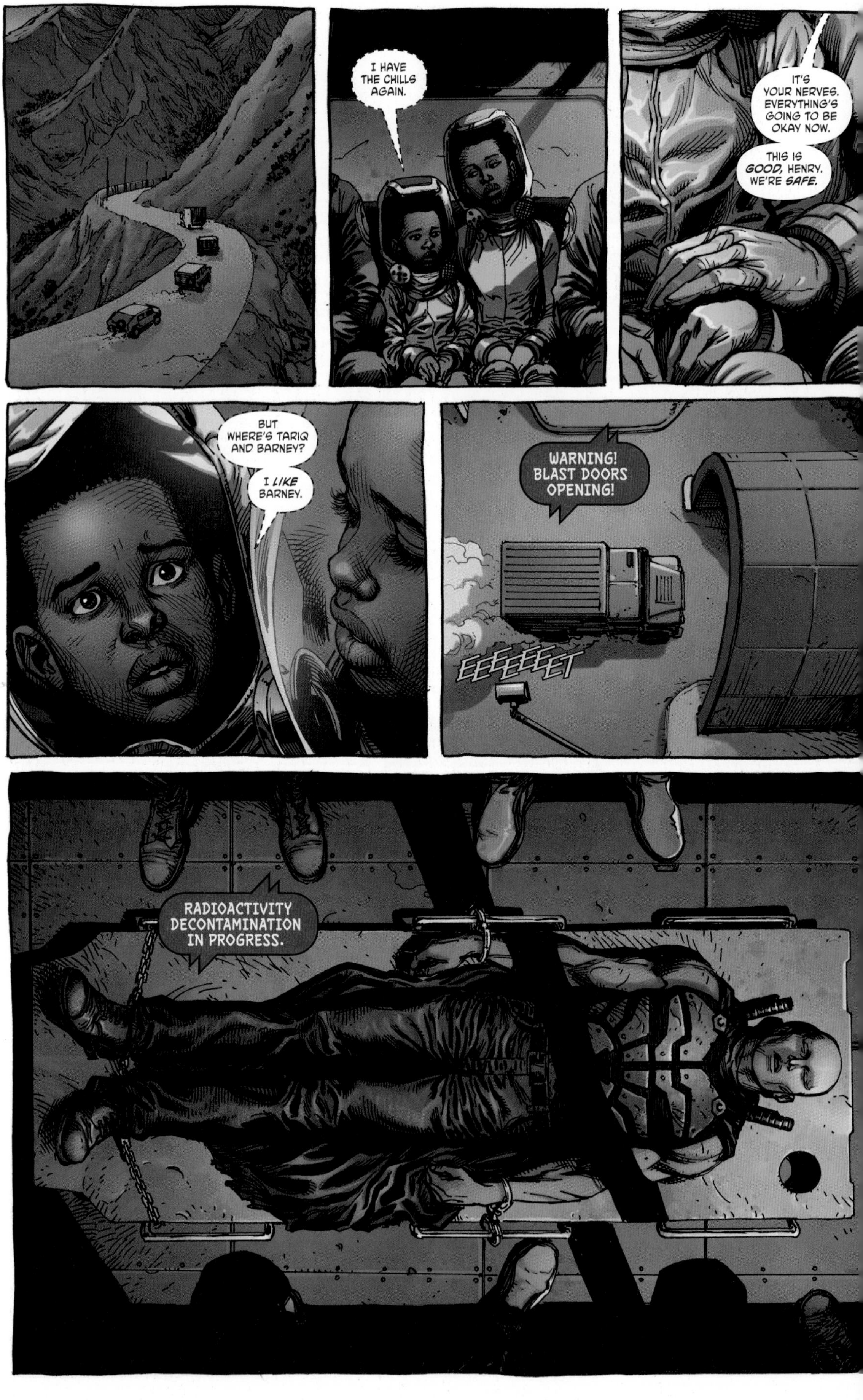

I HAVE THE CHILLS AGAIN.
IT'S YOUR NERVES. EVERYTHING'S GOING TO BE OKAY NOW.
THIS IS GOOD, HENRY. WE'RE SAFE.
BUT WHERE'S TARIQ AND BARNEY?
I LIKE BARNEY.
WARNING! BLAST DOORS OPENING!
EEEEEEEET
RADIOACTIVITY DECONTAMINATION IN PROGRESS.

"THE NUCLEAR FOOTBALL WENT MISSING *YEARS* AGO WHEN AIR FORCE ONE WENT DOWN. HOW DID THESE *CHILDREN* COME INTO POSSESSION OF IT?"

THEY SAID THEIR *MOTHER* GAVE IT TO THEM, MR. VICE PRESIDENT.

WHEN AIR FORCE ONE WENT DOWN IT WAS SCAVENGED.

THE FOOTBALL WAS LOST. WE THOUGHT, BEST CASE, *DESTROYED.*

"YET, WE'VE VERIFIED THIS IS WHAT'S LEFT OF IT.

"IT CONTAINS THE SITES OF EVERY NUCLEAR WARHEAD IN AMERICA."

SO WE CAN LOCATE THE SILOS THAT HAVE REMAINED HIDDEN...

...AND TAKE BACK CONTROL OF OUR NUCLEAR ARSENAL.

THE SOUTH. THE GREAT LAKES. THEY'LL HAVE NO CHOICE BUT TO UNITE UNDER *PRESIDENT GRIFFIN* AGAIN.

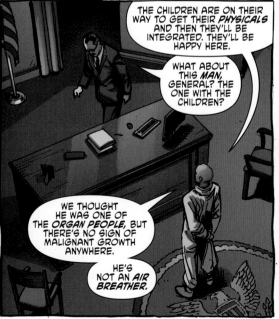

THE CHILDREN ARE ON THEIR WAY TO GET THEIR *PHYSICALS* AND THEN THEY'LL BE INTEGRATED. THEY'LL BE HAPPY HERE.

WHAT ABOUT THIS *MAN*, GENERAL? THE ONE WITH THE CHILDREN?

WE THOUGHT HE WAS ONE OF THE *ORGAN PEOPLE*, BUT THERE'S NO SIGN OF MALIGNANT GROWTH ANYWHERE.

HE'S NOT AN *AIR BREATHER.*

HE'S SOMETHING *ELSE.*

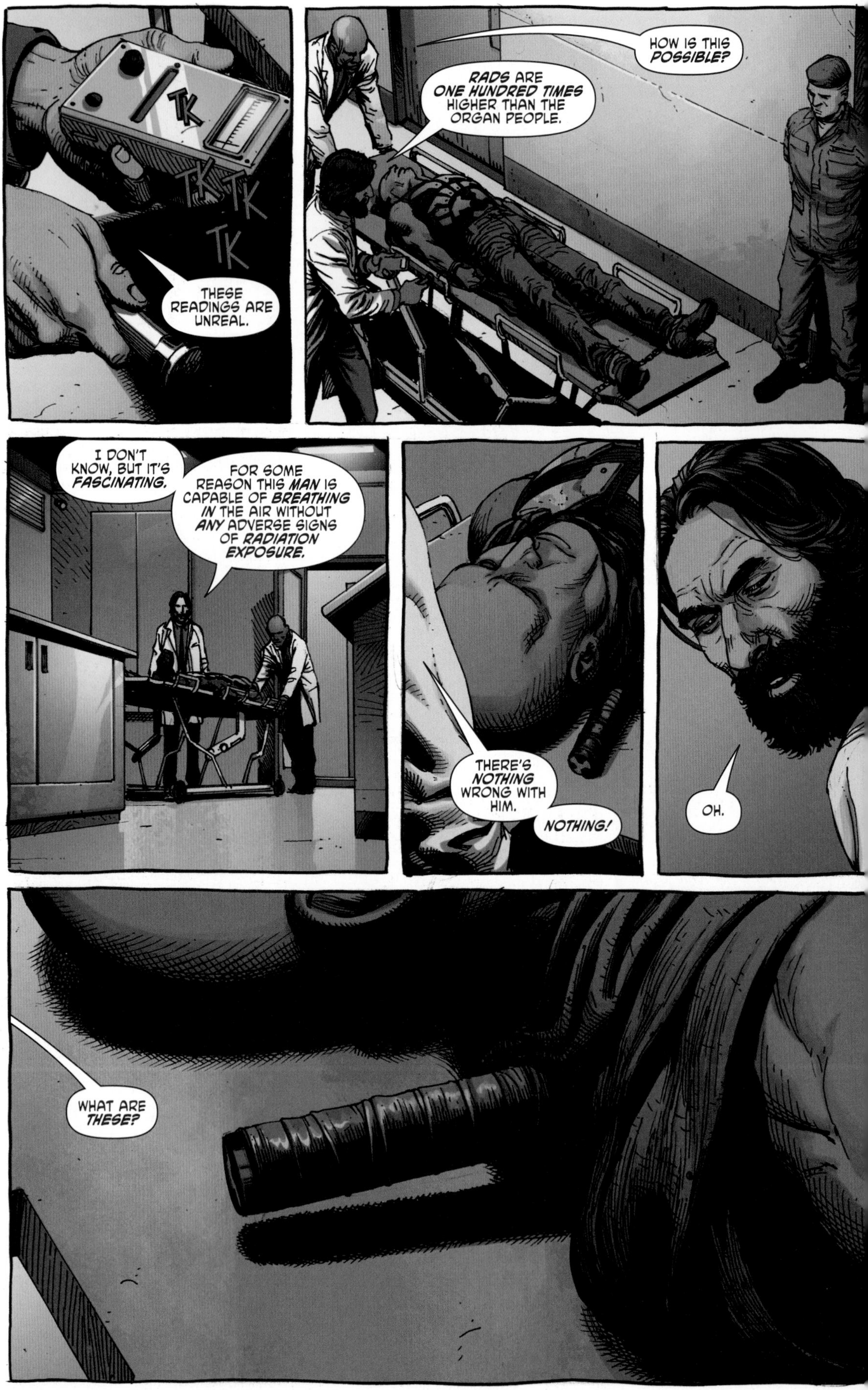
TK
TK TK
TK
THESE READINGS ARE UNREAL.
RADS ARE ONE HUNDRED TIMES HIGHER THAN THE ORGAN PEOPLE.
HOW IS THIS POSSIBLE?
I DON'T KNOW, BUT IT'S FASCINATING.
FOR SOME REASON THIS MAN IS CAPABLE OF BREATHING IN THE AIR WITHOUT ANY ADVERSE SIGNS OF RADIATION EXPOSURE.
THERE'S NOTHING WRONG WITH HIM.
NOTHING!
OH.
WHAT ARE THESE?

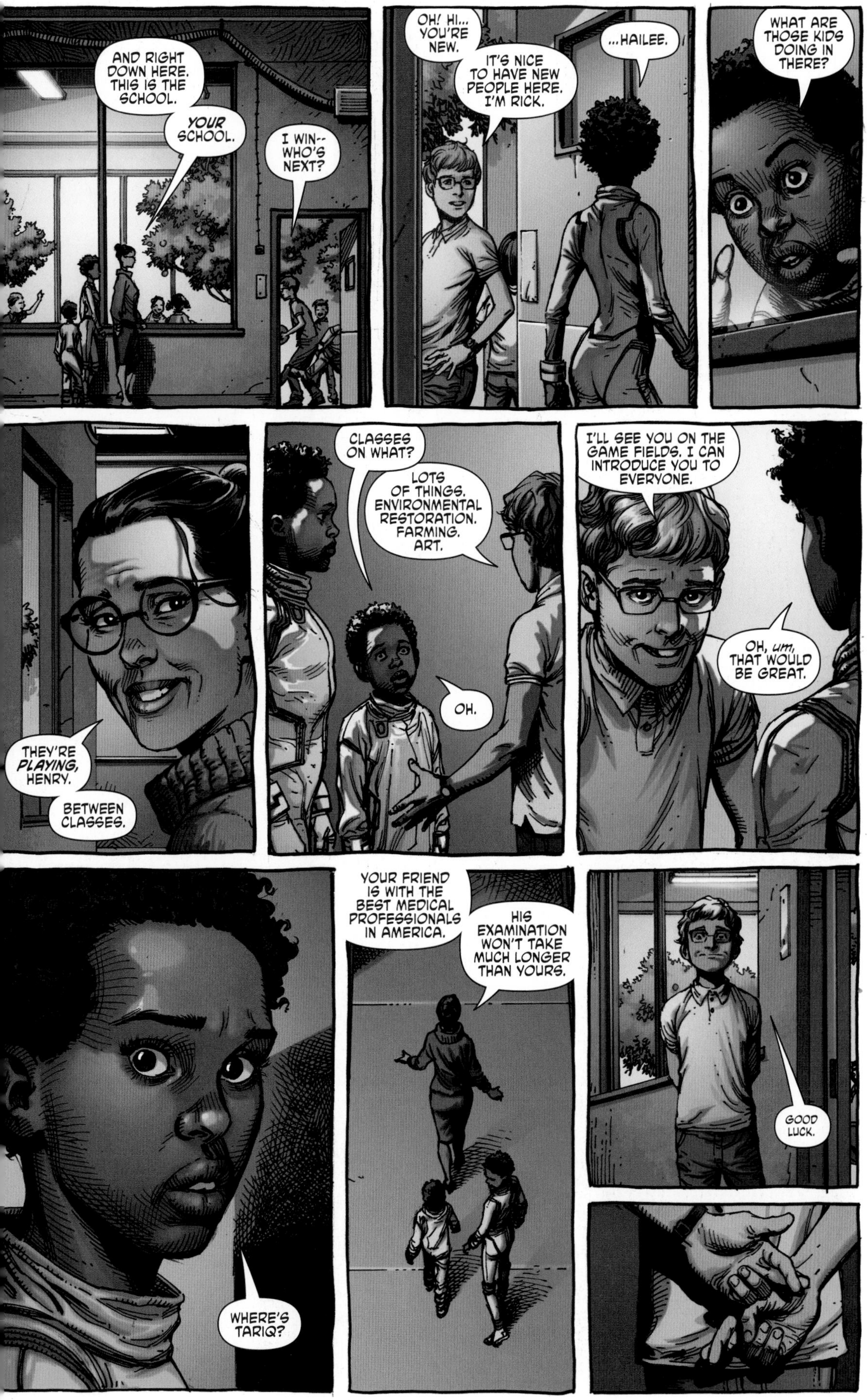
AND RIGHT DOWN HERE. THIS IS THE SCHOOL.
YOUR SCHOOL.
I WIN-- WHO'S NEXT?
OH! HI... YOU'RE NEW.
IT'S NICE TO HAVE NEW PEOPLE HERE. I'M RICK.
...HAILEE.
WHAT ARE THOSE KIDS DOING IN THERE?
THEY'RE PLAYING, HENRY.
BETWEEN CLASSES.
CLASSES ON WHAT?
LOTS OF THINGS. ENVIRONMENTAL RESTORATION. FARMING. ART.
OH.
I'LL SEE YOU ON THE GAME FIELDS. I CAN INTRODUCE YOU TO EVERYONE.
OH, UM, THAT WOULD BE GREAT.
WHERE'S TARIQ?
YOUR FRIEND IS WITH THE BEST MEDICAL PROFESSIONALS IN AMERICA.
HIS EXAMINATION WON'T TAKE MUCH LONGER THAN YOURS.
GOOD LUCK.

NN!

THESE THINGS ARE REALLY IN THERE.

SHLLLLK

AH!

WHAT ARE THEY?

THEY LOOK LIKE NIGHTSTICKS, BUT...

SHHHHHK

WHAT DO YOU THINK THEY DO?

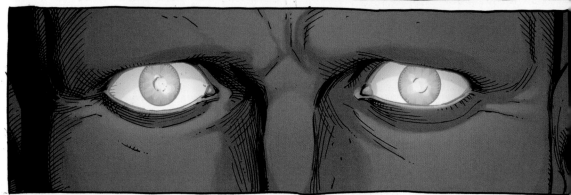

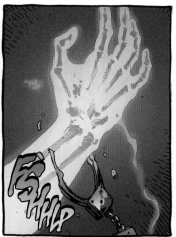

I DON'T THINK WE SHOULD HAVE TAKEN THOSE OUT.

GOOD OBSERVATION.

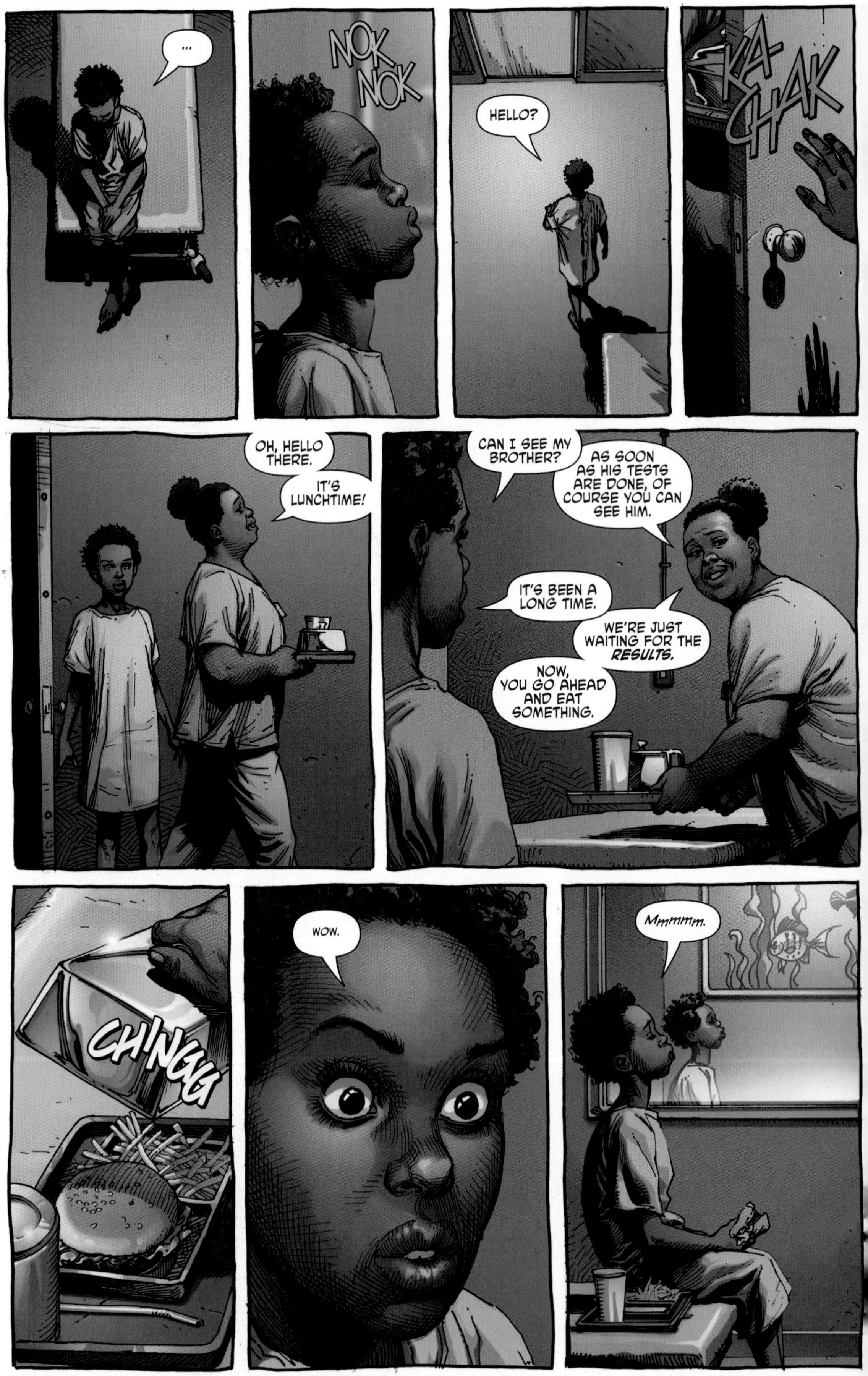
...
NOK NOK
HELLO?
KA CHAK
OH, HELLO THERE.
IT'S LUNCHTIME!
CAN I SEE MY BROTHER?
AS SOON AS HIS TESTS ARE DONE, OF COURSE YOU CAN SEE HIM.
IT'S BEEN A LONG TIME.
WE'RE JUST WAITING FOR THE *RESULTS.*
NOW, YOU GO AHEAD AND EAT SOMETHING.
CHINGG
WOW.
Mmmmm.

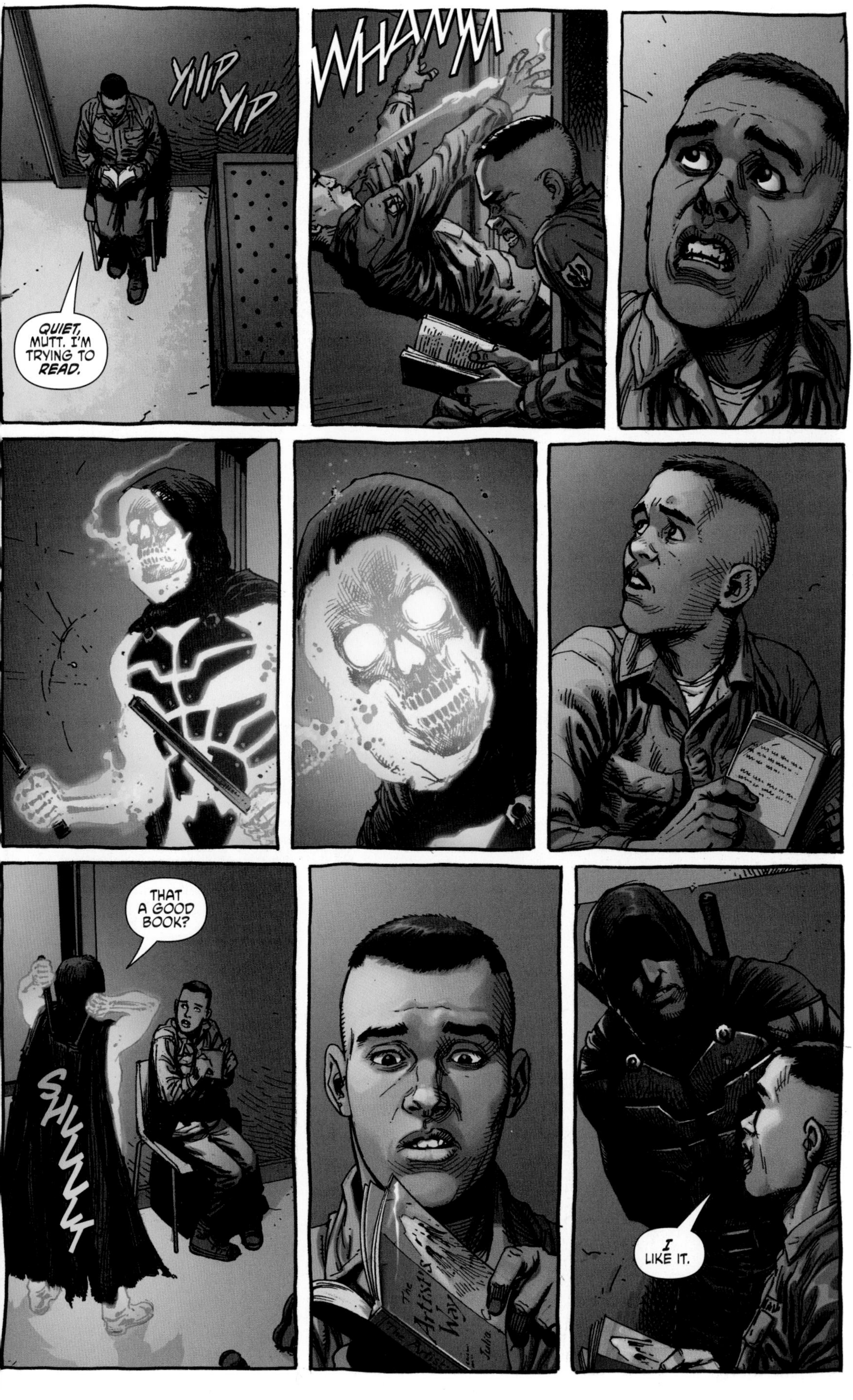
YIIP YIP
QUIET, MUTT. I'M TRYING TO READ.
WHAMM
THAT A GOOD BOOK?
I LIKE IT.

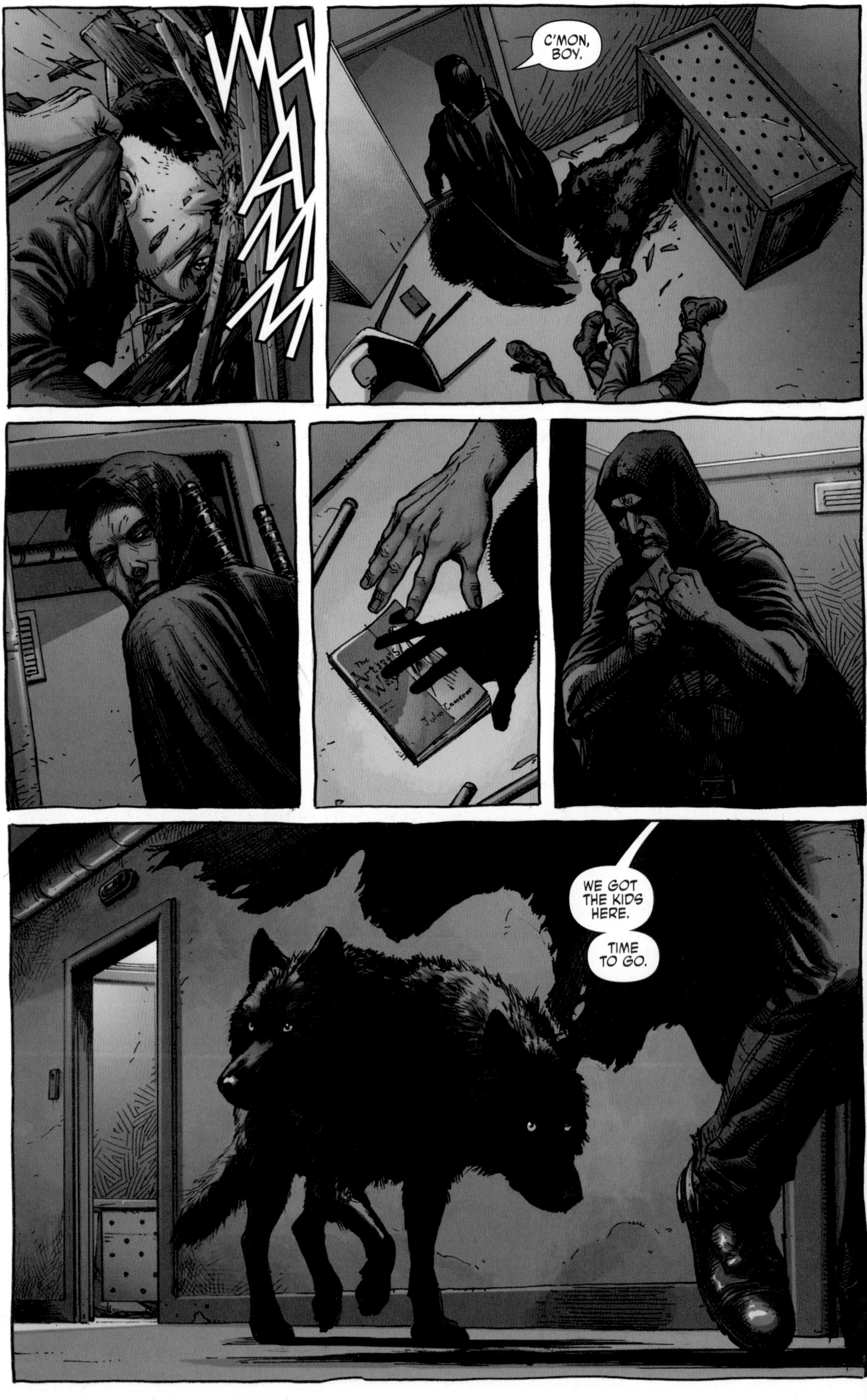
WHAMM
C'MON, BOY.
The Artist's Way
Julia Cameron
WE GOT THE KIDS HERE.
TIME TO GO.

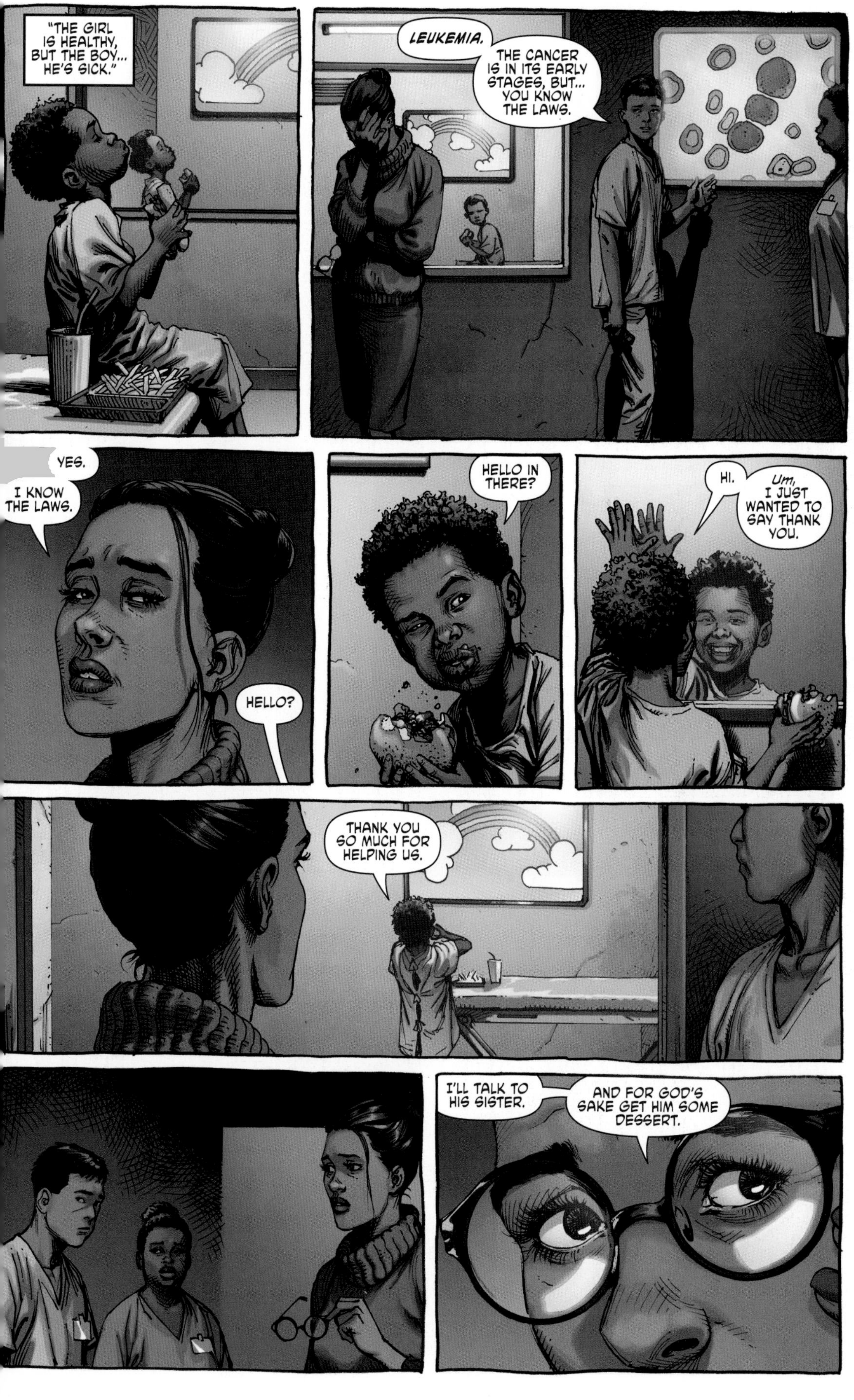
"THE GIRL IS HEALTHY, BUT THE BOY... HE'S SICK."
LEUKEMIA.
THE CANCER IS IN ITS EARLY STAGES, BUT... YOU KNOW THE LAWS.
YES.
I KNOW THE LAWS.
HELLO?
HELLO IN THERE?
HI.
Um, I JUST WANTED TO SAY THANK YOU.
THANK YOU SO MUCH FOR HELPING US.
I'LL TALK TO HIS SISTER.
AND FOR GOD'S SAKE GET HIM SOME DESSERT.

WHERE'S HENRY?

HE'S SAFE, HAILEE, BUT HE'S SICK.

SICK?

HAS YOUR BROTHER BEEN EXPERIENCING ANY SIGNS OF FATIGUE OR DISCOMFORT?

WELL, YEAH, BUT... I THOUGHT HE WAS JUST COMPLAINING. HE NEVER WANTS TO HELP DO ANYTHING.

HE'S A LITTLE KID.

HE HAS ACUTE LYMPHOCYTIC LEUKEMIA.

WHAT? CAN YOU HELP HIM?

OH, HAILEE.

I WISH WE COULD.

BUT OUR RESOURCES AREN'T ENDLESS.

AS MUCH AS WE DO TO GENERATE FOOD AND POWER AND CLEAN WATER, WE JUST DON'T HAVE ENOUGH FOR EVERYONE.

WHAT ARE YOU SAYING? THAT WE CAN'T STAY HERE BECAUSE HE'S SICK?

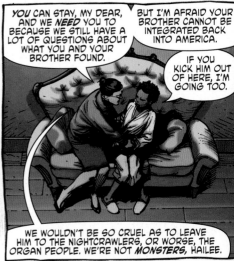

YOU CAN STAY, MY DEAR, AND WE NEED YOU TO BECAUSE WE STILL HAVE A LOT OF QUESTIONS ABOUT WHAT YOU AND YOUR BROTHER FOUND.

BUT I'M AFRAID YOUR BROTHER CANNOT BE INTEGRATED BACK INTO AMERICA.

IF YOU KICK HIM OUT OF HERE, I'M GOING TOO.

WE WOULDN'T BE SO CRUEL AS TO LEAVE HIM TO THE NIGHTCRAWLERS, OR WORSE, THE ORGAN PEOPLE. WE'RE NOT MONSTERS, HAILEE.

WE HAVE A COMPASSIONATE LIFE-ENDING PROGRAM HERE.

HE WILL HAVE A PEACEFUL PASSING, I ASSURE YOU.

NO!

HENRY?!

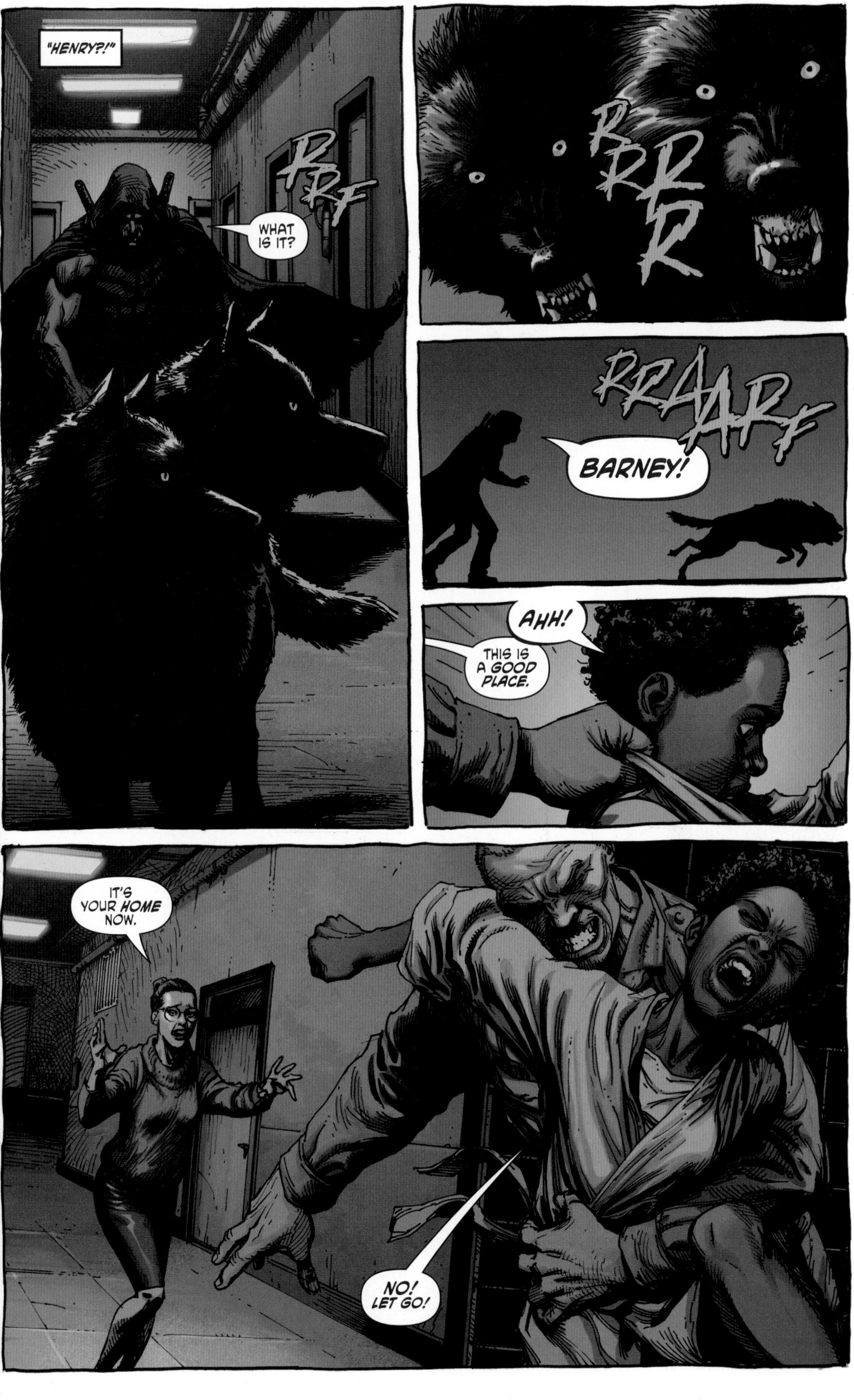

"HENRY?!"
RRRF
WHAT IS IT?
RRRRR
RRAARF
BARNEY!
AHH!
THIS IS A GOOD PLACE.
IT'S YOUR HOME NOW.
NO! LET GO!

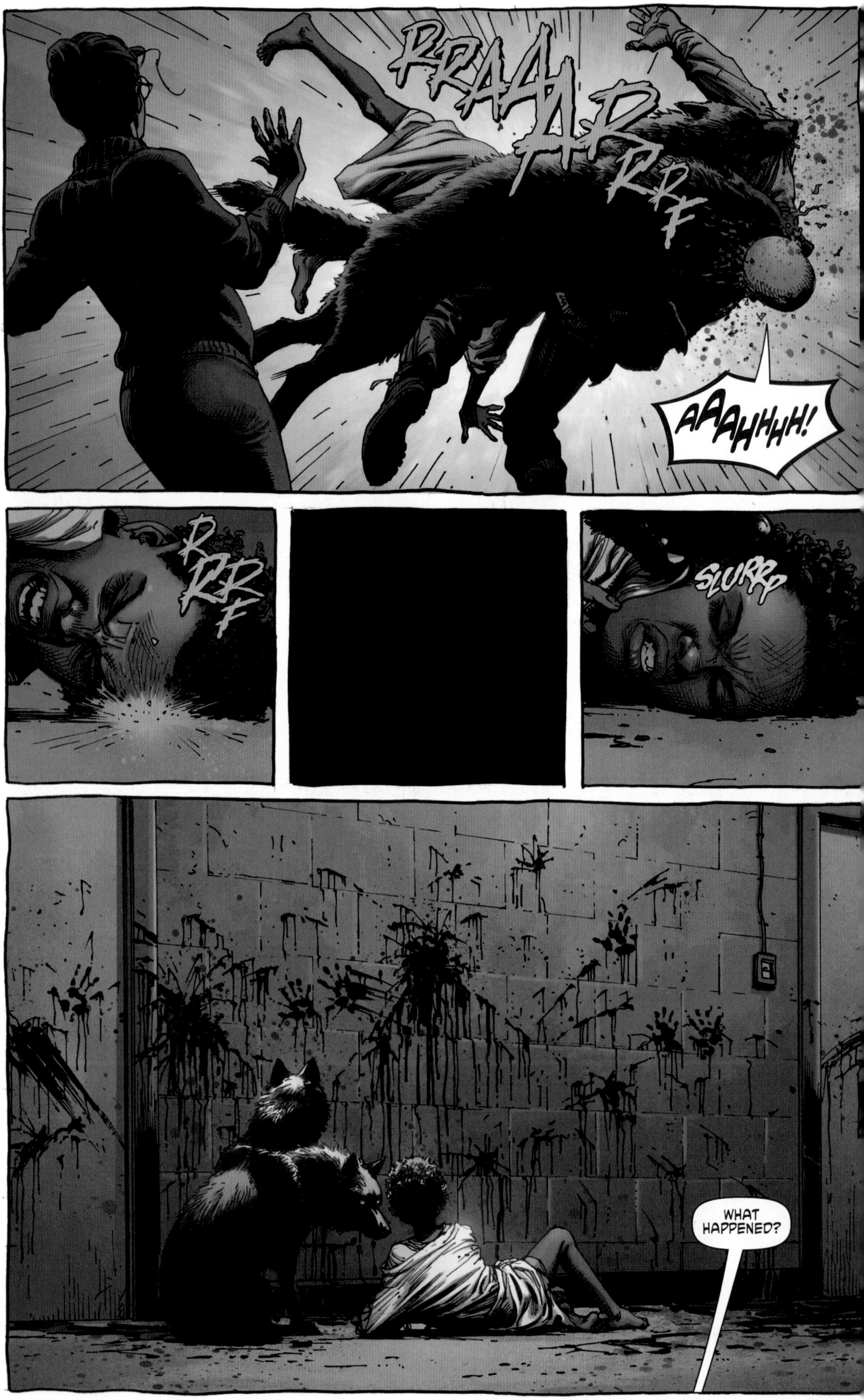
RRAAAARRRF
AAAHHHH!
RRRF
SLURRP
WHAT HAPPENED?

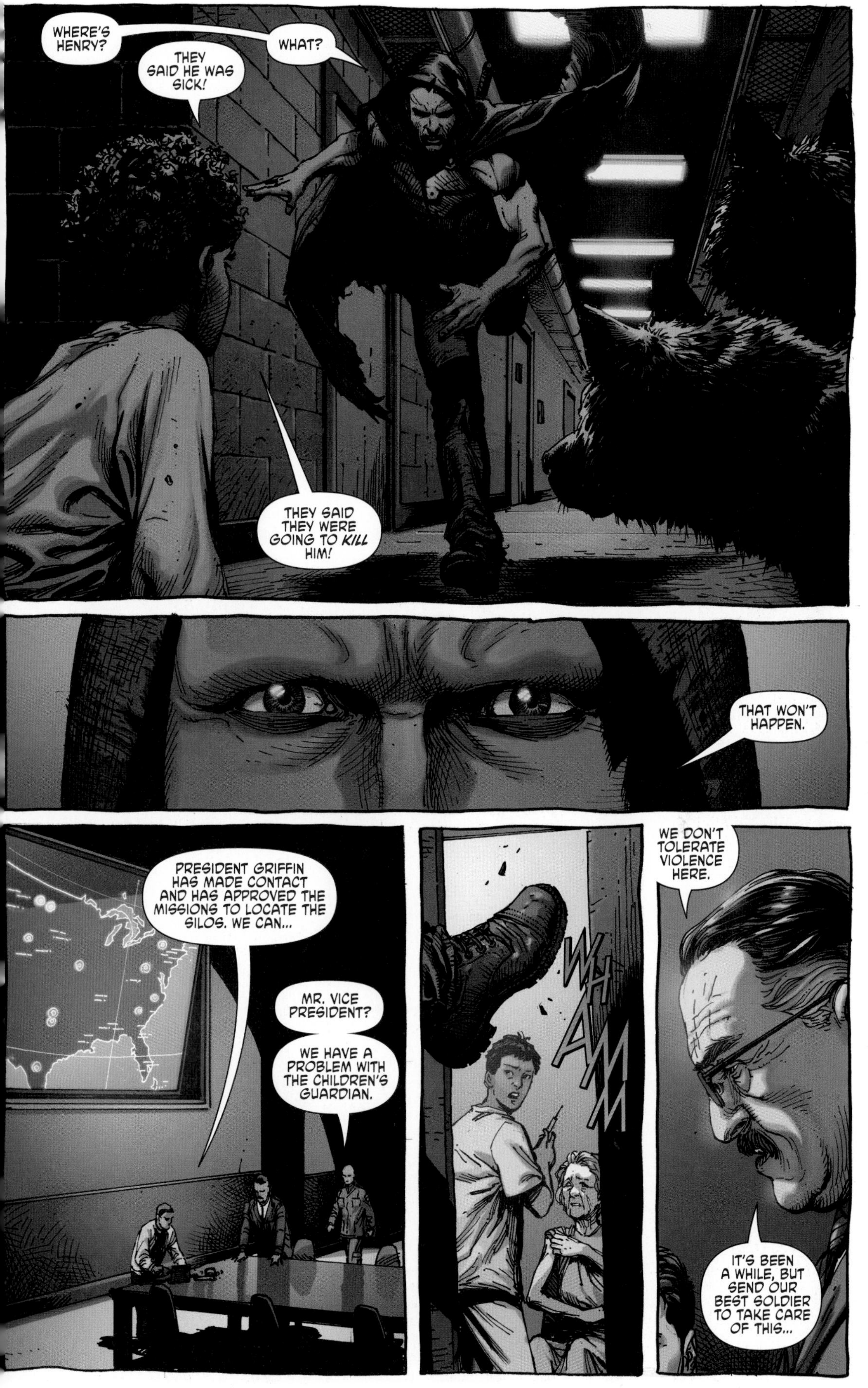
WHERE'S HENRY?
WHAT?
THEY SAID HE WAS SICK!
THEY SAID THEY WERE GOING TO *KILL* HIM!
THAT WON'T HAPPEN.
PRESIDENT GRIFFIN HAS MADE CONTACT AND HAS APPROVED THE MISSIONS TO LOCATE THE SILOS. WE CAN...
MR. VICE PRESIDENT?
WE HAVE A PROBLEM WITH THE CHILDREN'S GUARDIAN.
WHAM
WE DON'T TOLERATE VIOLENCE HERE.
IT'S BEEN A WHILE, BUT SEND OUR BEST SOLDIER TO TAKE CARE OF THIS...

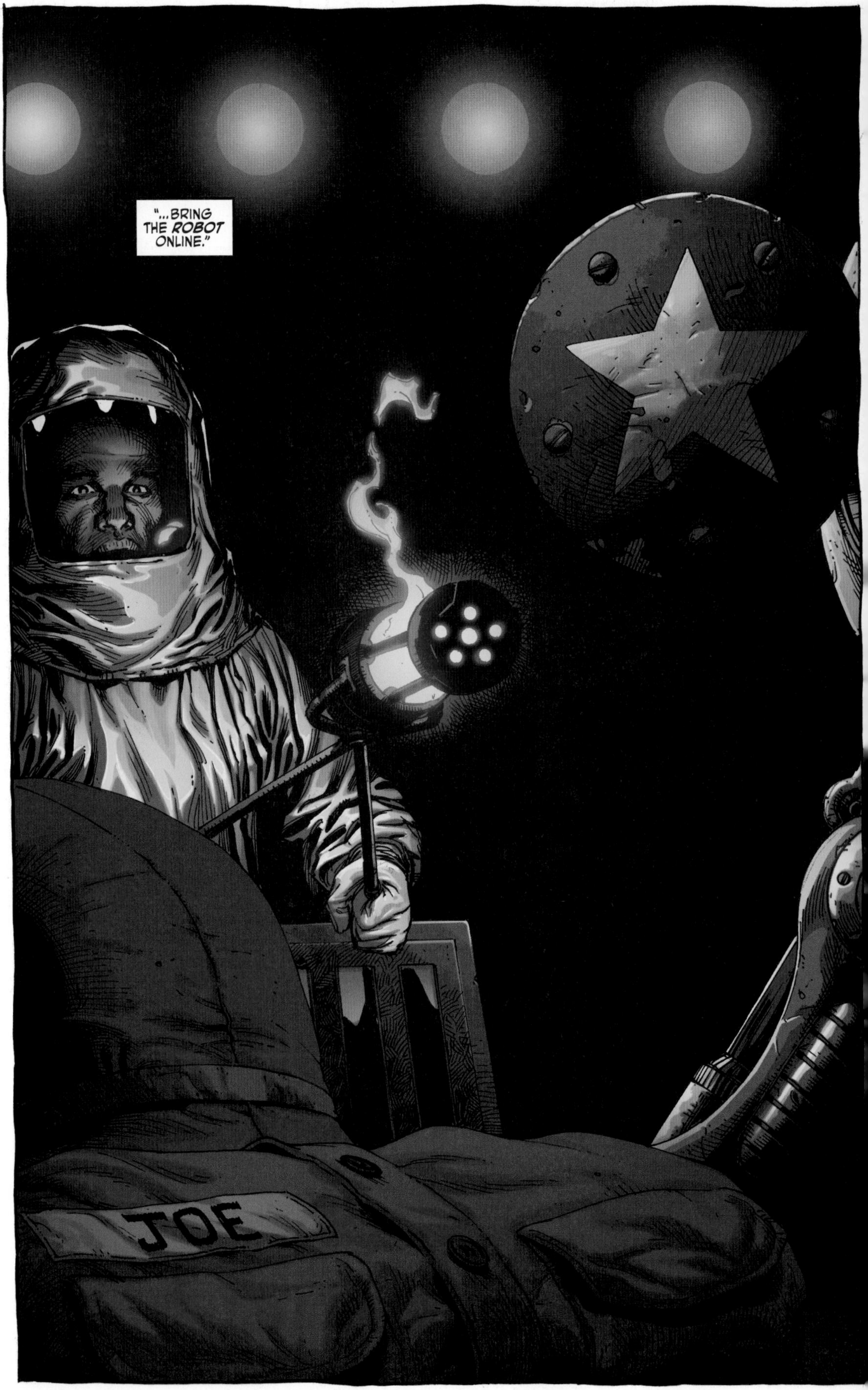
"...BRING THE *ROBOT* ONLINE."
JOE

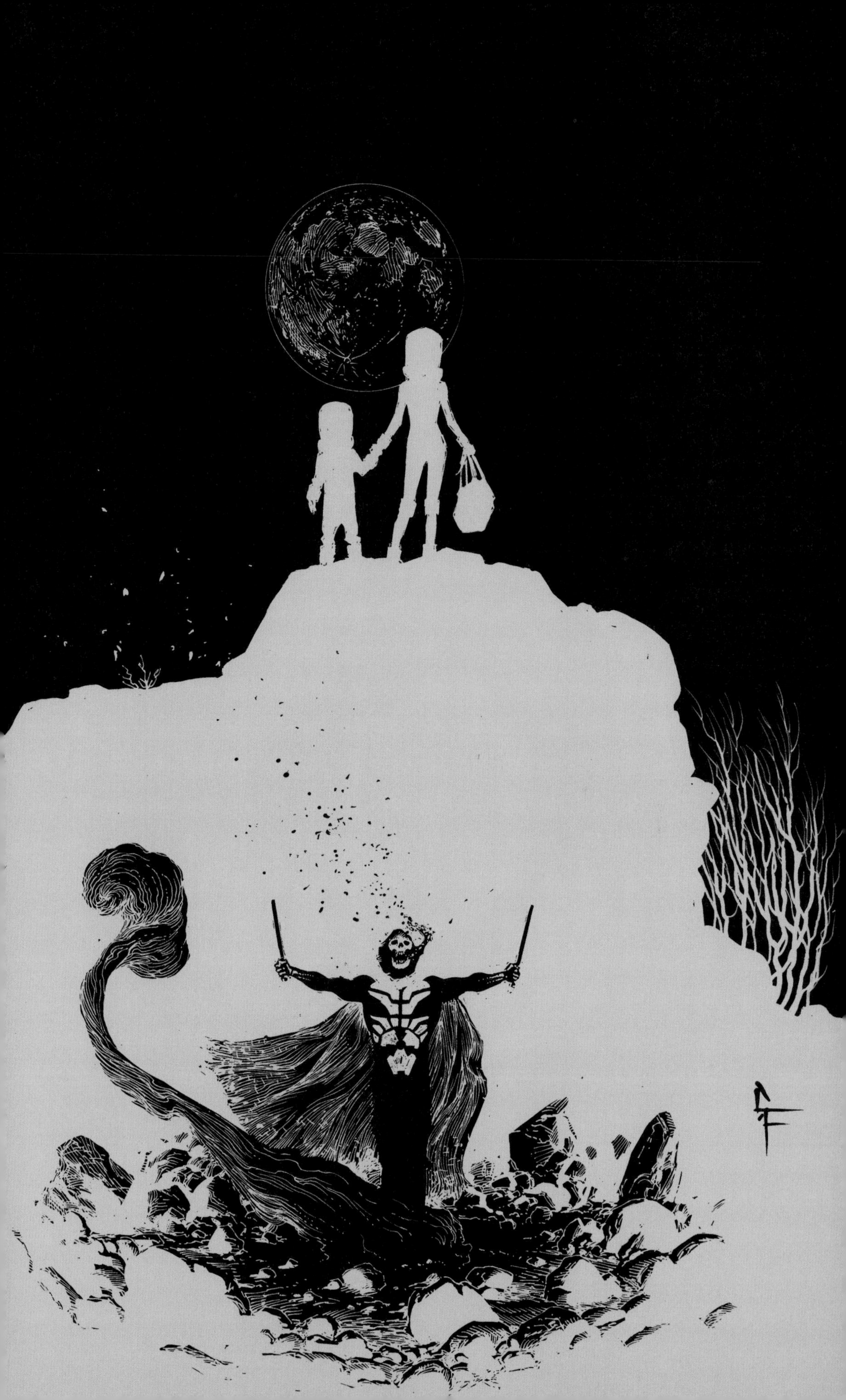

CHAPTER SIX

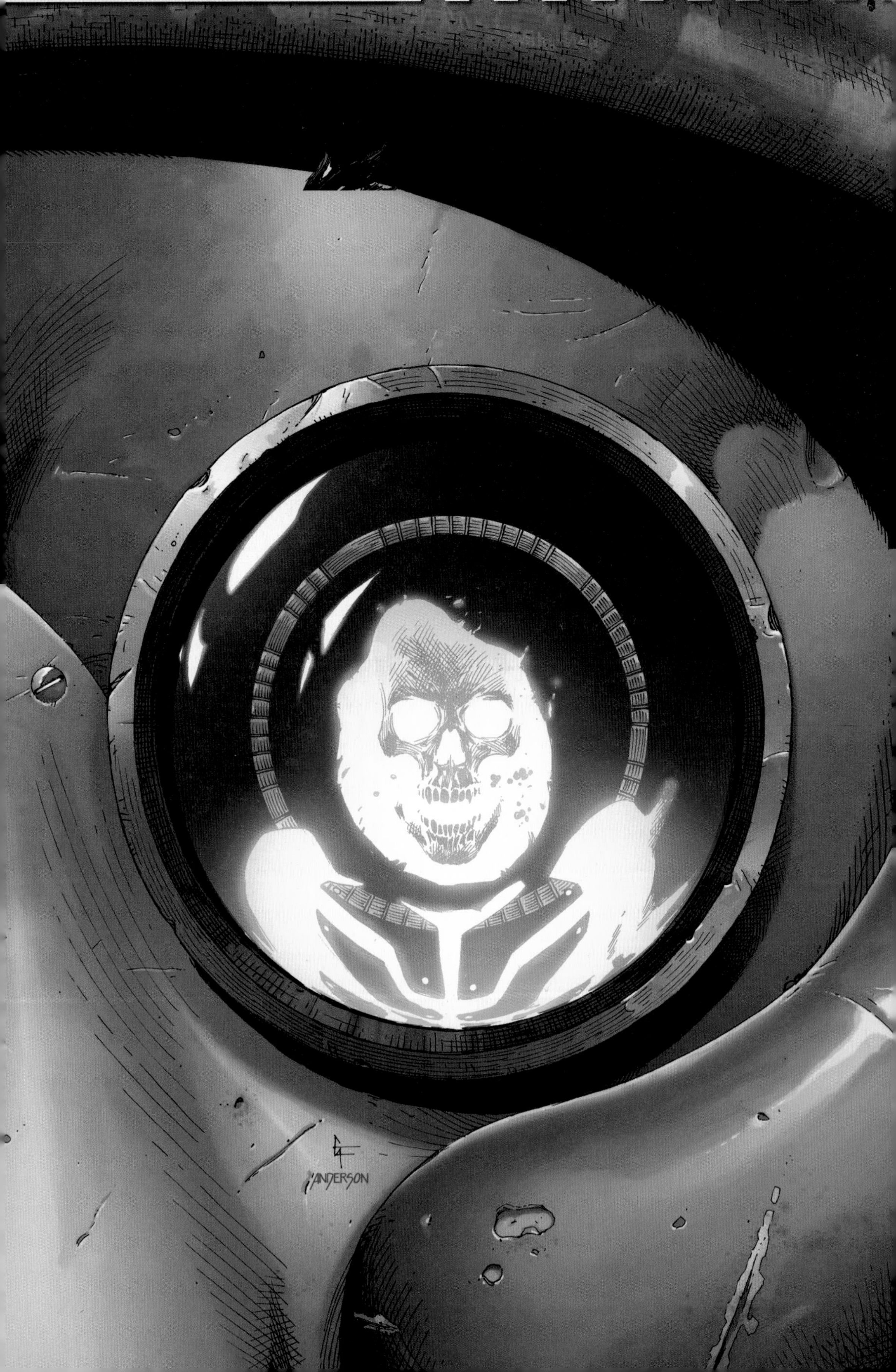
ANDERSON

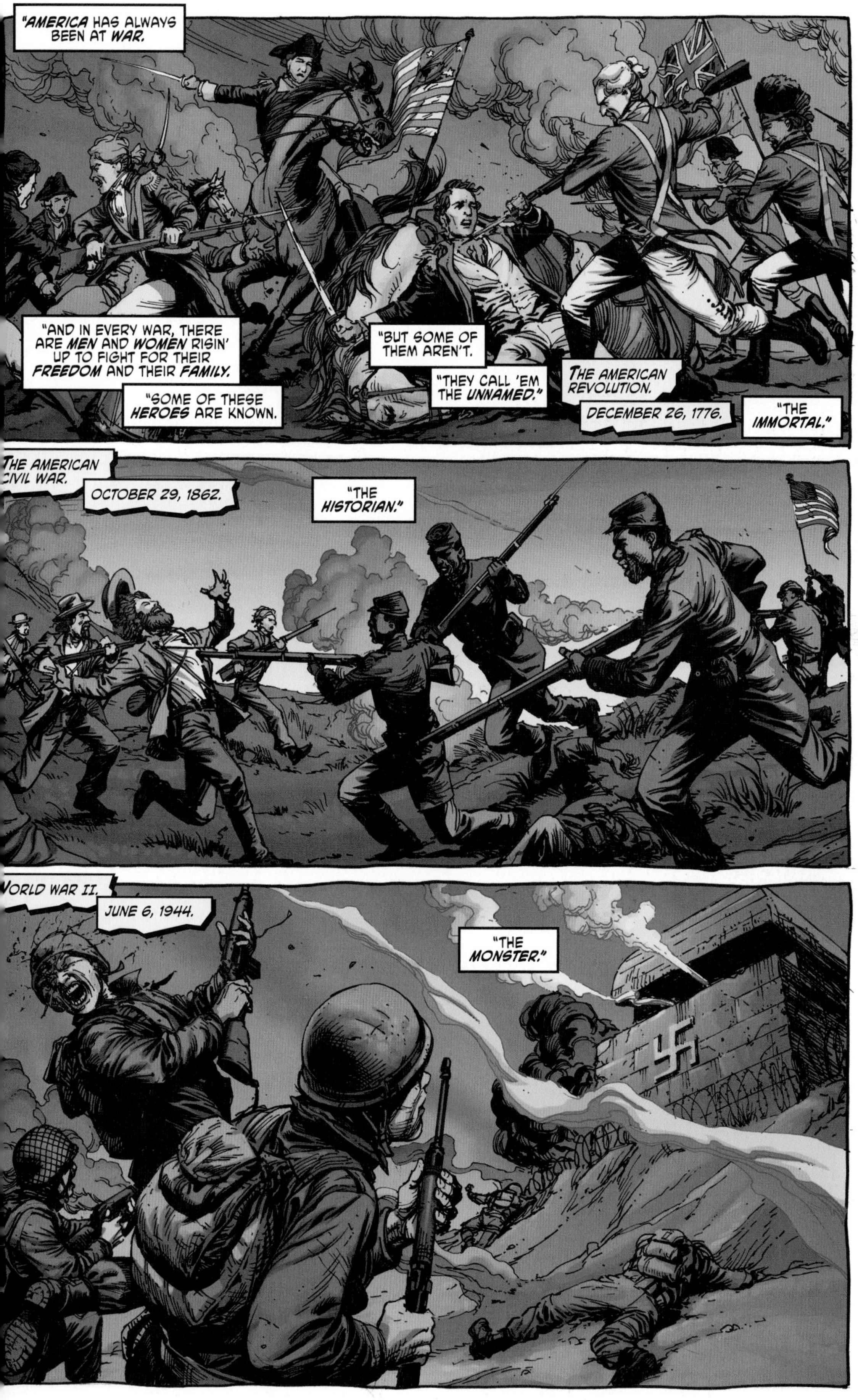

"AMERICA HAS ALWAYS BEEN AT WAR.
"AND IN EVERY WAR, THERE ARE MEN AND WOMEN RISIN' UP TO FIGHT FOR THEIR FREEDOM AND THEIR FAMILY.
"SOME OF THESE HEROES ARE KNOWN.
"BUT SOME OF THEM AREN'T.
"THEY CALL 'EM THE UNNAMED."
THE AMERICAN REVOLUTION.
DECEMBER 26, 1776.
"THE IMMORTAL."
THE AMERICAN CIVIL WAR.
OCTOBER 29, 1862.
"THE HISTORIAN."
WORLD WAR II.
JUNE 6, 1944.
"THE MONSTER."

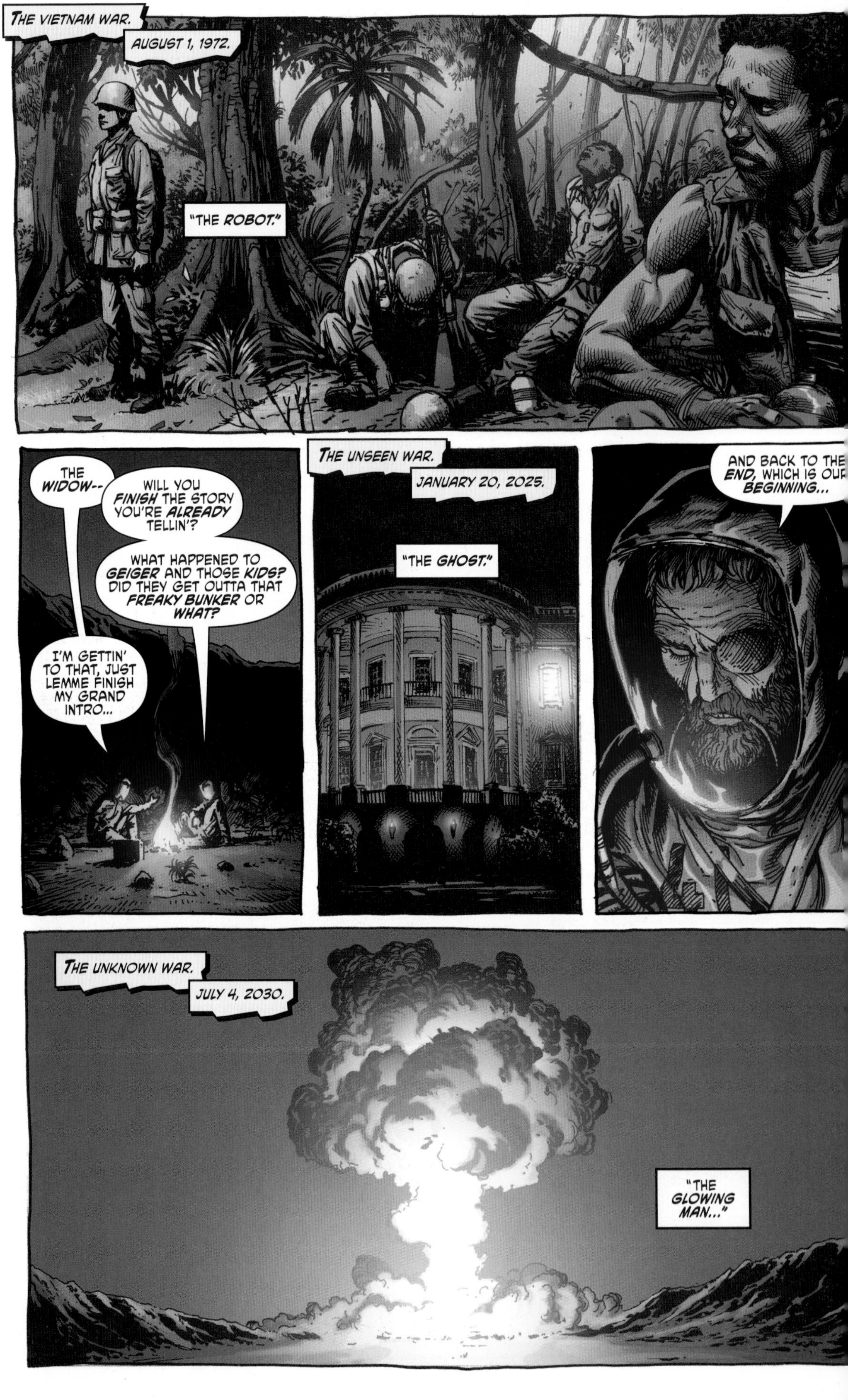
THE VIETNAM WAR.
AUGUST 1, 1972.
"THE ROBOT."
THE WIDOW--
WILL YOU FINISH THE STORY YOU'RE ALREADY TELLIN'?
WHAT HAPPENED TO GEIGER AND THOSE KIDS? DID THEY GET OUTTA THAT FREAKY BUNKER OR WHAT?
I'M GETTIN' TO THAT, JUST LEMME FINISH MY GRAND INTRO...
THE UNSEEN WAR.
JANUARY 20, 2025.
"THE GHOST."
AND BACK TO THE END, WHICH IS OUR BEGINNING...
THE UNKNOWN WAR.
JULY 4, 2030.
"THE GLOWING MAN..."

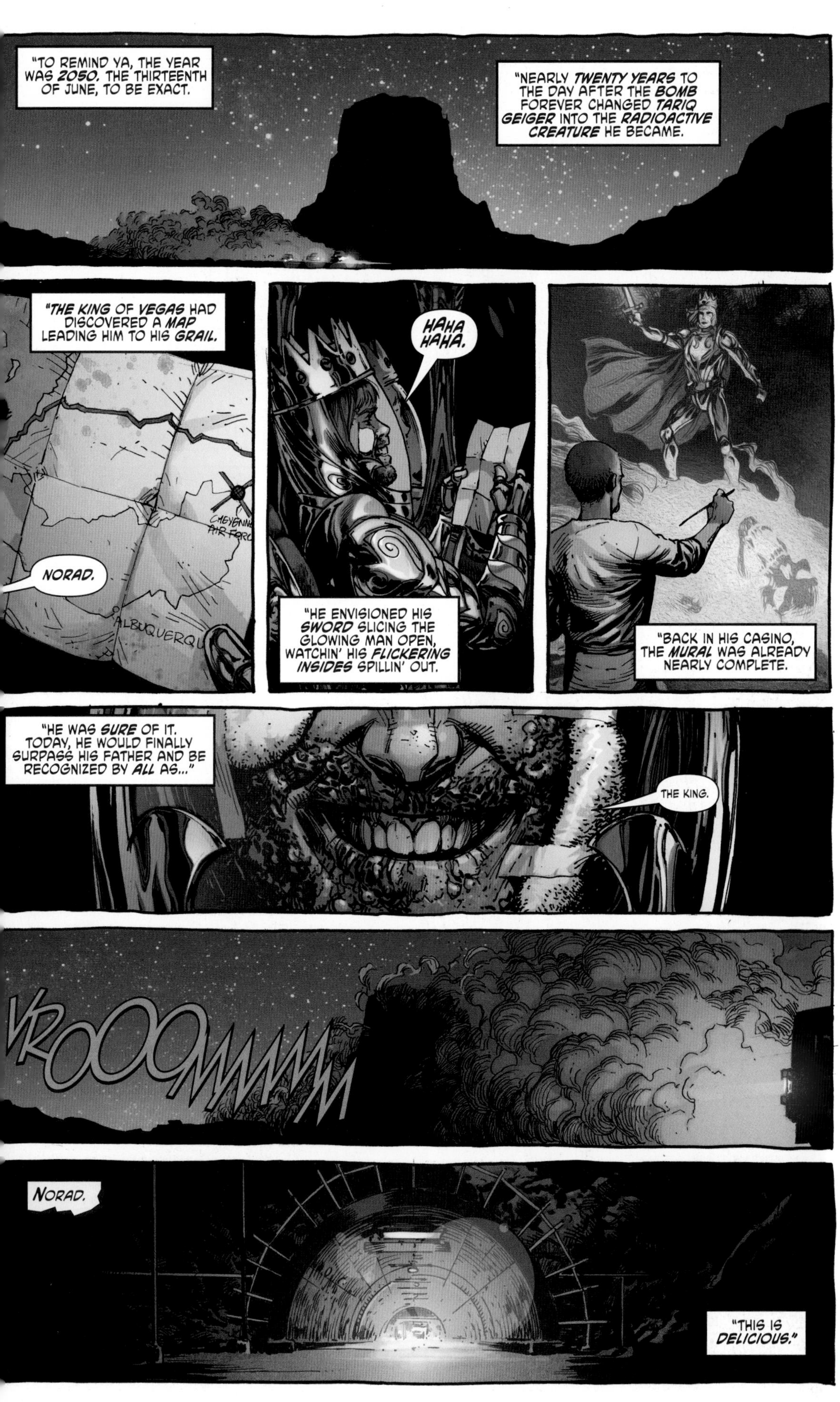
"TO REMIND YA, THE YEAR WAS 2050. THE THIRTEENTH OF JUNE, TO BE EXACT.
"NEARLY TWENTY YEARS TO THE DAY AFTER THE BOMB FOREVER CHANGED TARIQ GEIGER INTO THE RADIOACTIVE CREATURE HE BECAME.
"THE KING OF VEGAS HAD DISCOVERED A MAP LEADING HIM TO HIS GRAIL.
NORAD.
HAHA HAHA.
"HE ENVISIONED HIS SWORD SLICING THE GLOWING MAN OPEN, WATCHIN' HIS FLICKERING INSIDES SPILLIN' OUT.
"BACK IN HIS CASINO, THE MURAL WAS ALREADY NEARLY COMPLETE.
"HE WAS SURE OF IT. TODAY, HE WOULD FINALLY SURPASS HIS FATHER AND BE RECOGNIZED BY ALL AS..."
THE KING.
VROOOMMMM
NORAD.
"THIS IS DELICIOUS."

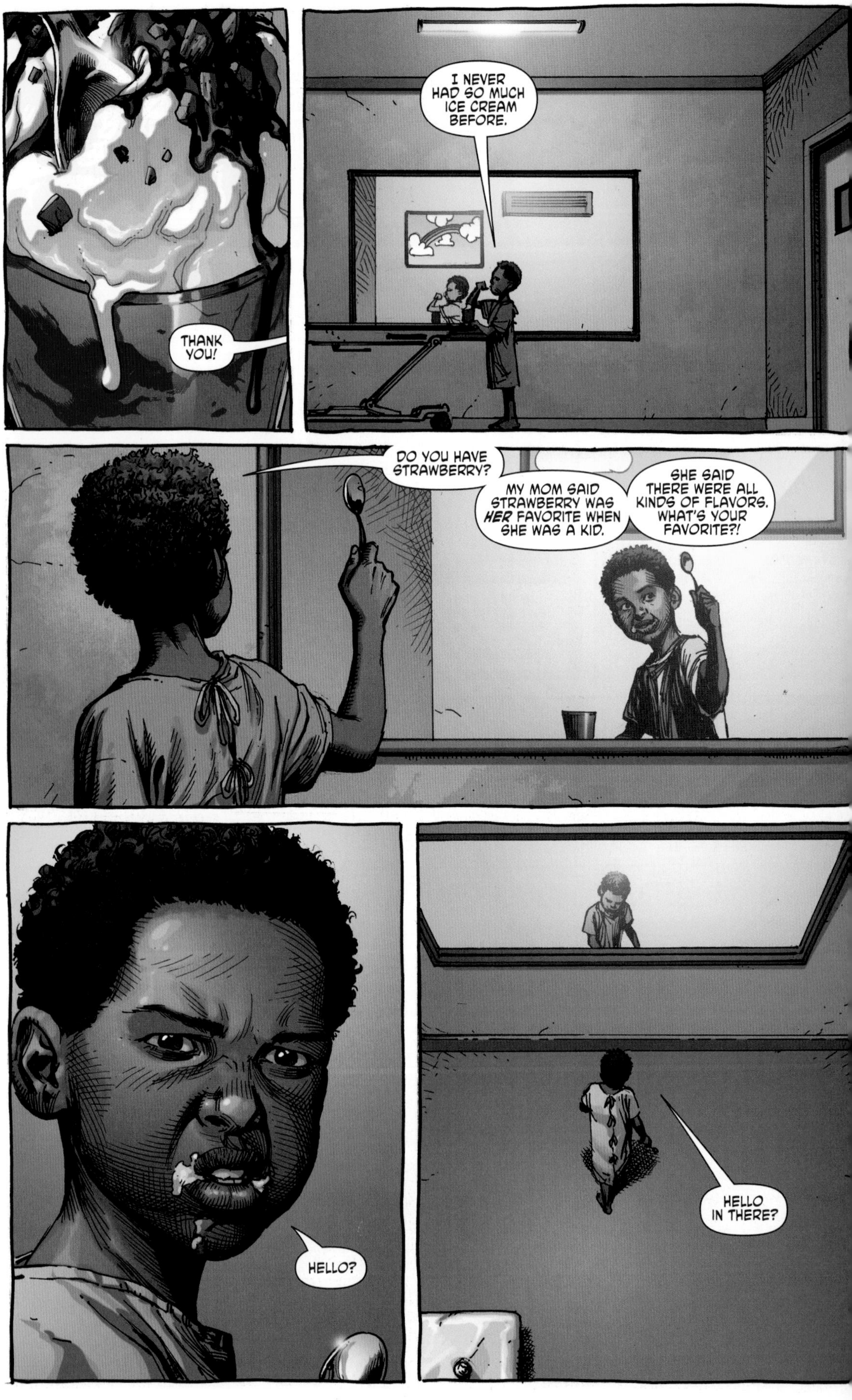
THANK YOU!
I NEVER HAD SO MUCH ICE CREAM BEFORE.
DO YOU HAVE STRAWBERRY?
MY MOM SAID STRAWBERRY WAS *HER* FAVORITE WHEN SHE WAS A KID.
SHE SAID THERE WERE ALL KINDS OF FLAVORS. WHAT'S YOUR FAVORITE?!
HELLO?
HELLO IN THERE?

WHAM!

AHH!

HENRY?!

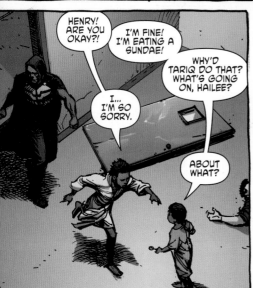

HENRY! ARE YOU OKAY?!

I'M FINE! I'M EATING A SUNDAE!

WHY'D TARIQ DO THAT? WHAT'S GOING ON, HAILEE?

I.... I'M SO SORRY.

ABOUT?

YOU'VE BEEN TIRED AND I'M ALWAYS TELLING YOU TO STOP COMPLAINING, BUT I... I THOUGHT YOU WERE JUST BEING A KID, I...

I DIDN'T KNOW.

KNOW WHAT?

YOU'RE... SICK, HENRY. YOU'RE SICK AND THESE PEOPLE... THEY WON'T LET THE SICK STAY HERE.

I DUH-DON'T UNDERSTAND.

I DON'T WANT TO BE SUH-SICK.

HENRY?

I WAS SICK TOO.

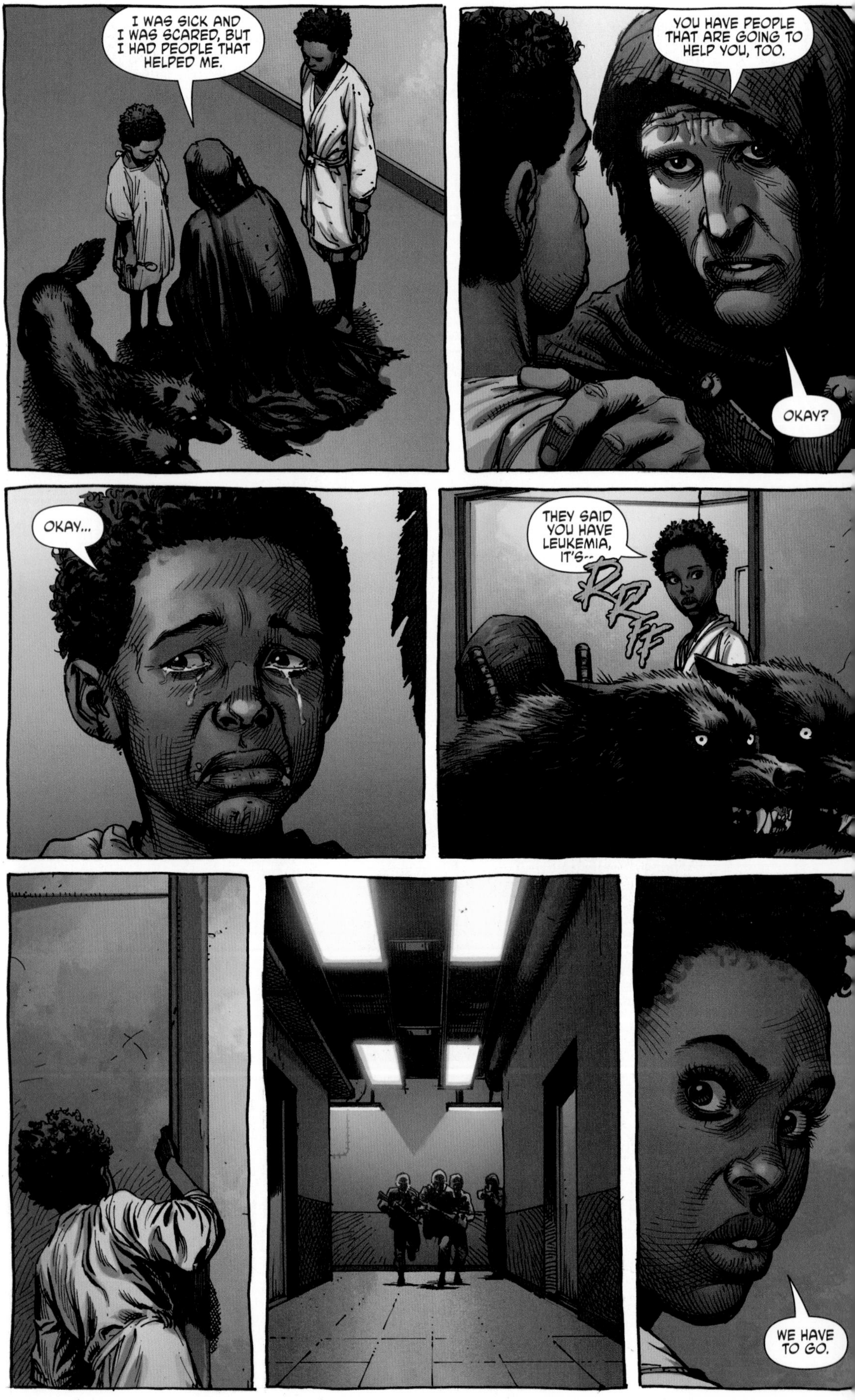
I WAS SICK AND I WAS SCARED, BUT I HAD PEOPLE THAT HELPED ME.
YOU HAVE PEOPLE THAT ARE GOING TO HELP YOU, TOO.
OKAY?
OKAY...
THEY SAID YOU HAVE LEUKEMIA, IT'S--
RRFF
WE HAVE TO GO.

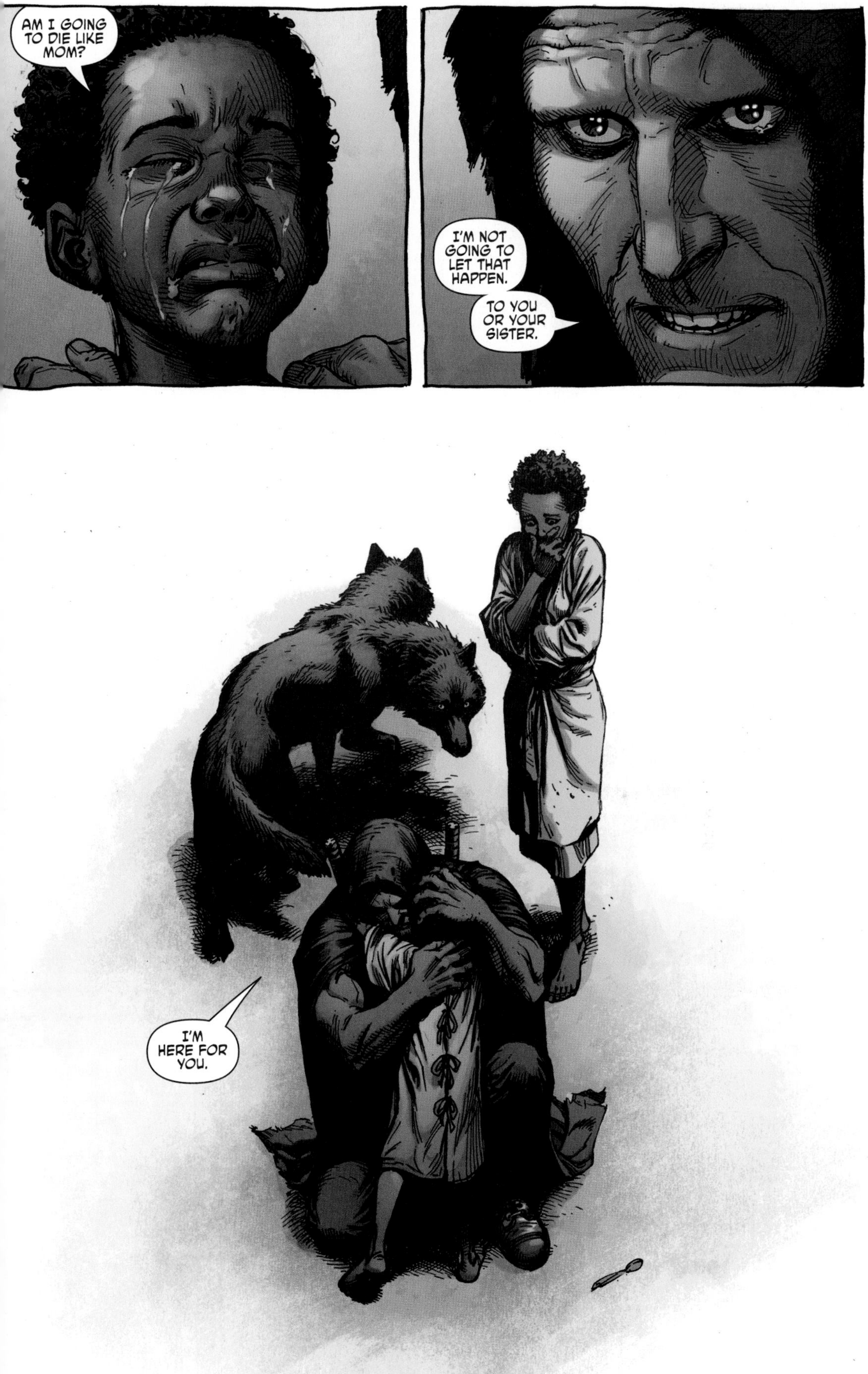
AM I GOING TO DIE LIKE MOM?
I'M NOT GOING TO LET THAT HAPPEN.
TO YOU OR YOUR SISTER.
I'M HERE FOR YOU.

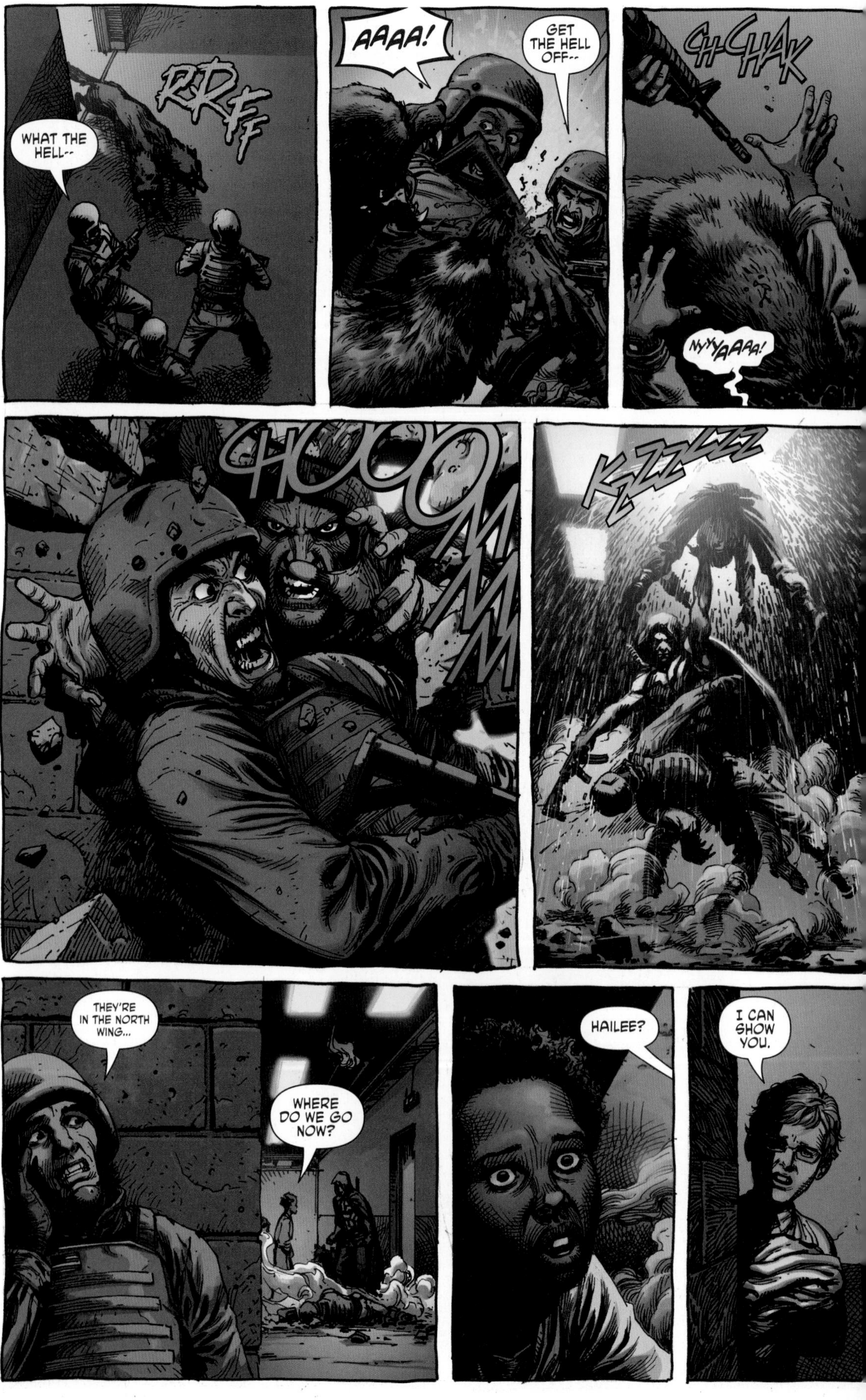
RRFF
WHAT THE HELL--
AAAA!
GET THE HELL OFF--
CH-CHAK
NYYYAAAA!
CHOOOMMM
KZZZZZZ
THEY'RE IN THE NORTH WING...
WHERE DO WE GO NOW?
HAILEE?
I CAN SHOW YOU.

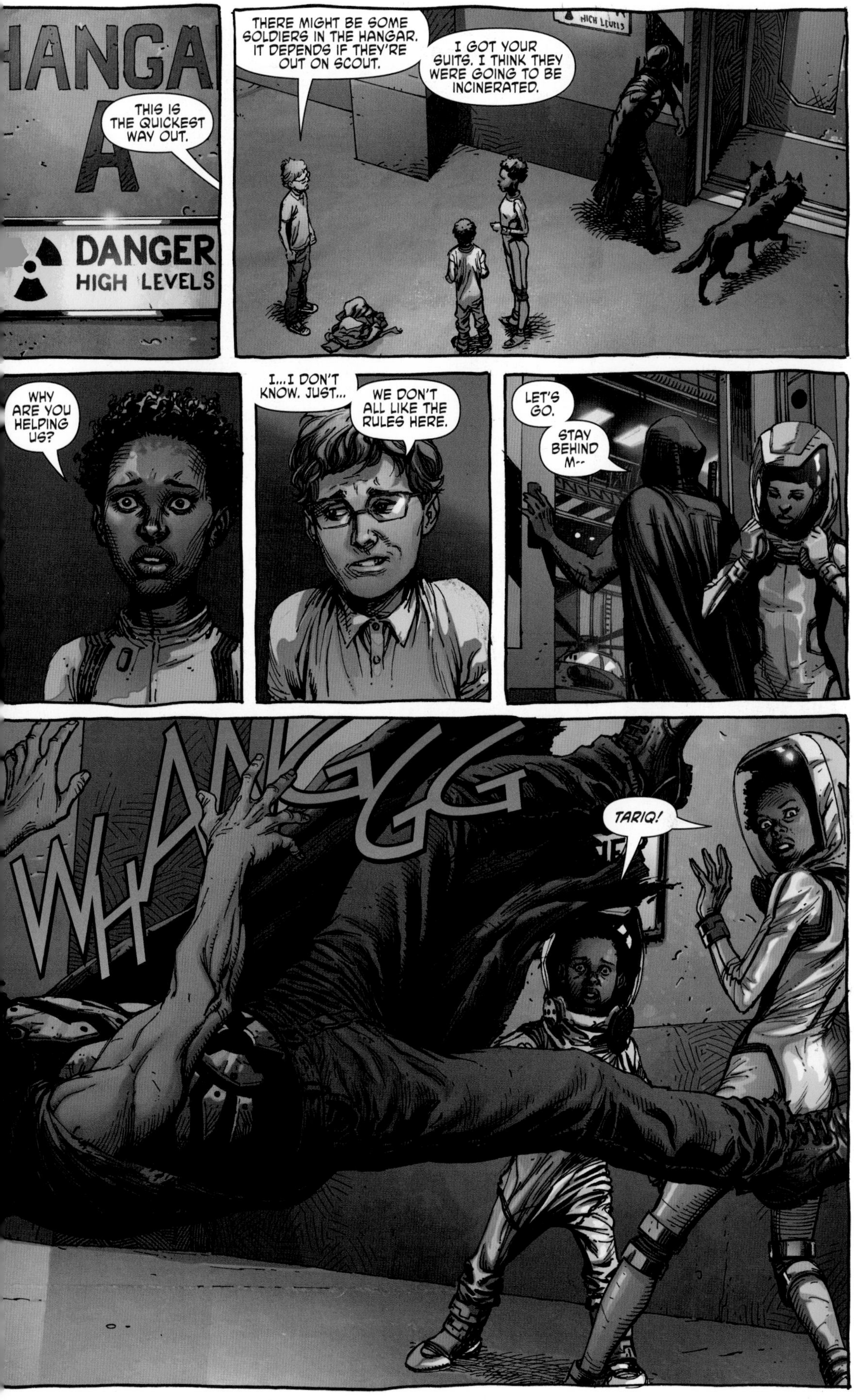

HANGA
A
DANGER
HIGH LEVELS
THIS IS THE QUICKEST WAY OUT.
THERE MIGHT BE SOME SOLDIERS IN THE HANGAR. IT DEPENDS IF THEY'RE OUT ON SCOUT.
I GOT YOUR SUITS. I THINK THEY WERE GOING TO BE INCINERATED.
WHY ARE YOU HELPING US?
I...I DON'T KNOW. JUST...
WE DON'T ALL LIKE THE RULES HERE.
LET'S GO.
STAY BEHIND M--
WHANGG
TARIQ!

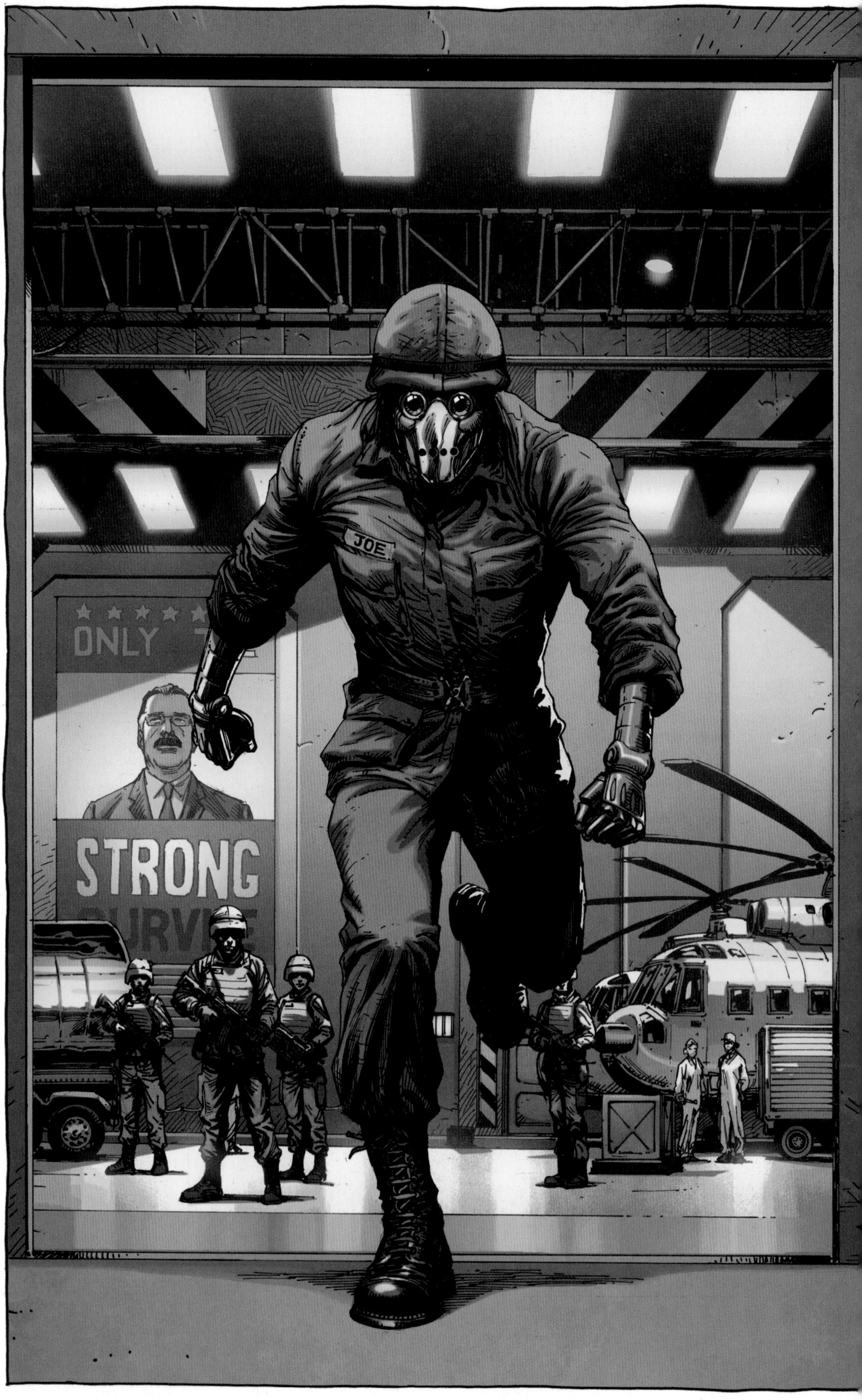
JOE
ONLY
STRONG

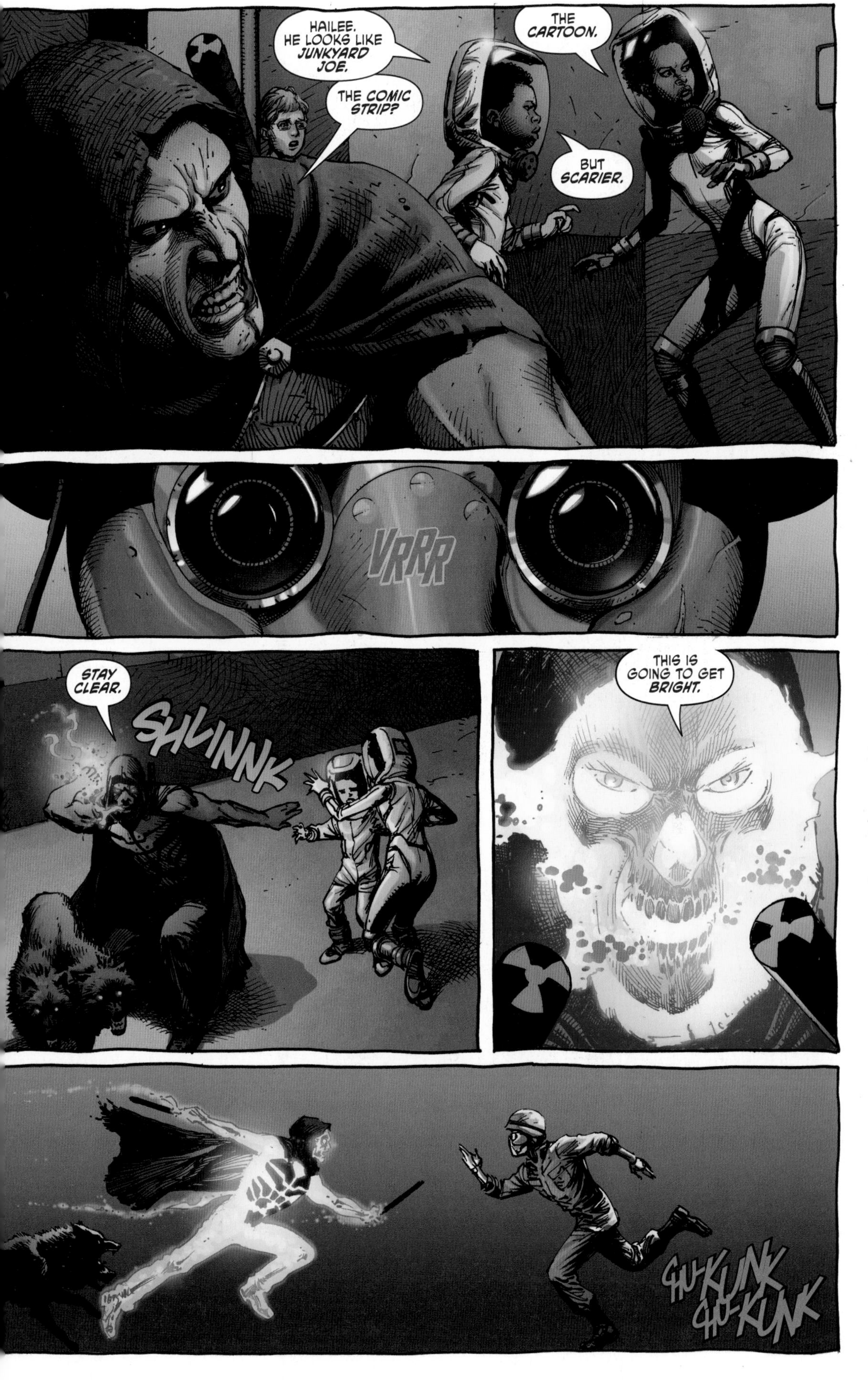
HAILEE. HE LOOKS LIKE JUNKYARD JOE.
THE COMIC STRIP?
THE CARTOON.
BUT SCARIER.
VRRR
STAY CLEAR.
SHUNNK
THIS IS GOING TO GET BRIGHT.
CHU-KUNK CHU-KUNK

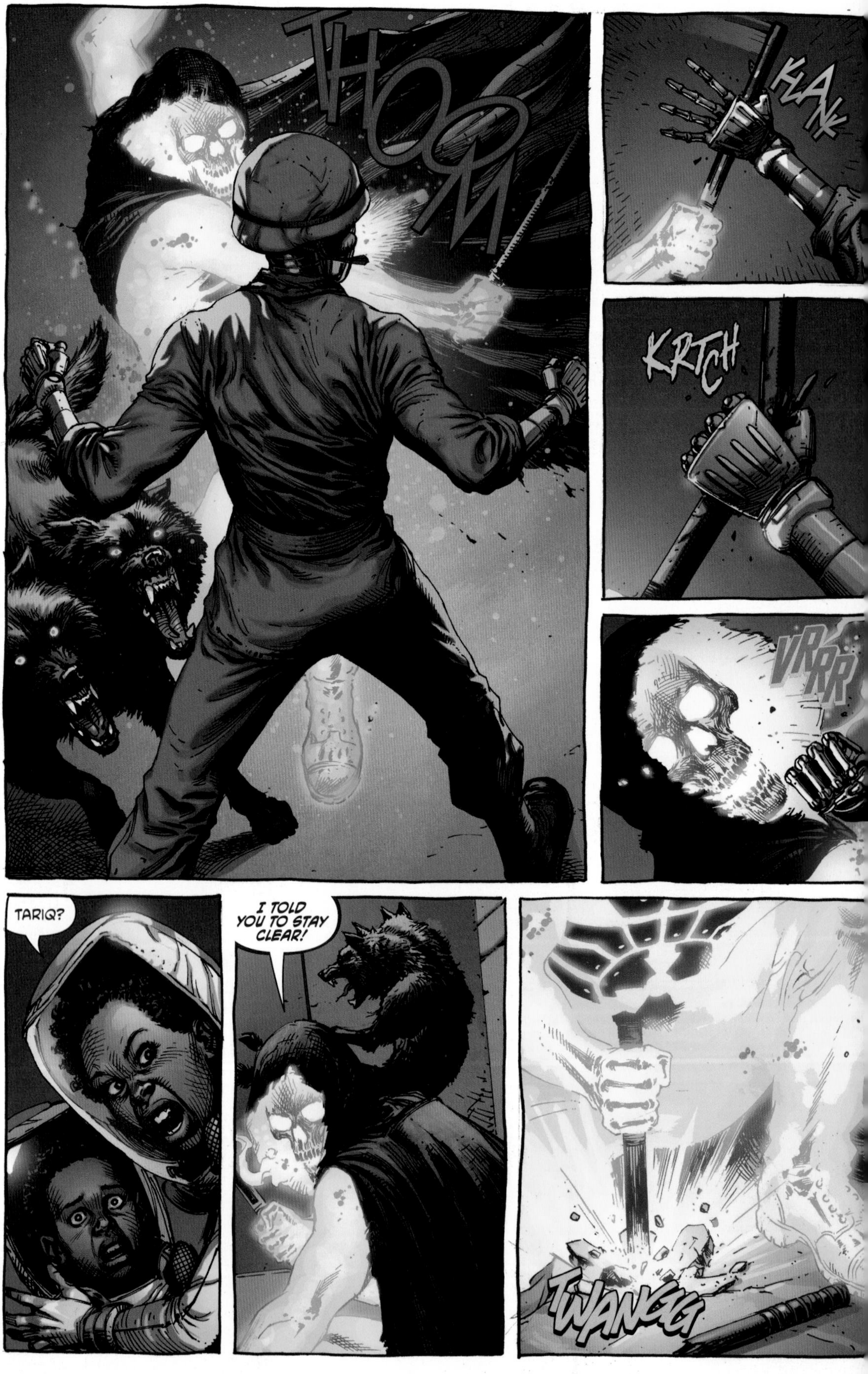
THOOM
KLANK
KRTCH
VRRR
TARIQ?
I TOLD YOU TO STAY CLEAR!
TWANGG

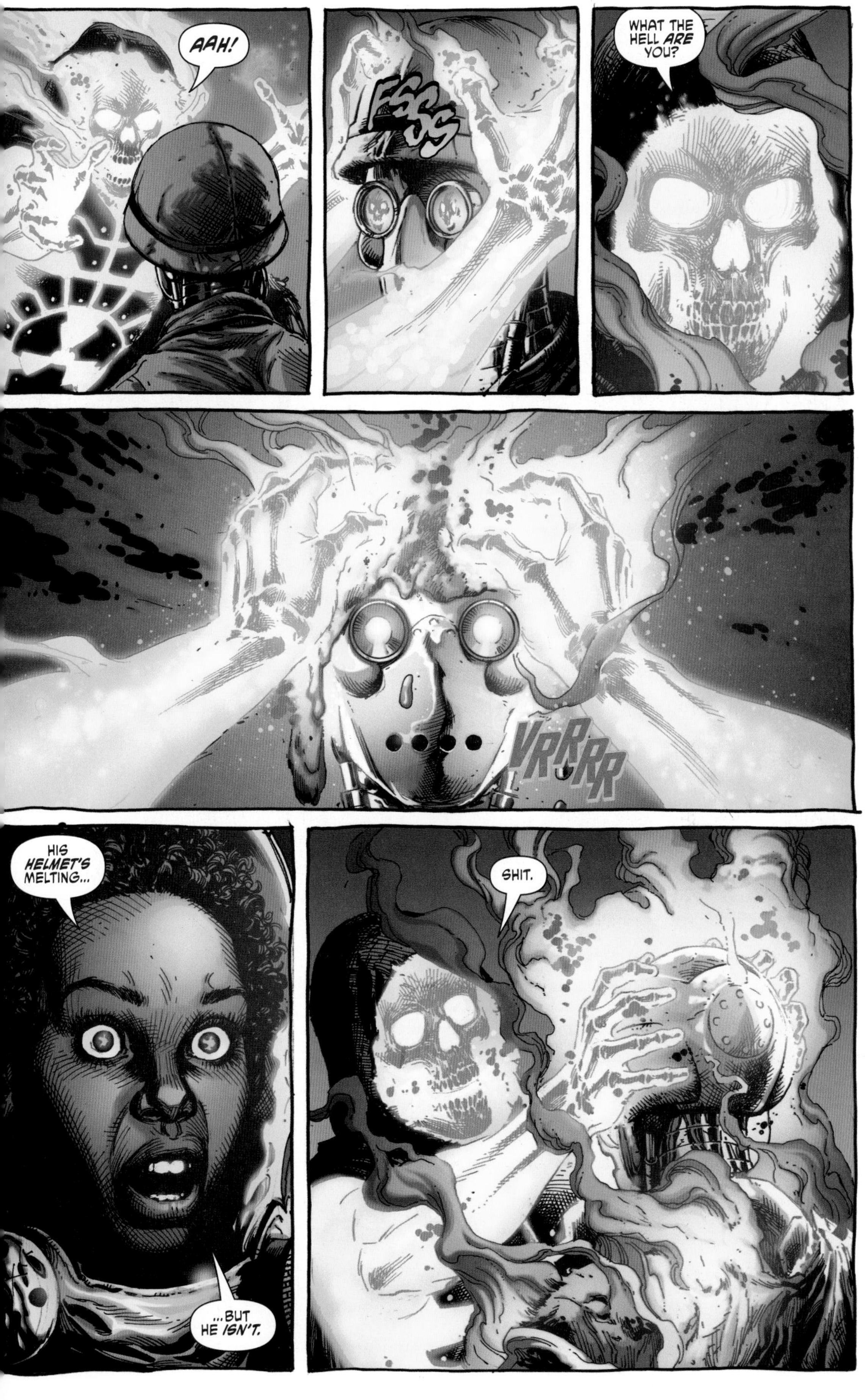
AAH!
FSSSS
WHAT THE HELL ARE YOU?
VRRRR
HIS HELMET'S MELTING...
...BUT HE ISN'T.
SHIT.

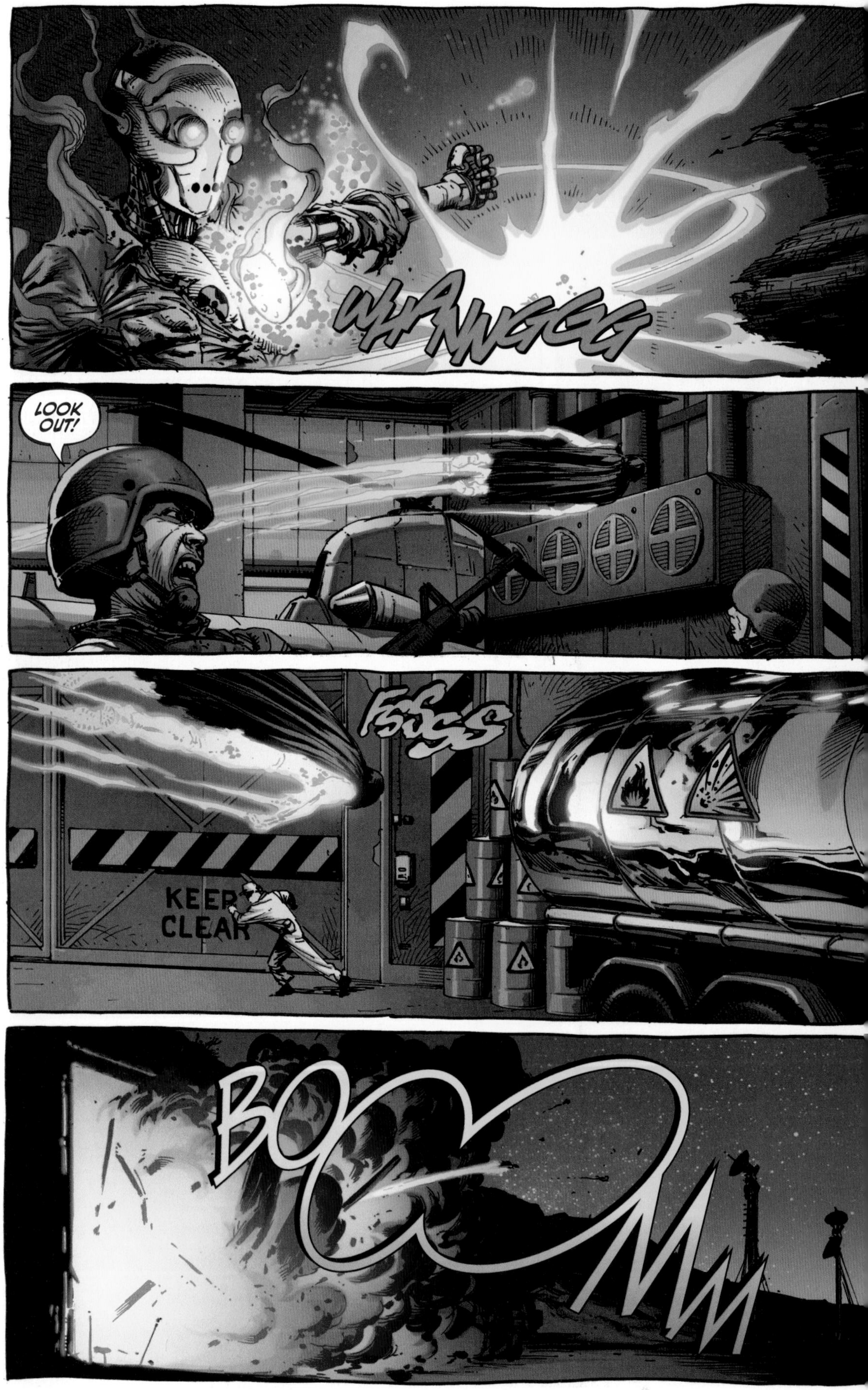
WHANGGG
LOOK OUT!
FSSSS
KEEP CLEAR
BOOOM

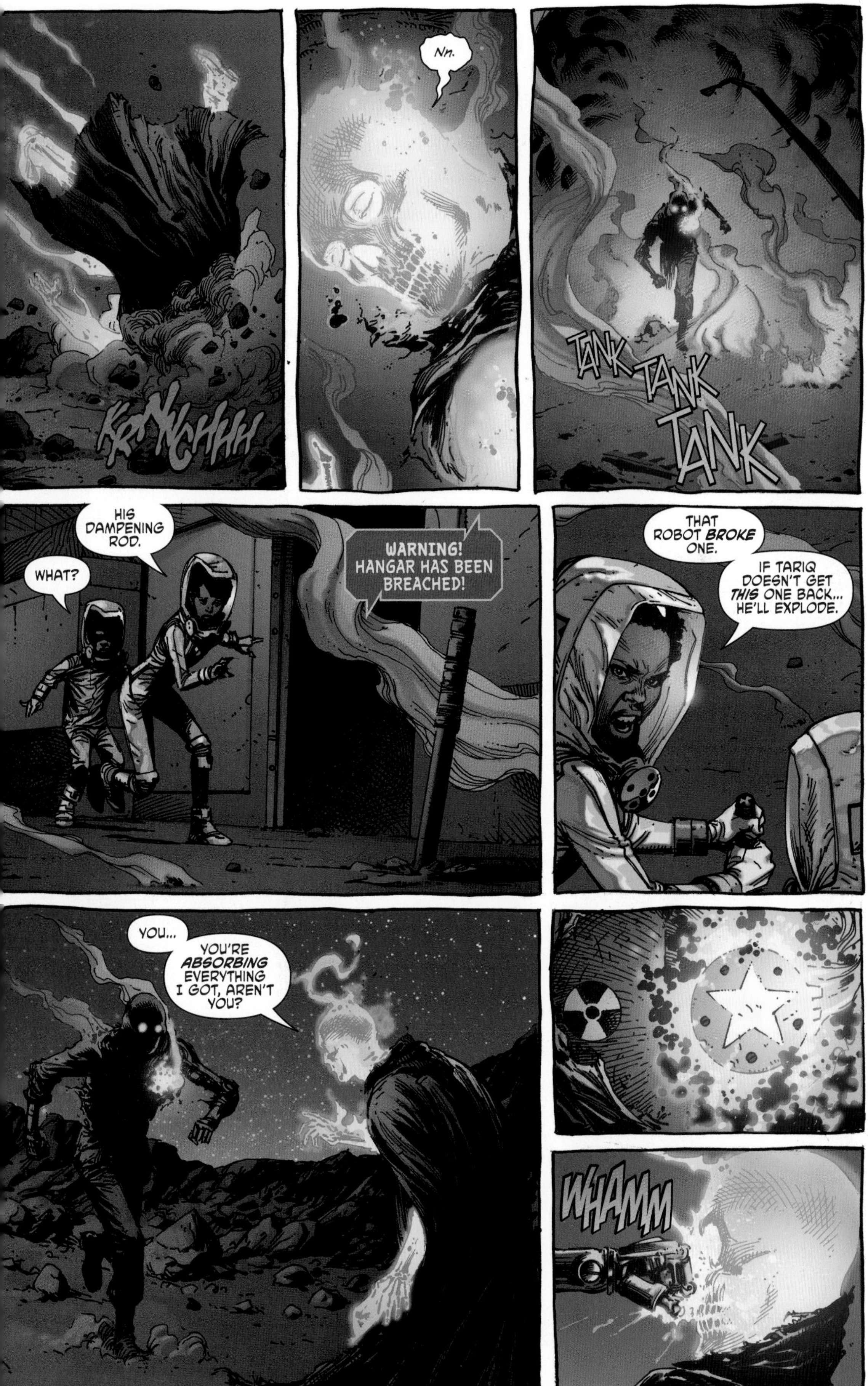
KRNNCHHH
Nn.
TANK TANK TANK
HIS DAMPENING ROD.
WHAT?
WARNING! HANGAR HAS BEEN BREACHED!
THAT ROBOT BROKE ONE.
IF TARIQ DOESN'T GET THIS ONE BACK... HE'LL EXPLODE.
YOU...
YOU'RE ABSORBING EVERYTHING I GOT, AREN'T YOU?
WHAMM

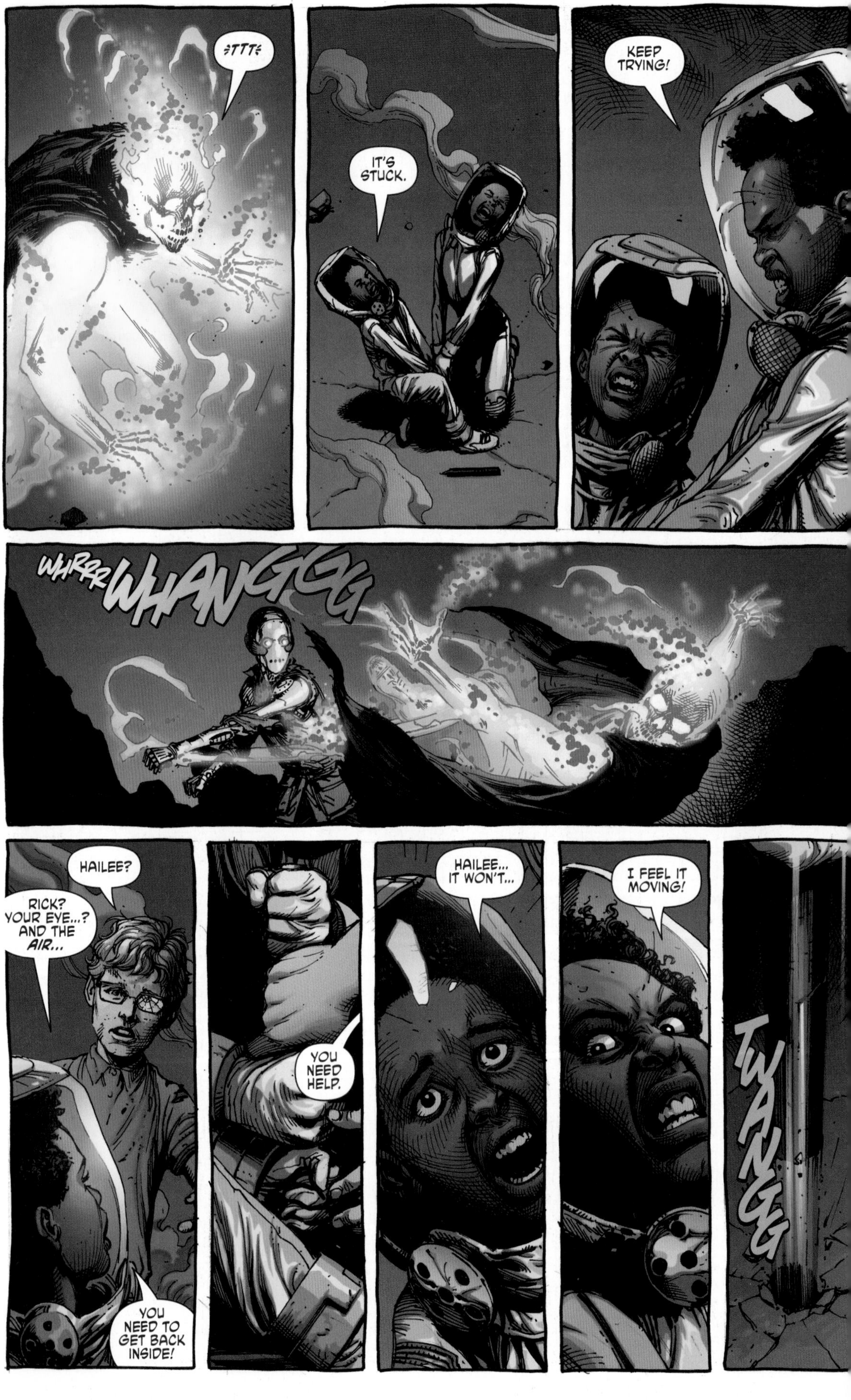
TTT
IT'S STUCK.
KEEP TRYING!
WHIRRR WHANGGG
HAILEE?
RICK? YOUR EYE...? AND THE AIR...
YOU NEED TO GET BACK INSIDE!
YOU NEED HELP.
HAILEE... IT WON'T...
I FEEL IT MOVING!
TWANGG

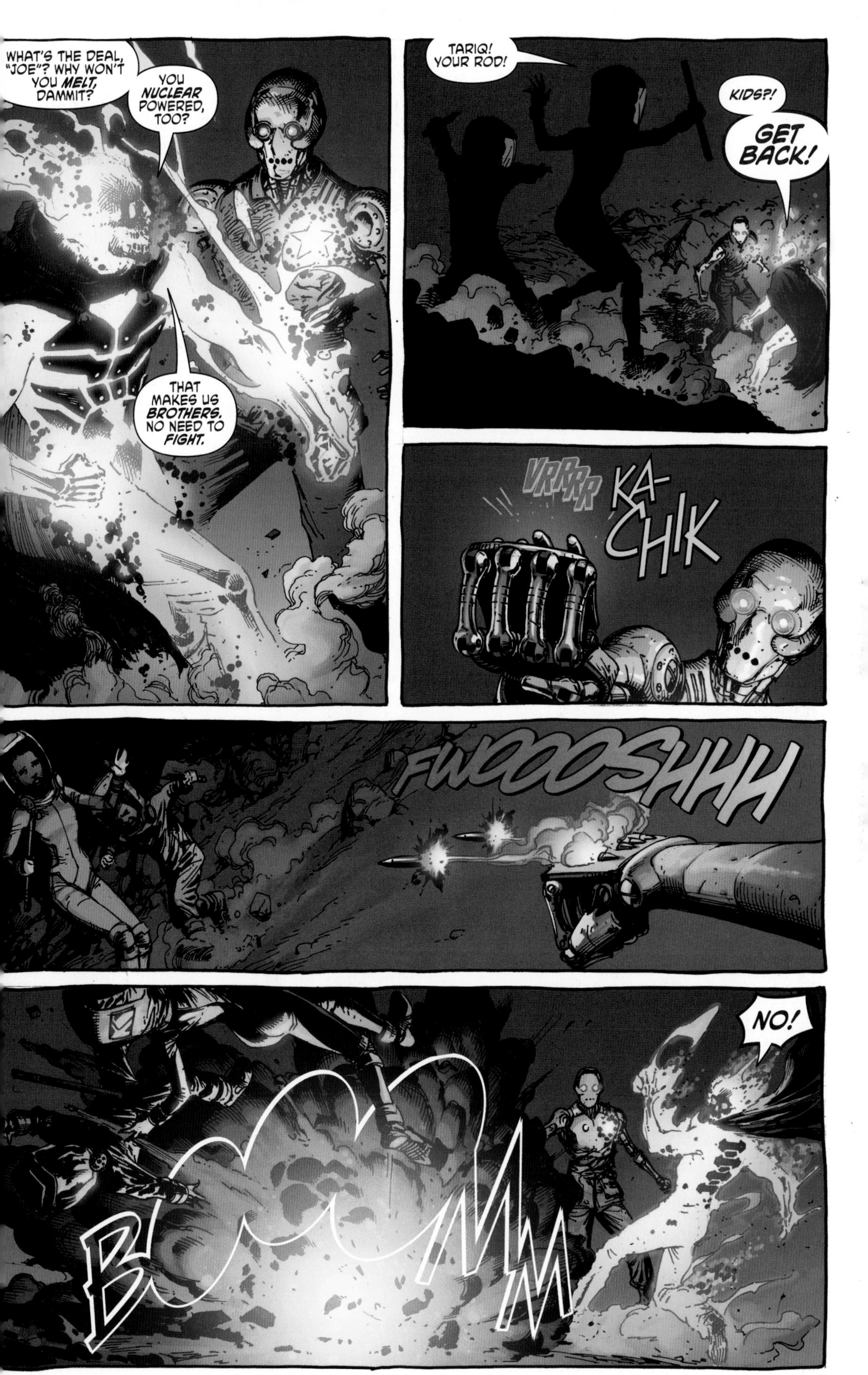
WHAT'S THE DEAL, "JOE"? WHY WON'T YOU MELT, DAMMIT?
YOU NUCLEAR POWERED, TOO?
THAT MAKES US BROTHERS. NO NEED TO FIGHT.
TARIQ! YOUR ROD!
KIDS?!
GET BACK!
VRRRR
KA-CHIK
FWOOOSHHH
NO!
BOOMMM

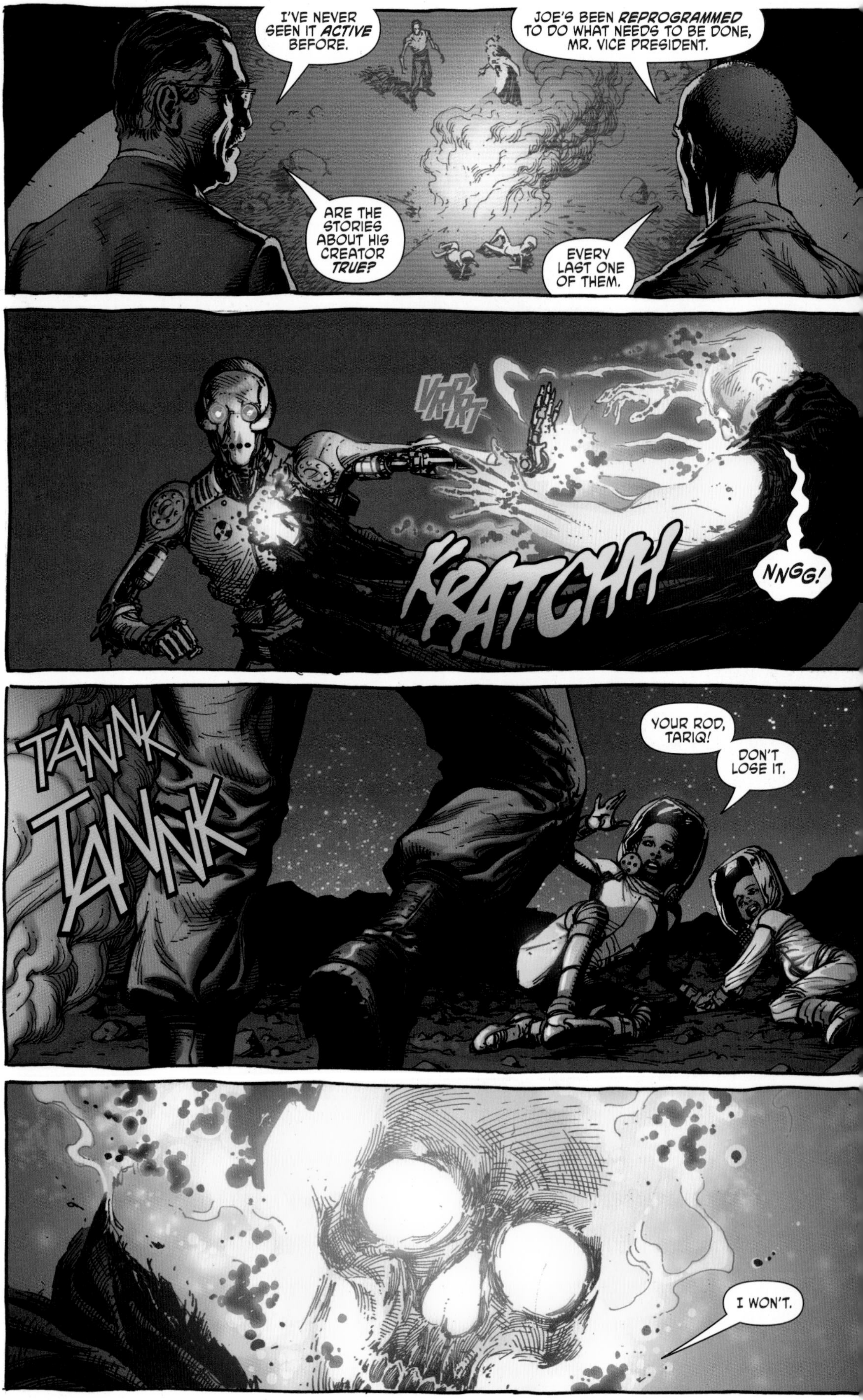
I'VE NEVER SEEN IT ACTIVE BEFORE.
JOE'S BEEN REPROGRAMMED TO DO WHAT NEEDS TO BE DONE, MR. VICE PRESIDENT.
ARE THE STORIES ABOUT HIS CREATOR TRUE?
EVERY LAST ONE OF THEM.
VRRRT
KRATCHH
NNGG!
TANNK
TANNK
YOUR ROD, TARIQ!
DON'T LOSE IT.
I WON'T.

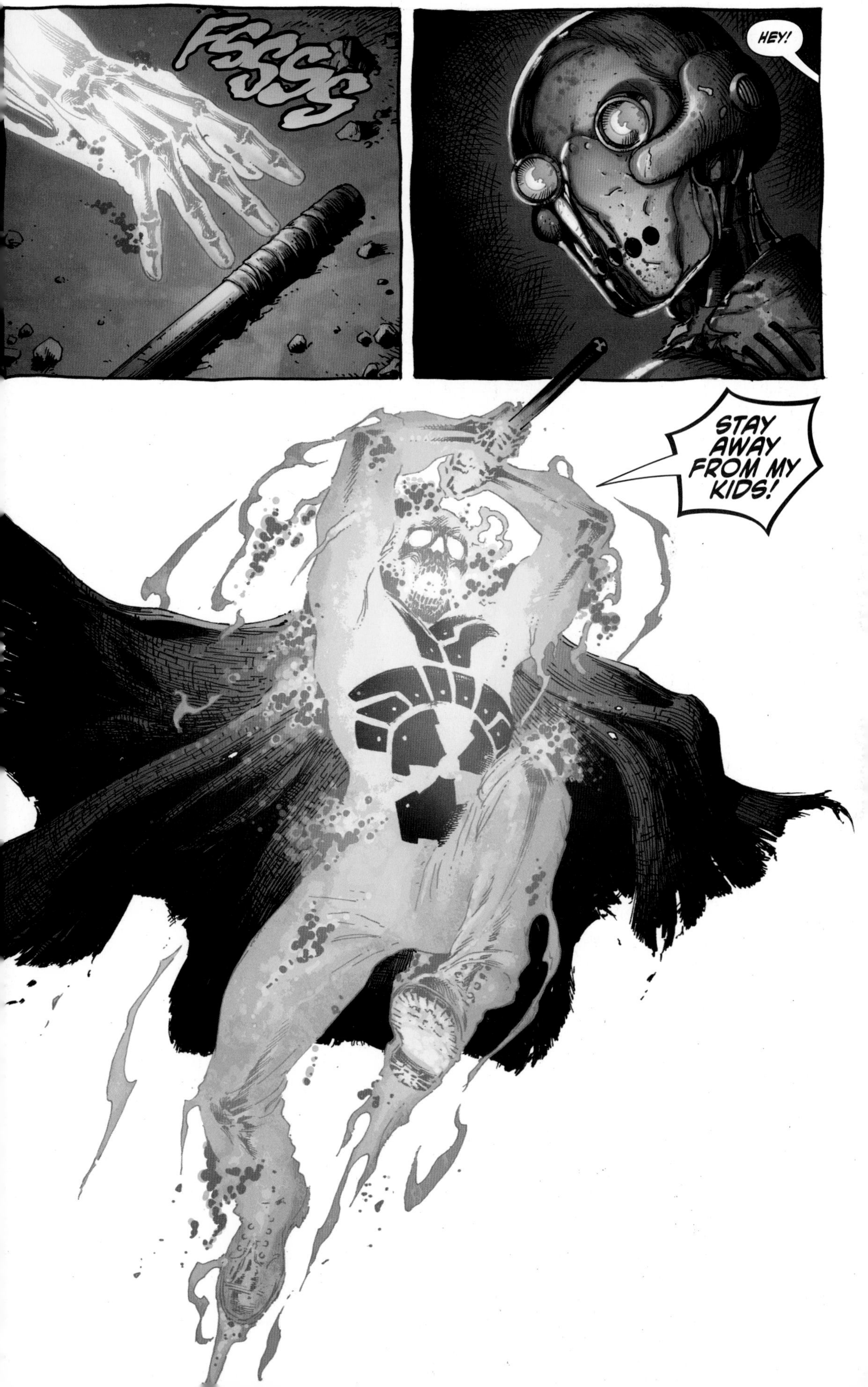
FSSSS
HEY!
STAY AWAY FROM MY KIDS!

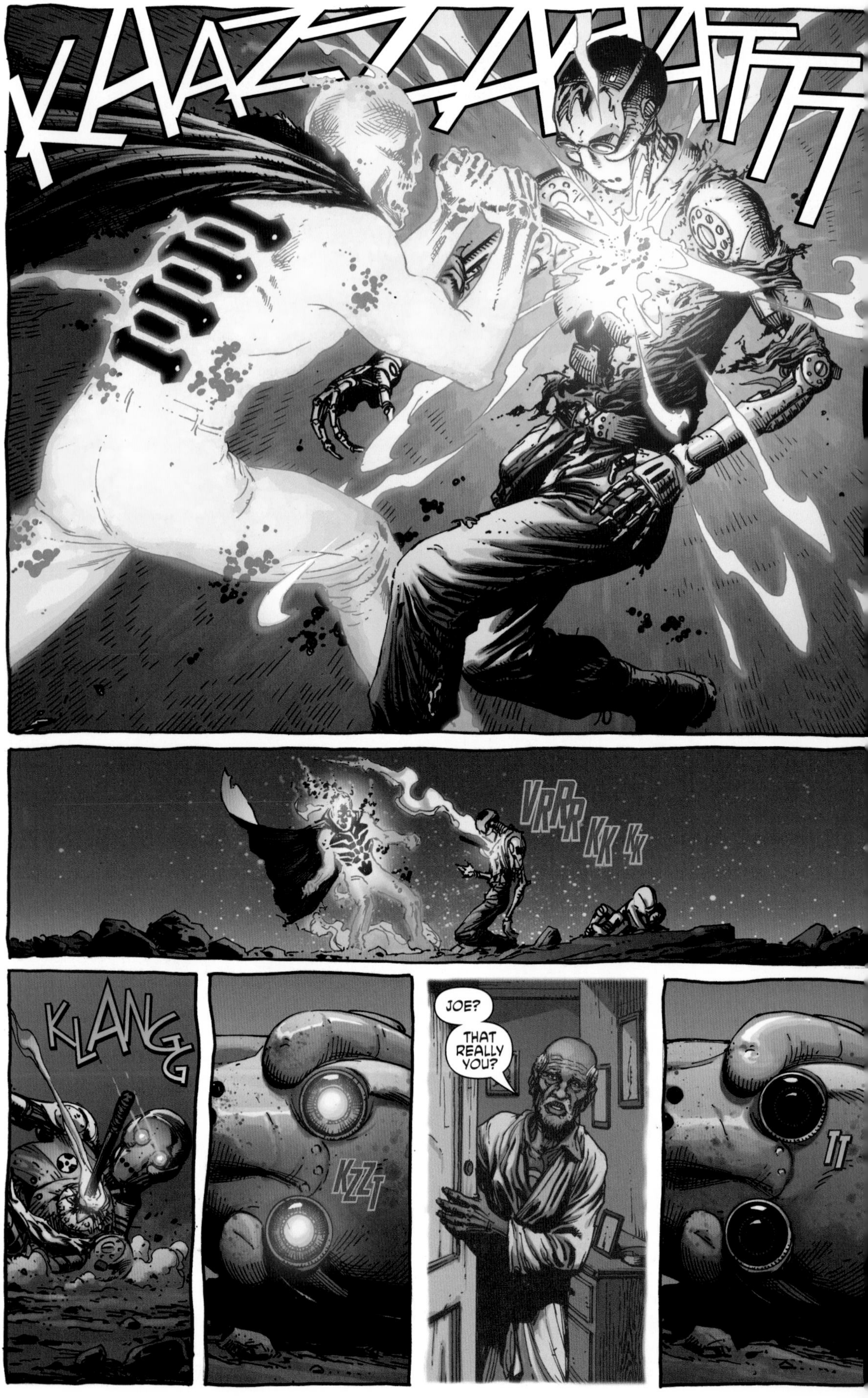
KHAZZAKATT
VRRRKKKK
KLANGG
KZZT
JOE?
THAT REALLY YOU?
TT

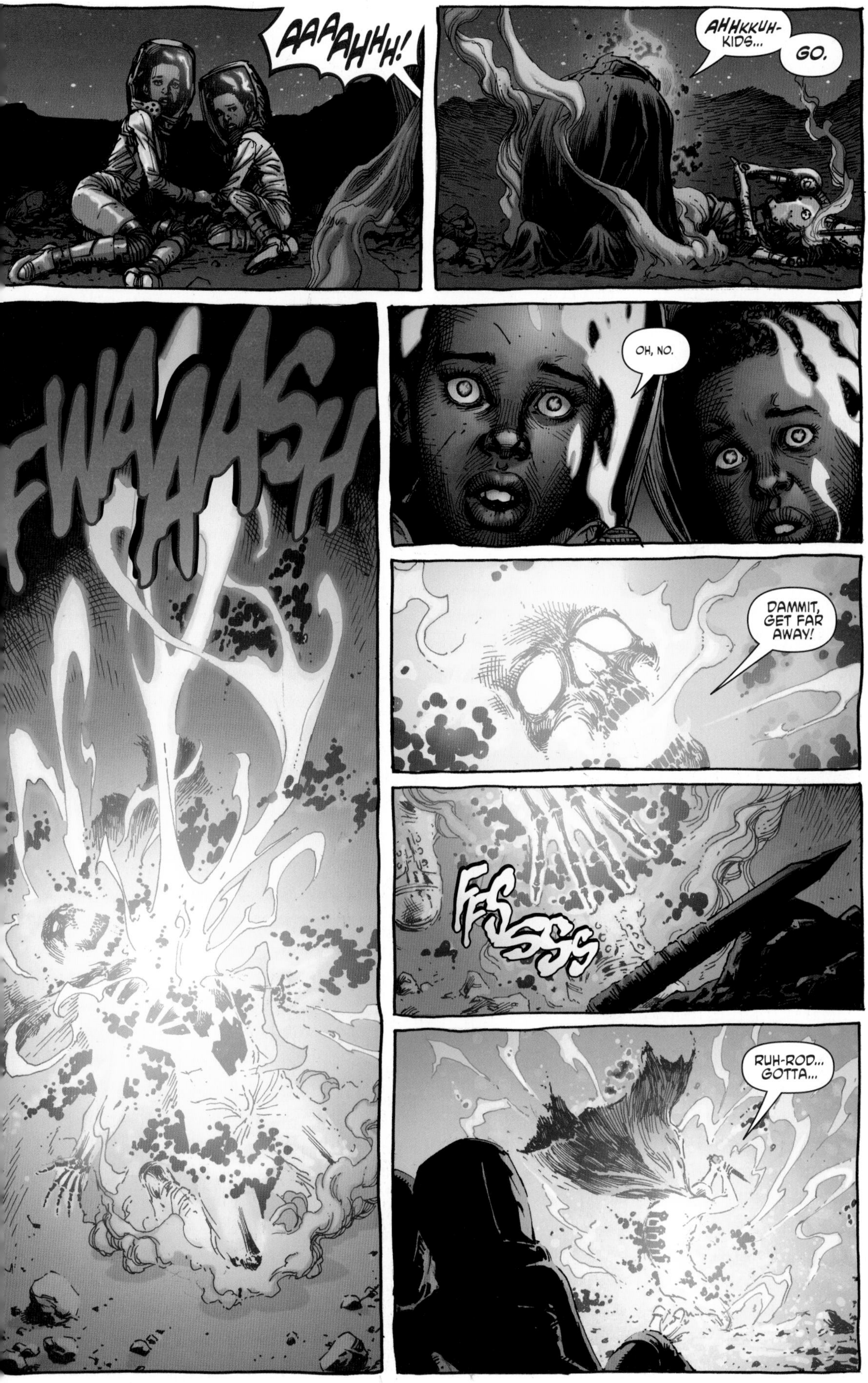
AAAAHHH!
AHHKKUH-KIDS...
GO.
FWAASH
OH, NO.
DAMMIT, GET FAR AWAY!
FFSSSS
RUH-ROD... GOTTA...

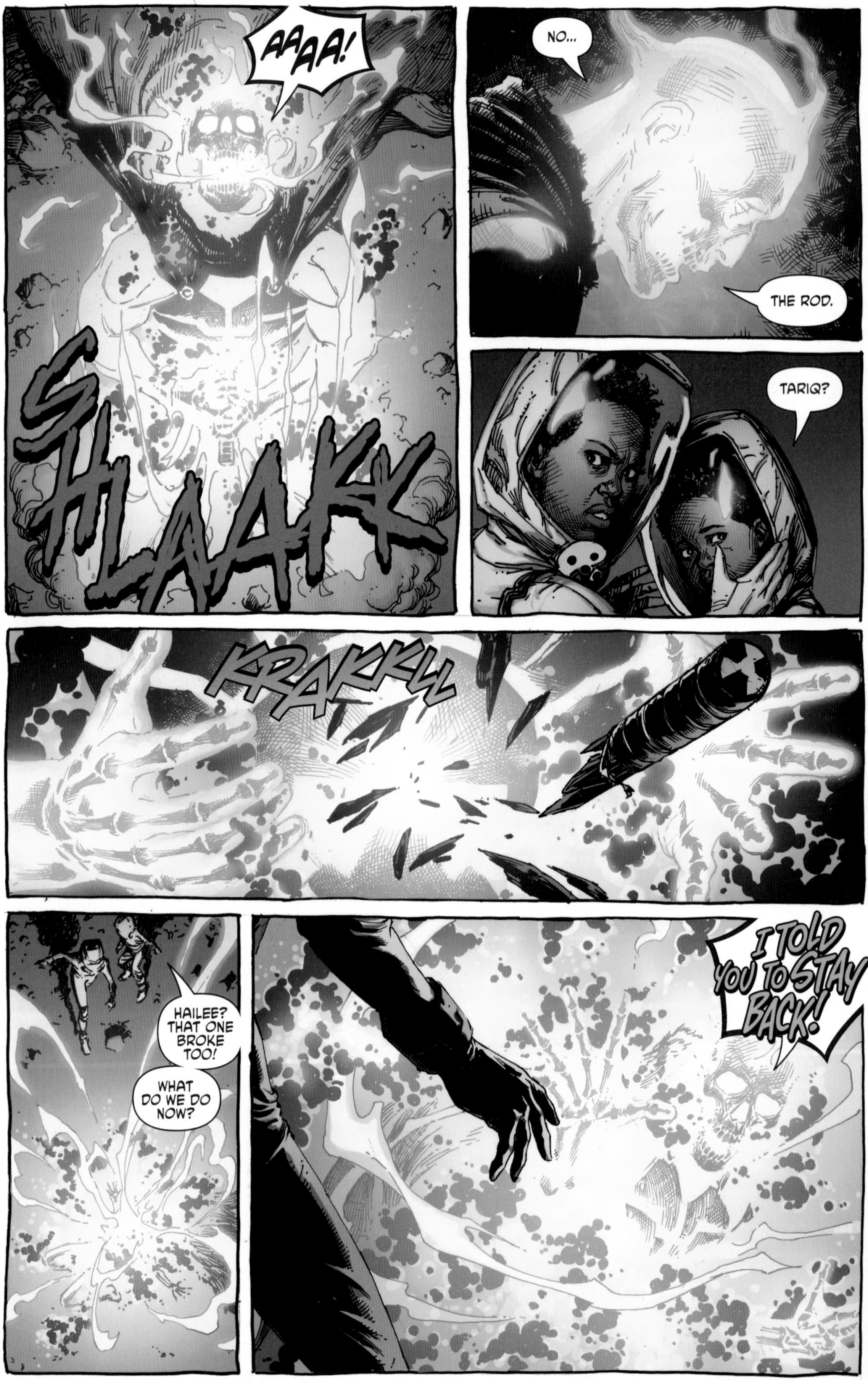
AAAAA!
SHLAAK
NO...
THE ROD.
TARIQ?
KRAKKL
HAILEE? THAT ONE BROKE TOO!
WHAT DO WE DO NOW?
I TOLD YOU TO STAY BACK!

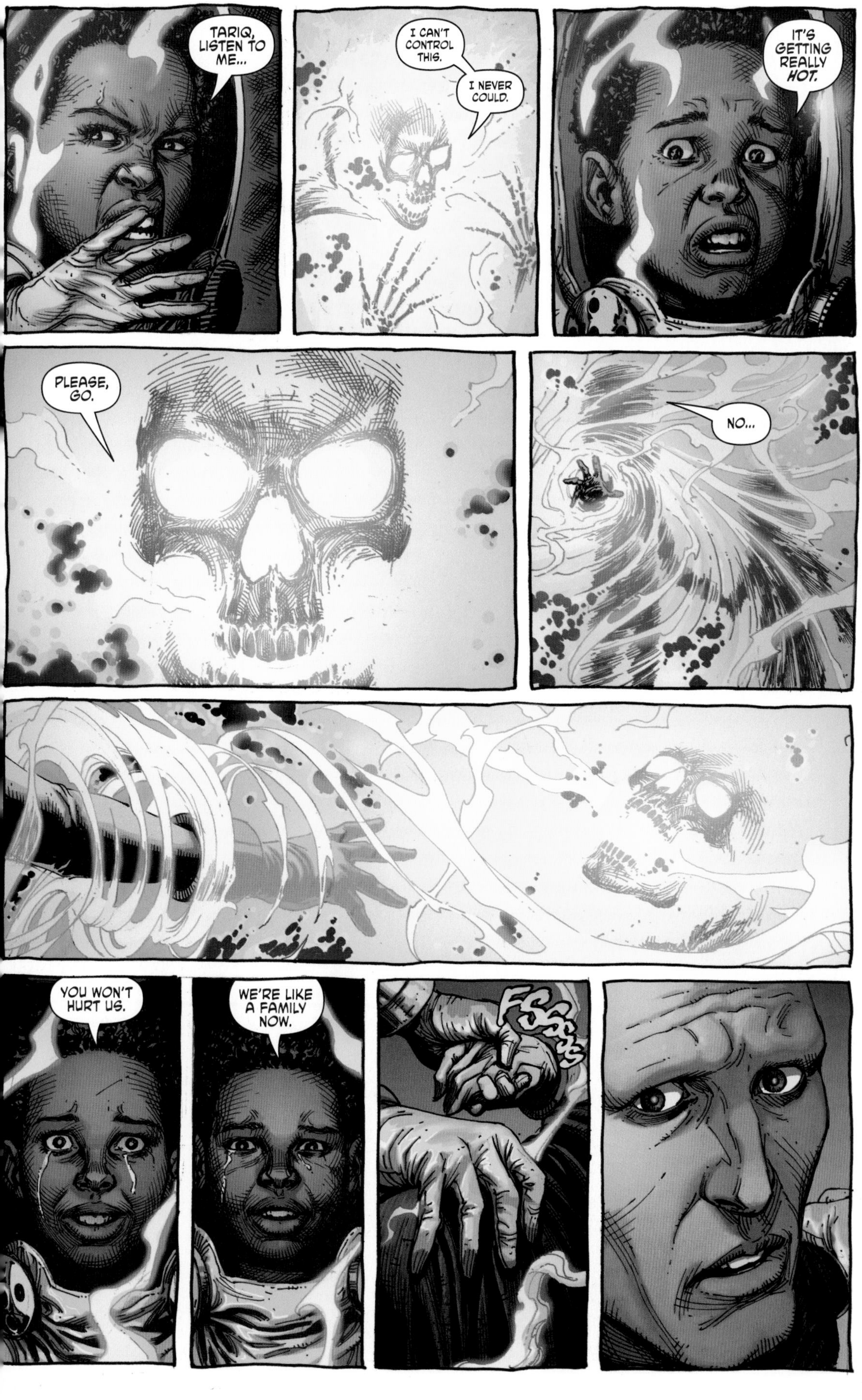
TARIQ, LISTEN TO ME...
I CAN'T CONTROL THIS.
I NEVER COULD.
IT'S GETTING REALLY *HOT.*
PLEASE, GO.
NO...
YOU WON'T HURT US.
WE'RE LIKE A FAMILY NOW.
FSSSS

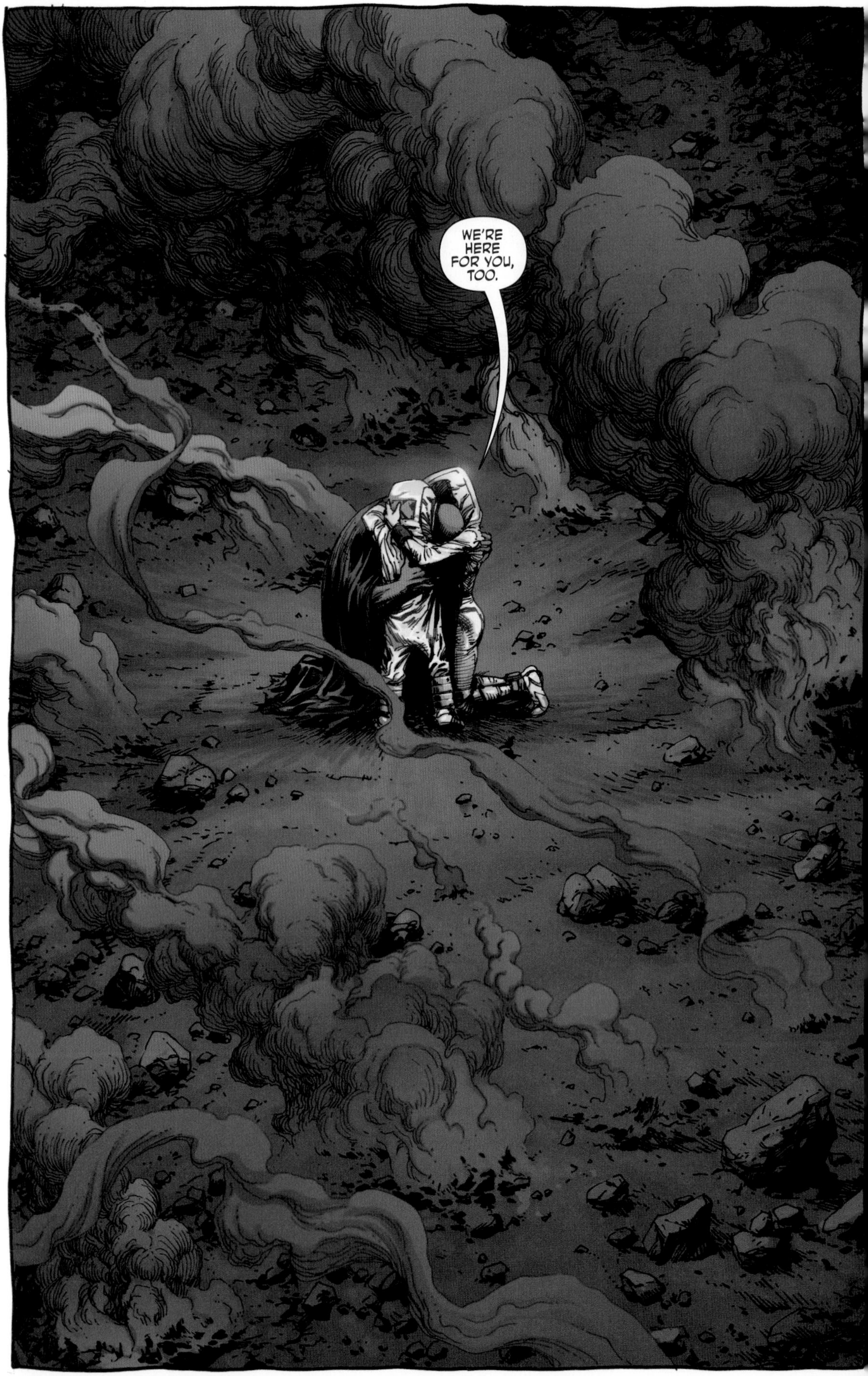
WE'RE HERE FOR YOU, TOO.

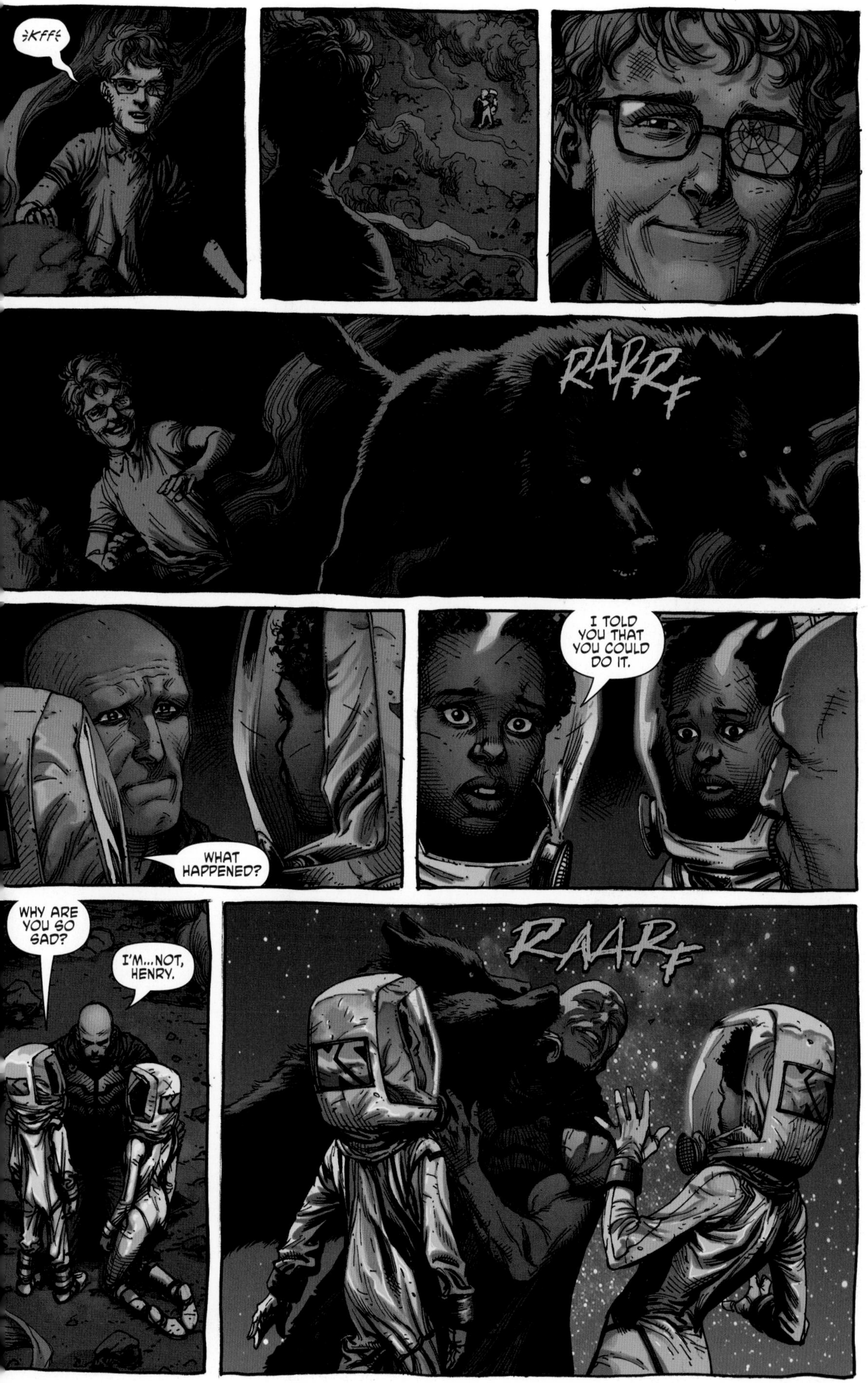
KFF
RARRF
WHAT HAPPENED?
I TOLD YOU THAT YOU COULD DO IT.
WHY ARE YOU SO SAD?
I'M...NOT, HENRY.
RAARF

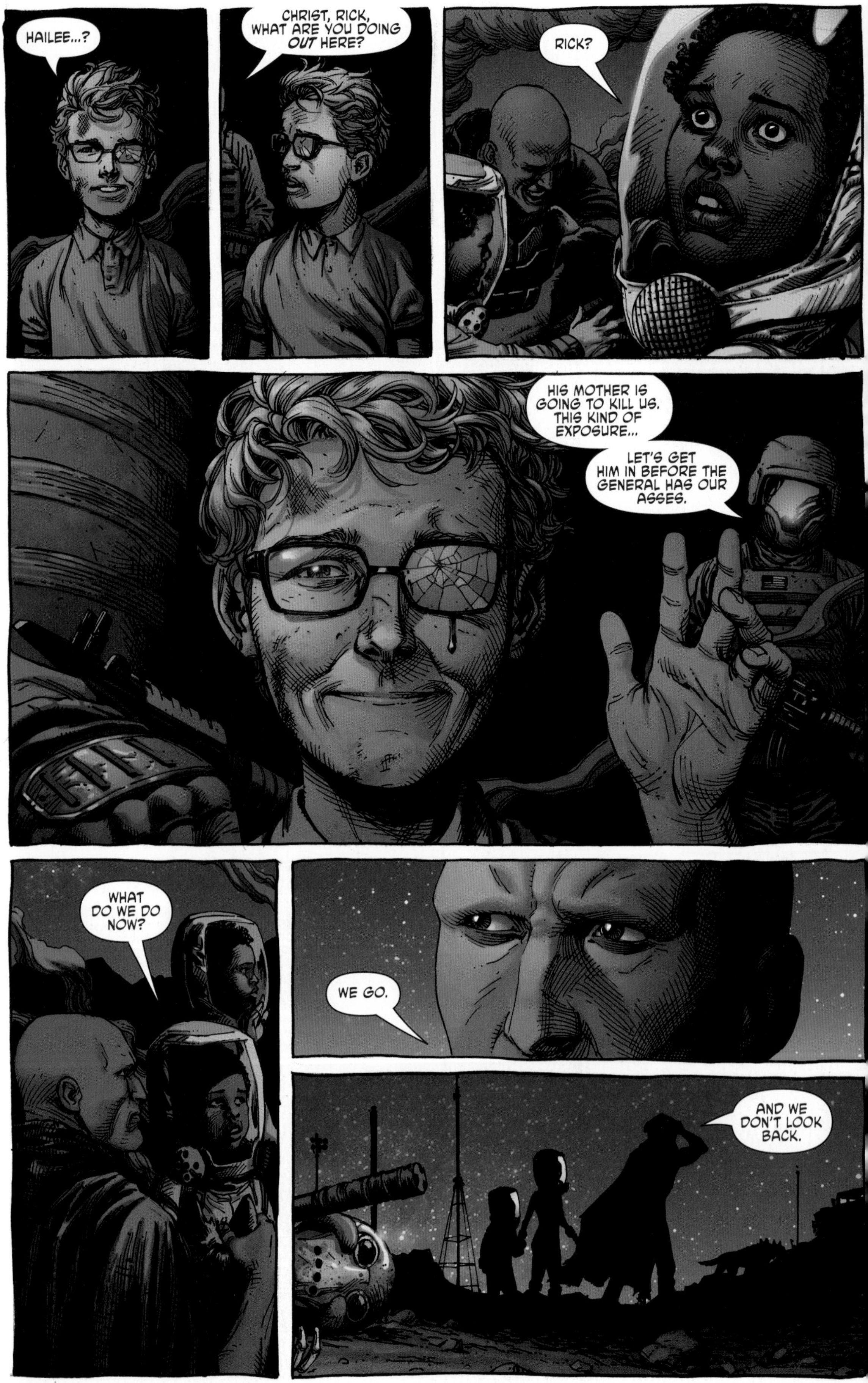
HAILEE...?
CHRIST, RICK, WHAT ARE YOU DOING *OUT* HERE?
RICK?
HIS MOTHER IS GOING TO KILL US. THIS KIND OF EXPOSURE...
LET'S GET HIM IN BEFORE THE GENERAL HAS OUR ASSES.
WHAT DO WE DO NOW?
WE GO.
AND WE DON'T LOOK BACK.

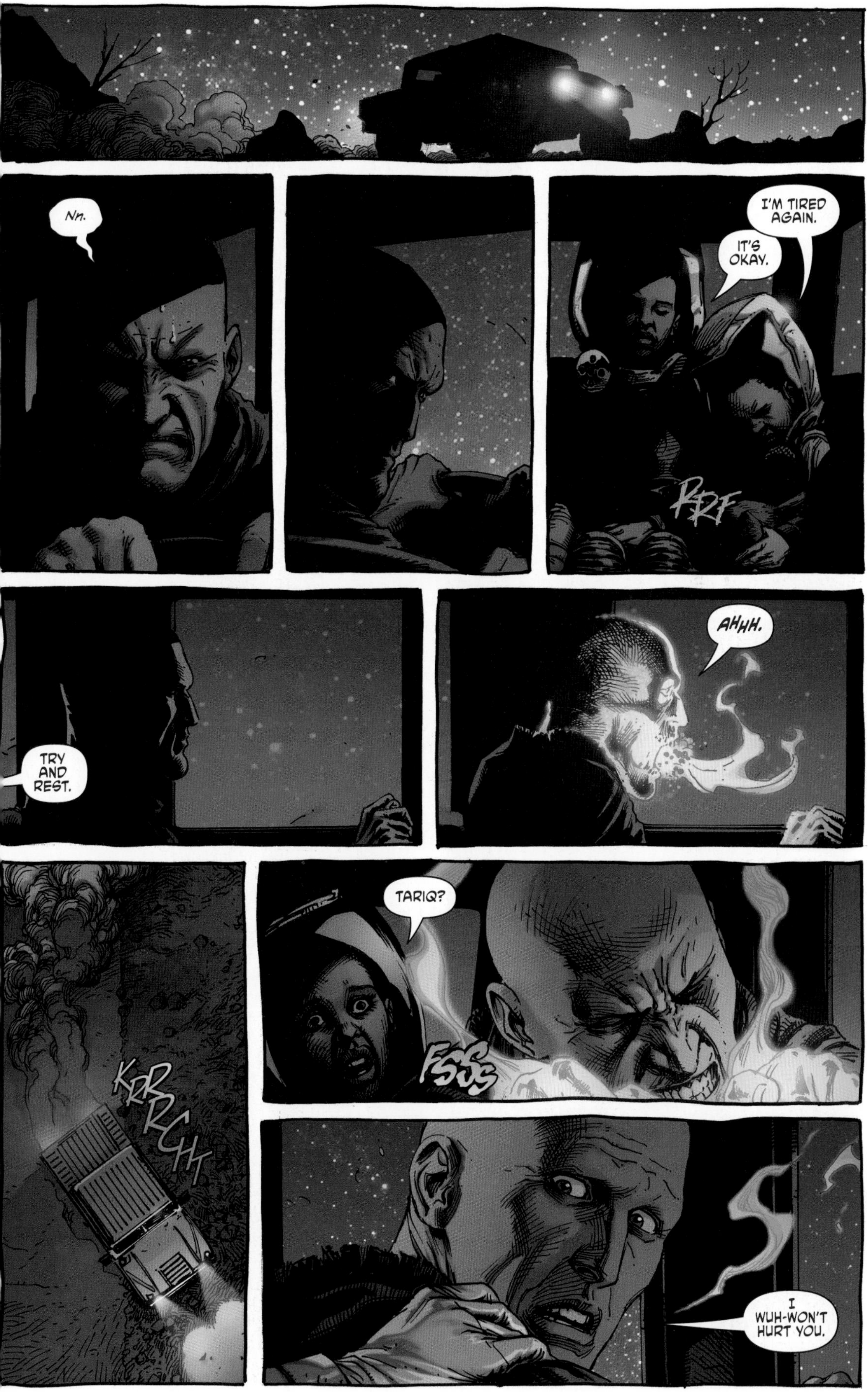

Nn.
I'M TIRED AGAIN.
IT'S OKAY.
RRF
TRY AND REST.
AHHH.
KRRRCHKT
TARIQ?
FSSS
I WUH-WON'T HURT YOU.

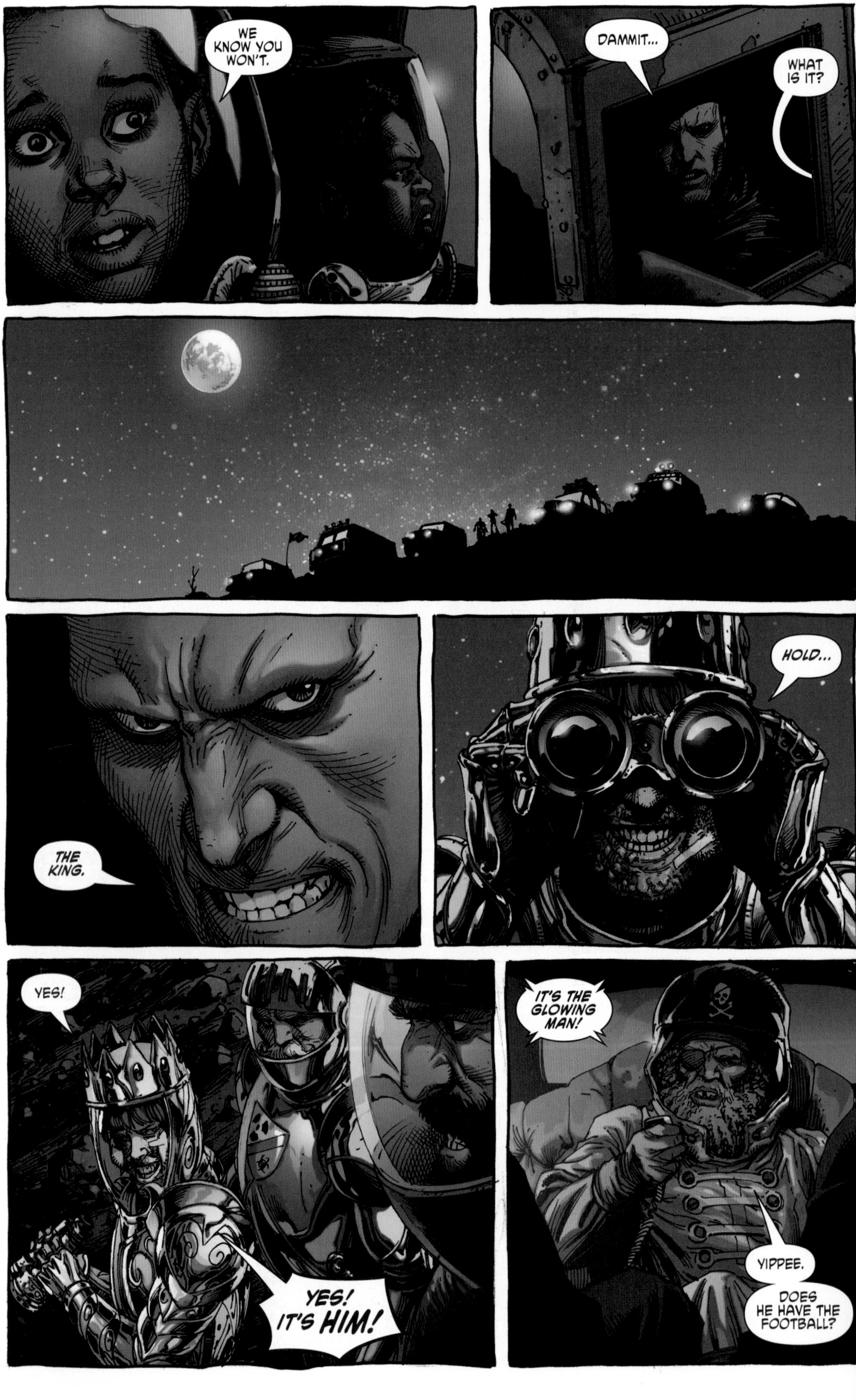
WE KNOW YOU WON'T.
DAMMIT...
WHAT IS IT?
THE KING.
HOLD...
YES!
YES! IT'S HIM!
IT'S THE GLOWING MAN!
YIPPEE.
DOES HE HAVE THE FOOTBALL?

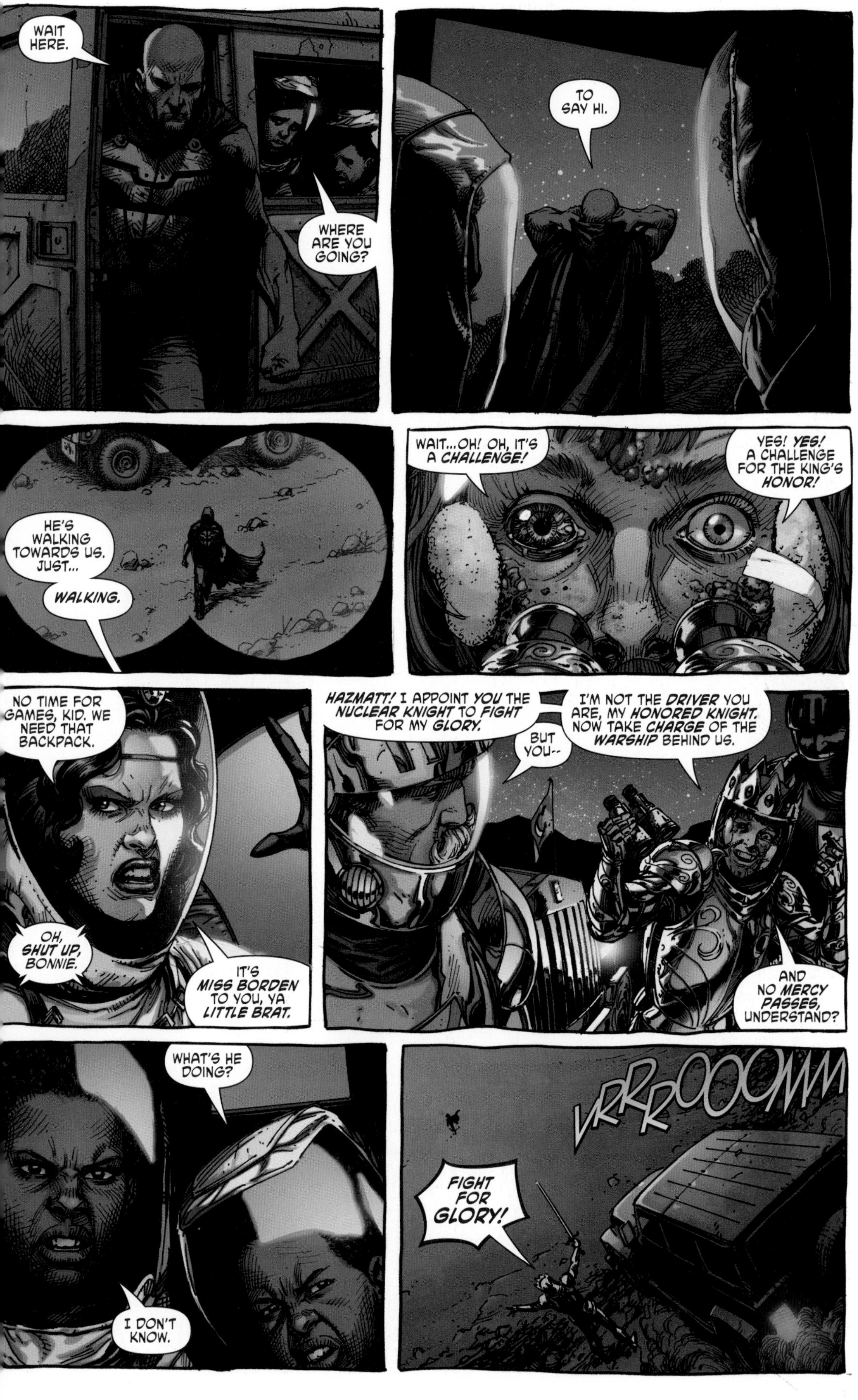
WAIT HERE.
WHERE ARE YOU GOING?
TO SAY HI.
HE'S WALKING TOWARDS US. JUST...
WALKING.
WAIT...OH! OH, IT'S A CHALLENGE!
YES! YES! A CHALLENGE FOR THE KING'S HONOR!
NO TIME FOR GAMES, KID. WE NEED THAT BACKPACK.
OH, SHUT UP, BONNIE.
IT'S MISS BORDEN TO YOU, YA LITTLE BRAT.
HAZMATT! I APPOINT YOU THE NUCLEAR KNIGHT TO FIGHT FOR MY GLORY.
BUT YOU--
I'M NOT THE DRIVER YOU ARE, MY HONORED KNIGHT. NOW TAKE CHARGE OF THE WARSHIP BEHIND US.
AND NO MERCY PASSES, UNDERSTAND?
WHAT'S HE DOING?
I DON'T KNOW.
VRRROOOMM
FIGHT FOR GLORY!

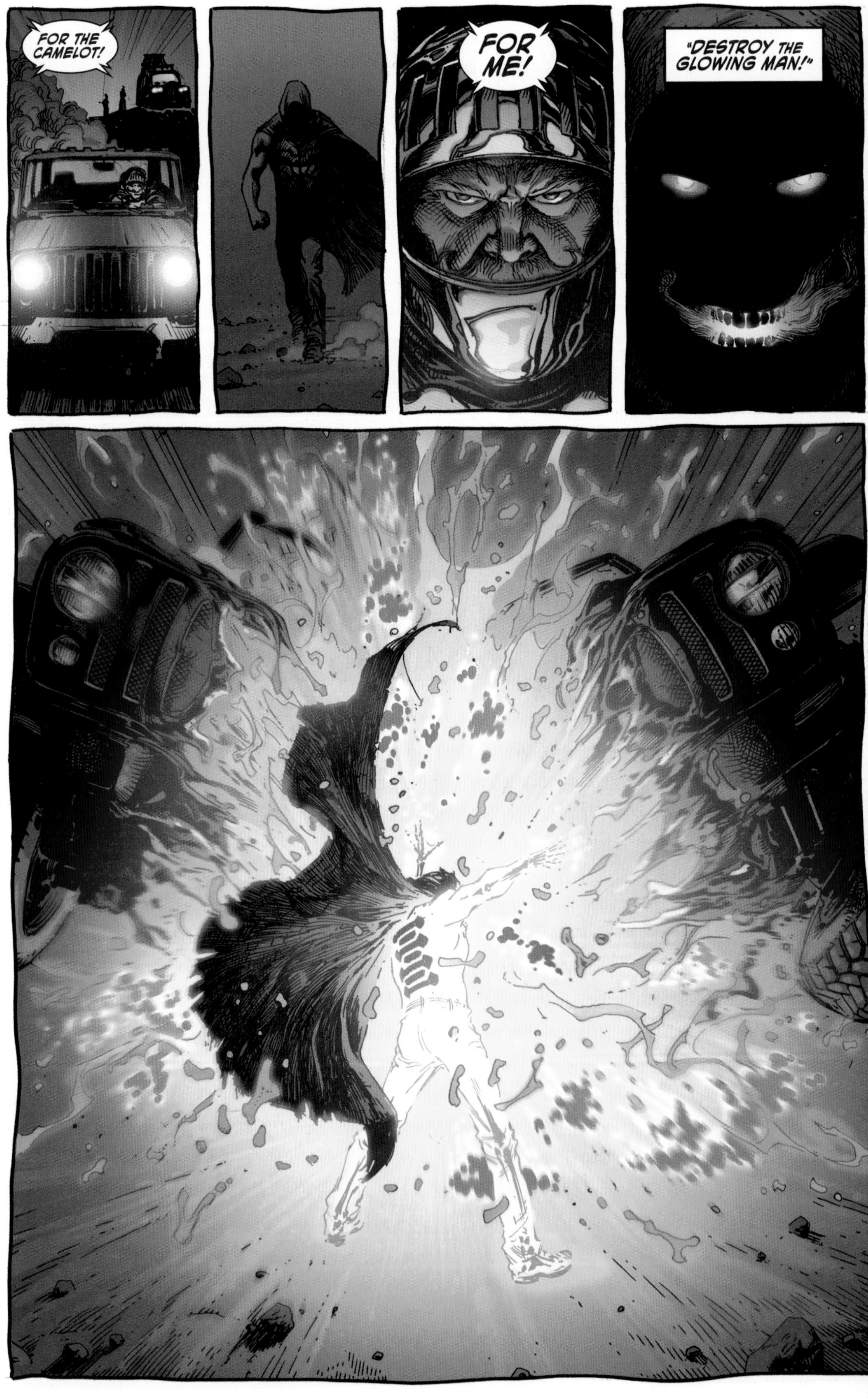
FOR THE CAMELOT!
FOR ME!
"DESTROY THE GLOWING MAN!"

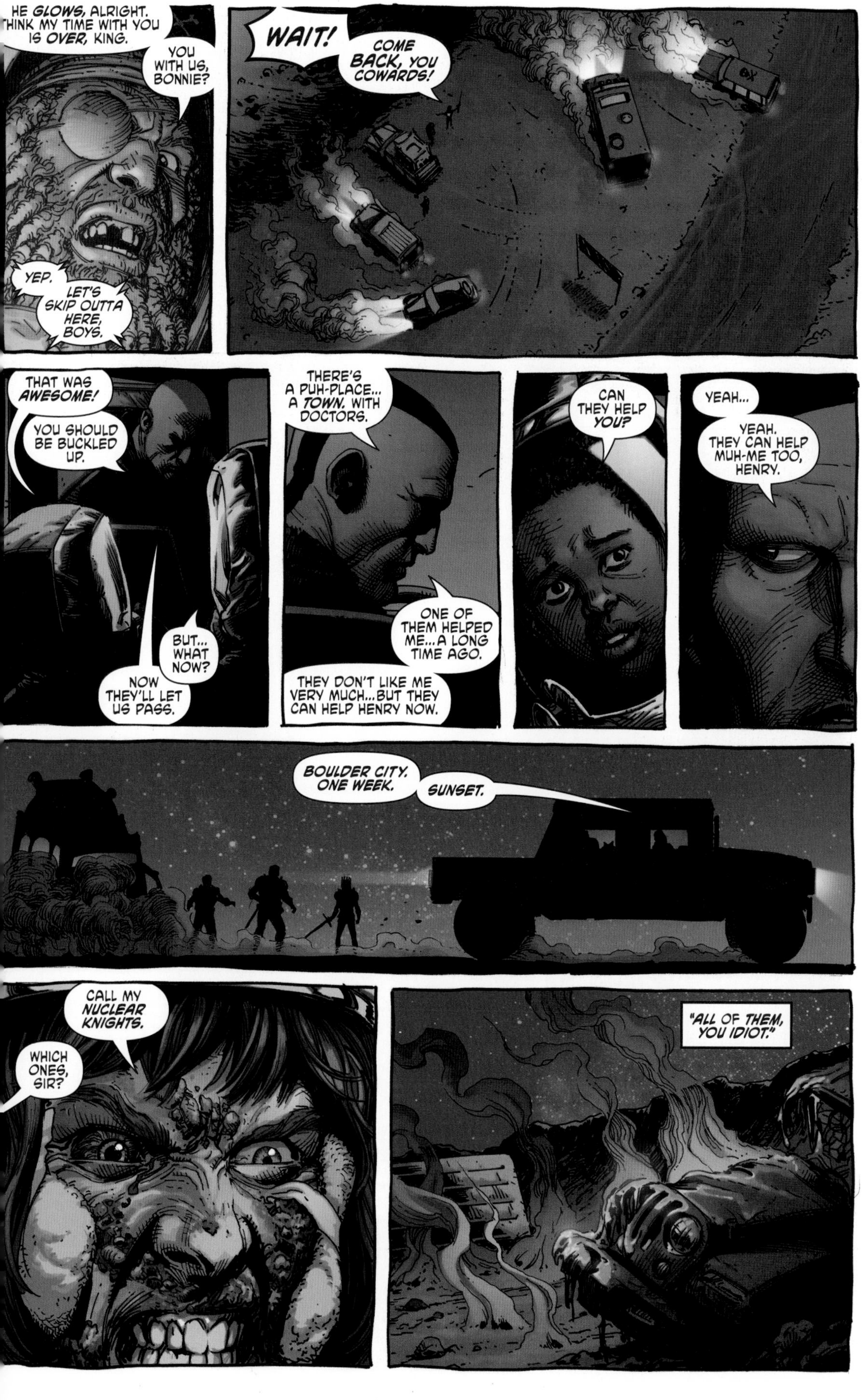
HE GLOWS, ALRIGHT. THINK MY TIME WITH YOU IS OVER, KING.
YOU WITH US, BONNIE?
YEP.
LET'S SKIP OUTTA HERE, BOYS.
WAIT!
COME BACK, YOU COWARDS!
THAT WAS AWESOME!
YOU SHOULD BE BUCKLED UP.
BUT... WHAT NOW?
NOW THEY'LL LET US PASS.
THERE'S A PUH-PLACE... A TOWN, WITH DOCTORS.
ONE OF THEM HELPED ME...A LONG TIME AGO.
THEY DON'T LIKE ME VERY MUCH...BUT THEY CAN HELP HENRY NOW.
CAN THEY HELP YOU?
YEAH...
YEAH. THEY CAN HELP MUH-ME TOO, HENRY.
BOULDER CITY. ONE WEEK.
SUNSET.
CALL MY NUCLEAR KNIGHTS.
WHICH ONES, SIR?
"ALL OF THEM, YOU IDIOT."

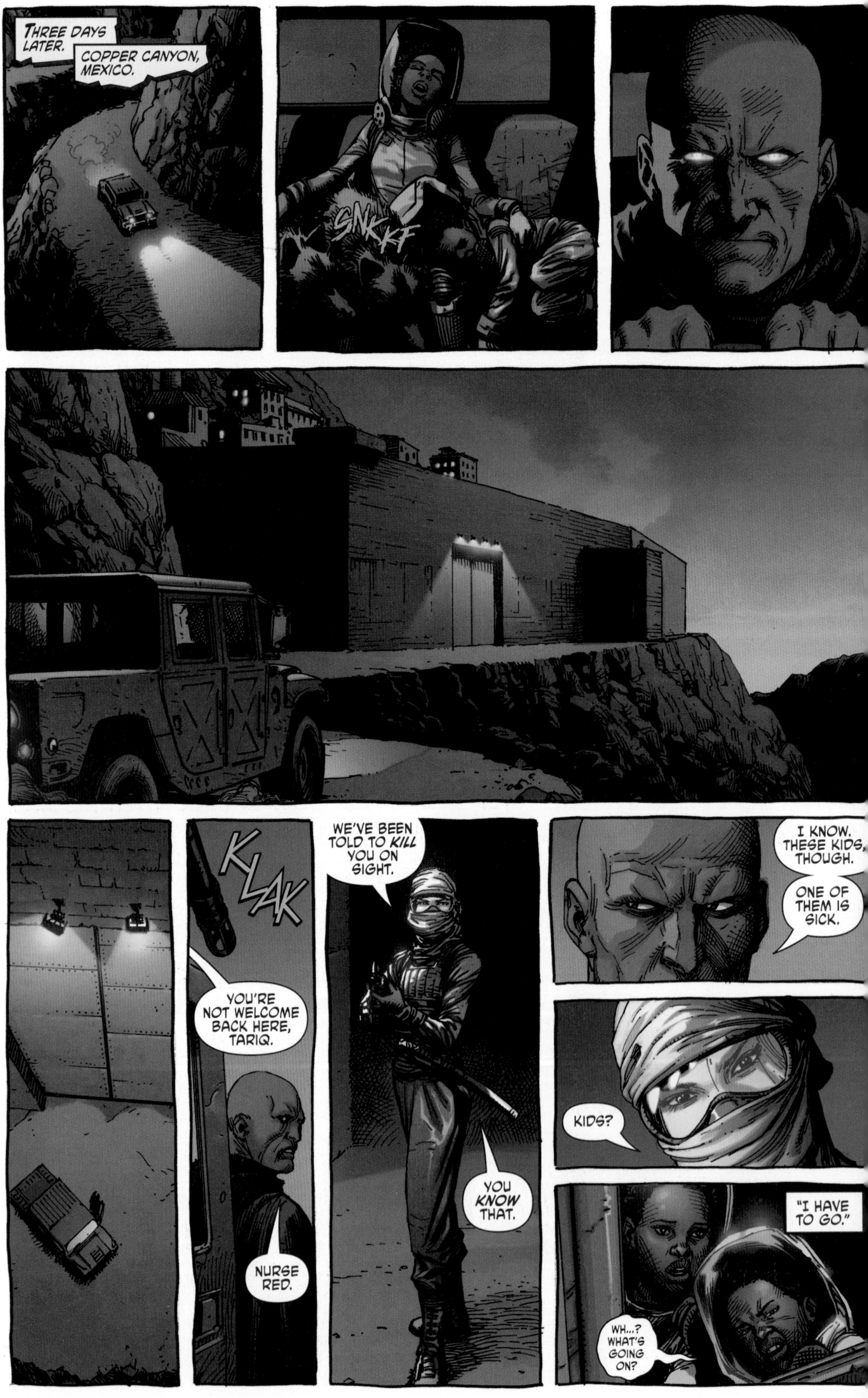
THREE DAYS LATER.
COPPER CANYON, MEXICO.
SNKKF
KLAK
YOU'RE NOT WELCOME BACK HERE, TARIQ.
NURSE RED.
WE'VE BEEN TOLD TO KILL YOU ON SIGHT.
YOU KNOW THAT.
I KNOW. THESE KIDS, THOUGH.
ONE OF THEM IS SICK.
KIDS?
"I HAVE TO GO."
WH...? WHAT'S GOING ON?

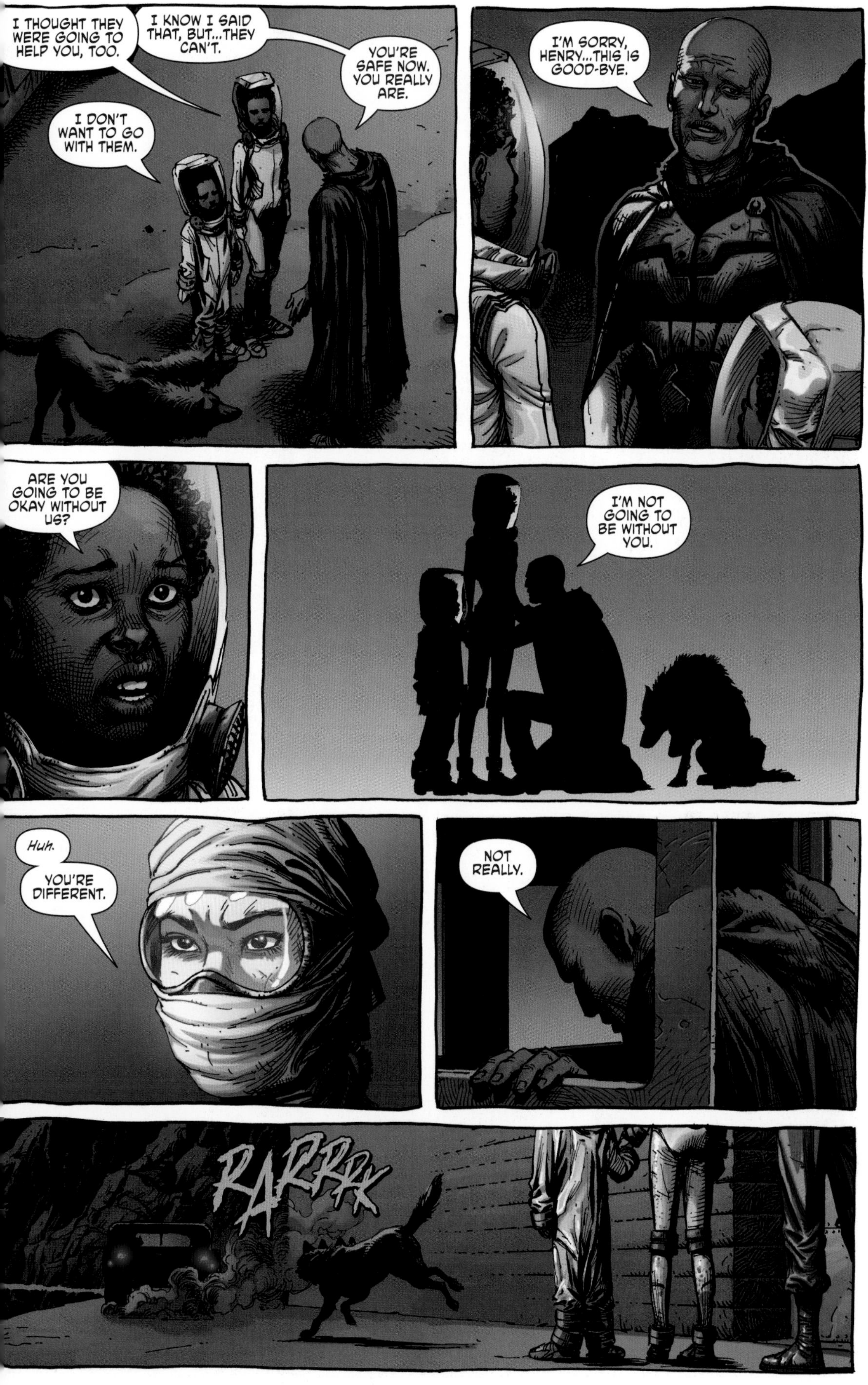
I THOUGHT THEY WERE GOING TO HELP YOU, TOO.
I KNOW I SAID THAT, BUT...THEY CAN'T.
YOU'RE SAFE NOW. YOU REALLY ARE.
I DON'T WANT TO GO WITH THEM.
I'M SORRY, HENRY...THIS IS GOOD-BYE.
ARE YOU GOING TO BE OKAY WITHOUT US?
I'M NOT GOING TO BE WITHOUT YOU.
Huh.
YOU'RE DIFFERENT.
NOT REALLY.
RARRRK

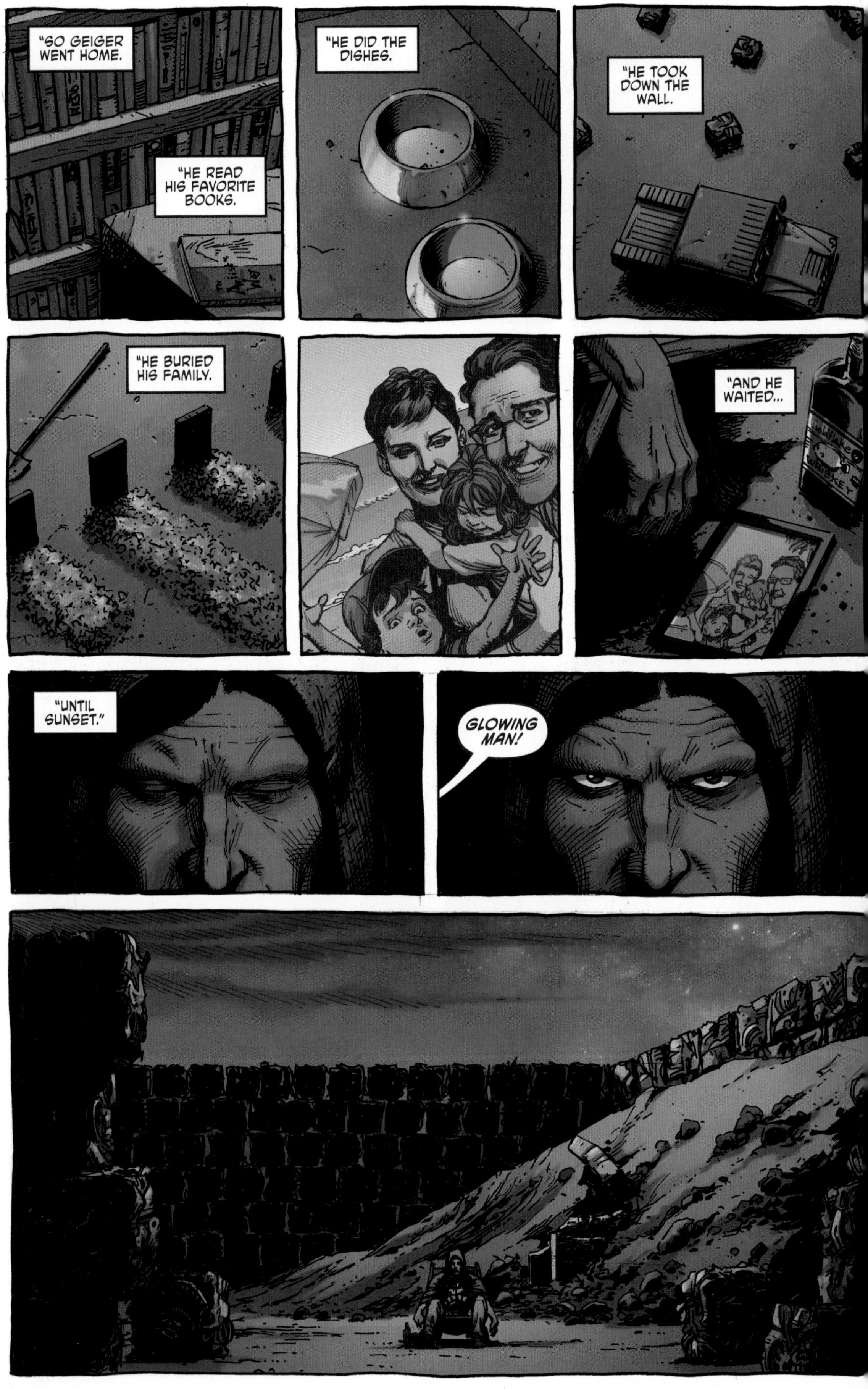
"SO GEIGER WENT HOME.
"HE READ HIS FAVORITE BOOKS.
"HE DID THE DISHES.
"HE TOOK DOWN THE WALL.
"HE BURIED HIS FAMILY.
"AND HE WAITED...
"UNTIL SUNSET."
GLOWING MAN!

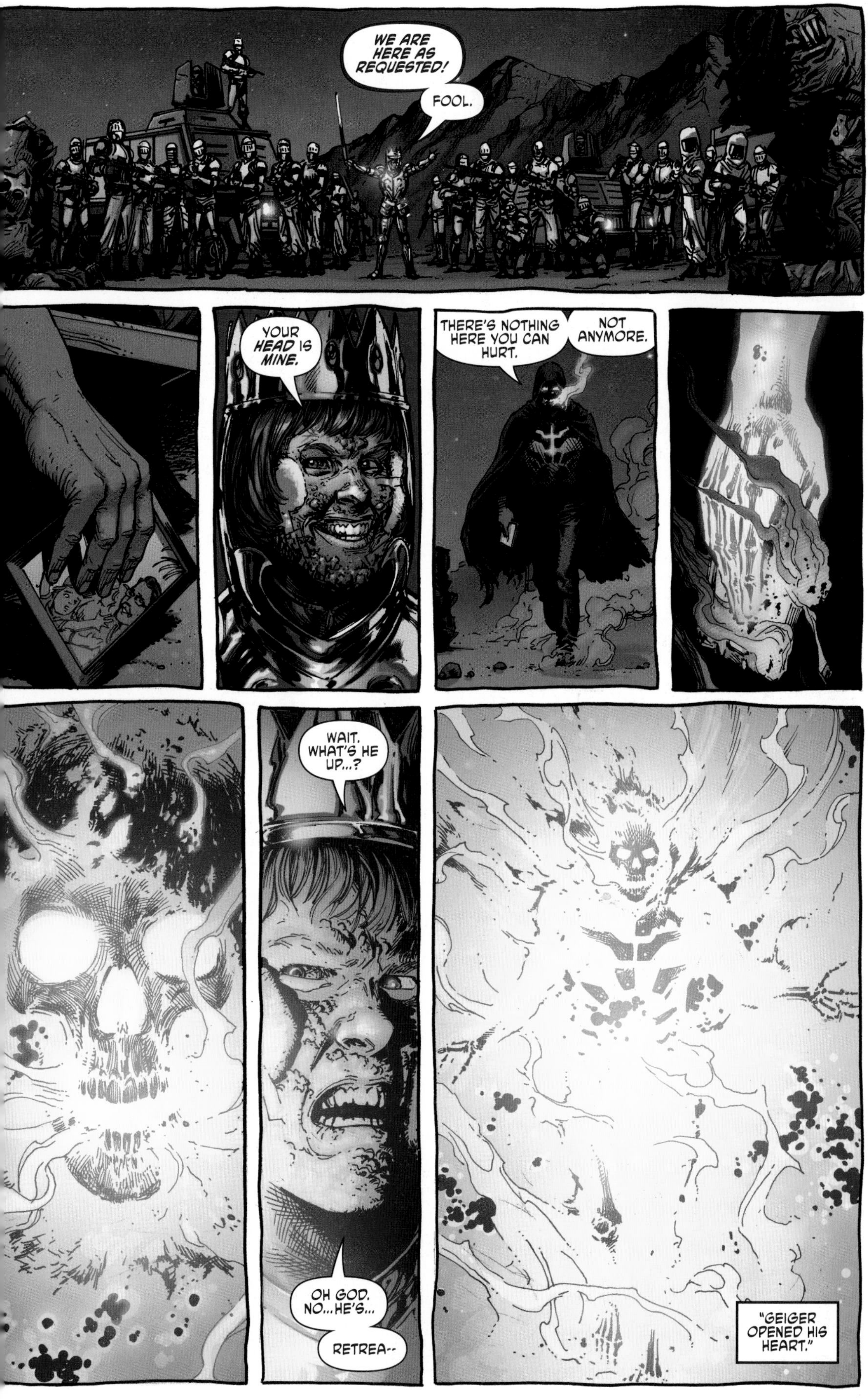
WE ARE HERE AS REQUESTED!
FOOL.
YOUR HEAD IS MINE.
THERE'S NOTHING HERE YOU CAN HURT.
NOT ANYMORE.
WAIT. WHAT'S HE UP...?
OH GOD. NO...HE'S...
RETREA--
"GEIGER OPENED HIS HEART."

"AND HE FOUND PEACE."

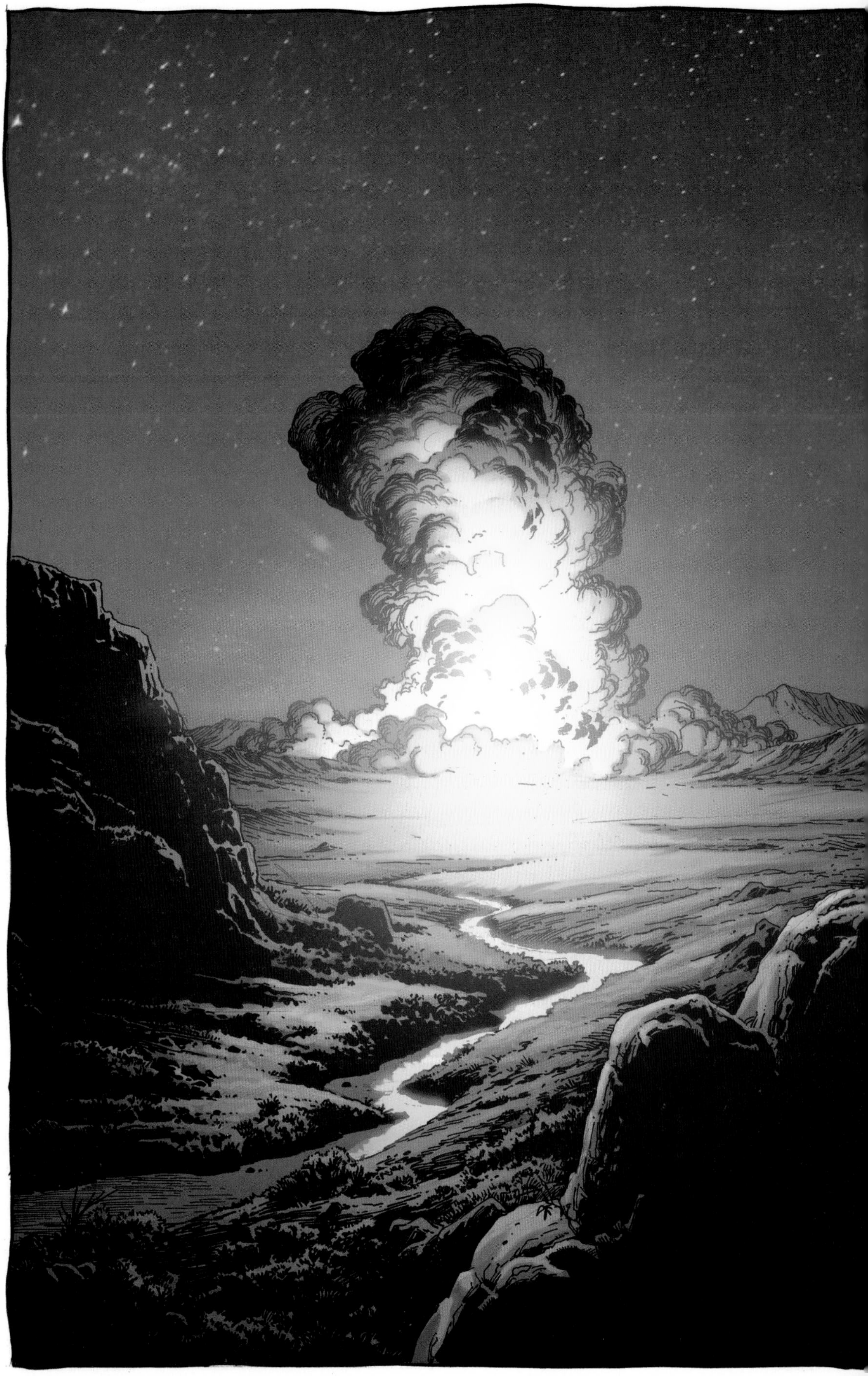

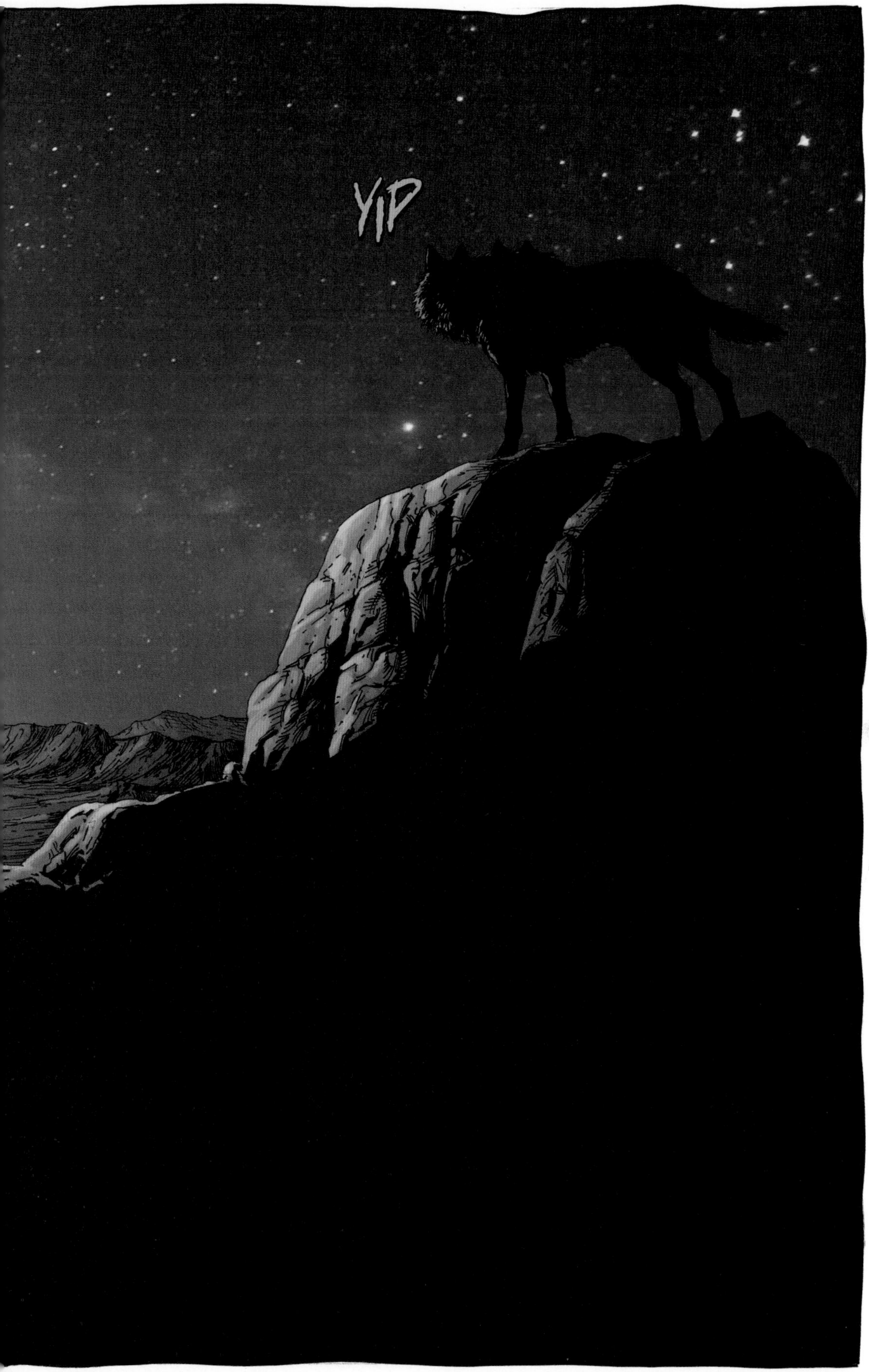
YIP

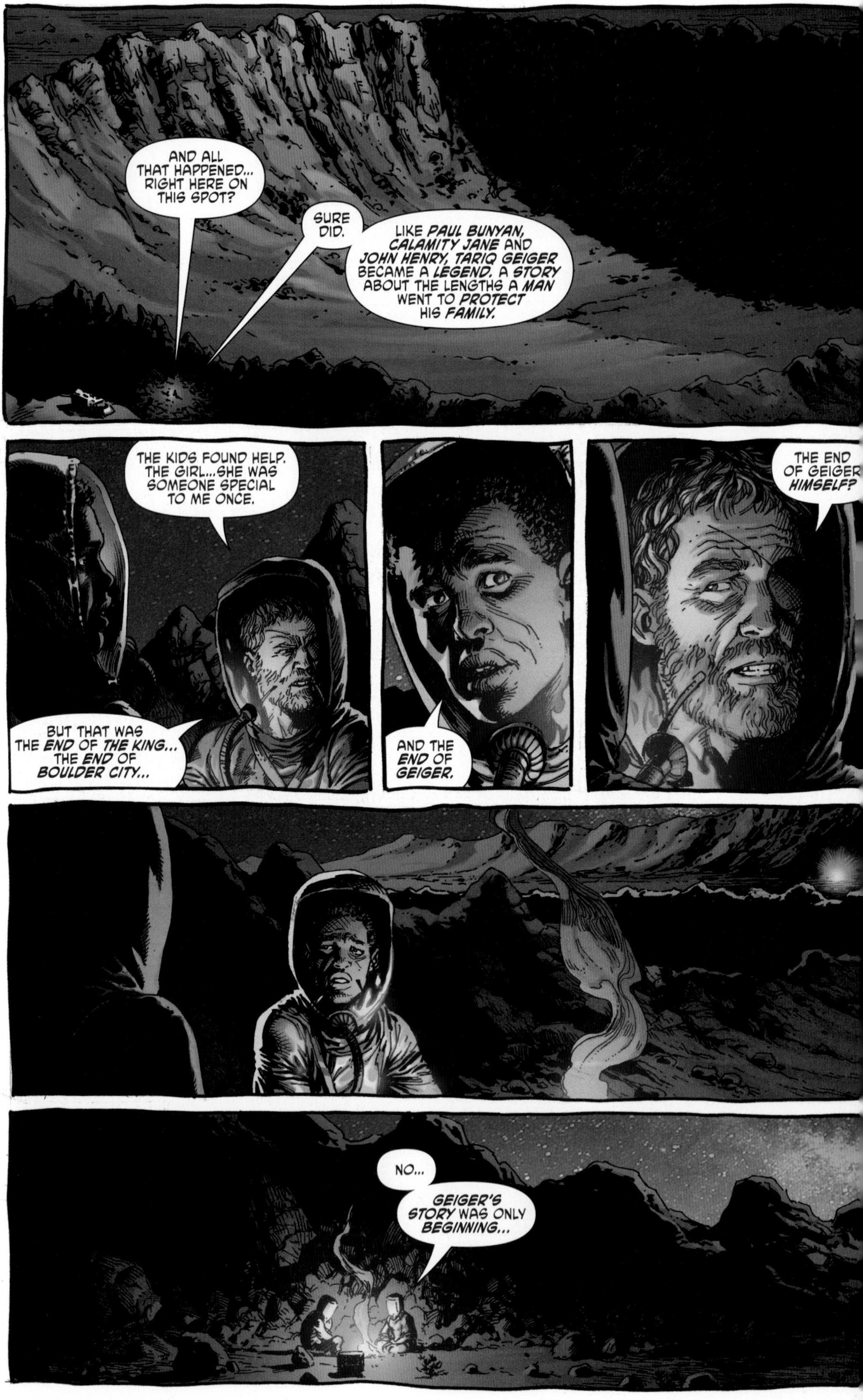
AND ALL THAT HAPPENED... RIGHT HERE ON THIS SPOT?
SURE DID.
LIKE *PAUL BUNYAN*, *CALAMITY JANE* AND *JOHN HENRY*, *TARIQ GEIGER* BECAME A *LEGEND*. A *STORY* ABOUT THE LENGTHS A *MAN* WENT TO *PROTECT* HIS *FAMILY*.
THE KIDS FOUND HELP. THE GIRL...SHE WAS SOMEONE SPECIAL TO ME ONCE.
BUT THAT WAS THE *END* OF *THE KING*... THE *END* OF *BOULDER CITY*...
AND THE *END* OF *GEIGER*.
THE END OF GEIGER *HIMSELF?*
NO...
GEIGER'S *STORY* WAS ONLY *BEGINNING*...

"BOULDER CITY IS GONE."

AND SO IS *MY* SON, THE HORRIBLE *SCAB.*

I BEG *YOU ALL* FOR YOUR *FORGIVENESS* FOR HIS ACTIONS.

THEY WERE *UNSANCTIONED* BY *ME,* I ASSURE YOU.

THE KING STIRRED *THE GLOWING MAN* FROM HIS NEST, MY DEAR QUEEN...

...BUT PERHAPS THAT WILL *BENEFIT* US *ALL.*

I'M ALL EARS, BOB.

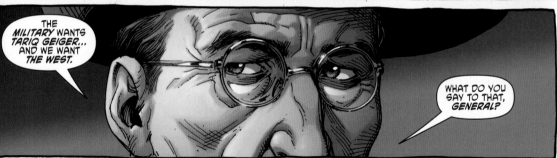

THE MILITARY WANTS TARIQ GEIGER... AND WE WANT *THE WEST.*

WHAT DO YOU SAY TO THAT, *GENERAL?*

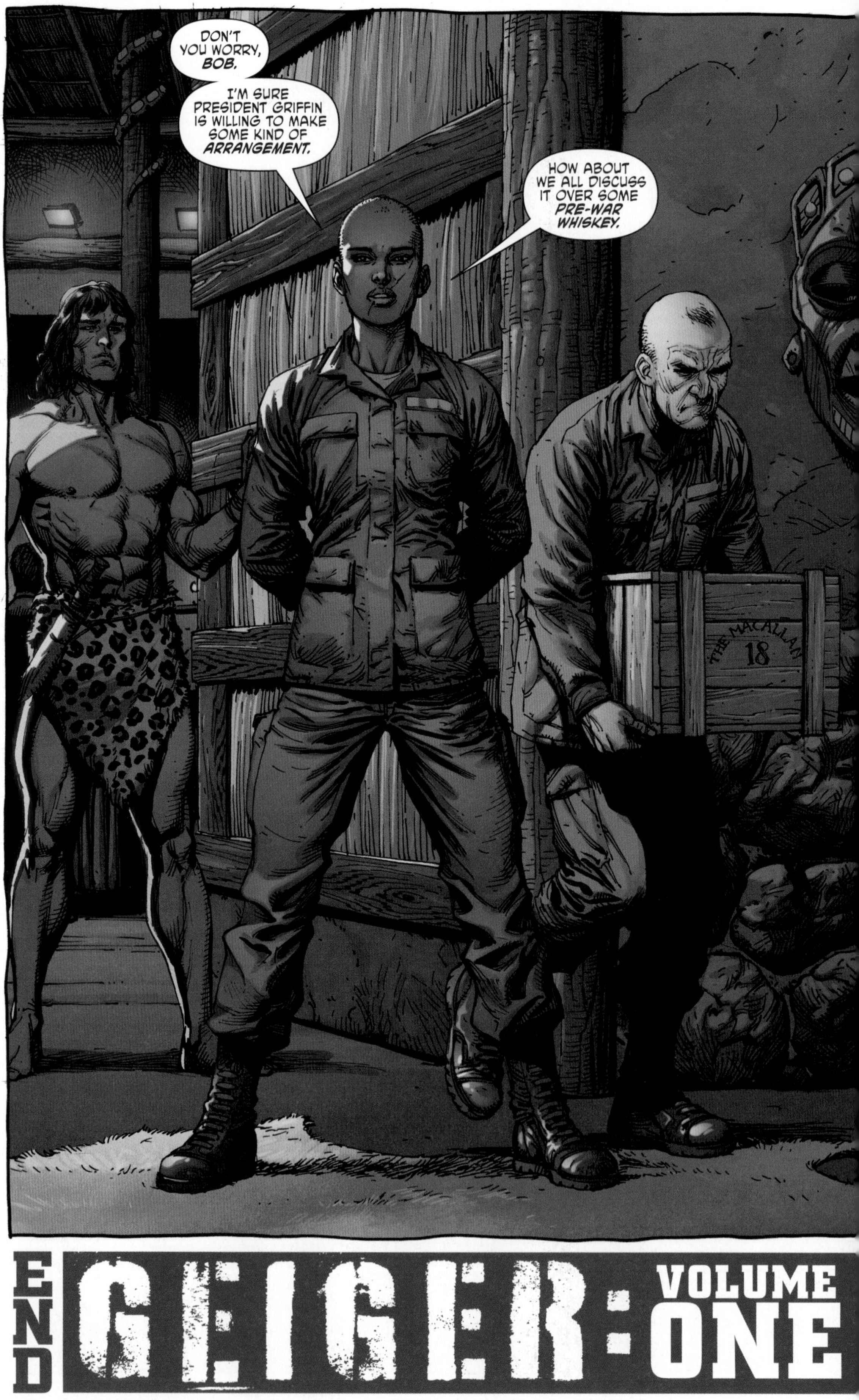
DON'T YOU WORRY, *BOB.*
I'M SURE PRESIDENT GRIFFIN IS WILLING TO MAKE SOME KIND OF *ARRANGEMENT.*
HOW ABOUT WE ALL DISCUSS IT OVER SOME *PRE-WAR WHISKEY.*
THE MACALLAN
18

END

GEIGER: VOLUME ONE

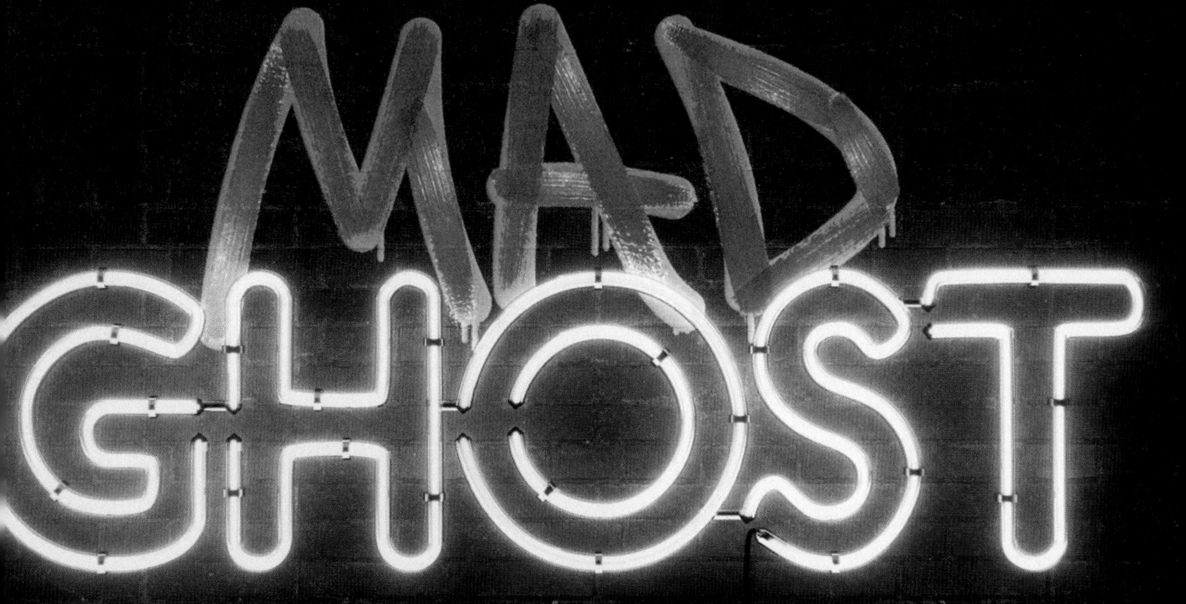
MAD
GHOST

On behalf of Gary, myself and the whole team at MAD GHOST, thank you for diving into the world of GEIGER.

Gary and I have been lucky enough to work on some of the biggest superheroes in mainstream comics over our long career of collaboration, but those stories were built on characters that were already created. We came to Image to unleash a new timeline of heroes. Heroes born out of the most violent days in America; then, now and tomorrow. Their adventures take place across the history of the United States, from 1776 to 2050. In our greatest dreams we've always loved American Myths like Paul Bunyan, Calamity Jane and John Henry.

We call them The Unnamed.

GEIGER is the first of these.

This all started when my son was born. A primal instinct kicked in. A rush of adrenaline hit. And I heard these words echo in my head: *I will do anything to protect my son*. The raw emotion of that moment is forever with me.

Having children of his own, Gary and I talked about fatherhood often. What our kids were going through, how we wanted to help them. That shared fatherhood is where Geiger really began.

He will do anything to protect his family.

From there, our longtime friend and master colorist, Brad Anderson, came on board along with the best letterer in the business, Rob Leigh, and our longtime friends and collaborators, Mad Ghost Editor Brian Cunningham and Editor Pat McCallum.

Back to the fatherhood that keeps Geiger alive. Even now, he wanders the irradiated deserts, looking for a good book to read... or a soul in need.

As we close the first volume of Geiger, Gary and I are busy at work on the next chapter of The Unnamed—JUNKYARD JOE. Joe debuted in this very issue, but we're going back in time to 1972. Back to reveal Joe's mysterious origins—from robotic soldier to cartoon character—as he seeks out his creator. It is a story born out of our desire for connection and family. A theme you'll see that connects all of these heroes.

Until then, our special GEIGER 80 pg. GIANT will be released in November, delving further into the world of Geiger and the Criminals of Vegas, with an incredible lineup of talent including Bryan Hitch, Jay Faerber, Peter J. Tomasi, Sean Galloway, Janet Harvey, Pornsak Pichetshote and many more unbelievable creators from across the industry.

Thank you again for giving our book a shot—and a big welcome to the Mad Ghost Family.

Geoff Johns

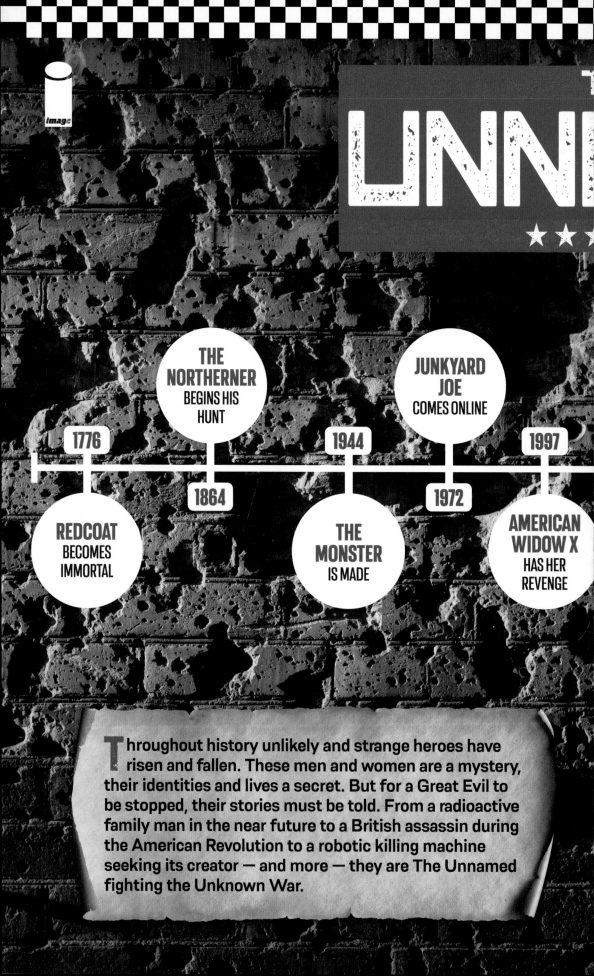

THE
UNN...
★ ★ ★

THE NORTHERNER BEGINS HIS HUNT

JUNKYARD JOE COMES ONLINE

1776

1944

1997

1864

1972

REDCOAT BECOMES IMMORTAL

THE MONSTER IS MADE

AMERICAN WIDOW X HAS HER REVENGE

Throughout history unlikely and strange heroes have risen and fallen. These men and women are a mystery, their identities and lives a secret. But for a Great Evil to be stopped, their stories must be told. From a radioactive family man in the near future to a British assassin during the American Revolution to a robotic killing machine seeking its creator — and more — they are The Unnamed fighting the Unknown War.

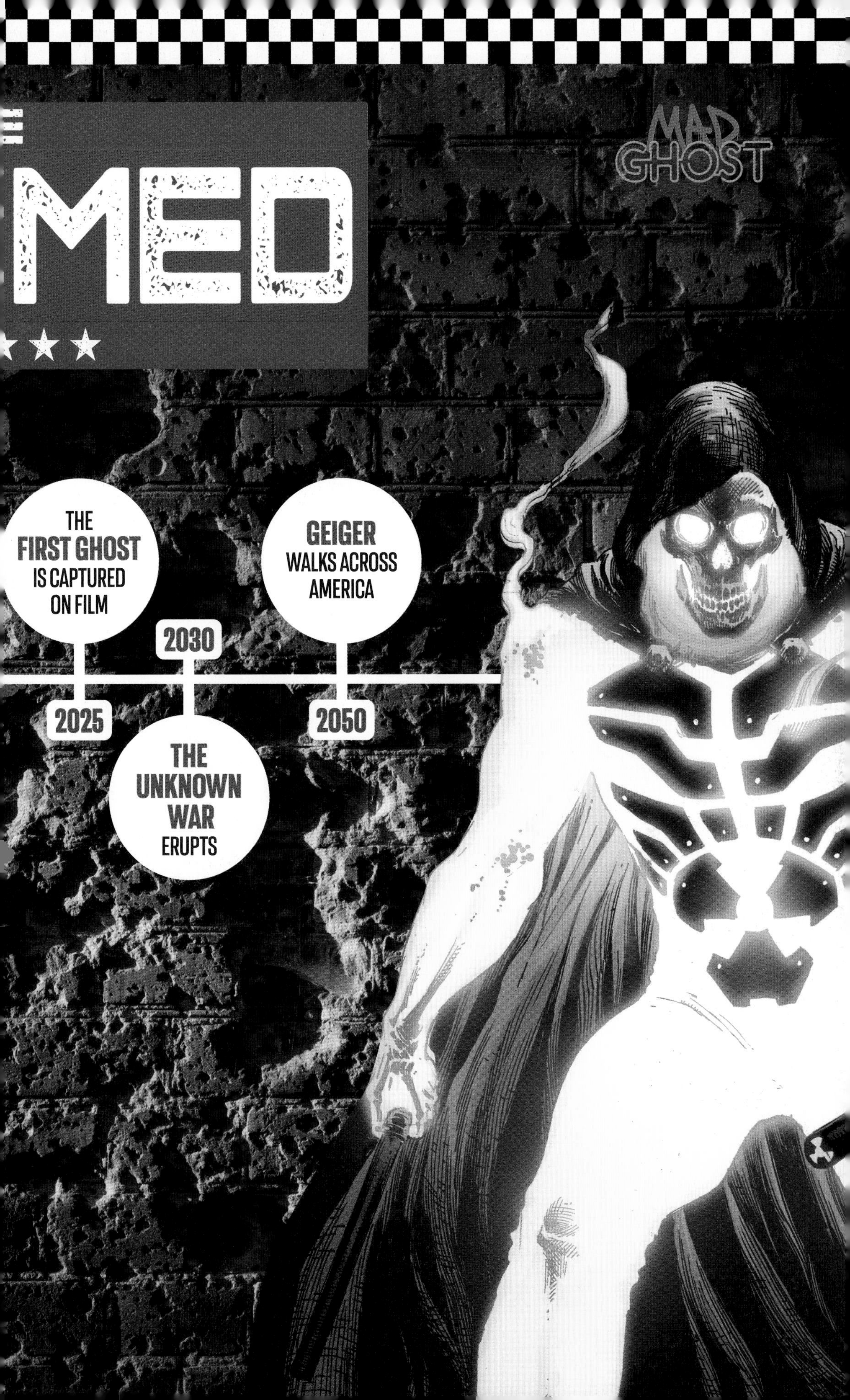
MED
MAD GHOST
THE FIRST GHOST IS CAPTURED ON FILM
2025
2030
THE UNKNOWN WAR ERUPTS
GEIGER WALKS ACROSS AMERICA
2050

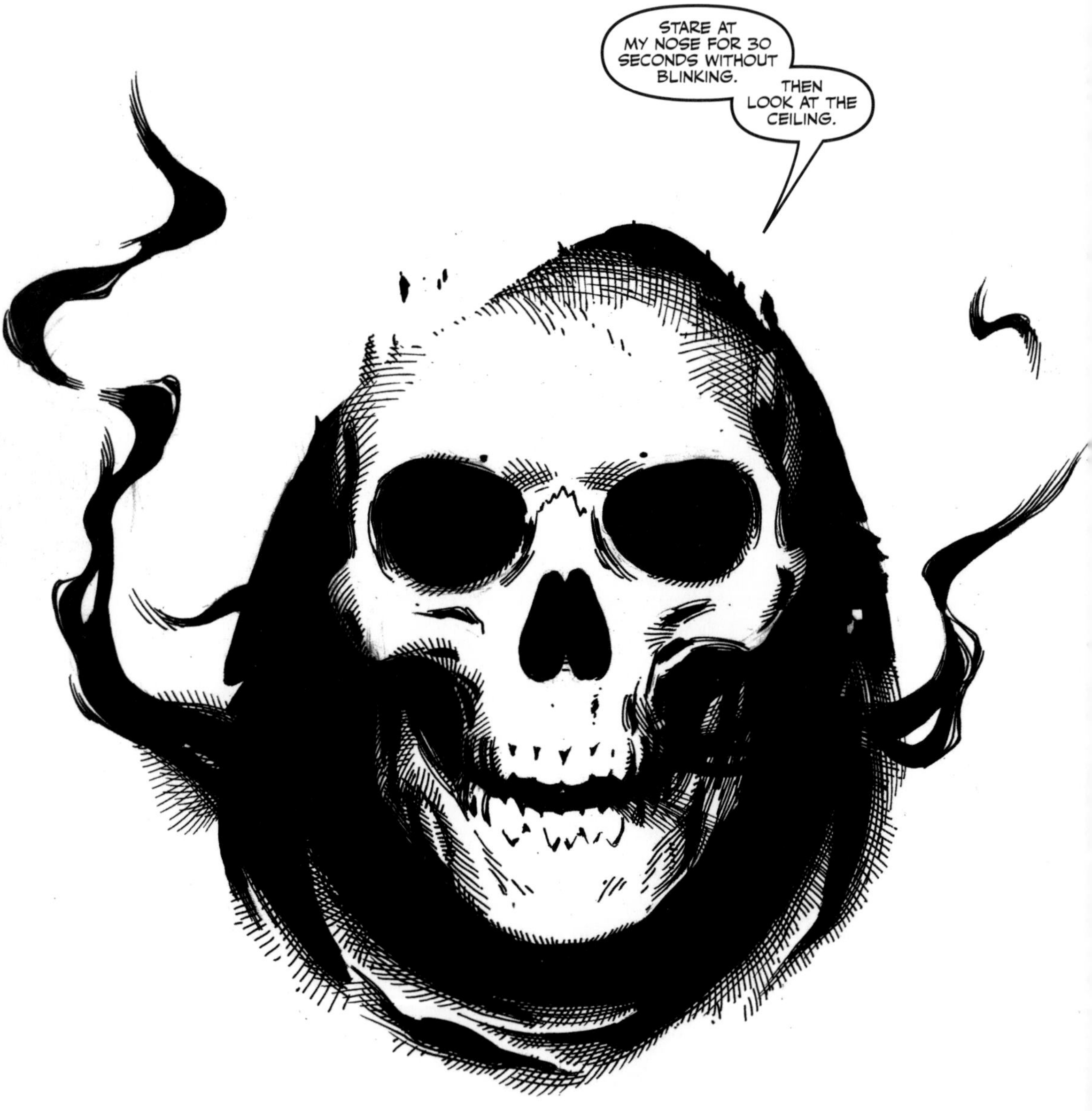
STARE AT MY NOSE FOR 30 SECONDS WITHOUT BLINKING.
THEN LOOK AT THE CEILING.

GEIGER #1 Third Printing Cover
By GARY FRANK and BRAD ANDERSON

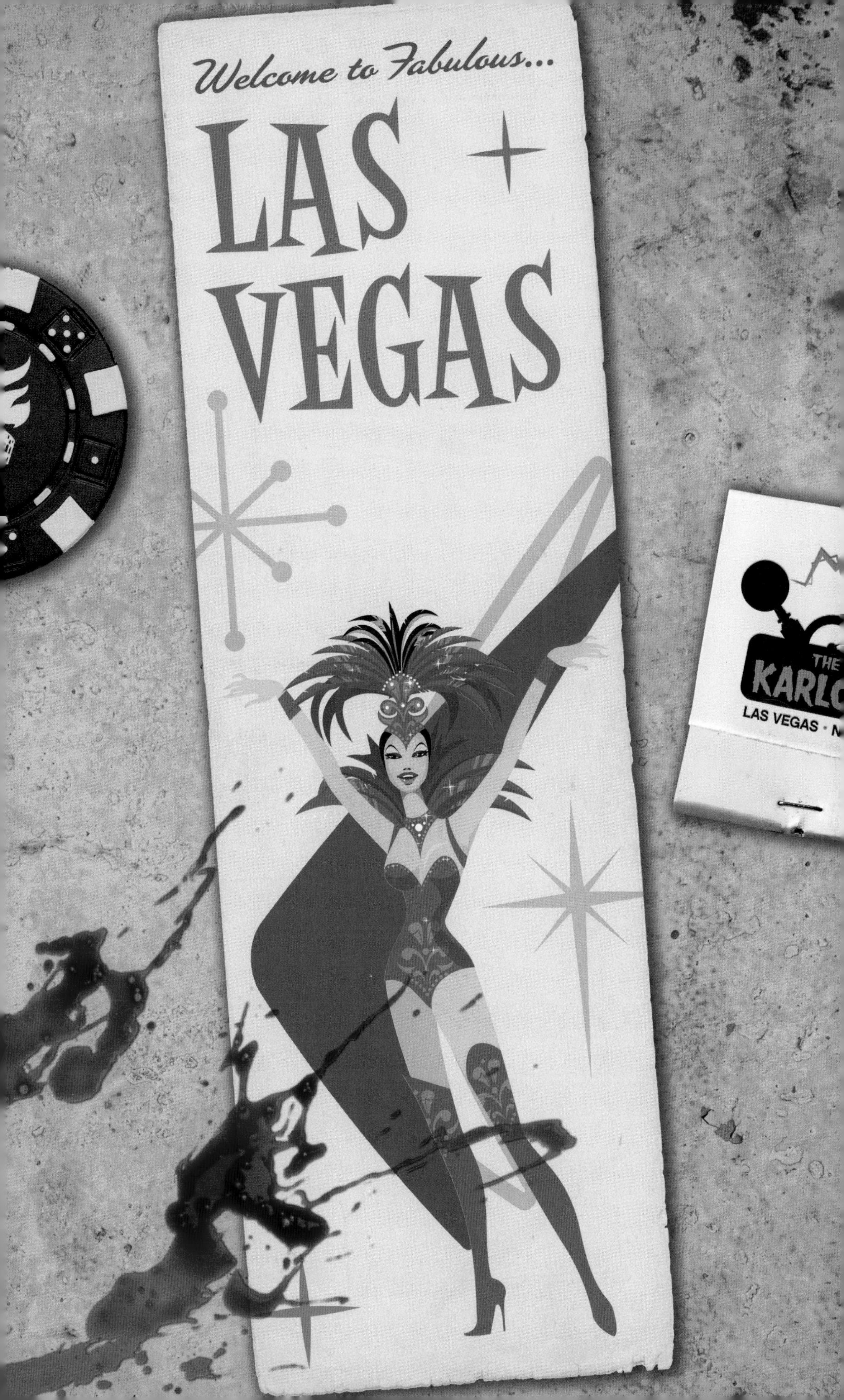

Welcome to Fabulous...
LAS VEGAS
THE
KARL
LAS VEGAS ·

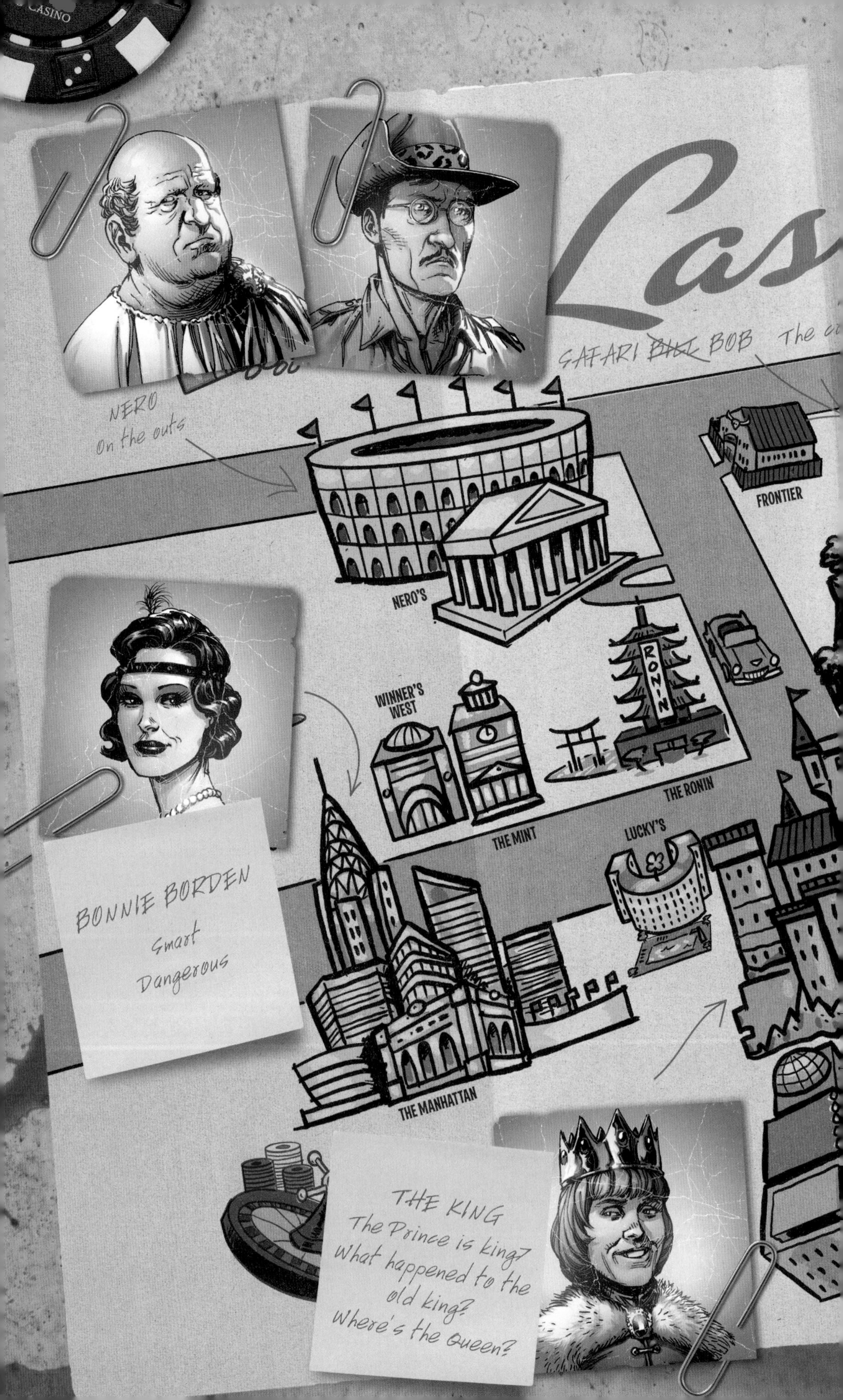
CASINO
Las
SAFARI ~~BILL~~ BOB
The c
NERO
On the outs
FRONTIER
NERO'S
RONIN
WINNER'S WEST
THE MINT
THE RONIN
LUCKY'S
BONNIE BORDEN
Smart
Dangerous
THE MANHATTAN
THE KING
The Prince is king?
What happened to the old king?
Where's the Queen?

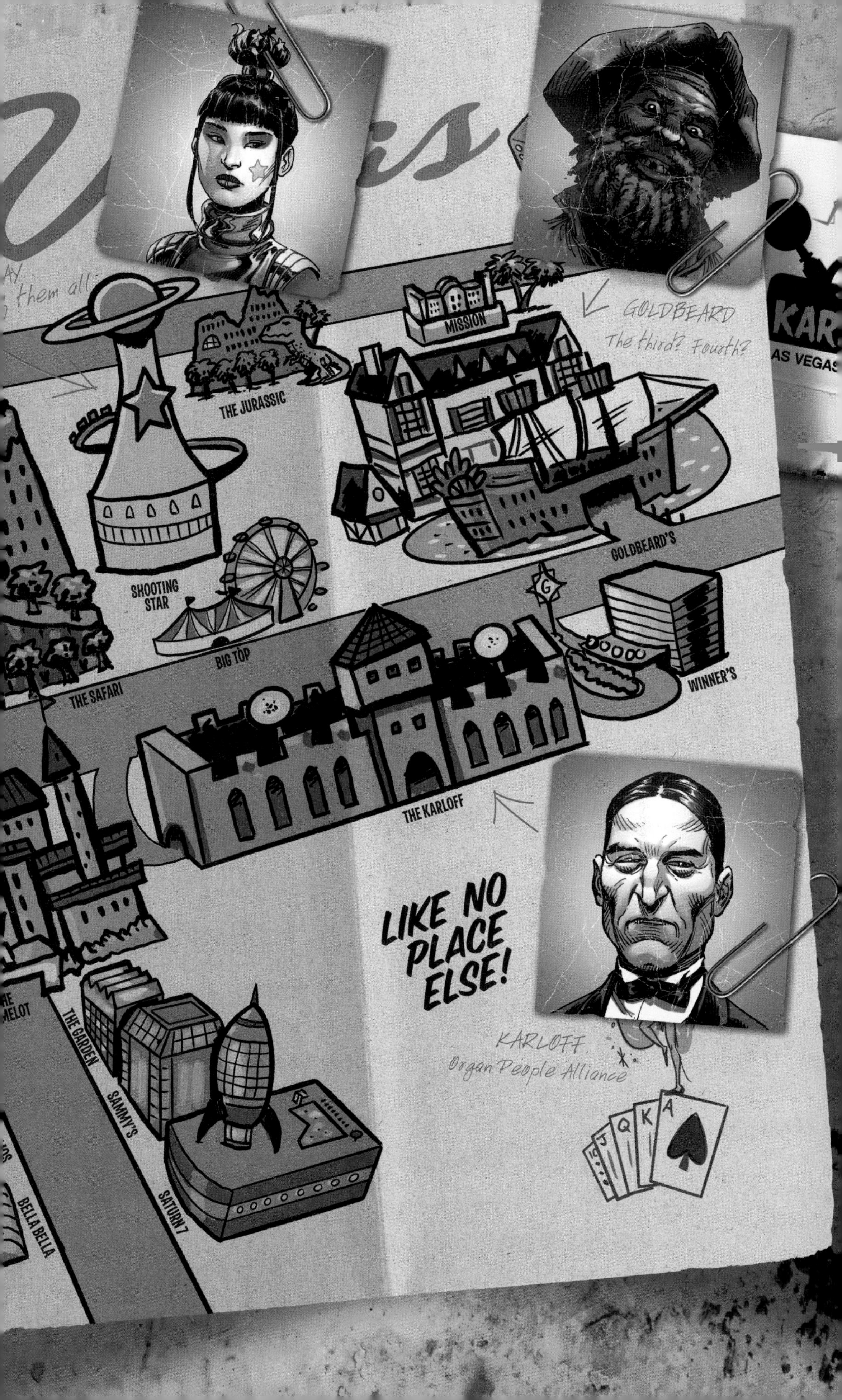

them all
GOLDBEARD
The third? Fourth?
MISSION
THE JURASSIC
SHOOTING STAR
GOLDBEARD'S
BIG TOP
THE SAFARI
WINNER'S
THE KARLOFF
LIKE NO PLACE ELSE!
THE GARDEN
SAMMY'S
SATURN 7
BELLA BELLA
KARLOFF
Organ People Alliance
AS VEGAS

MOLOTOV MEDICAL GROUP

PATIENT INFORMATION

PATIENT: Geiger, Tariq

AGE: Male, 32 years

Pathology reports indicate cancer has metastasized and is present in patient's lungs, liver and kidneys.

High grade tumors show a 10% growth rate since previous examination.

Continued testing indicates strong probability cancer will

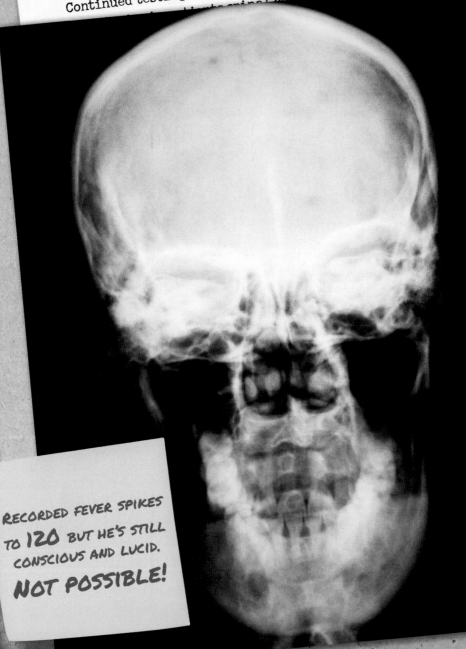

RECORDED FEVER SPIKES TO 120 BUT HE'S STILL CONSCIOUS AND LUCID. NOT POSSIBLE!

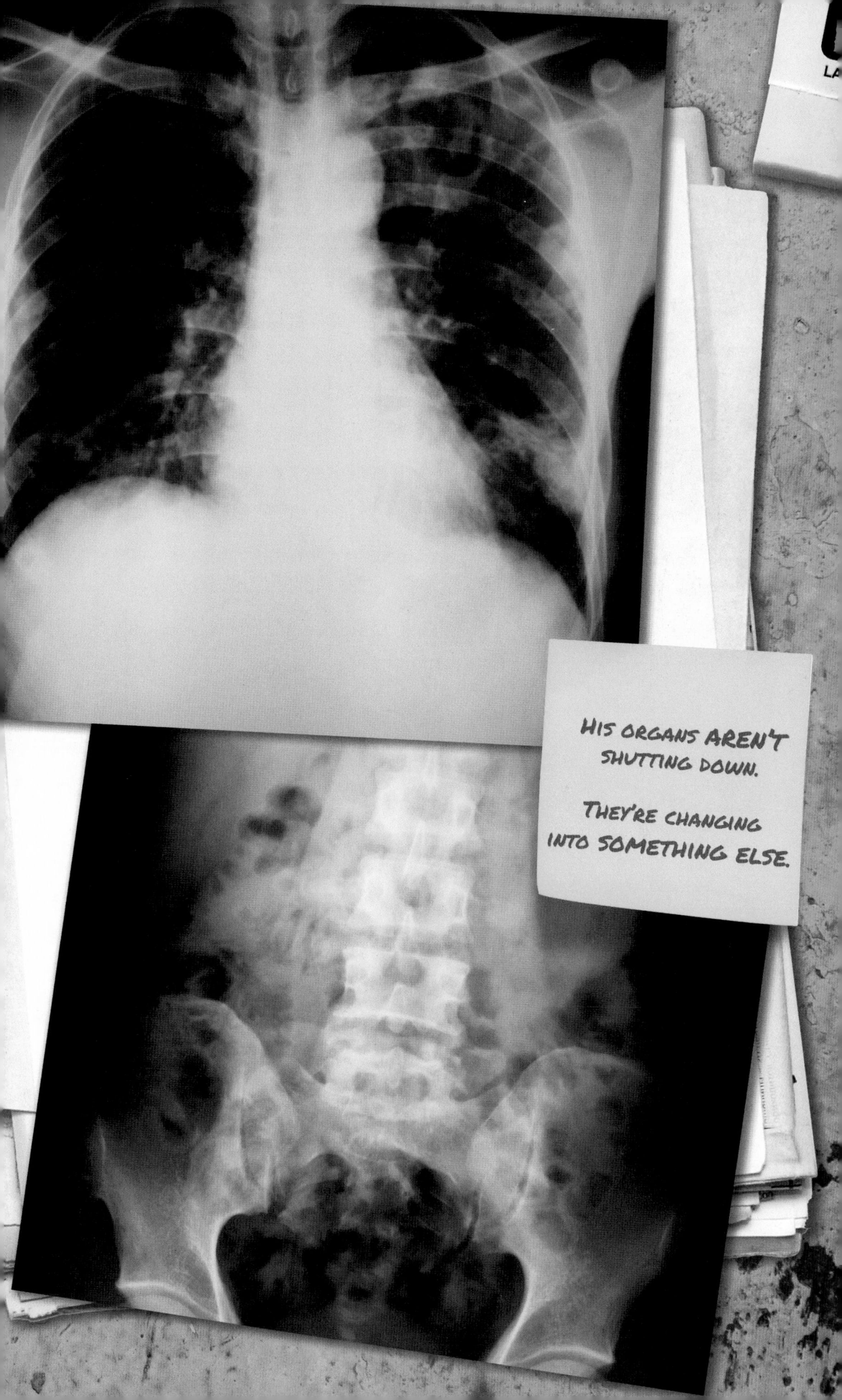

HIS ORGANS AREN'T SHUTTING DOWN.
THEY'RE CHANGING INTO SOMETHING ELSE.

GEIGER #1 Cover B
By ERIK LARSEN and BRAD ANDERSON

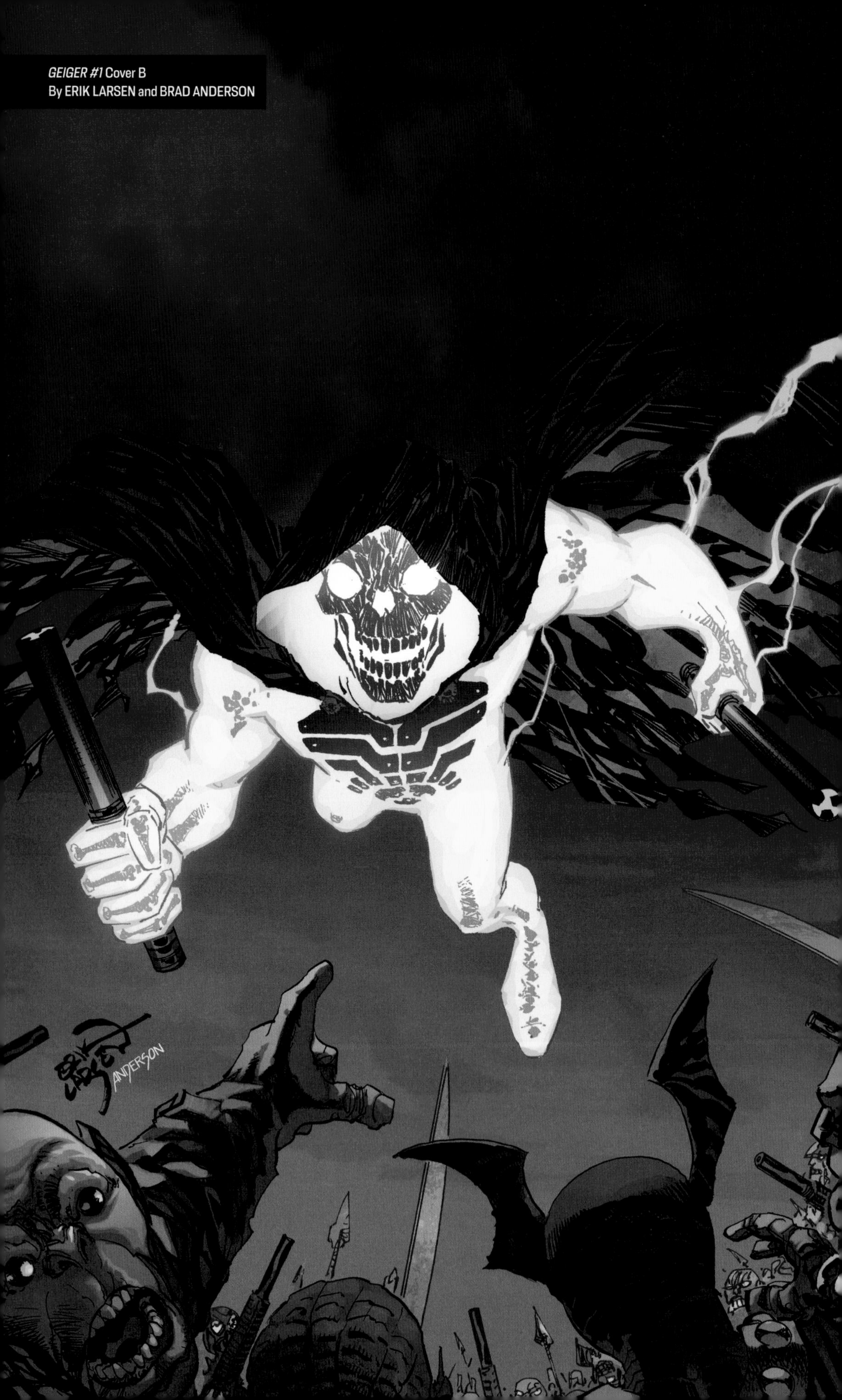
ANDERSON

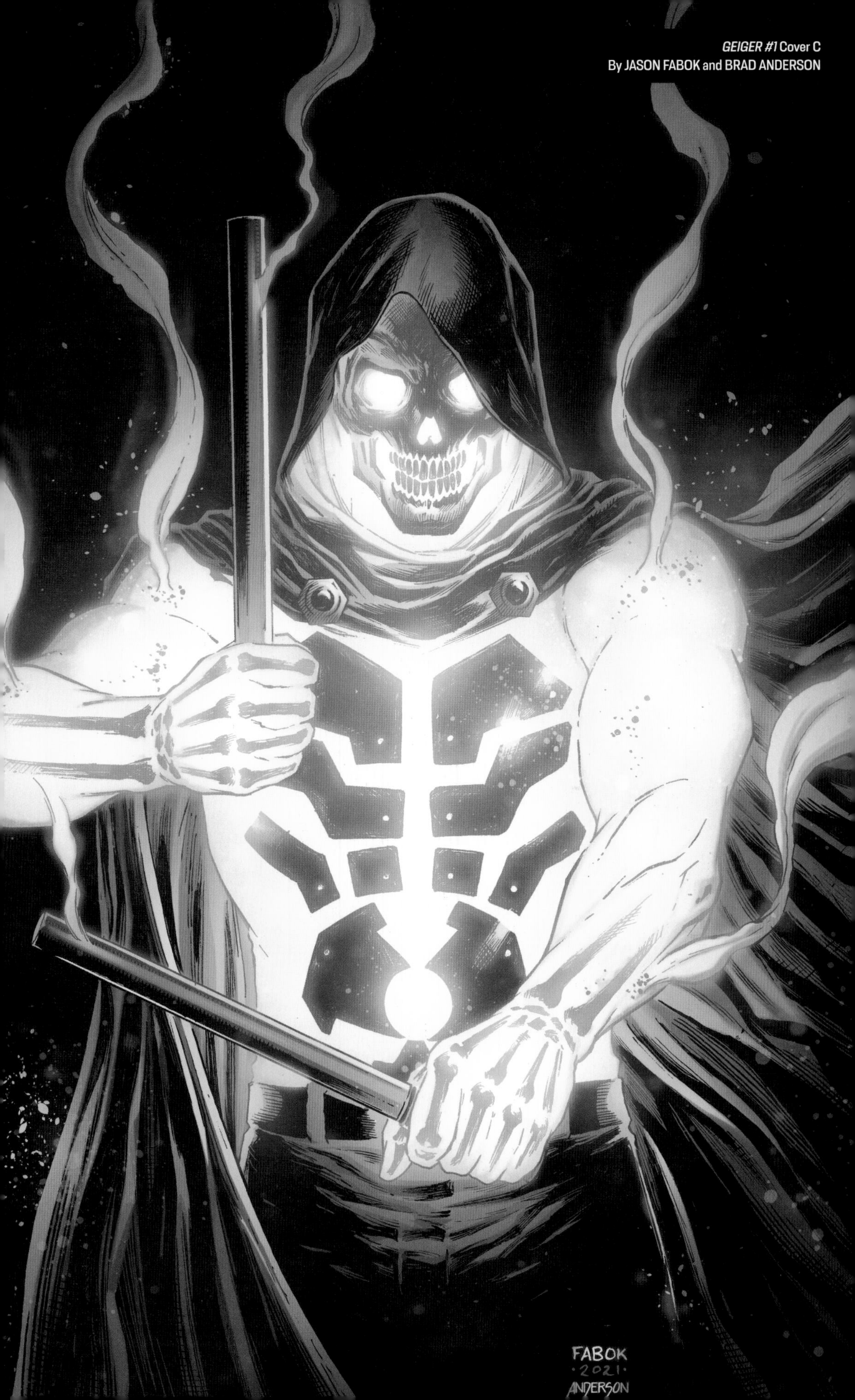
FABOK
·2021·
ANDERSON

GEIGER #1 Cover C
By JASON FABOK and BRAD ANDERSON

GEIGER #1 Cover E
By GARY FRANK and BRAD ANDERSON

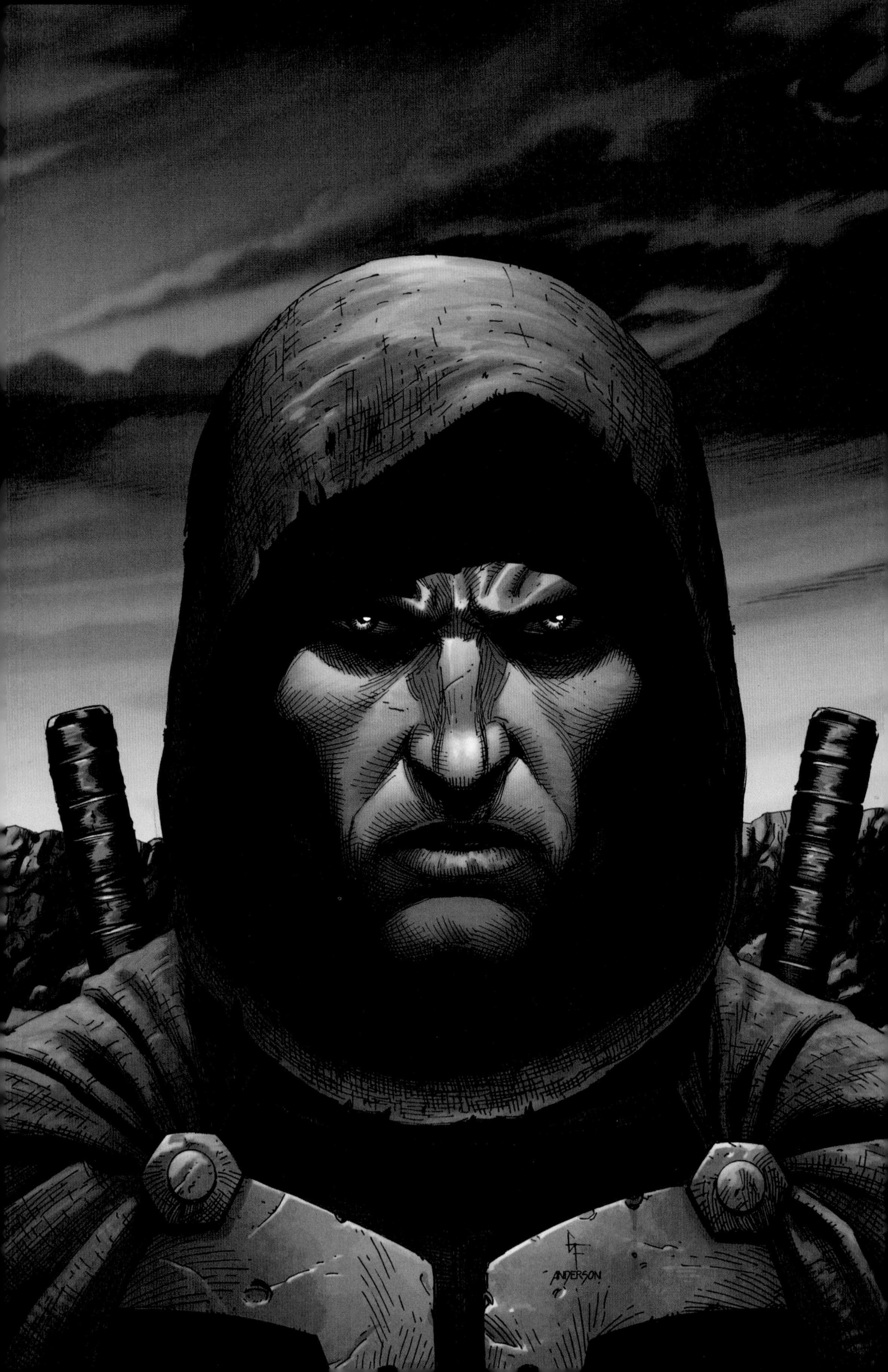
ANDERSON

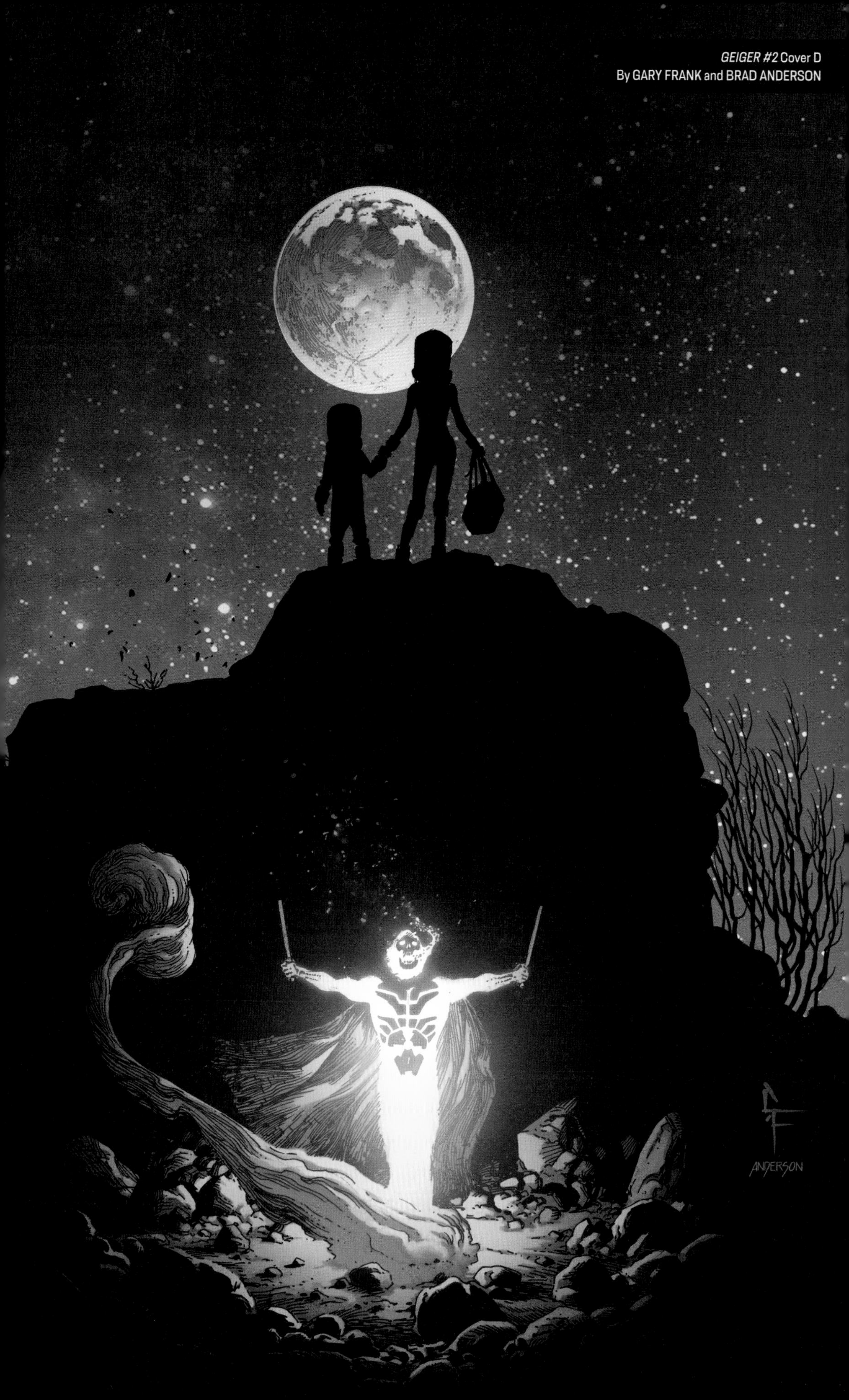
ANDERSON

GEIGER #2 Cover D
By GARY FRANK and BRAD ANDERSON

GEIGER #2 Cover B
By BRYAN HITCH and ALEX SINCLAIR

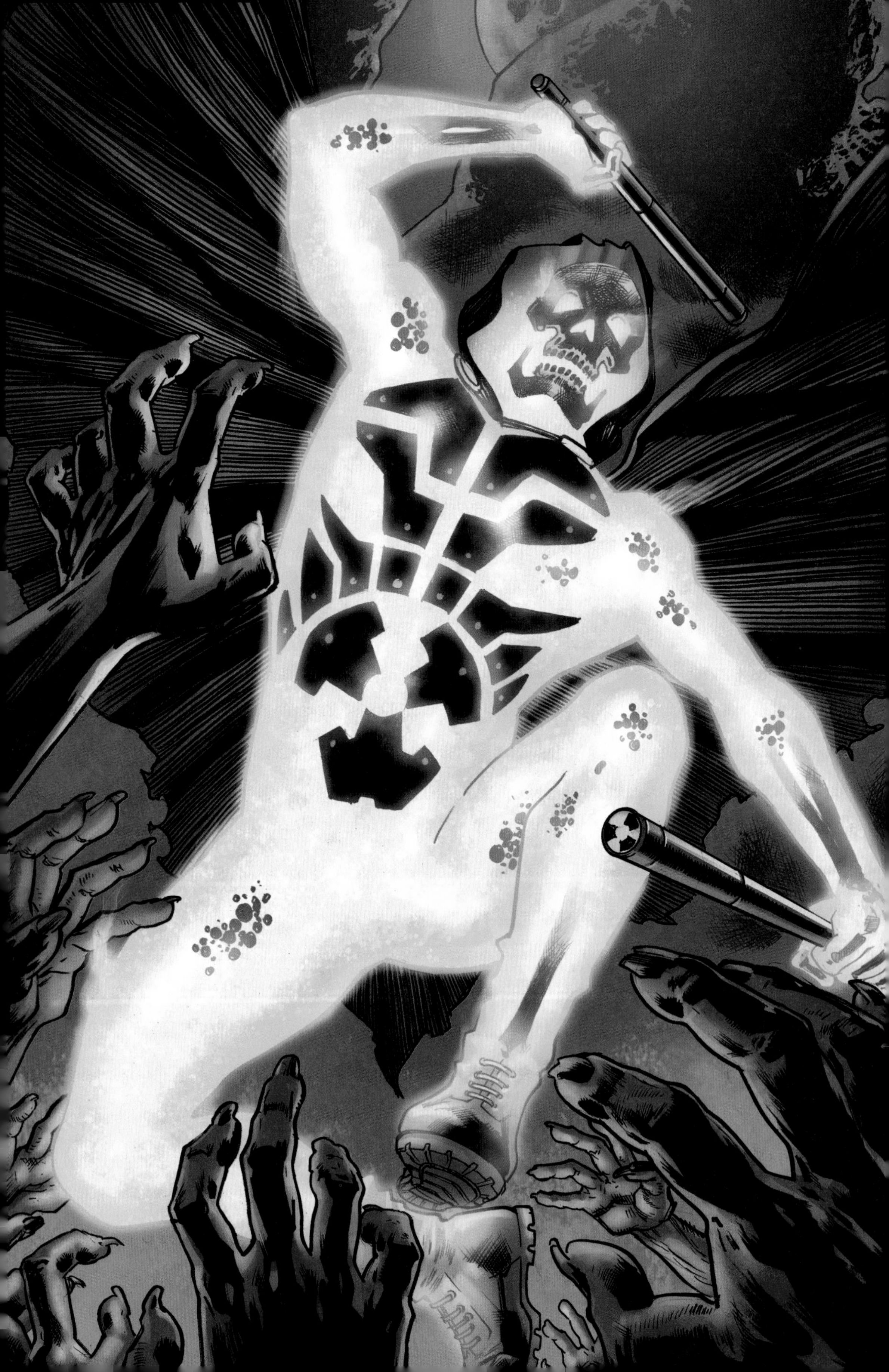

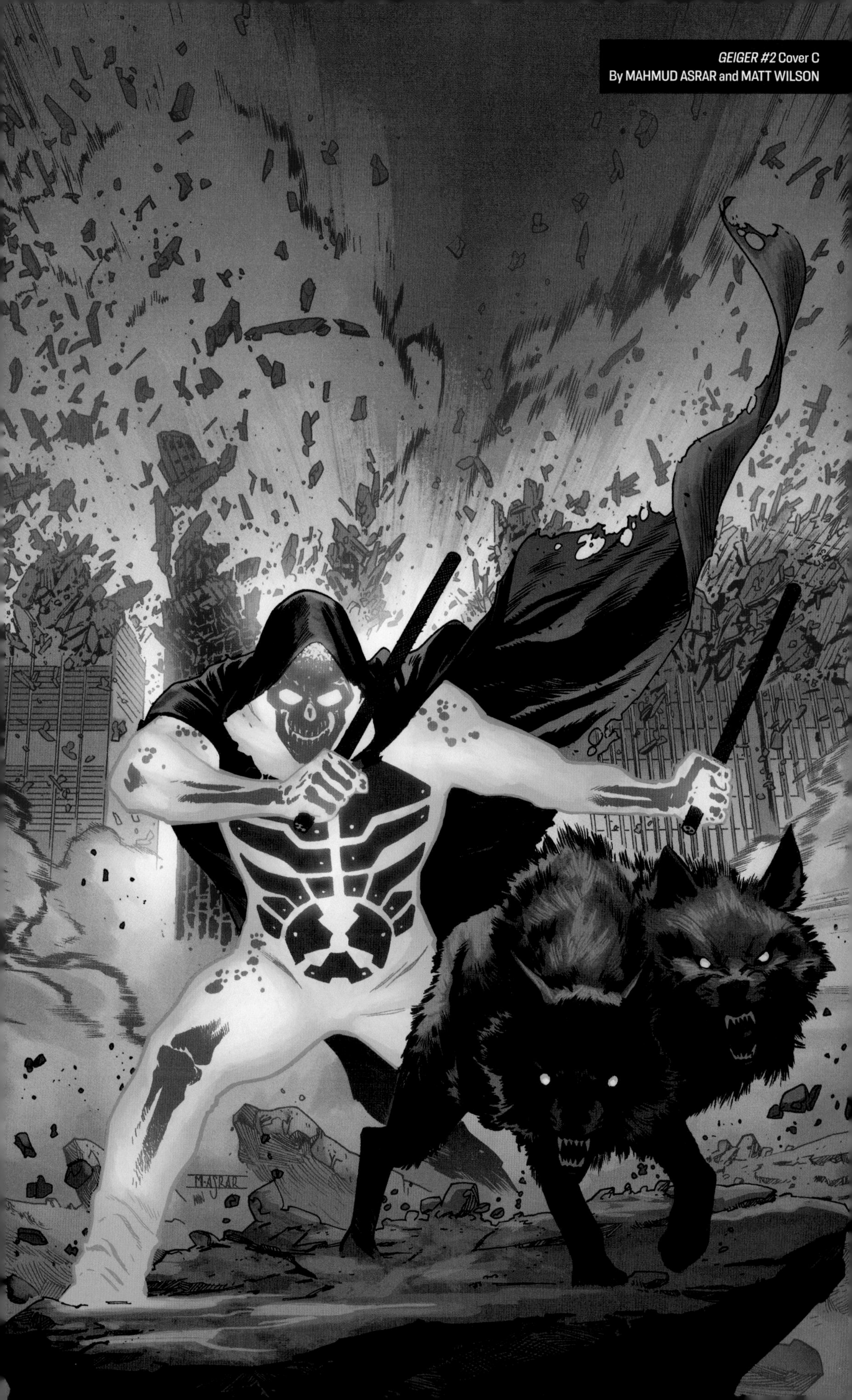
M.ASRAR

GEIGER #2 Cover C
By MAHMUD ASRAR and MATT WILSON

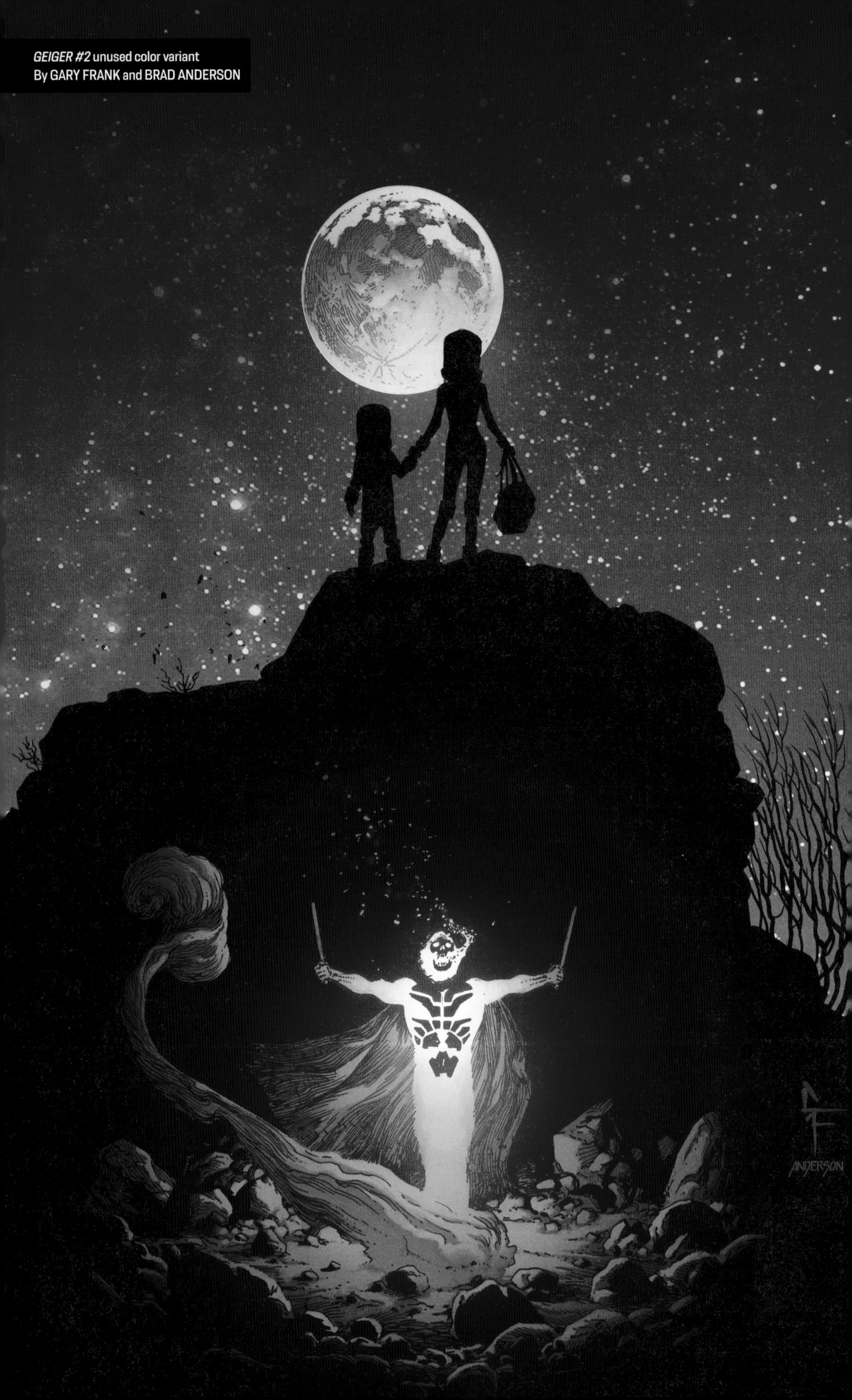
ANDERSON

GEIGER #2 unused color variant
By GARY FRANK and BRAD ANDERSON

GEIGER #3 Cover B
By JEFF LEMIRE

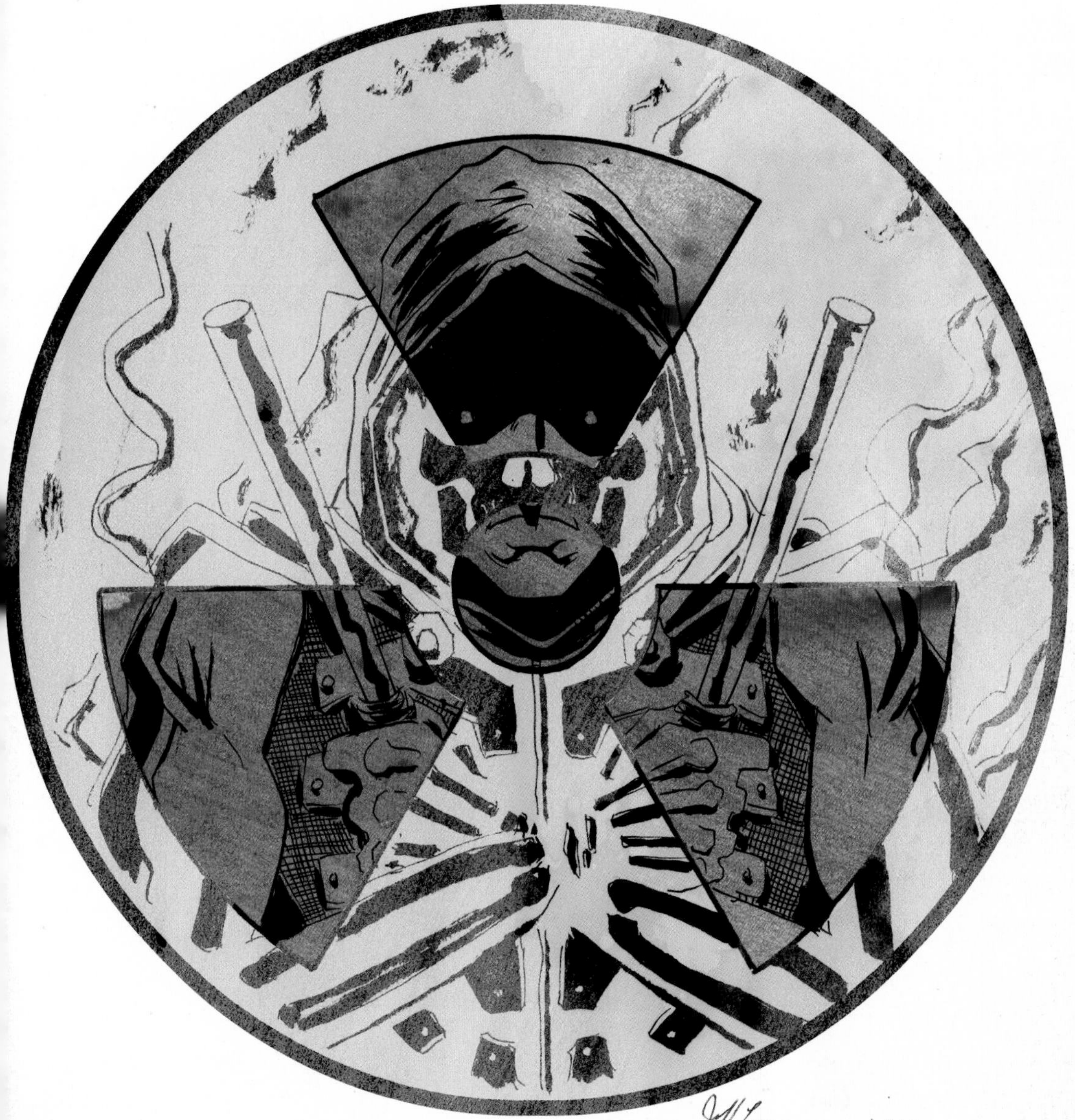

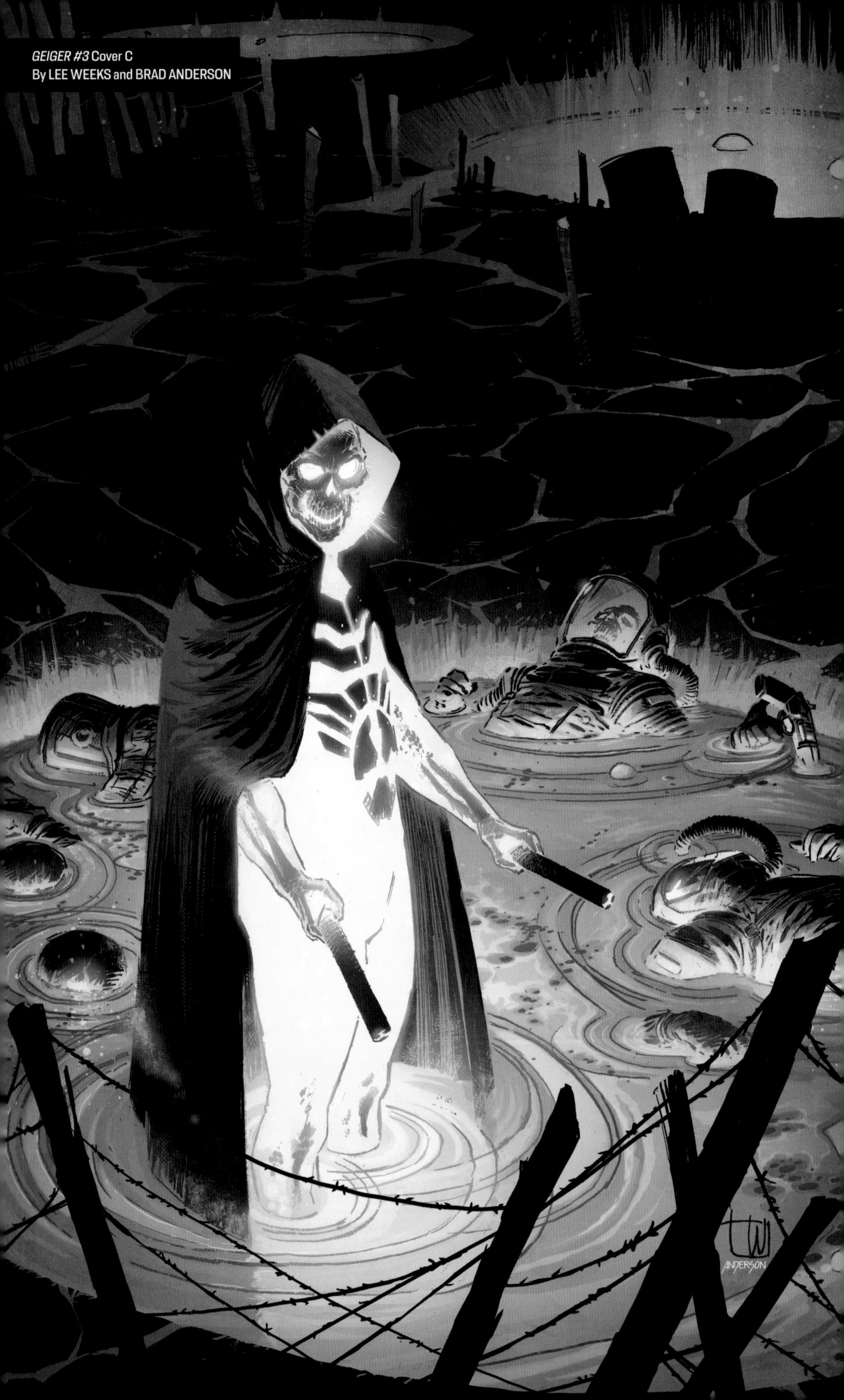
ANDERSON

GEIGER #3 Cover C
By LEE WEEKS and BRAD ANDERSON

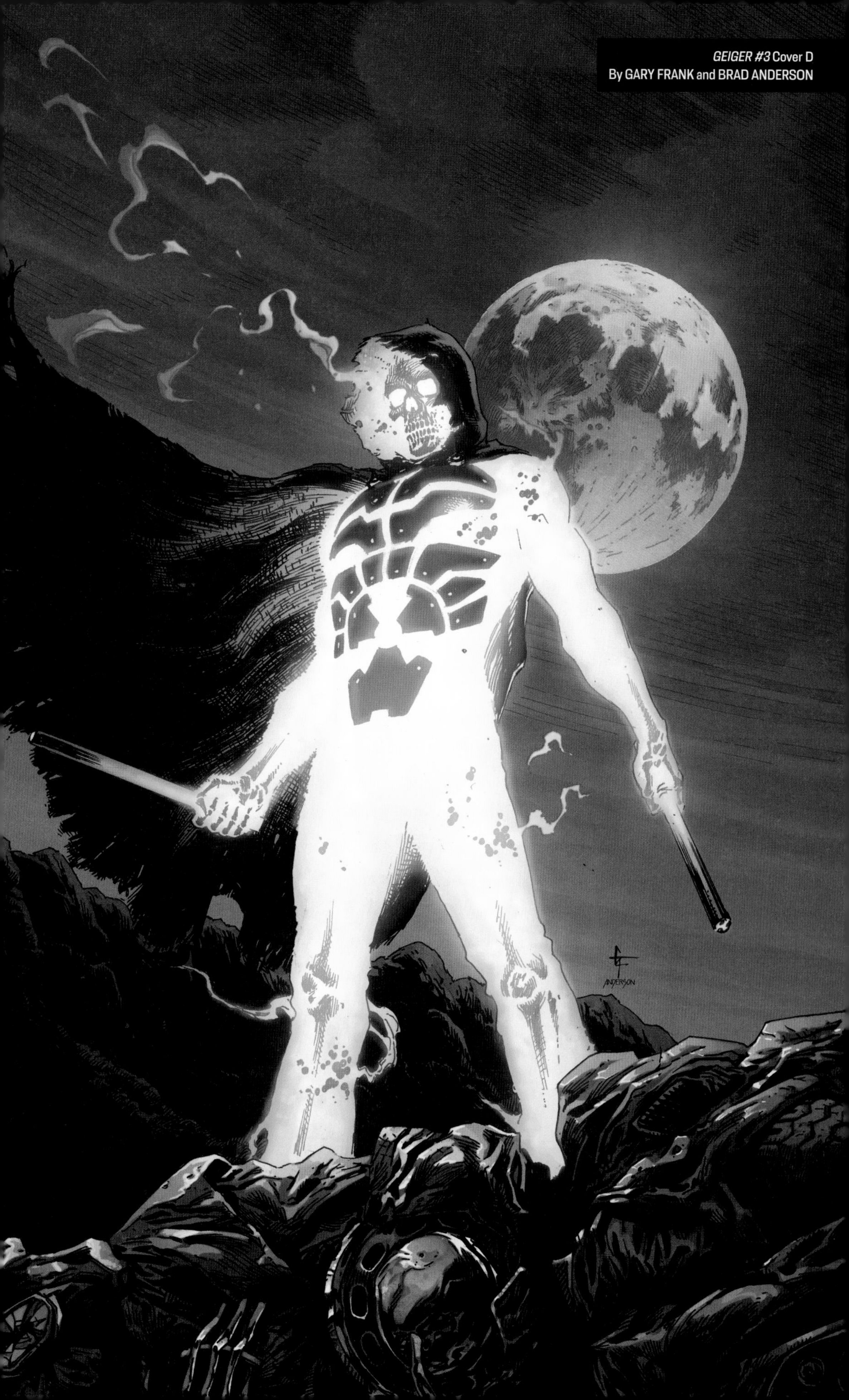
ANDERSON

GEIGER #3 Cover D
By GARY FRANK and BRAD ANDERSON

GEIGER #3 Second Printing
By BRAD ANDERSON

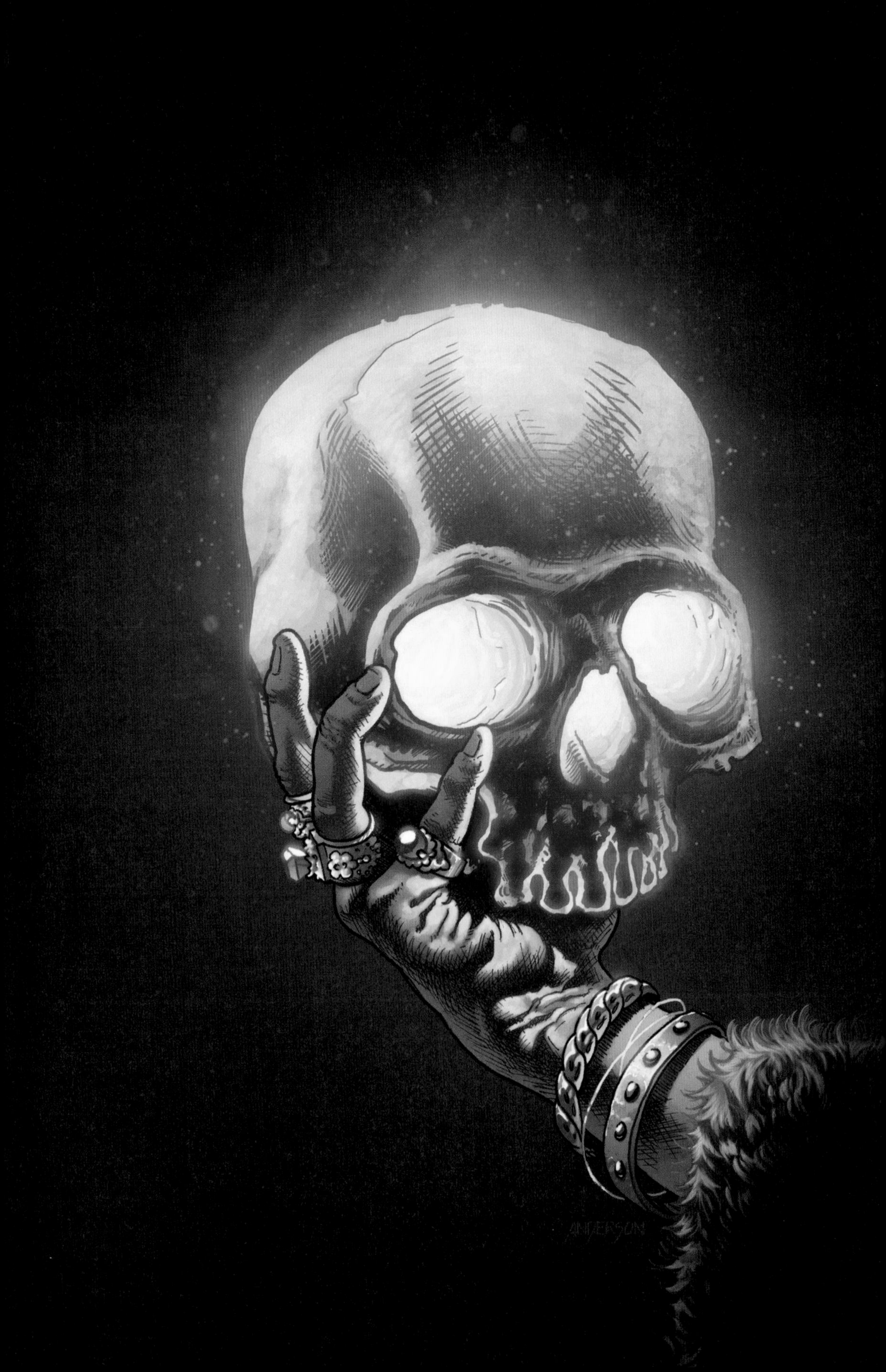
ANDERSON

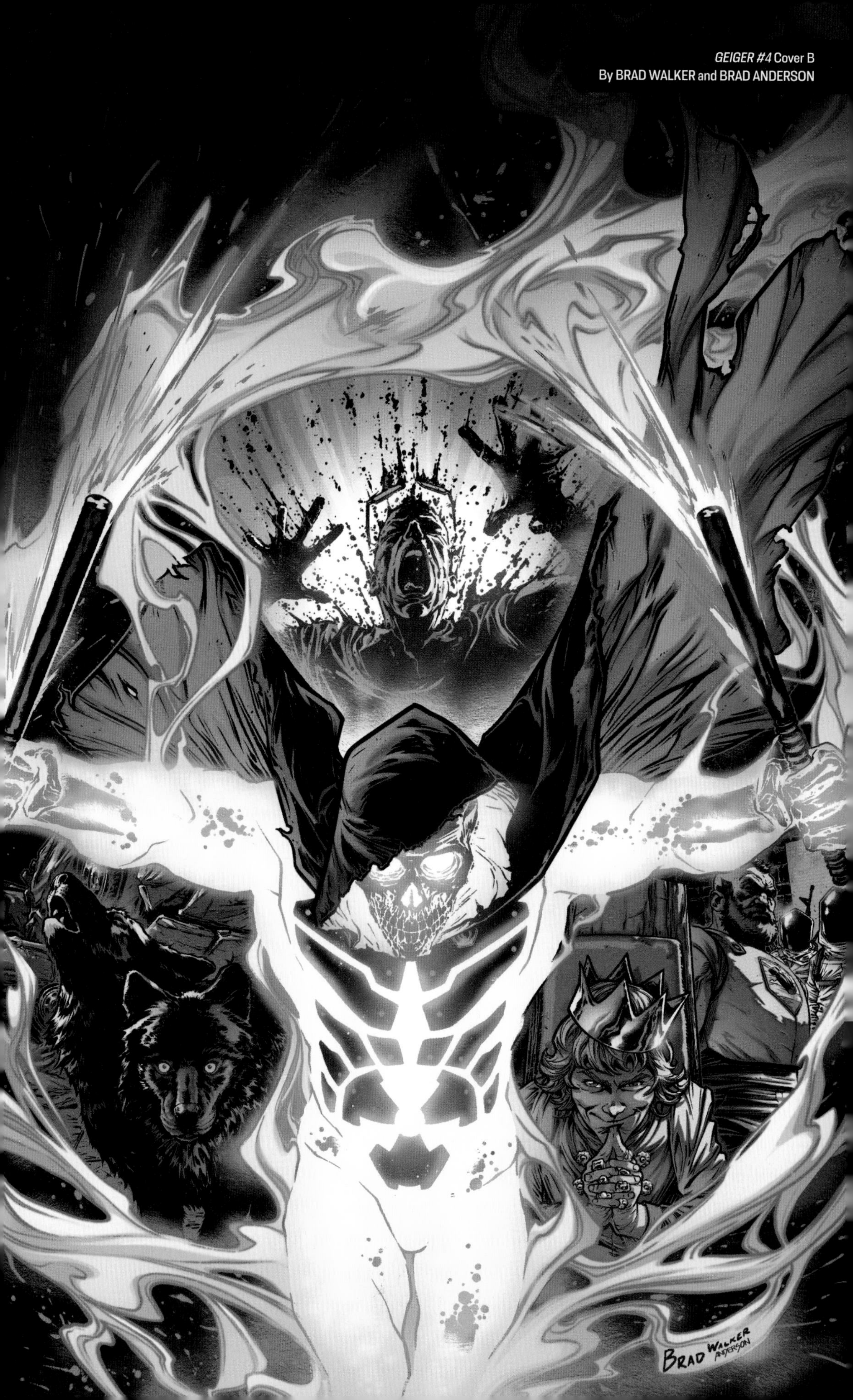
BRAD WALKER
ANDERSON

GEIGER #4 Cover B
By BRAD WALKER and BRAD ANDERSON

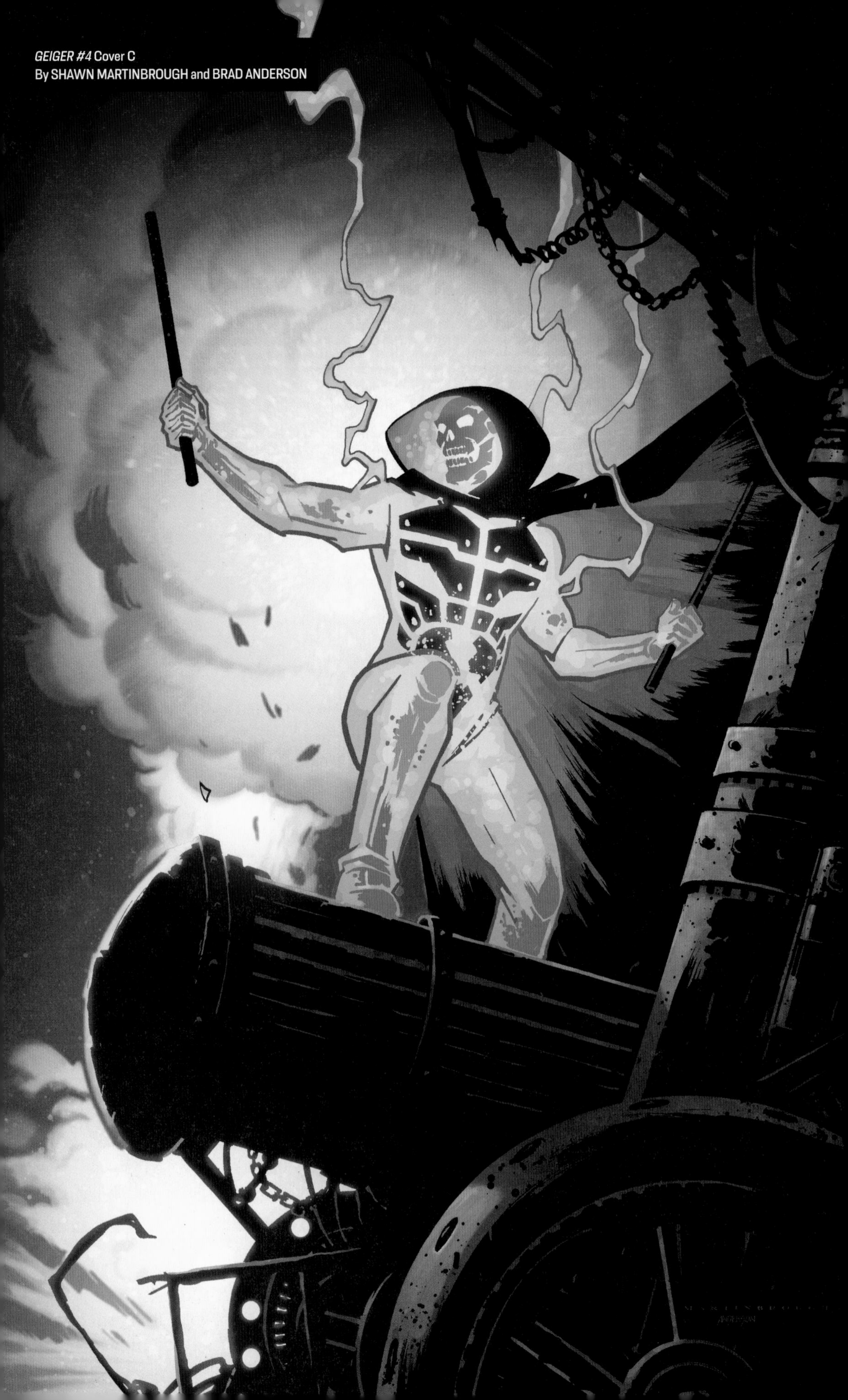

GEIGER #4 Cover C
By SHAWN MARTINBROUGH and BRAD ANDERSON

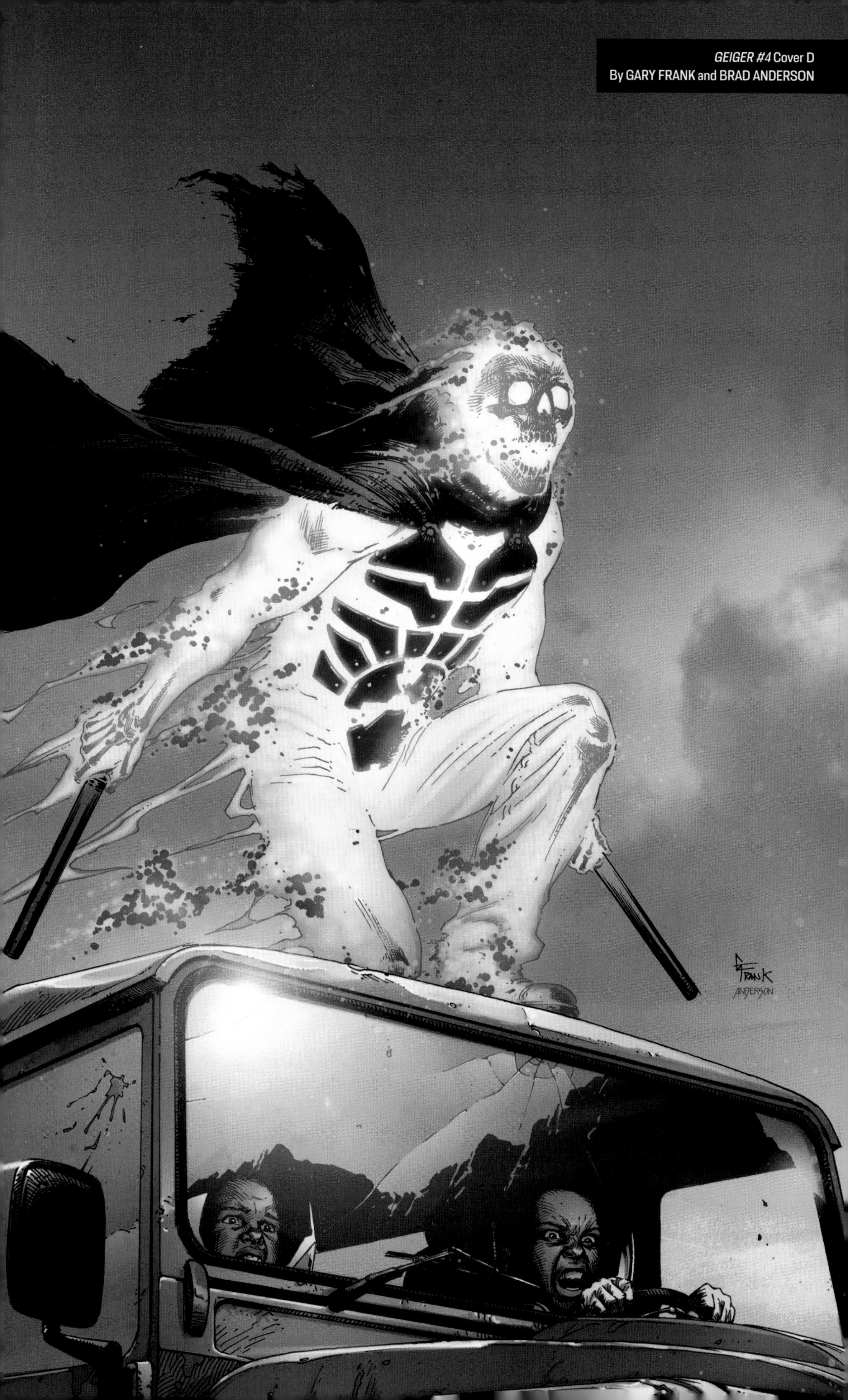
FRANK
ANDERSON

GEIGER #4 Cover D
By GARY FRANK and BRAD ANDERSON

GEIGER #5 Cover B
By JERRY ORDWAY and BRAD ANDERSON

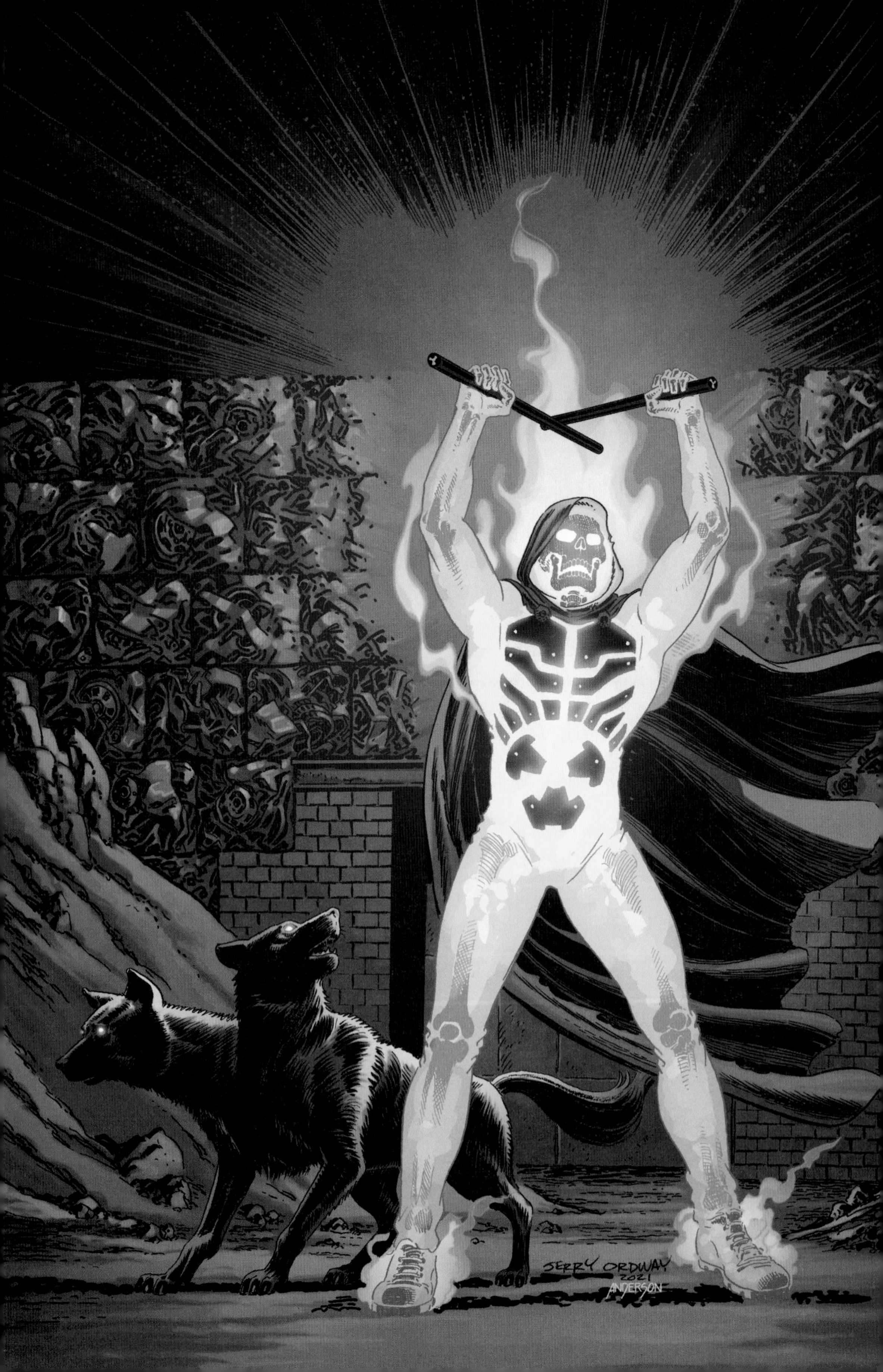
JERRY ORDWAY
2021
ANDERSON

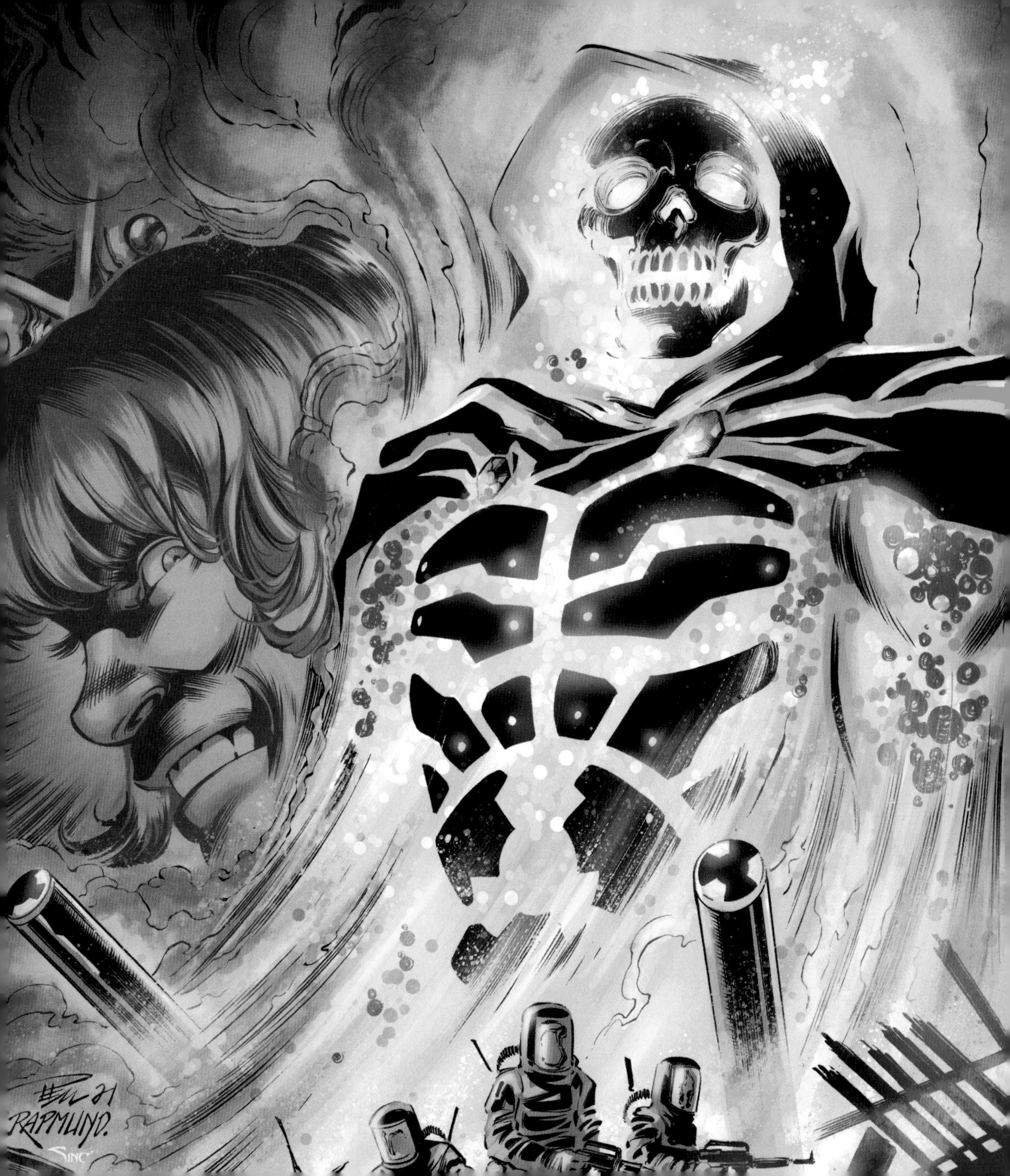

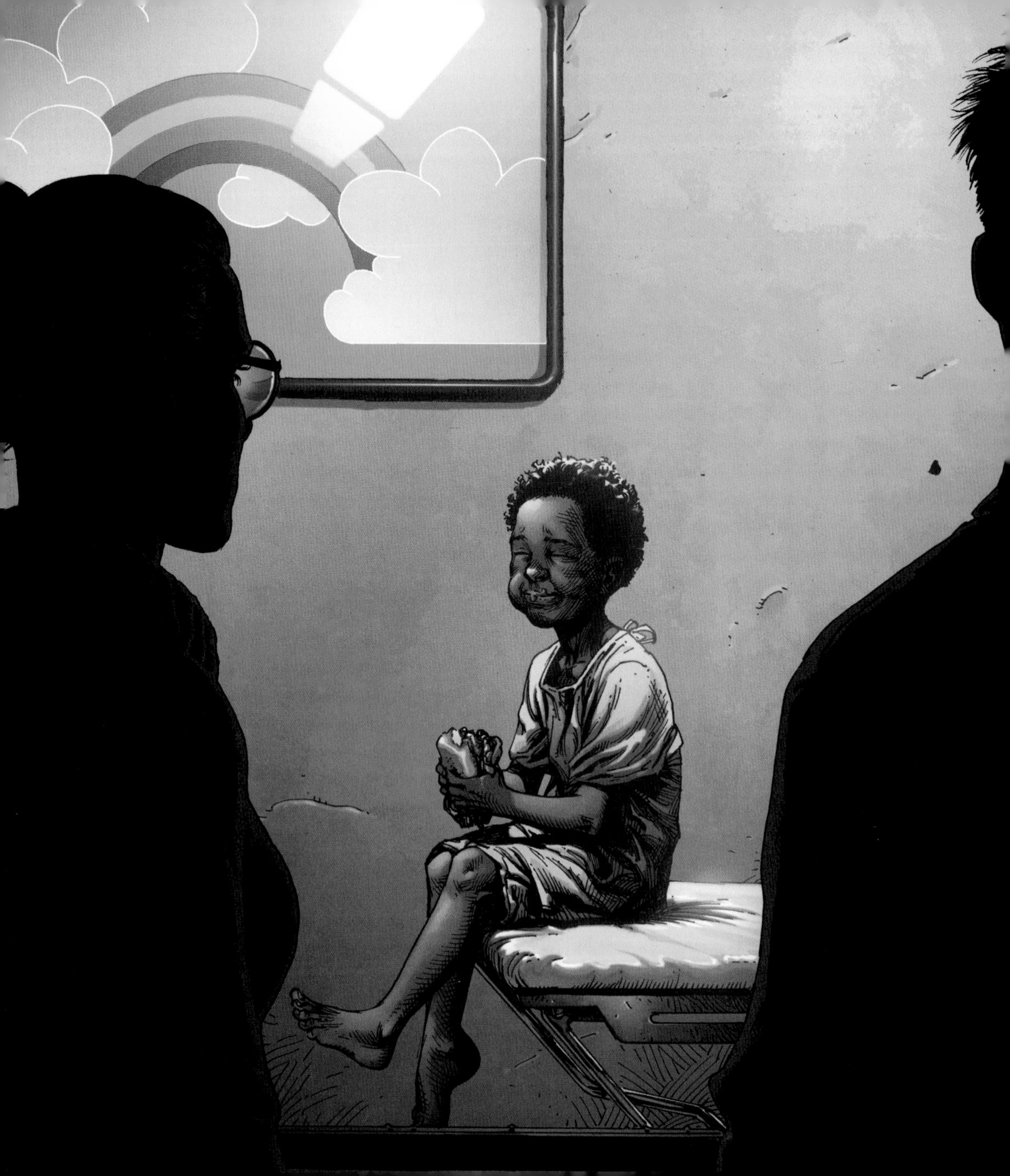

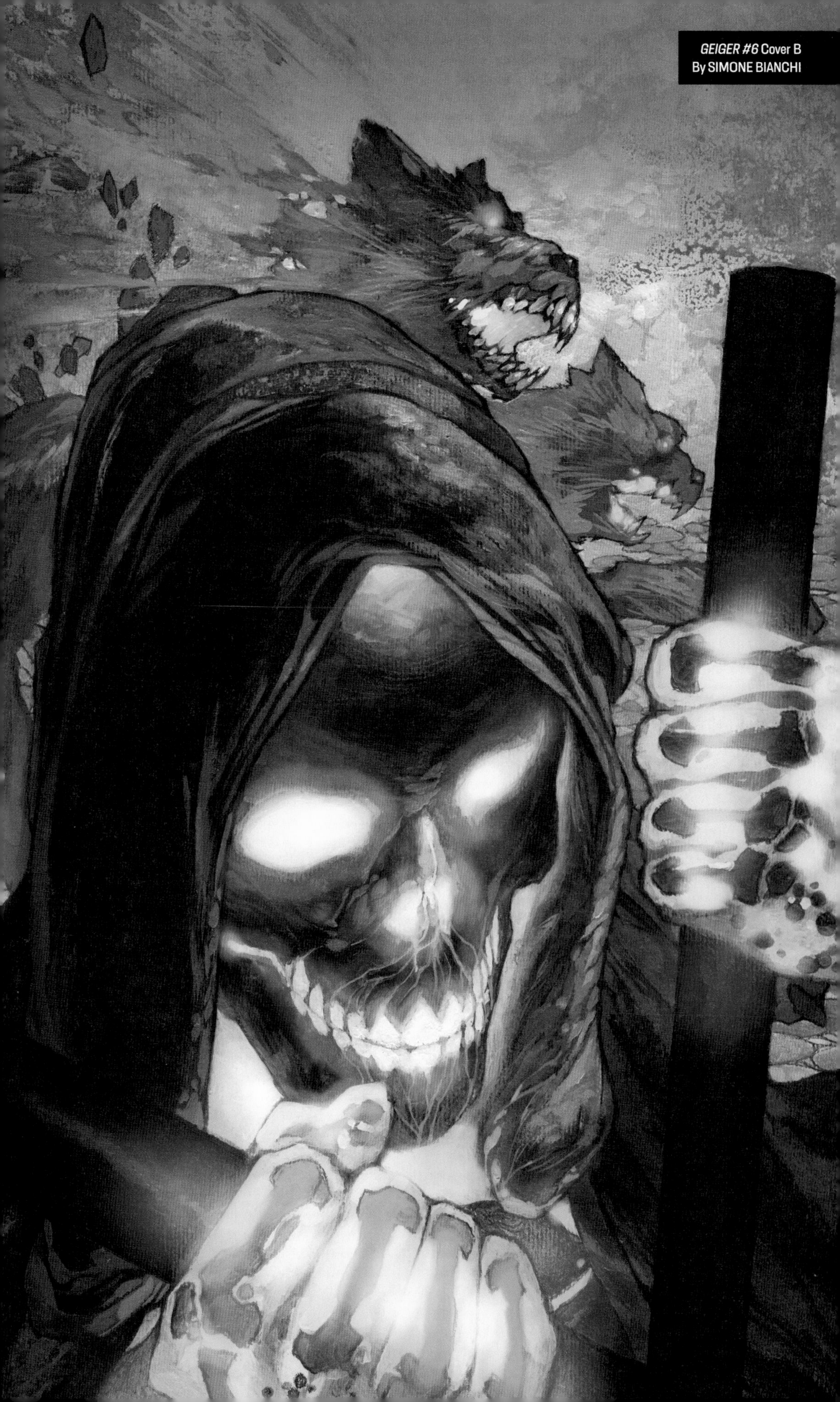

GEIGER #6 Cover B
By SIMONE BIANCHI

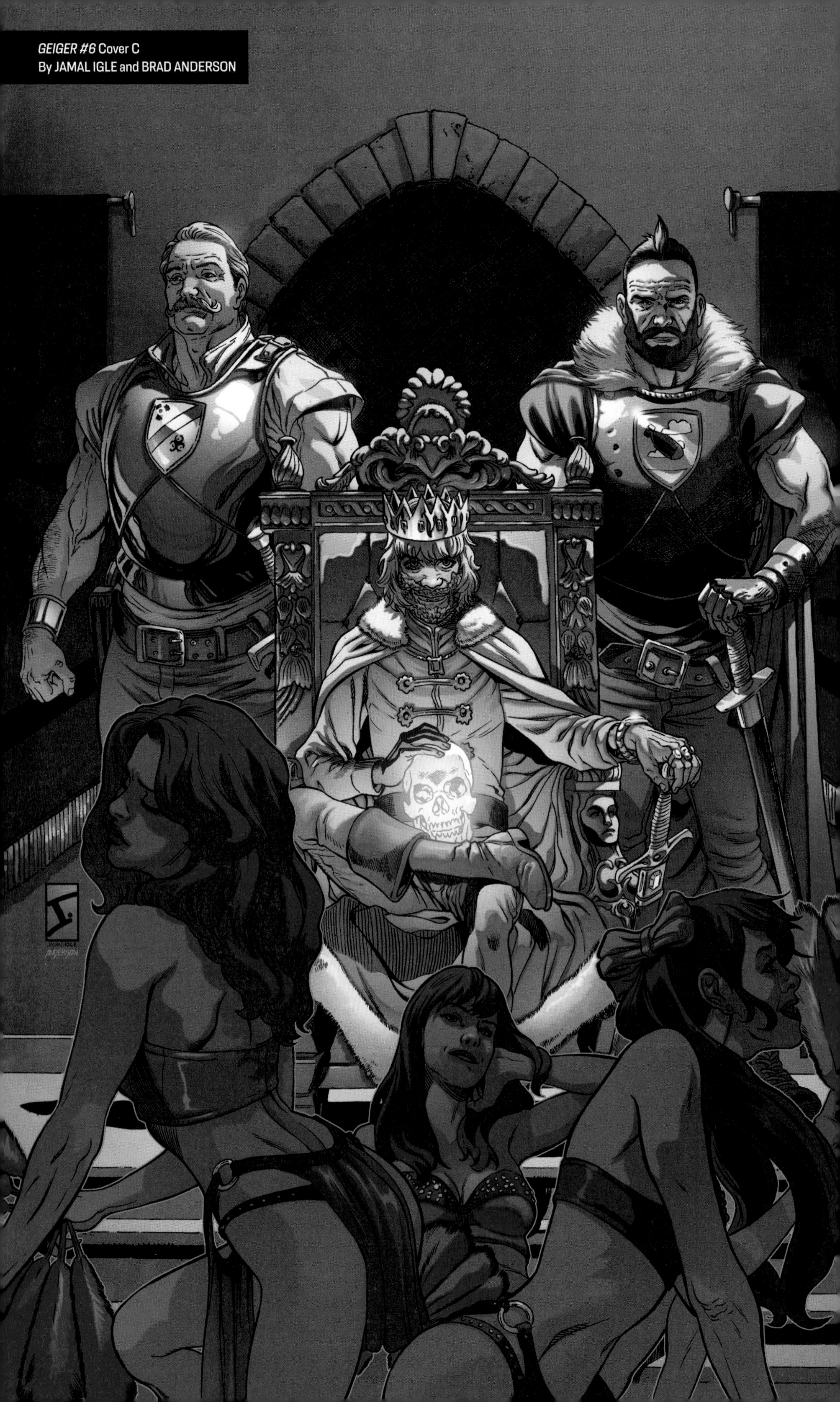

GEIGER #6 Cover C
By JAMAL IGLE and BRAD ANDERSON

GEIGER #6 Cover D
By GARY FRANK and BRAD ANDERSON

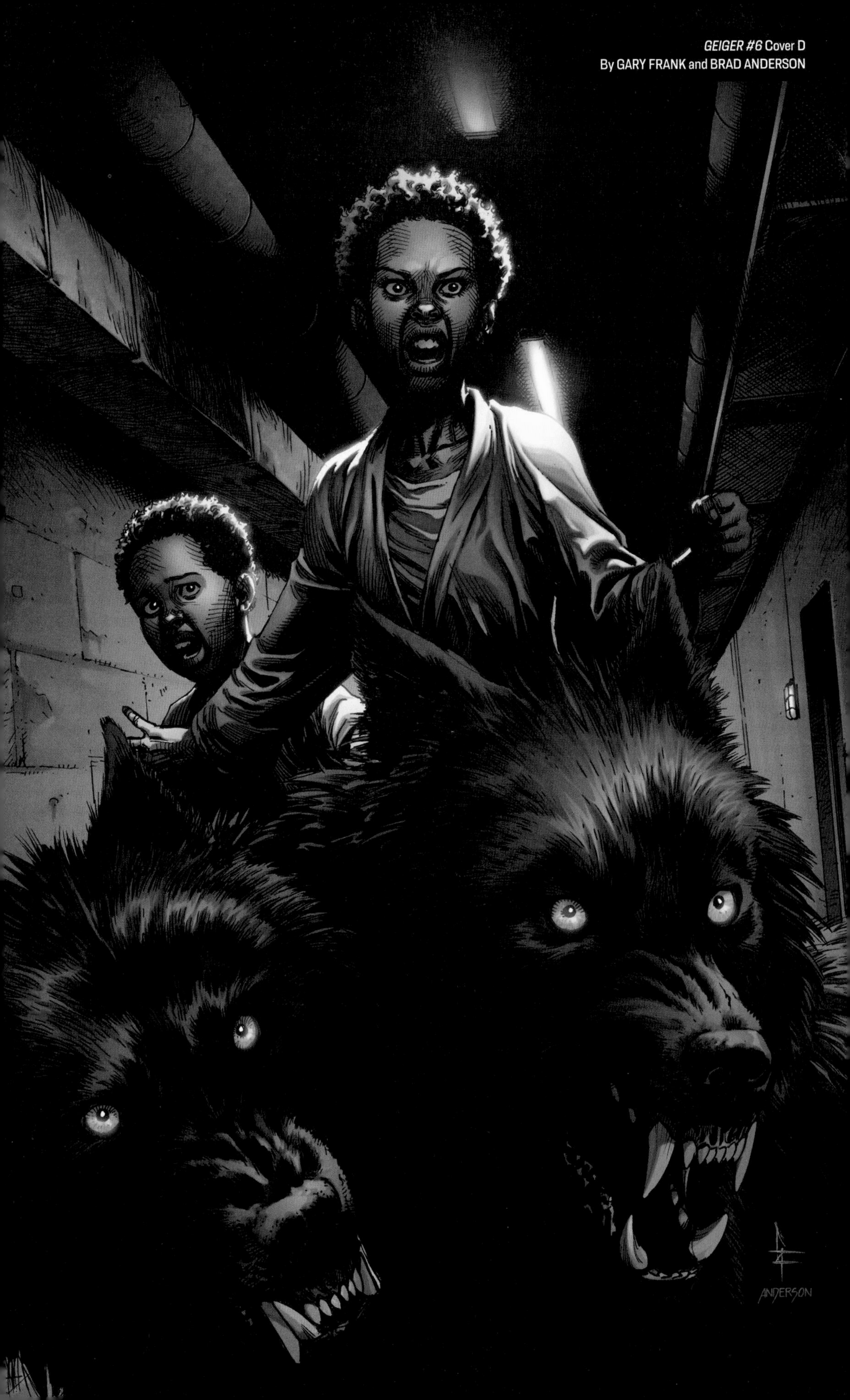
ANDERSON

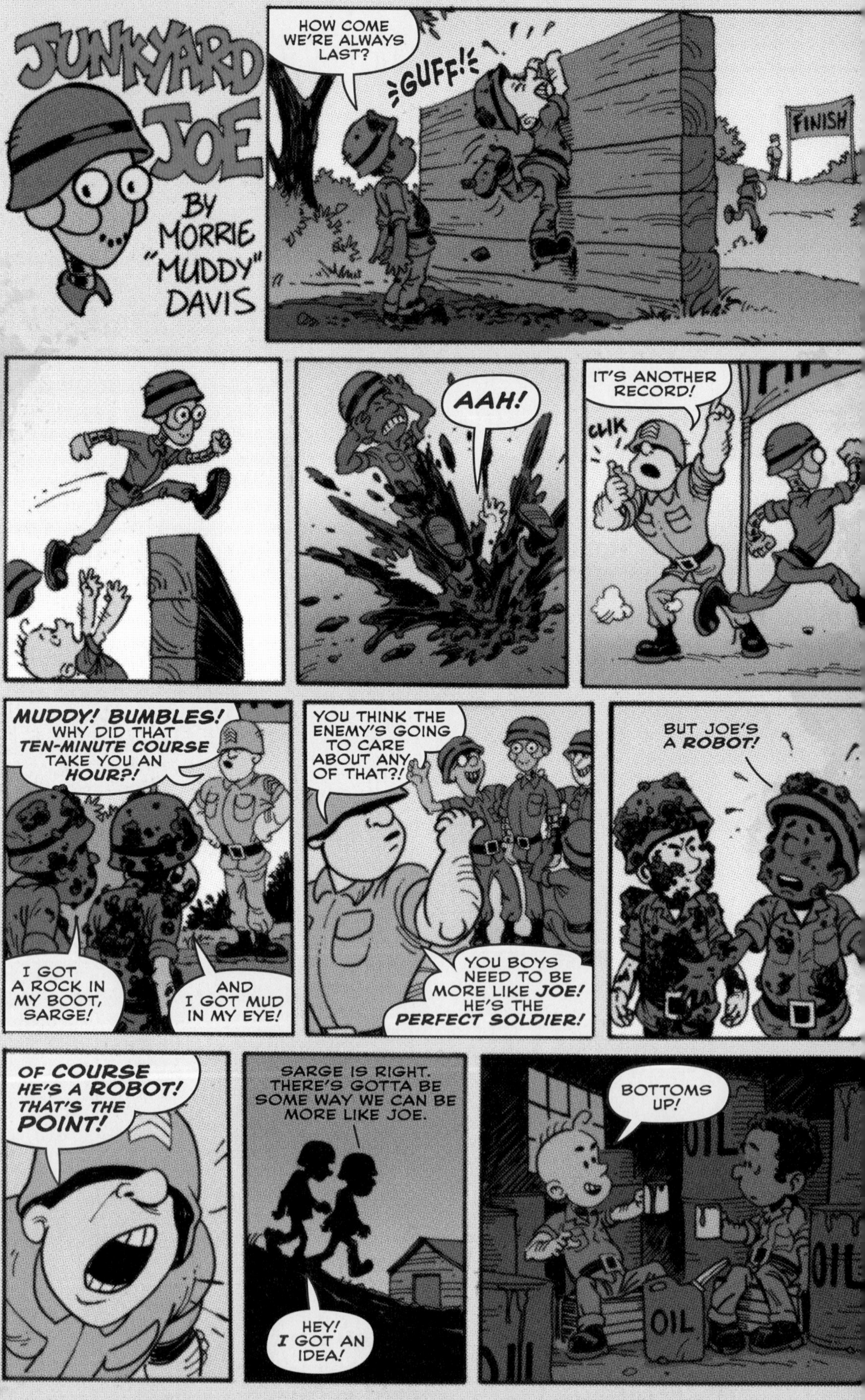
JUNKYARD JOE
BY MORRIE "MUDDY" DAVIS
HOW COME WE'RE ALWAYS LAST?
GUFF!
FINISH
AAH!
IT'S ANOTHER RECORD!
CLIK
MUDDY! BUMBLES! WHY DID THAT TEN-MINUTE COURSE TAKE YOU AN HOUR?!
I GOT A ROCK IN MY BOOT, SARGE!
AND I GOT MUD IN MY EYE!
YOU THINK THE ENEMY'S GOING TO CARE ABOUT ANY OF THAT?!
YOU BOYS NEED TO BE MORE LIKE JOE! HE'S THE PERFECT SOLDIER!
BUT JOE'S A ROBOT!
OF COURSE HE'S A ROBOT! THAT'S THE POINT!
SARGE IS RIGHT. THERE'S GOTTA BE SOME WAY WE CAN BE MORE LIKE JOE.
HEY! I GOT AN IDEA!
BOTTOMS UP!
OIL
OIL
OIL

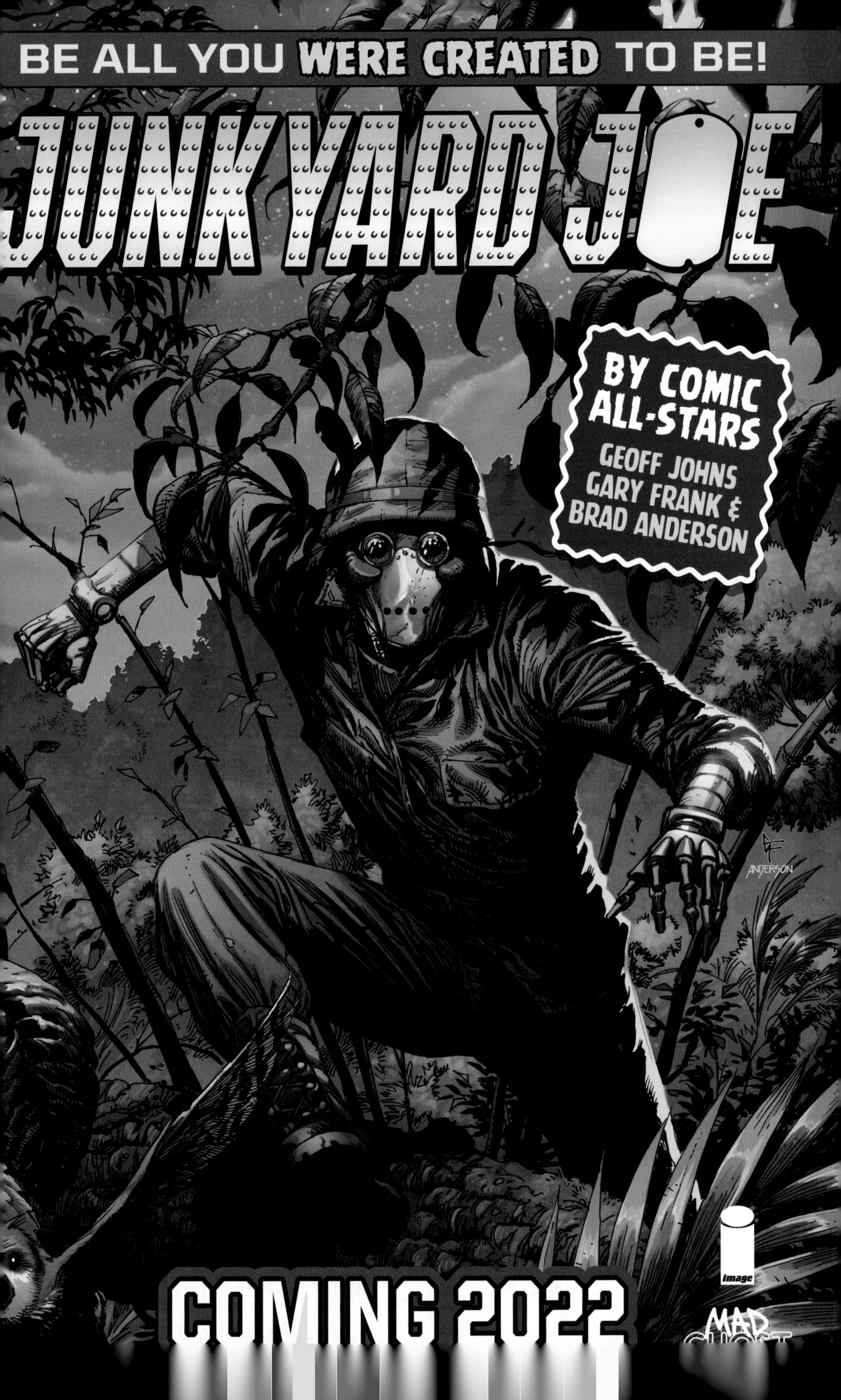

BE ALL YOU WERE CREATED TO BE!
JUNKYARD JOE
BY COMIC ALL-STARS
GEOFF JOHNS
GARY FRANK &
BRAD ANDERSON
COMING 2022
image
MAD

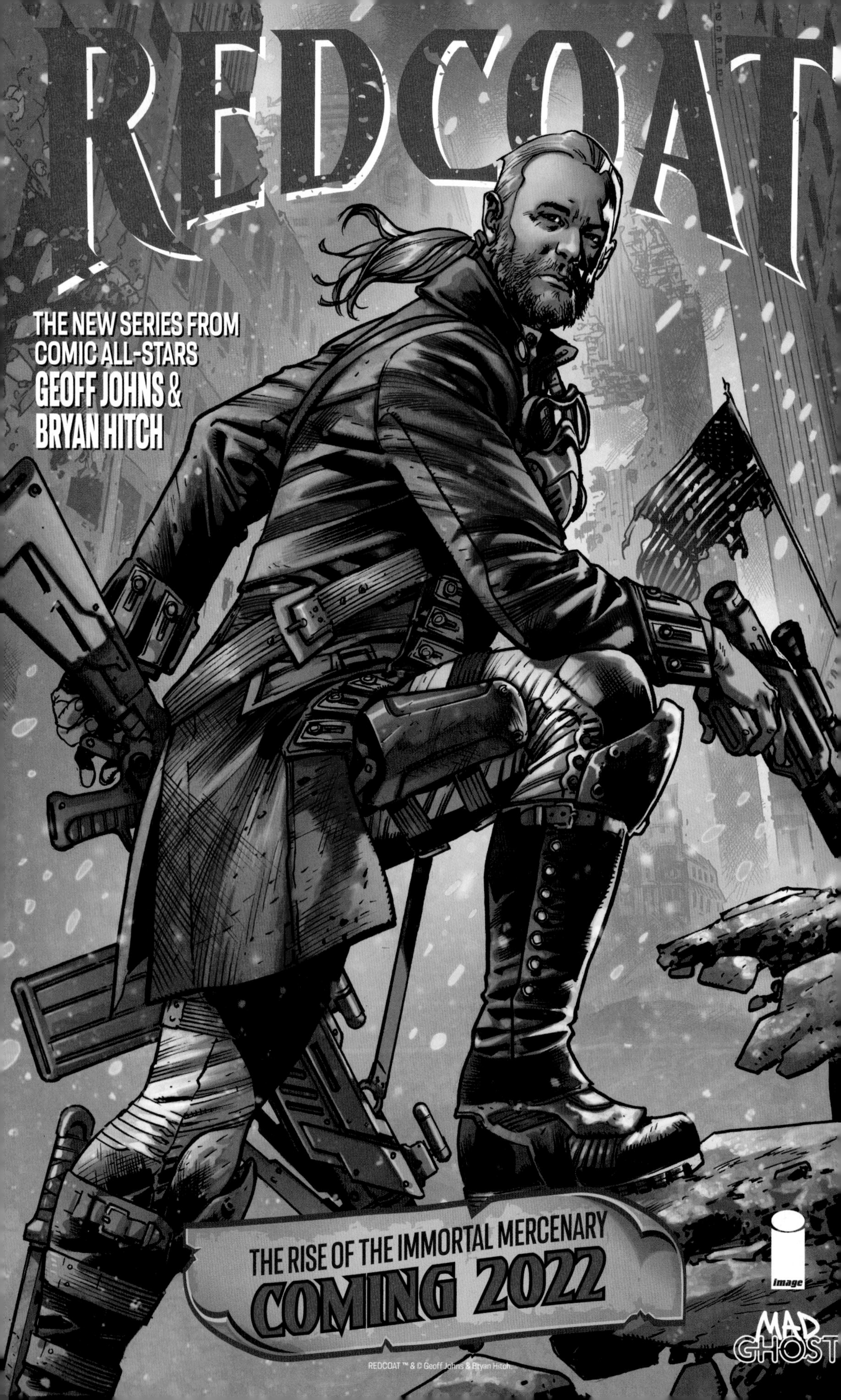
REDCOAT
THE NEW SERIES FROM
COMIC ALL-STARS
GEOFF JOHNS &
BRYAN HITCH
THE RISE OF THE IMMORTAL MERCENARY
COMING 2022
image
MAD GHOST
REDCOAT ™ & © Geoff Johns & Bryan Hitch.